HANS JOACHIM IWAND ON CHURCH AND SOCIETY

T&T Clark Enquiries in Theological Ethics

Series editors

Brian Brock

Susan F. Parsons

HANS JOACHIM IWAND ON CHURCH AND SOCIETY

Opened by the Kingdom of God

Edited by
Benjamin Haupt
Michael Basse
Gerard den Hertog
Christian Neddens

Translated by
Christian Einertson

t&tclark

LONDON • NEW YORK • OXFORD • NEW DELHI • SYDNEY

T&T CLARK
Bloomsbury Publishing Plc
50 Bedford Square, London, WC1B 3DP, UK
1385 Broadway, New York, NY 10018, USA
29 Earlsfort Terrace, Dublin 2, Ireland

BLOOMSBURY, T&T CLARK and the T&T Clark logo are trademarks of Bloomsbury Publishing Plc

First published in Great Britain 2023
Paperback edition published 2024

Copyright © Benjamin Haupt, Michael Basse, Gerard den Hertog and Christian Neddens, 2023

Benjamin Haupt, Michael Basse, Gerard den Hertog and Christian Neddens have asserted their right under the Copyright, Designs and Patents Act, 1988, to be identified as Authors of this work.

All rights reserved. No part of this publication may be reproduced or transmitted in any form or by any means, electronic or mechanical, including photocopying, recording, or any information storage or retrieval system, without prior permission in writing from the publishers.

Bloomsbury Publishing Plc does not have any control over, or responsibility for, any third-party websites referred to or in this book. All internet addresses given in this book were correct at the time of going to press. The author and publisher regret any inconvenience caused if addresses have changed or sites have ceased to exist, but can accept no responsibility for any such changes.

A catalogue record for this book is available from the British Library.

Library of Congress Cataloging-in-Publication Data
Names: Iwand, Hans Joachim, 1899-1960, author. | Haupt, Benjamin, editor. | Basse, Michael, editor. | Hertog, Gerard Cornelis den, 1949- editor. | Neddens, Christian, 1972- editor. | Einertson, Christian, translator.
Title: Hans Joachim Iwand on church and society : opened by the Kingdom of God / edited by Benjamin Haupt, Michael Basse, Gerard den Hertog, Christian Neddens ; translated by Christian Einertson.
Description: London ; New York : T&T Clark, 2022. | Series: T&T Clark enquiries in theological ethics | Includes bibliographical references and index. |
Identifiers: LCCN 2022036253 (print) | LCCN 2022036254 (ebook) | ISBN 9780567700032 (hardback) | ISBN 9780567701732 (paperback) | ISBN 9780567700049 (pdf) | ISBN 9780567700056 (epub)
Subjects: LCSH: Iwand, Hans Joachim, 1899-1960–Translations into English. | Church and the world. | Christian life–Lutheran authors. | Lutheran Church–Doctrines.
Classification: LCC BX4827.I93 I93 2022 (print) | LCC BX4827.I93 (ebook) | DDC 230/.41–dc23/eng/20221205
LC record available at https://lccn.loc.gov/2022036253
LC ebook record available at https://lccn.loc.gov/2022036254

ISBN: HB: 978-0-5677-0003-2
PB: 978-0-5677-0173-2
ePDF: 978-0-5677-0004-9
ePUB: 978-0-5677-0005-6

Series: T&T Clark Enquiries in Theological Ethics

Typeset by Deanta Global Publishing Services, Chennai, India

To find out more about our authors and books visit www.bloomsbury.com and sign up for our newsletters.

CONTENTS

Foreword from a North American Context — vii
Foreword from a Continental European Context — ix
A Note on the Translation — xii
List of Abbreviations — xiii

INTRODUCTION — 1

Chapter 1
THE PREACHING OF THE LAW — 13

Chapter 2
THE OBJECTIVITY OF THE THEOLOGICAL TASK — 35

Chapter 3
SED ORIGINALE PER HOMINEM UNUM: A CONTRIBUTION TO
THE DOCTRINE OF MAN — 47

Chapter 4
LOVE AS THE FOUNDATION AND LIMIT OF FREEDOM — 65

Chapter 5
THE BIBLE AND THE SOCIAL QUESTION — 77

Chapter 6
CHURCH AND SOCIETY — 107

Chapter 7
TOWARD A THEOLOGICAL RATIONALE FOR PROTEST AGAINST
THE GOVERNMENT — 127

Chapter 8
AGAINST THE MISUSE OF THE *PRO ME* AS A METHODOLOGICAL
PRINCIPLE IN THEOLOGY — 139

Chapter 9
ESTATE AND SACRAMENT — 147

Chapter 10
ON THE ORIGIN OF LUTHER'S CONCEPT OF THE CHURCH:
A CRITICAL CONTRIBUTION TO KARL HOLL'S ESSAY OF THE
SAME NAME   171

Chapter 11
THEOLOGIA CRUCIS: COMPOSED FOR THE CONVENTION IN
BEIENRODE IN THE FALL OF 1959   205

Chapter 12
THE FREEDOM OF THE CHRISTIAN AND THE BONDAGE OF
THE WILL   221

List of Contributors   241
Index   242

FOREWORD FROM A NORTH AMERICAN CONTEXT
HANS JOACHIM IWAND, A VOICE FOR THIS TIME

The moral bonds that have held our society together seem to be loosing, losing their hold on the thinking of many. The search for simple solutions has led us to applaud leadership that strives for ever tighter control in conformity to a worldview at odds with fundamental Christian values of respect for all God's human creatures. Leaders in society play on fears and cultivate a sense of defensiveness that accents our differences rather than our common humanity. In pursuit of reasserting our nation's prestige and place, some leaders are succeeding only in isolating us from the family of nations.

Into this situation emerged a young theological voice in the 1930s, that of Hans Joachim Iwand. His absorption of the way of thinking about the world proclaimed by Martin Luther began with the little Hans Joachim's learning Luther's Small Catechism and matured with his development as a Luther scholar. As a follower of the sixteenth-century reformer, Iwand applied Luther's insights to the complex world that he experienced in the National Socialist Third Reich and in the postwar period in a Europe set at odds by rival powers. His contributions to Luther's understanding of the righteousness of God and the theology of the cross, as well as God's Word delivered as law and as gospel, framed within his dialogue with Karl Barth and other contemporaries, provide valuable insights more than half a century after his death. In addition, his insights into the Christian reaction to the foibles and failures of society and of the church as a part of society should stimulate and cultivate Christian witness in the midst of the debates over ordering the public arena in every nation and ecclesiastical culture around the world in the twenty-first century.

Iwand left secondary education in East Prussia in 1934 to assume a professorship at the Herder Institut, a university for the German-speaking Baltic population, but his opposition to National Socialist inference in the church soon led to his dismissal. He taught at several of the underground theological training centers of the Confessing Church until 1938, when he was imprisoned for four months. Thereafter, he served as a parish pastor until the defeat of the Third Reich and became professor of systematic theology in Göttingen in 1946. Six years later he accepted a professorship at the University of Bonn and taught there until his death.

Iwand's Christ-centered trust in the presence and power of God, exercised through his accusing law and his life-giving gospel, brought key insights from Luther into the context of the world in which Iwand felt called to give witness to the crucified one. His investigation of the precise significance of Luther's understanding of the righteousness of God and his unconditionally given gift of righteousness through Christ's death and resurrection continues to enrich our understanding of the reformer's central insights. Iwand's perceptive reading of Luther's *On Bound Choice* accentuated the necessity of the Holy Spirit's effecting the turning of every sinner who repents back to God, who in Jesus Christ conquered sin and death by dying and rising. Iwand focused on Luther's theology of the cross and its careful drawing of the line between God Hidden and God Revealed. He recognized that the hiddenness of the majesty of God differs from his revealing himself in Christ and his cross, where God has demonstrated his wisdom and power in what those apart from faith in Christ call foolishness and weakness.

Iwand's own historical experience in the struggle against the National Socialist ideology of race and the use of political power of the most vicious sort led him also to dedicate much of his energy to speaking to the role of Christians in seeking to strive for the social justice which the prophets of the Old Testament and Jesus and Paul in the New Testament affirmed as a goal of all whom the Holy Spirit gathers around the cross. His insistence of a clear distinction of law and gospel without separating the two permitted him to speak clearly to this world and to the abuse of the very concept of law in both National Socialist ideology and the Cultural Christian affirmation of many of its values in the proclamation and pronouncements of the "German Christians."

God's law brings sinners to repentance, Iwand taught. The repentant trust God's gospel that bestows righteousness and childhood as a member of God's own family through the forgiveness of sins Christ claimed for his people in dying and rising. The repentant believe God when he says, "you are righteous." Convinced of our righteous identity, we live as God wants us to live. We seek to love our neighbors out of the new identity that centers in fearing, loving, and trusting God with heart, soul, mind, and strength.

With this conviction Iwand offers guidance that rises above the situation of German believers, European believers, more than a half century ago. His words point to ways in which English-speaking believers in North America, the UK, South Africa, Australia, or wherever on earth God has placed them can in the twenty-first century repudiate the values of our cultures that worship the toys that give us pleasure and the freedom that permits us to do things "my way." Iwand's proclamation of God's Word assists believers in finding ways to confess and act out God's gift of righteousness in Christ in our ever-changing societies.

Twenty-first-century Christians live in a very different historical-cultural situation than Iwand's, but his insights call twenty-first-century Christians to repentance and to trusting the Word of God that bestows righteousness upon them. That empowers us to act with courage and insight to aid our fellow citizens with the pressing problems that materialism and individualism have lured us into trusting what God has made rather than the Creator. Iwand's words are words for today.

Robert Kolb
Concordia Seminary, St. Louis United States

FOREWORD FROM A CONTINENTAL EUROPEAN CONTEXT

The publication of this collection of essays of Hans Joachim Iwand in English definitely marks a milestone in the reception of his theology. It is not the first text of Iwand that is published in English translation: his short but content-full book on Martin Luther's doctrine of the righteousness of faith preceded this volume and, in a sense, paved its way (Hans Joachim Iwand, *The Righteousness of Faith According to Luther*, ed. Virgil Thompson, trans. Randi Lundell [Eugene, OR: Wipf & Stock, 2008]). However, the present volume exemplifies how the study of Luther's theology inspired and enabled Iwand in dealing critically with urgent issues in church, society, and politics. This is probably why more than sixty years after his death he is far from forgotten in Europe. On the contrary, Iwand's theological heritage is alive and shows itself inspiring, helpful, and challenging for new generations, creating even wider interest. This might also be why there appears to be interest in his theology in the English-speaking world.

It is worth mentioning that Iwand started his "conquest" of the Americas in the Spanish-speaking South. In 2015 a translation of a number of his texts was published in Spanish to serve Protestant Christians and theologians in Latin America: Daniel C. Beros (ed./transl.), *Hans J. Iwand: Justicia de la fe. Estudios sobre la Teología de Martín Lutero y de la Reforma Evangélica del Siglo XVI*, Buenos Aires 2015. With this present volume, Iwand firmly sets foot ashore in North America and among English speakers worldwide.

The question may arise: Why only now, why just now, more than sixty years after his death? There is no simple and clear answer to that question. It is a fact that, thanks to personal and theological relationships with theologians on the European continent, colleagues in both North America and the UK have become acquainted with and interested in Iwand's theology. The reason, therefore, is not so much that Iwand addresses themes and topics that are of direct actual interest for us, but it is more the critical, reformational way of his doing theology that gives insights and shows perspectives in what is at stake in present-day society. Iwand definitely belonged to the theologians who, at the beginning of the twentieth century, in his case after the First World War, "discovered" the young Luther. And yet, in bringing the young Wittenberg professor of theology to the fore, the distance of four or five centuries fades away, and we hear a message for our times. This explains why Iwand still appeals to new generations. However, the language difference showed itself to remain a real obstacle. That is why the initiative was taken to publish a collection of Iwand texts in English.

What kind of book is this, and why is the selection of articles as it is here? It is not so much a bundling of papers with related themes. That was how, after Hans Iwand's early death in 1960, his (by then mainly yet unpublished) work was edited in six volumes as *Nachgelassene Werke* (1962–74), later in four volumes (thus far) as *Nachgelassene Werke Neue Folge* (1998–2004), and further accompanied by the collected "Preaching Studies" Iwand wrote for the *Göttinger Predigtmeditationen*.

In the meantime, a desire arose to publish a book that could serve as a good introduction to the theology of Iwand. In 1979 Peter Sänger carefully composed a representative selection of letters of Iwand, interwoven with a short biography, and also a number of lectures and preaching studies of him (Hans Joachim Iwand, *Briefe, Vorträge, Predigtmeditationen. Eine Auswahl, herausgegeben von P.-P. Sänger*, Berlin 1979). Although the distribution was strictly limited to the German Democratic Republic and "socialist countries abroad," this book found its way to the Western world as well and functioned as an "appetizer" for a new generation.

This volume aims in the same direction as Sänger's choice of texts did, albeit this time not for a German readership that has access to the already elsewhere published Iwand texts but for an English readership that hardly knows Iwand, yet has heard of him enough to be interested in his theology. In view of them the texts for this volume were chosen. Five or even six texts—if we count "The Preaching of the Law" among them—are Luther studies, four texts show Iwand's dealing with social ethics, and in two texts we meet Iwand as the systematic theologian he was. Thus, the focus in this volume is on Iwand as Luther specialist and as engaged "public theologian."

It deserves mentioning that several texts on Luther in this volume were published by Gerhard Sauter in the very same year that Sänger's anthology appeared (Hans Joachim Iwand, *Glaubensgerechtigkeit. Gesammelte Aufsätze II* [herausgegeben von Gerhard Sauter], Theologische Bücherei 64, München 1979[1]). This edition was developed according to the highest scientific standards and intended to reintroduce Iwand in the discussion of the theology of Luther. In four texts of this volume, we have greatly profited from his excellent annotations.

Therefore, Peter Sänger stands for the first collection of Iwand texts in terms of an introduction in his "theologische Existenz heute," as is this volume as well, and Gerhard Sauter for the careful annotation and publication of Iwand's studies on Luther, which is one of the two main focuses of this book. It is for this reason that we mention the names of both Peter Sänger and Gerhard Sauter with reverence and gratitude.

With great respect and gratitude, I address here, on behalf of the board of the "Hans Iwand Stiftung," a special word of thanks to Christian Einertson, Ben Haupt, and Tobias Schütze. Christian Einertson translated the texts of Iwand into English, supported and critically scrutinized by Michael Basse, Christian Neddens, and myself. The three of us were impressed by the clear, concise, and understandable translation Christian Einertson put on the table. He definitely succeeded in transferring the thoughts of Iwand into good English. I guess the reader will not notice what it took to achieve that and just that is probably the best compliment. It was most helpful that Tobias Schütze critically commented on the translations and suggested alternatives; he also assisted in verifying many quotations, especially the Luther passages in the American edition. Ben Haupt did the editorial work, reviewing the translations, proposing suggestions for bottlenecks, and bringing the texts to a unified format. And he did so in an excellent way! So, the three of them, Ben, Christian, and Tobias deserve great acknowledgment for what they accomplished!

Gerard den Hertog
President of the Hans Iwand Stiftung

A Note on the Translation

The translators and editors have had to make several decisions on how to translate concepts and terms, which often carry philosophical implications given Iwand's extensive reading in philosophy and his careful articulations in light of the intellectual history. Some words like *Anfechtung* and *Weltanschauung* are well-known as difficult to translate into English and have thus been left in their original German. One word, in particular, in Iwand's writings that is notoriously challenging to translate is *geistig*. Iwand used the word often in his writings in the 1950s. It refers to German Idealism, especially Hegel, and the term is contrary to "materialistic" as in Marxism. English-speaking Hegelian scholars have disputed whether the word is best translated as "intellectual," "mental," or "spiritual." Upon Anthony King's recommendation in a chapter he wrote specifically on the challenges of translating *geistig* into English, we have chosen to translate the word as "cultural" because in English that word captures the intellectual, mental and spiritual spheres as well as the potential for those spheres to become instantiated in the material world through art, theater, film, or literature.[1] It should also be noted that in addition to the main introduction to this volume, each chapter contains a brief introduction written by the Continental European editor responsible for editing that chapter. These introductions are italicized at the beginning of each chapter and conclude with the editor's initials in parentheses. It should also be noted that square brackets and parentheses are used intentionally throughout the chapters. When parenthetical material in the chapter is original to Iwand, it is included in parentheses as in Iwand's original. When parenthetical material or additional footnotes have been added by an editor, that material has been placed in square brackets.

---

1. Anthony King, "Hegel and the Concept of Geist," in *The Structure of Social Theory* (New York: Routledge, 2004).

ABBREVIATIONS

ANF	*Ante-Nicene Fathers*
Ap	"Apology" in: *The Book of Concord*
BSELK	*Die Bekenntnisschriften der Evangelisch-Lutherischen Kirche*, 2014
CA	"Confessio Augustana" or "Augsburg Confession" in: *The Book of Concord*
CSEL	*Corpus Scriptorum Ecclesiasticorum Latinorum*
FC Ep	"Formula of Concord: Epitome" in: *The Book of Concord*
KW	*The Book of Concord*, ed. Robert Kolb and Timothy Wengert
LC	"Large Catechism" in: *The Book of Concord*
LSB	*Lutheran Service Book*
LW	*Luther's Works American Edition*
PL	*Patrologia Latina (Migne)*
SA	"*Smalcald Articles*" in: *The Book of Concord*
WA	*Luthers Werke, Weimarer Ausgabe*

Iwand Publications

GA I	Hans Joachim Iwand, *Um den rechten Glauben*, Gesammelte Aufsätze, vol. 1, ed. Karl Gerhard Steck, *Theologische Bücherei*, vol. 9 (Munich: Christian Kaiser Verlag, 1959); cited: Iwand, *Um den rechten Glauben*, GA I.
GA II	Hans Joachim Iwand, *Glaubensgerechtigkeit*, Gesammelte Aufsätze, vol. 2, ed. Gerhard Sauter, *Theologische Bücherei*, vol. 64 (Munich: Christian Kaiser Verlag, 1979); cited: Iwand, *Glaubensgerechtigkeit*, GA II.
NW I	Hans Joachim Iwand, *Glauben und Wissen*, Nachgelassene Werke, vol. 1, ed. Helmut Gollwitzer (Munich: Christian Kaiser Verlag, 1962); cited: Iwand, *Glauben und Wissen*, NW I.
NW II	Hans Joachim Iwand, *Vorträge und Aufsätze*, Nachgelassene Werke, vol. 2, ed. Dieter Schellong and Karl Gerhard Steck (Munich: Christian Kaiser Verlag, 1966); cited: Iwand, *Vorträge und Aufsätze*, NW II.
NW III	Hans Joachim Iwand, *Ausgewählte Predigten*, Nachgelassene Werke, vol. 3, ed. Hans Helmut Eßer and Helmut Gollwitzer (Munich: Christian Kaiser Verlag, 1963); cited: Iwand, *Ausgewählte Predigten*, NW III.
NW IV	Hans Joachim Iwand, *Gesetz und Evangelium*, Nachgelassene Werke, vol. 4, ed. Walter Kreck (Munich: Christian Kaiser Verlag, 1964); cited: Iwand, *Gesetz und Evangelium*, NW IV.

NW V	Hans Joachim Iwand, *Luthers Theologie*, Nachgelassene Werke, vol. 5, ed. Johann Haar (Munich: Christian Kaiser Verlag, 1974); cited: Iwand, *Luthers Theologie*, NW V.
NW VI	Hans Joachim Iwand, *Briefe an Rudolf Hermann*, Nachgelassene Werke, vol. 6, ed. Karl Gerhard Steck (Munich: Christian Kaiser Verlag, 1964); cited: Iwand, *Briefe an Rudolf Hermann*, NW VI.
NWN I	Hans Joachim Iwand, *Kirche und Gesellschaft*, Nachgelassene Werke Neue Folge, vol. 1, ed. Ekkehard Börsch (Gütersloh: Gütersloher Verlagshaus, 1998); cited: Iwand, *Kirche und Gesellschaft*, NWN I.
NWN II	Hans Joachim Iwand, *Christologie. Die Umkehrung des Menschen zur Menschlichkeit*, Nachgelassene Werke Neue Folge, vol. 2, ed. Eberhard Lempp and Edgar Thaidigsmann (Gütersloh: Gütersloher Verlagshaus, 1999); cited: Iwand, *Christologie*, NWN II.
NWN III	Hans Joachim Iwand, *Theologiegeschichte im neunzehnten und zwanzigsten Jahrhundert. Väter und Söhne*, Nachgelassene Werke Neue Folge, vol. 3, ed. Gerard C. den Hertog (Gütersloh: Gütersloher Verlagshaus, 2001); cited: Iwand, *Theologiegeschichte*, NWN III.
NWN V	Hans Joachim Iwand, *Predigten und Predigtlehre*, Nachgelassene Werke Neue Folge, vol. 5, ed. Albrecht Grözinger, Bertold Klappert, Rudolf Landau and Jürgen Seim (Gütersloh: Gütersloher Verlagshaus, 2004); cited: Iwand, *Predigten und Predigtlehre*, NWN V.

Hans Joachim Iwand, *Predigtmeditationen*, ed. Helmut Gollwitzer (Göttingen: Vandenhoeck & Ruprecht, 1963); cited: Iwand, *Predigtmeditationen* I.

Hans Joachim Iwand, *Predigtmeditationen* II (Göttingen: Vandenhoeck & Ruprecht, 1973); cited: Iwand, *Predigtmeditationen* II.

Hans Joachim Iwand, *Briefe, Vorträge, Predigtmeditationen: Eine Auswahl*, ed. Peter-Paul Sänger (Berlin: Evangelische Verlagsanstalt, 1979); cited: Iwand, *Briefe, Vorträge, Predigtmeditationen*.

Hans Joachim Iwand, *Dogmatik-Vorlesungen 1957–1960. Ausgewählte Texte zur Prinzipienlehre, Schöpfungslehre, Rechtfertigungslehre, Christologie und Ekklesiologie mit Einführungen*, ed. Thomas Bergfeld and Edgar Thaidigsmann, Arbeiten zur Historischen und Systematischen Theologie, vol. 18 (Berlin / Wien / Zürich / London: LIT-Verlag, 2013).

Hans Joachim Iwand, *Frieden mit dem Osten: Texte 1933–1959*, ed. Gerard C. den Hertog (Munich: Christian Kaiser Verlag, 1988).

INTRODUCTION

Benjamin Haupt

Hans Joachim Iwand was once described by Gustaf Wingren as the best Lutheran theologian of the twentieth century.[1] Around the turn of the millennium and more than forty years after Iwand's death, Jürgen Moltmann wrote that "the time had come to discover Hans Joachim Iwand and to gauge the wide-ranging consequences of his theological findings."[2] Gerhard Forde extolled Iwand as "a peerless defender of the doctrine of justification by faith."[3] Nevertheless, up until now only one monograph of Iwand's writing has been translated into English, *The Righteousness of Faith According to Luther*.[4]

A peer of Karl Barth and Dietrich Bonhoeffer, Iwand lived through the tumultuous Second World War and was jailed for some time because of his attitude to Hitler's church policy. There was not only some critical distance between Bonhoeffer and Iwand but also several important similarities. The main difference is that while Bonhoeffer from 1938 expanded his opposition to commitment in the conspiracy cell within the counterintelligence of the Wehrmacht, Iwand restricted his opposition to the realm of church and distanced himself that year from Karl Barth because of the political implications of his booklet *Rechtfertigung und Recht*.[5]

In the face of the secularization of society from the outside and the collapse of many institutional church structures from the inside, Iwand brought forth a mature reflection on Luther's theology which addressed his contemporary situation.[6] While

---

1. James Nestingen, "Introduction," in *The Captivation of the Will* (Grand Rapids: Eerdmans, 2005), 20.

2. Jürgen Moltmann, "Hans Joachim Iwand entdecken," *Evangelische Theologie*, 60 (2000): 230.

3. Gerhard Forde, "The Exodus from Virtue to Grace: Justification by Faith Today," *Interpretation*, January 1980, 32.

4. Hans Joachim Iwand, *The Righteousness of Faith According to Luther*, ed. Virgil Thompson, trans. Randi Lundell (Eugene, OR: Wipf & Stock, 2008).

5. Karl Barth, *Rechtfertigung und Recht* (Theologische Studien H. 1) (Zürich: Theologischer Verlag Zürich, 1938). The English translation of Barth's work bears the title "Church and State" to denote its general topic. Karl Barth, *Church and State*, trans. G. Ronald Howe (Greenville, SC: Smyth & Helwys, 1991).

6. For English introductions to the thought of Iwand, cf. Gregory A. Walter, "Hans Joachim Iwand (1899-1960)," in *Twentieth-Century Lutheran Theologians*, ed. Mark

most of Iwand's reception into English has focused on his doctrinal reflections on justification by faith (and rightly so since this was central to his conception of the Christian faith), his writings also explored the vast ramifications of this doctrine for Christian faith and life. While Iwand's overall work on the theology of Martin Luther during the time of the Luther renaissance has been appreciated for its timely articulation of the doctrine of justification for the modern world, it was actually Iwand's insights into the implications of justification particularly for the intersection of church and society that have been recognized as a distinct contribution to the study of Luther.[7] This volume brings together a selection of Iwand's essays on this intersection of church and society as theological reflections on Luther's teachings on society, justification, and the theology of the cross. Iwand critiques herein the Lutheran understanding of the two kingdoms, in the way it was conceptualized in the nineteenth century, and charts a new way forward for understanding Luther's theology and the way it addresses Christian life within society. Most importantly, Iwand discusses church and society which have so often been seen as closed to one another and argues instead how they have been and continue to be opened up to each other by the kingdom of God.

The interwovenness of Iwand's reading of Luther and his reflection on what was going on in church and society will speak for itself in a brief overview of the texts in this volume. The first chapter, "The Preaching of the Law" (1934), shows how Iwand, in opposition to the German Christian heresy, loosens the ties between the law of God and the structures of political life by presenting a Lutheran view of the law, which is as critical as the Barmen Declaration of 1934, but from a slightly different perspective. The year after Iwand gave a lecture, "The Objectivity of the Theological Task" (1935), in which he elaborates on what it means to do theology in strict concentration on Jesus Christ, the living Lord. Iwand underscores that the unity of truth and reality of the Word of God brings together the theology of the cross and the church militant.

Eight years later, at a stage in the Second World War in which the inevitable defeat of Germany already was obvious, Iwand wrote an essay on Luther's anthropology that can be regarded as a preliminary exercise in how to confess guilt: "*Sed originale per hominem unum*: A Contribution to the Doctrine of Man" (1943). However, in the aftermath of the war Iwand recognized that the tendency in Western German society showed itself reluctant to face the past and instead focused on the political issues of the relation between church and state. The problematic and unfruitful character of this trend is brought to the fore in the "Darmstädter Wort" of the Council of Brethren of the Confessing Church of August 1947, for which Iwand

---

C. Mattes (Göttingen: Vandenhoeck & Ruprecht, 2013) and Timothy J. Schueler, "Hans Joachim Iwand's Interpretation of the Lutheran Understanding of the Law and Its Relevance for Preaching" (Unpublished M.Th. thesis written for James Nestingen at Luther Northwestern Seminary, 1989).

7. Bernhard Lohse, *Martin Luther: An Introduction to His Life and Work* (Minneapolis: Fortress Press, 1986), 142–3.

wrote the first draft. As a theologian who owed his fundamental insights to Luther, Iwand observed the refusal to look upon the past in confession and conversion as a token of self-justification, instead of entrusting oneself to God's forgiveness and renewal in Jesus Christ. This stance in Western German society at that time also became obvious in the accusation of Dietrich Bonhoeffer and his fellow conspirators of committing high treason in planning an attack on Adolf Hitler in order to end the war. Together with his colleague in the Faculty of Theology in Göttingen, Iwand was invited by the Brunswick court to deliver a theological assessment on this issue. His paper "Toward a Theological Rationale for Protest Against the Government" shows how he diagnosed the fixation of political ethics on the relation of church and state to be the fundamental flaw.

In the early 1950s Iwand was deeply engaged in rethinking the responsibility of the church in and for society. The church cannot and should not stick to the secular insistence of the separation of church and politics but should take up her own responsibility, as is implicated in the gospel of Jesus Christ. Iwand's own diagnosis and his new perspective can easily be recognized in the titles of a few texts and lectures on "church and society," one of which is contained in this volume. In "The Bible and the Social Question" (1951) he elaborates on the implications of the biblical account of the events of the life, death, and resurrection of Jesus Christ and the outpouring of the Holy Spirit for the particular perspective of Christians on society and for the way they should deal with its problems and challenges. Resisting the approach that a "neutral" concept of liberty can provide the Western world with real freedom, Iwand makes explicit in his political meditation on the parable of the Good Samaritan, "Love as Foundation and Boundary of Freedom" (1951), that the only solid foundation for freedom can be found in acknowledging and practicing the true "freedom of the Christian" in not looking away from those who are in real danger and in standing by those who are in real need.

By the end of the 1950s Iwand's engagement of society does not wane in the face of the new challenges of the world (dis)order, that is, the Cold War. Instead, he again studies Luther intensively to discover where and how things went wrong in a particular branch of Lutheranism and its development of a distinct approach to the theology of Luther. By doing so, Iwand digs up the critical and fruitful impulses that still are in it but had nevertheless remained undetected. It is the central statement of his short but very important paper "Against the Misuse of the *pro me* as Methodological Principle in Theology" (1954) that Luther's *Theses de fide* show us how the *assertiones*—the true and firm theological statements according to the Gospel—can free Western society in the midst of the twentieth century from its own "Babylonian captivity." In his essay "Estate and Sacrament" (1957) Iwand is again in search of the particular misunderstanding of Luther's teachings on church and state that had prevented what had become known as Protestant church and theology from actually protesting against Nazi politics. In his article "Toward a Development of Luther's Ecclesiology: A Rejoinder to the Essay of the Same Name by Karl Holl" (1957), Iwand expounds what the rediscovery of Luther's ecclesiology as part of the *theologia crucis* can imply, especially for renewing the perspective on the church and its role in society. In his paper "*Theologia crucis*" (1959) he assures that in going the way of the cross we are with our contemporaries and we can acknowledge what real faith is: not what we talk into ourselves but where we are really found by God in His redeeming and liberating work. In this a new way of thinking and doing ethics is implicated: not what we as moral individuals take for just, right, and good but the new ways God leads us, showing us ways where we thought there were none. The title of the last chapter in this volume, "The Freedom of the Christian and the Bondage of the Will" (1959), clearly shows that in Iwand's view the young Luther with his stress on the *servum arbitrium* is not an obsolete residual of the "Dark Middle Ages" but rather the interpreter of the Gospel we desperately need, because he shows the connection between the Gospel and our existence in a "liberating realization."

The German-language definitive biography of Hans Joachim Iwand begins with a brief reflection of Iwand himself on whether biography is a worthy genre in its own right.[8] In a lecture on Luther, Iwand once stated, "There is sometimes the danger with academics, that they isolate their teaching, that they actually try to form it into a system, and a timeless one at that. . . . All we end up hearing are their answers but not their questions."[9] Throughout the chapters of this volume, Iwand strives mightily to invite us into the questions he was wrestling with at the time. These questions are borne out of his multifaceted conversation with people in society as he sought to bring the ever-living Word of God to bear upon the situation. The following is a brief timeline of the life and thought of Hans Joachim Iwand.

Timeline

1899   On July 11, Hans Joachim Iwand is born as the first child to Pastor Otto Iwand and his wife Lydia Hermann in Schreibendorf, 25 miles south of Breslau (now Wrocław, Poland). There is no running water in the house of his birth and childhood.[10]

1910   Moves into the house of his grandfather, Moritz Iwand, in Görlitz to begin at the Gymnasium (middle school and high school education aimed at college prep).

1917   Finishes his college preparatory exams and enrolls in the fall at the University of Breslau to study evangelical theology. There he studies under several professors, among whom is Heinrich Scholz, a systematic theologian become philosopher. In Scholz's lectures on the philosophy

---

8. Jürgen Seim, *Hans Joachim Iwand: eine Biografie*, 2nd and expanded edition (Gütersloh: C. Kaiser/Gütersloher Verlagshaus, 1999).

9. Hans Joachim Iwand, *Luthers Theologie*, NW V, ed. J. Haar (Munich: Chr. Kaiser Verlag, 1974), 40.

10. This timeline follows the extensive German-language timeline in: Peter Sänger and Dieter Pauly, *Hans Joachim Iwand: Theologie in der Zeit* (Munich: Chr. Kaiser Verlag, 1992). It is supplemented by material from Seim and other sources as noted.

of religion, Iwand begins a lifelong project to hold faith and knowledge, theology and philosophy, together in a dynamic relationship.[11]

1918 Drafted into the Tenth Infantry Regiment and after training was stationed on the front lines. Later transferred to border patrol.

1919 After release from border patrol duty, returns to summer school in Breslau where he meets the young instructor Rudolf Hermann, with whom he would establish a lifelong friendship.

1920 Takes part in the Kapp-Putsch, a right-wing coups d'etat on the Reichstag. Goes into hiding for a time after this.

1921 In May 1921 Iwand in Upper-Silezia again fights in a *Freikorps* for conquering the *Annaberg* against the Poles, who refused to accept the outcome of the plebiscite on to which country the population wished to belong to. For his participation in this campaign Iwand received a decoration.[12]

Takes his first university exam and reveals to Rudolf Hermann, his lifelong mentor, that he wants to pursue academics as a career. Also begins his own independent study of Martin Luther. Spends some time at the University of Halle and then at seminary in Wittenberg. Begins to work as a private tutor (like the great scholars Kant, Schleiermacher, and Hölderlin) and has time to immerse himself in reading. Reads and is especially fascinated by Max Weber's three volumes on religious sociology alongside Luther's 1515/16 lectures on Romans and the Bible, especially the Gospel of John and 2 Corinthians.[13]

1923 Receives first academic post as "Studies Inspector" at the Luther House of the University of Königsberg (now Kaliningrad). Founded in 1919, the Luther House had places for twenty-one students to live and learn.

1924 Submits his dissertation in systematics and is promoted to Doctor of Theology. Meets Karl Barth for the first time when Barth comes to Königsberg to deliver a lecture entitled "Man's Word and God's Word in the Christian Sermon." After Iwand's death, Barth writes about Iwand, "I have known and loved him, since I . . . for the first time saw him in Königsberg. . . . The fire that burned in him had no equal."[14]

1926 Writes his second dissertation (*Habilitationsschrift*) on Luther's Christology and its relation to the doctrine of justification. Submits it just after the New Year in 1927 and thereby qualifies to become an instructor (*Privatdozent*) in the German university system at the University of Königsberg, among a prestigious theological faculty that would, during Iwand's time there,

---

11. Seim, *Hans Joachim Iwand*, 13.
12. Cf. Ibid., 25.
13. Seim, *Hans Joachim Iwand*, 27–8.
14. Ibid., 48.

include the New Testament professor Julius Schniewind (sixteen years Iwand's senior), the younger New Testament professor Günther Bornkamm, and the Old Testament professor Martin Noth. Iwand's lectures are not only full but overflowing.

1927   On March 5, marries Dr. of Jurisprudence Ilse Ehrhardt, daughter of the Jewish Christians Martha and Oskar Ehrhardt, professor of surgery in Königsberg. Hans and Ilse are blessed with five children—Annemone, Thomas, Peter, Malve, and Veronika.

1929   Completes his theological examination and is ordained as a pastor in the evangelical church of Königsberg.

1932   It is reported that three-fourths of the students at Iwand's *Lutherheim* are members of the *Sturmabteilung* (SA), a paramilitary group of stormtroopers, trying to "transform the *Lutherheim* into a SA-residence."[15] Despite his right-wing political orientation Iwand resists, which June 1933 would contribute to his dismissal by the German Christians.

1933   In April, called on to take a leading role in the preservation of the church and clergy which are beginning to fracture. At this time, the "Law for the Restoration of the Professional Civil Service" (*Gesetz zur Wiederherstellung des Berufsbeamtentums*) is signed into law preventing those of non-Aryan (Jewish) descent from serving in public positions, including in the church.

Gathers the East Prussian theologians against the Deutsche Christen, an organization founded in 1932 to advocate for church leaders aligned with the ideological principles of the Nazis in elections of the Church of the Old Prussian Union.

By June, removed from office as Director of the Lutherheim by German Christian (*deutsche Christen*) leadership and replaced. In the coming days, Iwand will be restored by the Nazi minister president of East Prussia, Erich Koch.

In November, founds alongside his colleague, Julius Schniewind, the Working Group for the Church (*kirchliche Arbeitsgemeinschaft*), the forerunner of the East Prussian Confessing Church.

1934   Begins to take part and a lead role in gatherings of the Confessing Church.

Publishes the first chapter of this volume, "The Preaching of the Law" (*Die Predigt des Gesetzes*), in the periodical *Evangelische Theologie* founded by Karl Barth.

Is forced out of the Lutherheim in October. Leaves Königsberg in November for Riga, Latvia, to accept a call to become Instructor of New Testament at the Herder Institute.

---

15. Cf. Ibid., 112.

1935　The East Prussian Confessing Church decides to form its own commission for theological examination.

Publishes "The Objectivity of the Theological Task" (*Die Sachlichkeit der theologischen Arbeit*) in the first issue of a new journal *Pamphlets for the Evangelical Church in the East* (*Flugschriften für die evangelische Kirche im Osten*), founded by Günther Bornkamm, his former theological colleague in Königsberg, and Kurt von Grot.

Just months after his arrival in Riga, the Herder Institute dissolves their contract with Iwand due to a reduction in force. He remains in his position to lecture until May. In August, the family moves back to the Königsberg region to a town called Blöstau (now Wischnjowka).

Founds a small practical seminary (*Predigerseminar*) in Blöstau with sixteen students and an assistant, Gerhard Friedrich, for the evangelical church of the Old Prussian Union.

1936　In January, the new Blöstau seminary is dedicated with participation by Martin Niemöller.

1937　Begins his lectures on law and gospel in the spring.

In May, Iwand is expelled by the Gestapo from East Prussia; he therefore has to leave Blöstau and Königsberg and to search for another location for the seminary. Until the closure of all the "illegal" declared institutions of the Confessing Church in September 1937, the seminary finds a shelter in the village Paradies (near modern-day Jordanowo, Poland). After the final closure of the seminary Iwand finds a refuge for his East Prussian seminary students and his family in Dortmund.[16]

In mid December he is jailed again along with his assistant and all thirteen students for a week.

1938　By April, the seminary is forced by the authorities in Dortmund to close. Shortly thereafter Iwand is called by the elders of the St. Mary's Church in Dortmund to be their pastor. The Gestapo, however, overrules the congregation's call and instead puts Iwand back in prison.

In July, the congregation in Dortmund prevails and is allowed to call Iwand who has now been released from prison. He will serve this congregation until after the end of the war.

Around the same time as the Kristallnacht (November 9–10, 1938) Iwand is again jailed and is not released until the following March. This is the last time he is jailed.

1939　Is visited in July by Dietrich Bonhoeffer, who is leading in Finkenwalde another practical seminary (*Predigerseminar*) akin to the one Iwand led in Blöstau. During this meeting, they discuss Bonhoeffer's interest in pacifism

---

16. Ibid., 205f.

of which Iwand remains somewhat skeptical.[17] He will recall in 1957 that he eventually came to agree with Bonhoeffer's position on pacifism.

In September, travels to see friends in Posen (now Poznań, Poland) shortly after Hitler's invasion of Poland which begins the Second World War. There he sees firsthand the devastation of Hitler's aggression.

Begins to ask whether questions of soteriology may be losing their salience in the midst of societal upheavals and doubles down on dogmatic rather than ethical investigations. Begins work on a long form essay to address soteriology from Luther's perspective.

1941   Publishes a 100 page overview of Luther's conception of the Christian faith in an essay addressed primarily to laity entitled "The Righteousness of Faith According to Luther" in another theological journal founded by Karl Barth, *Theologische Existenz Heute*. This brought him widespread notoriety throughout Germany. The essay is dedicated to Martin Niemöller who is at the time imprisoned in the Dachau concentration camp.[18]

1942   Writes his friend Günther Bornkamm a scathing critique of Bultmann's 1941 essays on demythologization arguing that "The Bible is the book of humanity and not written merely for the small horizon of 19th, let alone 20th, century Europe."[19]

1943   Writes the essay "*Sed originale per hominem unum*: A Contribution to the Doctrine of Man" for the sixtieth birthday of his former Königsberg colleague, Julius Schniewind. The essay is intended as an entry for a Festschrift but is not able to be published as such during the war. The essay is first published after the war in 1946 along with those of Günther Bornkamm and Martin Noth in *Evangelische Theologie*.[20]

1944   On the night of October 6–7, Dortmund is bombed. The Iwand parsonage is destroyed down to the basement ceiling. Fire burns much of the rest of many homes. The family barely escape the bombing with their lives. Most of Iwand's library and personal papers are also destroyed.[21] Of the 4,000 members living in the parish of St. Mary's before the war, only 100 remain. Although he and his family move north of the city center, Iwand continues weekly services in the area for those able to attend.

1945   Holds his farewell sermon as pastor in Dortmund after the end of the war in October. In November, he takes up a new academic post at the University of Göttingen in systematic theology.

---

17. Seim, *Hans Joachim Iwand*, 245.
18. Schueler, "Hans Joachim Iwand's Interpretation," 12.
19. "Die Bibel ist das Buch der Menschheit und nicht einfach für den kleinen Horizont des 19. oder gar des 20. Europäischen Jahrhunderts geschrieben." Seim, *Hans Joachim Iwand*, 272.
20. Seim, *Hans Joachim Iwand*, 279.
21. Ibid., 288–9.

1947 Begins writing meditations on the pericopal texts to help pastors in their preaching. He is eventually joined in writing these meditations by other colleagues at Göttingen including Gerhard von Rad, Joachim Jeremias, Günther Bornkamm, and Otto Weber. These become known as the "Göttinger Predigtmeditationen" and are published regularly in the journal *Pastoraltheologie*.

1948 Takes part in a number of meetings to restructure the church, including a meeting where he led on the topic "The Church and the Dissolution of the Orders of Society."

1949 Gives a lecture entitled "The Refugee Question as Religious Question" and later this year founds a home for refugees near the east-west border in Beienrode called "House of the Helping Hands." Ilse Iwand is responsible for the realization of this new home primarily for young widows. When he is invited to pray at an event in Dortmund commemorating the slaughter of 300 women and men on Good Friday of 1944, he writes a personal letter to a friend about his attendance, "I will again be on my own among people that other theologians are rarely among, but I do not want to write them off. 'Better' people do not concern themselves with these poor Jews and communists, that is, until something terrible happens again."[22]

1950 The 49-year-old Ilse Iwand, Hans' wife, dies of an aggressive form of breast cancer on December 21.

1951 Publishes "Love as Foundation and Boundary of Freedom" in the Roman Catholic sociopolitical periodical *Frankfurter Hefte*, under the direction of his friend Eugen Kogon. Begins teaching on the subject of "church and society" and gives a lecture entitled "The Bible and the Social Question" in London.

1952 Takes up a new academic post in Bonn to lead the evangelical theological faculty at the university. Publishes "The Bible and the Social Question" in the periodical *Junge Kirche* and the essay "Church and Society" in a "Festschrift" dedicated to Martin Niemöller. Also begins to lecture on a pressing question in the postwar period, whether there was any theological legitimacy to the evangelical protest and attempted coups against the Nazi government. When Major General Otto Ernst Remer pressed for sentencing for evangelical Christians associated with such resistance to the Nazi government, Iwand and his colleague Ernst Wolf were called upon to offer a theological opinion. Following these events, the essay "Toward a Theological Rationale for Protest Against the Government" was published in the following year.

1954 Presents the strongly perceived essay "Against the Misuse of the *pro me* as Methodological Principle in Theology" at the German Evangelical Theologians' conference. At a conference in Stockholm to work on

---

22. Ibid., 368–70.

international relations and attended by representatives from East and West Germany, South America, Australia, Eastern Europe, Eastern Asia, France, and England, Iwand meets the novelist Anna Seghers and the philosopher Georg Lukács. In his speech on the closing day of the conference, he says that he does not want to live in a different world from Seghers or Lukács. "We do not want to split the world into those who are held to be legitimate and those who are considered illegitimate. For that is essentially inhumanity."[23]

1957   Speaks at a church gathering in Berlin-Spandau, where he recalls his conversation with Dietrich Bonhoeffer and states that he was not born into his views on pacifism but rather was born into a nationalist-minded Prussian pastor's home. Through his experiences with National Socialism he was won over to Bonhoeffer's perspective on this.[24]

1960   Writes one of his last essays as an open letter to the Synod Convention of the evangelical church in Germany. Here he argues that atomic armament is evil and that atomic weapons are "the preparation for the assassination of humankind."[25] On April 29, Iwand suffers a stroke. On May 2, he dies in Bonn and then is buried beside his wife in a park next to the House of Helping Hands in Beienrode. Hans Joachim Iwand was a man who stood between East and West as a theologian of the cross. In the funeral, Ernst Burdach preaches on 2 Cor. 6:9 "As dying, and behold, we live" and proclaims, "This Theology of the Cross was the center of his thinking, and it shaped his life."[26]

Having given a snapshot of the life of Hans Joachim Iwand and how he himself navigated the intersection of church and society, we turn now to an overview of his thought, especially as it found witness in his writings. Charles Taylor has recently written of "itineraries" toward the end of his comprehensive study *The Secular Age*, which itself serves as a meditation on the conversation between church and society. Taylor holds before his readers Christians who were travelling various "itineraries" through the modern age and yet kept the faith.[27] Such itineraries are described as those staying in the center between the extremes of a spirituality of dwelling (traditionalists) and a spirituality of seeking (progressives). Taylor's main example of such an itinerary is Bede Griffiths who chronicled his intellectual life and conversion to Roman Catholicism after reading thoroughly among modern authors.

---

23. Ibid., 470–1.
24. Ibid., 11.
25. Schueler, "Hans Joachim Iwand's Interpretation," 19.
26. Seim, *Hans Joachim Iwand*, 1.
27. Charles Taylor, *A Secular Age* (Cambridge, MA: Belknap Press of Harvard University Press, 2007), esp. 745ff.

In many ways, Hans Joachim Iwand's life and thought follow a similar itinerary but more along an evangelical/Lutheran trajectory. Iwand is by no means a mere repristinator of Luther. He insists that the very Gospel itself is "no timeless truth" as if it could just be taken off a shelf as a museum relic.[28] The God who justifies sinners through the cross of Christ was at the heart of Iwand's theology. This happens in Iwand's thinking only in real time as the living God engages concrete people in real situations, not via a timeless, eternal, abstract set of thoughts to which human beings must ascend. Whether in his essays in this volume, his correspondence, or his preaching meditations, Iwand insists that the Word of God is the voice of a living and active God which calls people in every age to proclaim it as a word for today.

As a modern person and twentieth-century academic, Iwand was by no means content to keep the Word of God cordoned off to the realm of private religious experience or even just to the corporate religious experience in the sanctuary. Iwand was conversant with the philosophers and theologians of his day in a deeply engaged manner and yet was himself deeply beholden to a Christianity that was far older and more orthodox. He dug deeply into Martin Luther's theology and scriptural exegesis in order to bring it into conversation with his own life and times. And yet, in doing so he insists that the Bible is not just a word for the nineteenth or twentieth centuries but for all of humanity living in every age.

Iwand's itinerary can most clearly be grasped in his unique view of church and society. For him, these were two communities, entities, or estates (Stände) which were both being opened to the other by a third entity, the kingdom of God. Typical conceptions of a Lutheran view of the two kingdoms teaching have often left matters of the left hand such as society to be separated from religious concerns of the right hand. This scenario may have been one mode of expression for Luther but in an age of a still existing unity in an enchanted or believing age. In the late modern Cartesian, Kantian world in which most people, secular and religious alike, believe in a separation of church and state, the two kingdoms teaching becomes only a religious justification for the status quo. Put another way, the two kingdoms approach to discussing issues of church and society is often co-opted by the culture to insist that Christians keep their views to themselves. Capitulating to this status quo leads Christians to quarantine themselves unknowingly from all things related to society. Iwand was an observant reader of Kant and Hegel and other influential philosophers of the modern age and understood the danger these philosophers posed to Christians utilizing the two kingdoms doctrine. He thus brings out another way of discussing Luther's view of church and society based on Luther's teaching of the estates. This insight of Luther is a view that brings church and society back into engagement with one another. This may at first seem only to bring about a clash between these two estates, and Iwand agrees that there will be clashing. And yet, the kingdom of God in opening these two estates to one another also brings new opportunities for rapprochement and reengagement, precisely in ways that had been impossible before.

---

28. Cf. "Church and Society" in this volume.

Chapter 1

THE PREACHING OF THE LAW

Originally published as Hans Joachim Iwand, "Die Predigt des Gesetzes," *Evangelische Theologie* 1 (1934): 55-78; also in Hans Joachim Iwand, *Glaubensgerechtigkeit*, GA II, ed. Gerhard Sauter, Theologische Bücherei 64 (Munich: Christian Kaiser Verlag, 1979), 145-70.

In the first volume of Evangelische Theologie, *the new periodical of Karl Barth and the theologians who were congenial with his rejection of the "natural theology" of the* Deutsche Christen *(German Christians), Hans Joachim Iwand contributed an article on the pressing theme of the preaching of the Gospel. This journal was established as a kind of replacement for the periodical* Zwischen den Zeiten, *the appearance of which had stopped after Friedrich Gogarten joined the German Christians in 1933. So, the fact that Iwand published in* Evangelische Theologie *was a clear statement of his stance in the theological discussions of the time. It is noteworthy that until 1933 Iwand felt himself more aligned with Gogarten than with Barth and up until then widely agreed with Gogarten's view of the relation between church and state. Whereas Gogarten in his 1933 booklet "Einheit von Evangelium und Volkstum?" ("Unity of Gospel and Nationhood?") linked the Law in the church directly with the fundamental principles of the new Nazi state, Iwand dissects these, in order to articulate that the preaching of the Law not be blurred and blemished with political intentions.* (GdH)

The whole force of this topic is in the word "preaching." It is precisely because we know other forms of legislation and other possible ways to live under the Law that the preaching of the law is a thing unto itself. For the preaching of the law means an event that comes from God, means that God makes his will known, means that it is given to us to hear what God wills in our life. Here the law is subsumed into the Word—what's more, it is transformed into the Word. Certainly, it is the *nomos* that we hear, but the one we hear is the Lord even of this *nomos*. For we do not believe in the *nomos* but rather in the promise of the one who wills to give the person the law in his heart. This is why one thing must be certain above all else: the preaching of the law is the proclamation of God's will, not in the timelessness of the law as it is hewn in stone or able to be handed down word for word [cf. 2 Corinthians 3:3ff.] but rather in the presence of the God who is speaking to us. For "The word is near you, in your mouth and in your heart" (Rom. 10:8).

The preaching of the law must be a proclamation that both awakens belief and is believable. It is only able to be such a proclamation if it itself comes from Jesus Christ. Only the preaching of the law that comes from him leads to him; it is only credible if it adheres to the cycle of the law. Every other understanding of the law must end up at the same place where the Jews' understanding of the law ended up: "We have a law, and according to that law he ought to die" (Jn 19:7). This is why the preaching of the law can only be serious where it is not understood as *praeparatio ad gratiam*[1] but rather where it is itself a part of the whole of the good news. To give and interpret laws is a part of human activity in the world; the pagans can do it just as well as Christians. But the preaching of the law is only possible because we belong to God and are his possession—indeed, only because of that reality. "Unless the Lord builds the house, those who build it labor in vain" (Ps. 127:1). In the proclamation and interpretation of the law, we must be grounded in that saving act of God in Jesus Christ that claims the world as his own possession, the act that is the only firm foundation of the law. We must not dare to preach the law—and people would have good reason to close their ears—if this presupposition were not true and if it were not also our presupposition when we speak to people, and if we did not believe—because we may and must believe it in Jesus Christ—that those to whom God speaks are already his possession, already his elect. And if, in spite of it all, this presupposition does not constrain the preaching of the law but spreads it, if this presupposition does not narrow the preaching of the law to a particular set of people who in their own presumptuousness fancy themselves the elect but rather brings it about that the law applies to everyone—pagans and Jews, wicked and good, the pious no less than the children of the world—then it is not because the meaning of the law is universally comprehensible. For this comprehensibility of the law is definitely *not* the point of contact for the proclamation (of the Gospel),[2] is *not* the point where God makes contact; rather, the preaching of the

---

1. [The "preparation for grace, that is, for the reception of grace" is the precondition for God's salvation that must be present in man according to scholastic teaching (cf. Thomas Aquinas, *Summa Theologica* I-II, q 112 a 2–5); this view was affirmed in the Council of Trent's decree concerning justification (cf. Heinrich Denzinger and Peter Hünermann [ed.], *Enchiridion Symbolorum, Definitionum et Declarationum de rebus fidei et morum*, 43rd ed. (San Francisco: Ignatius Press, 2012), nr. 1525f.

In his interpretation of Galatians 3:24f., Luther says that the law prepares for grace, "For the Law, as I have said, prepares for grace in that it reveals and increases sin; it humbles the proud, so that they long for Christ's help" (Martin Luther, *Lectures on Galatians* (1519), LW 27, 279; WA 2, 529,7-9). On Galatians 3:19, "Thus, the law is a preparation for grace" (Martin Luther, *Lectures on Galatians* (1535), LW 26, 314; WA 40/1, 488,2f.). Cf. "And consequently, the law also assists the promise with its office; even though it does not justify, it is nevertheless a sweet servant that drives a person towards justification" (LW 26, 315; WA 40/1, 489,8-10).]

2. [Here Iwand is alluding to the controversy between Karl Barth, Emil Brunner, Rudolf Bultmann, and Friedrich Gogarten at the beginning of the 1930s concerning the point of

Law applies to all precisely because God loves the world in Jesus Christ (cf. Jn 3:16). The wonder of God's love, not the moral sensibility of *Homo sapiens*, is the point of contact for what God has to say even and precisely as the one who has a claim to the world. For as Luther once wrote in his thesis: "*Amor Dei non invenit, Sed Creat suum Diligibile.*"³

Since the proclamation of the law has such great things in mind, it must face opposition in this world and bear the scandal of the cross in itself. For what does this proclamation mean alongside the application of the law in state and society, discipline [*Erziehung*] and morals? Does it not at first become clear by this juxtaposition how little we accomplish? To say it quite crudely: if we waited until people obey God and do what they ought to out of this obedience, the world would fall into pieces. Precisely there lies our agonizing struggle [*Anfechtung*]. Precisely upon this visible failure soar the priest's desires to be allowed to apply the law with that dazzling authority that enchants his eye and his heart when observing the authoritarian state. He would also like to make fire come down from heaven over the unrepentant cities one time (cf. Gen. 19:24; Lk. 17:29) to punish the wicked one time, to reward the good, to confer the respect that the judgment of the state enjoys among people upon the judgment of God one time. Since the reality of the law also stands before his eyes in the state and the societal order—the reality of a law that is not only word but also power, that encounters not only the heart but also the body, that not only commands but also carries out that which it commands—since everything that the preacher is unable to do and is incapable of enforcing is therein able to be done and enforced, despair befalls him as to the uselessness of his task, the meaninglessness of his speaking. He experiences the weakness of the Word (cf. 1 Cor. 2:3f.) that has nothing behind itself and thus brings nothing before itself. He experiences in this the weakness of God himself (cf. 1 Cor. 1:25).

For therein lies the scandal of divine righteousness, that the same God who gives power to the prince to punish the violation of external orders of personal property, honor and freedom, body and life, at the very place where he makes his will immediately manifest, is so weak, so meek, so mild that he only calls, admonishes, entices, promises and threatens, pleads and implores, and remains hidden with all of this in the Word instead of forces the person to keep his commandments as the state forces him. God reveals himself in the Word. This means simultaneously and inevitably: he tolerates it that people overlook and mock, despise and bend his will. He lets it come to pass that they regard themselves as more powerful, freer, mightier than God himself. He lets it come to pass that they all sin before him

---

contact (the "preunderstanding") as a precondition for hearing the gospel. Cf. Wilhelm Link's report of the discussion, "contact," "preunderstanding," and the issue of "theological anthropology" in *Theologische Rundschau, Neue Folge*, Nr. 7 (1935): 205-54, reprinted in *Heidegger und die Theologie. Beginn und Fortgang der Diskussion*, ed. Gerhard Noller, Theologische Bücherei 38 (Munich: Christian Kaiser Verlag, 1967), 147-93.]

3. ["The love of God does not find, but creates, that which is pleasing to it."] Martin Luther, *Heidelberg Disputation* (1518), LW 31, 41; Thesis 28. WA 1, 365,1.

precisely in that place where, stripped of all his power, he speaks to their hearts, where no one judges but him, where no one speaks but him, where no one sees but him, where no one is encountered but him. It would be no proper preacher of the law who had not himself gotten a taste of the despair that this weakness of God brings with it. For this weakness is indeed nothing else but the weakness of our office, which means that we stand there like "the scum of the world" (1 Cor. 4:13). And if only we were to stand in this way, if only we would comprehend that we were then standing precisely in the course of salvation history, if only it would be true of us that "When reviled, we bless; when persecuted, we endure; when slandered, we entreat" (1 Cor. 4:12f.); mind you: if only both of these things applied to us, if only this comparison to our office could be found, if only we experienced the actuality of God in this way and none other!

Since the righteousness of God is always inferior to the world wherever it is truly *his* righteousness, the priesthood of all times and religions has continually dreamed the theocratic dream: the dream of erecting a law that makes people not into sinners but into righteous people, not into transgressors but into fulfillers—to found a kingdom that demonstrates the dominion of God in power and majesty before his worshippers and his enemies, his faithful, and his opponents. From that day when the Son of God heard the offer of world dominion from the mouth of the one who did *not* have the kingdoms of the world to give away (Mt. 4:8f. par.), the theocratic idea has, even for the church of Jesus Christ, continually been a great temptation to apostasy, to apostasy from faith into the desire for sight (cf. 2 Cor. 5:7), from expectation into grasping, from us relying on God to God relying on us. And no one who has to carry out the office of the law is secure in the face of that kind of lonely hour, about which it is written, "the devil took him to a very high mountain and showed him all the kingdoms of the world and their glory" (Mt. 4:8). Good for us if we do not forget in that hour that the servant is not greater than the master (cf. Mt. 10:24 par.) and that there is one who has already stood there before us and made the decision that we do not make anew but only accept obediently as something that is also binding for us—without argument, without consideration of pros and cons, without an appraisal of the opportunities that could open up for our service. For the one who stood there before us saw through the offer's deception and recognized that a dual service, a service of two masters, had been introduced here, the great minus sign before the parenthesis that necessarily turns all achievements that allure and call out to us into achievements of the opponent of God from the outset. Because the way that God made his Son go is truly the redemption of the world, the prince of this world constructs on the wayside the enchanting images of something that seems to be holiness, a dominion of God next to which and under which his kingdom can persist in all its glory. "*Imperium non est extra Ecclesiam, idest Christus non illuditur nisi in purpura.*"[4]

---

4. ["The dominion is not outside of the church, that is to say: Christ is only mocked in purple garments" Martin Luther, *Lectures on the Psalms* (1513/15), WA 5, 650,3f. On Psalm 22:19 (translation our own). (Here, Luther speaks of the relationship between the spiritual

1. The Preaching of the Law

The temptation to the apostasy to which the church is prone cannot be the temptation to unbelief, to naked, open godlessness. Rather, it is always the temptation to a faith that is no faith, to a worship that is secretly dominion, to a zeal for God that is secretly zeal on one's own behalf. The psychology of the priest is one of the most impressive chapters of the "Will to Power," not for the first time with Nietzsche[5] but rather long before him in the mouth of Jesus himself. And the fact that this is the case does not arise out of some accidental, distinct disposition of the individual; rather, it lies in the curse of the law [cf. Gal. 3:10] that has designated those who administer it and makes them receptive to the enchantment of a theocratic way of life, to the fantasy that is dreamed and preached, believed and enjoyed in the priesthood of all times and religions. It must be this way and will remain this way as long as the law's end and aim (cf. Rom. 10:4) are not made manifest, as long as we do not understand and interpret the law according to its end. For as long as we are missing insight into the meaning of the law, into the *usus legis*,[6] that can only be gained from there, all zeal for God's justice and power will work ruin, will the veil be placed over the face of the speaker and over the hearts of the hearer (cf. 2 Cor. 3:13ff.) that hides the end from us, will the sobriety be taken away that makes us immune to the blinding majesty of the law, the deception from Sinai.

We should be preachers of the law; we should bear the weakness of the Word in view of the display of power that is bestowed upon the law by the mighty in the world and make it so impressive, so weighty. For in order that the preacher would endure in his post as the caller of God and find his sufficiency in the Word, the promise is given to him that no other legislation can claim: that God wants to write his law in the heart of people and place it on their mind as the law of his people, his

---

and the temporal authority. In a letter to Rudolf Hermann of December 5, 1934 [Iwand, *Briefe an Rudolf Hermann*, NW VI, 263], Iwand mentions that he has read this sentence and feels that it is a confirmation of his worry for the church.)]

5. [Friedrich Nietzsche speaks of the "psychology of the priest" already at the beginning of his *Genealogy of Morality* (1887) in Friedrich Nietzsche. *Ecce Homo*, The Complete Works of Friedrich Nietzsche vol. 17 (New York: Russell & Russell, Inc., 1964), 118, then in *The Antichrist* (1888), in Friedrich Nietzsche, *The Antichrist* (New York: Alfred A Knopf, 1920), 139, and in fragments from the remains of the 1880s that later became known by the title *Will to Power*, for example: "The priest wishes to make it an understood thing that he is the *highest type* of man, that he rules—even over those who wield the power,—that he is invulnerable and unassailable,—that he is the *strongest power* in the community, not by any means to be replaced or undervalued." Friedrich Nietzsche, *The Will to Power: An Attempted Transvaluation of All Values*, The Complete Works of Friedrich Nietzsche vol. 14 (New York: Russell & Russell, Inc., 1964), 118. (Emphasis in the original.)]

6. [In the case of the "uses of the law," the theological function (*usus theologicus*) of the law, which convicts us of our sin and brings us to Christ (therefore following Galatians 3:24 it is also spoken of *usus paedagogicus*), is distinguished in Reformation theology from its task of arranging things in a political sense (*usus politicus*).]

possession. "And no longer shall each one teach his neighbor and each his brother, saying, 'Know the Lord,' for they shall all know me, from the least of them to the greatest" (Jer. 31:33-34). That is the promise that God gives the harbingers of his will along the way. That is why they seem so poor, because they are blessed with this promise. This is why they are condemned so long to silence, because they only get a hearing when all other lawgivers have reached the end of their craft. That is why there is such a mystery and wonder about the task of the preaching of the law, because a promise—even more than that, *the* promise—of God comes to fruition here. For the fulfillment of the preaching of the law is the freedom of the person from the law (cf. Rom. 8:2; Gal. 4:4ff.).

The freedom of the person from the law? It is no coincidence that no person understands this statement who does not know this freedom, who does not know it beginning with it being bestowed on him. The person in his finitude and his infinitude, the natural (1 Cor. 2:14) person set on himself knows only the freedom of the servant who mocks his chains. He only knows the freedom that runs off the tracks, only that freedom and none other. His life under the law is not freedom for him or else he would not seek the fullness of and reason for life in transgressions; and his transgressions are also not freedom for him or else he would not be ashamed of them and flee before them into the solitude of secretiveness. He gets an inkling of the great good of freedom in his inability to be free and cries out for it in the confession: "I do not do the good I want, but the evil I do not want is what I keep on doing" (Rom. 7:19). He suspects that only the free life deserves the name "life," he senses the morning air that surrounds this word, he has a deep-rooted feeling that the person's vocation is "freedom,"[7] but he only senses it when, like a prisoner, he grinds up against the chains that bind him to the dark place of his prison. These chains are the only tangible and perceptible reminder to him of his being free. Who bound him in this way? Who chained the rebel to the stone wall so that his heart would become spoils for the beasts?[8] Whoever it is, only the one who bound him can release him and only the one who forged the chains can break

---

7. [Fichte brings the conflict in the consciousness of freedom to expression in his *The Vocation of Man* in the following way: "Never impelled by any other motive than the desire after what can actually be realized in this world, there is for us no true freedom,—no freedom which holds the ground of its determination absolutely and entirely within itself. . . . We cannot have the slightest conception of true freedom because we do not ourselves possess it; when it is spoken of, we either bring down what is said to the level of our own notions, or at once declare all such talk to be nonsense. Without the idea of freedom, we are likewise without the faculty for another world." Johann Gottlieb Fichte, *The Vocation of Man*, trans. William Smith (London: John Chapman, 1848), 167. Available online: https://archive.org/details/vocationmantrby00fichgoog/page/n169/mode/2up?view=theater (accessed August 15, 2021).]

8. [According to Hesiod, this is what the legend of the punishment of Prometheus, who stole fire from the gods, describes: Zeus chained him, an eagle would daily eat his liver, which would grow back at night, until Heracles freed him.]

them. For the iron law of time reigns over this ill fate and only eternity can be a limit and gauge at this point.

Does being a preacher of the law not mean shaking these chains that bind the person to the earth, wherever they may be—wanted or unwanted? Does it not mean shaking the memory that must not be shaken if life in the here and now is to remain bearable? Does it not mean, wherever it may be, to speak the language that we cannot hear if we are to endure in the foreign land against which we must persist in work, steadfastness, and superior indifference? For where the law comes to my ear as the reminder from God, as the call into the primordial, into the state of childhood, into the truly dignified [*menschenwürdige*] life of the person, the life of love, of faith and hope (cf. 1 Cor. 13:13), then that law will be heavier than a thousand chains and places the whole burden of existence onto heart and conscience. Precisely because it is so good (cf. Rom. 7:16) and thinks so well of me, the law makes my existence unbearable. For it speaks to the person we are of purity of heart, of humility of spirit, of awe before the name that is above all names (Phil. 2:9), of service and the reverence that makes great and small, young and old, dwell together well (Ps. 133:1); it speaks of a brotherhood and an exchange of goods and hardships that makes us smile in view of the reality of life; and it speaks of a love of the sexes that only the youth apprehends. Being a preacher of the law always means—whether we know it or not, whether we believe it or pass right over it back to business as usual—to speak the speech of God into the world of people, this speech that the person understands only too well, the speech that reminds him of where he came from and where he is going, the speech that the person only seems not to understand because he does not want and is not permitted to understand. For who can hear it without despairing of it? And if someone should be able to, how could he boast in that (cf. Rom. 2:23)? For in so doing, he would only make manifest the hardness of his heart (cf. Mk 10:5). This speech of the law reaches into life like death, and the goodness that is made known in it is bitterer to the person than the bitterest agony. This is why people essentially agree with us before we begin to interpret the law and entreat us not to shout about their silent distress if we do not have a means to turn it. For "The whole head is sick, and the whole heart faint" (Isa. 1:5).

We know the excuses that the preaching of the law makes in such dire situations. We know it from the history of the church in former times just as we know it from the church's history in our days. However, this way out that seemingly makes the preaching of the law more fruitful because it makes it bearable, practical, useful, actually forms the germ of the most profound fragmentation of human community, the fragmentation into good and wicked, churchgoing and non-churchgoing, those who live under the law and those who are lawless, religious people and worldly people. For in the same moment when one makes the understanding of the law into the preserve of a particular social stratum, a class, a type of person, or a people, into the privilege of the so-called moral people, one creates on the other side—admittedly, without wanting to do so—a privileged lawlessness. The preaching of the law ceases to be proclamation under the authority of the divine mandate and turns into an interpretation of the law that makes it possible for a particular group of people—more precisely, for a sect—to hear the law and not to despair before it—simply because people thereby no longer have anything to do with God's law at all but rather because they are dealing with the law of their own existence as qualified in this way. They are confronted at best with the ideal of their potentialities but not with the Word of the Creator that calls the person by name. At best, they come across the bonds of community life but never across God's covenant of life with the human race. Then comes the hallmark of every nomistic distortion of faith in God: the law of God that should unite us all under a common condemnation (cf. Rom. 3:19f.) instead separates people into classes and estates. The dichotomy of good and evil, the great final mystery of our existence that is reserved to faith, becomes an intrapersonal, class-struggle, nationalist (*völkisch*), or racial issue. A humanity that wrongly imagines itself to be beyond good and evil[9] makes the enormous attempt to cope with that dichotomy by means of its own power. This is and remains the end of all false preaching of the law: that the blinded, misguided person takes up the struggle against evil out of his own absolute power, his own mental estimation, his own hubris; that he elucidates evil and tries to subject it as if it were like a thing within this world; that he no longer comprehends that there is only one way to break evil's claim to dominion, which is to subject oneself to God's claim to dominion. For the redemption of creation is nothing other than the true Lord coming into his own possession (cf. Jn 1:11).

This is why the First Commandment of all proclamation of the law is to proclaim God's law in such a way that it applies to everyone. No one is so depraved, so lost, so past civilization that he can no longer hear this word, for it is certainly the word that encounters him at the origin of his life. And no one is so good and noble, so believing and pious that he does not need to be frightened to the core of his being when the word of the law encounters him. No one has sunken down so deep, no one climbed so high, no one so far astray, no one has come so far that this word does not catch up with them all and call them back, call them to repentance! To a repentance that is just as difficult for the high and mighty as for the lowly, for the righteous as for the unrighteous, for those who push forward as for those who cannot go on any further—just as difficult for all of them because this call of the law is indeed the call to an impossible return to the origin, to the outset that is lost. Do we really still have an understanding today that the preaching of the law requires the impossible? That the "unless you turn and become like children" (Mt. 18:3) is latent within each individual demand of God? That we must continually respond to every commandment of God with the totally baffled question: "How can a person return to his mother's womb" (Jn 3:4)? That faith in the fulfillment of God's demand is nothing other than faith in the resurrection, in new birth, in new life? If our trust in God were only for this life, we are truly the most pitiable of all people (cf. 1 Cor. 15:19).

---

9. [Cf. Friedrich Nietzsche, *Beyond Good and Evil/On the Genealogy of Morality*, The Complete Works of Friedrich Nietzsche, vol. 8 (Stanford: Stanford University Press, 2014).]

This is how the preaching of the law goes if it proceeds from God, like a sudden shock through hard and soft hearts; it takes everyone as it finds him and reveals the same thing to them all: the place of the person before God as revealed once and for all in Jesus Christ. He is the "honest mirror"[10] in which we behold the truth of our human existence, our truth and yet a truth that we do not find in us but in relation to us, the truth that only becomes our truth and our self-awareness in faith in Jesus Christ. "Christ is the end of the law" (Rom. 10:4). This word of the Scriptures encompasses this gracious exchange of position: the one marked with the curse of the law (cf. Gal. 3:13) bears the features of the person, what we are in the secrecy of our conscience, in our being before God. ". . . *Qualis forma Christi patientis in oculis hominum, talis tua in oculis dei*, . . ."[11]

With all due theological rigor, it must be made sure that the law is only the way to self-awareness when it refers to the story and the cross of Jesus Christ in this way. All immediate self-awareness is delusion and deception; it possesses neither the truth of God nor the truth of man. Only where the person who we are before God stands before us as the one before whom all hills and valleys are made level (cf. Isa. 40:4) is the person encountered with the truth of himself, neither from within nor from without but from God. This is the aim of the law: to wrap the truth of the person and the truth of God together into one so that no one can despair of himself without at the same time believing in God and no one can believe in God without despairing of himself: "For the benefit of Christ's sufferings depends completely and entirely on man coming to a true knowledge of himself and becoming terror-stricken and slain before himself."[12]

Thus, the preaching of the law comes to fruition in the self-awareness of the person, and if there were no preaching of the law in the world, there would also be no way for the person to become aware of himself. The church owes the world this truth of the person concerning himself. We know that all those who want to help the person along other ways to the self-awareness that is indispensable to him will raise this objection to the church's claim: that the person would rather and can more easily look into a self-made mirror than into the face of God. We know that the *one*

---

10. ["Where one nail is driven through his hands and feet, thou shouldest eternally suffer such and even more painful nails; as will be also visited upon those who let Christ's sufferings be lost and fruitless as far as they are concerned. For this earnest mirror, Christ, will neither lie nor mock; whatever he says must be fully realized." John Nicholas Lenker, ed., *The Complete Sermons of Martin Luther*, vol. 1.2 (Grand Rapids: Baker Books, 2000), 186; WA 2,137, 32-36.]

11. ["Whatever form the suffering Christ has in the eyes of men, you have it in the eyes of God." (translation our own) Luther, *Operationes in Psalmos* (1519/21),] WA 5, 638,19f. On Psalm 22:19.

12. [Lenker, *The Complete Sermons of Martin Luther*, vol. 1.2, 186f.;] WA 2, 138,15-17. [Lenker translates the German word "fast" as "almost," which would be correct for modern German. In Luther's times however "fast" meant "completely" or "entirely," therefore his mistake was corrected in the quotation.]

way and the *one* truth is already becoming a scandal at this point because this *one* actuality of the person undercuts all potentialities in which he otherwise operates. But that is not so much what worries us. If only the church would understand in its proclamation *that the judgment concerning the revelatory character of Christianity is rendered already in the preaching of the law*, that it is only a half-thing and for that reason a lost cause from the outset if the law is surrendered to the relativism of historical and psychological conditions in order to assert Christianity's claim to absoluteness only later within the proclamation of the gospel!

The history of theology has demonstrated the untenability of this claim to absoluteness simply because the legion that makes this claim is already on the retreat, as there is no certainty of faith behind it but, at best, the will to surrender on the most favorable terms. If the law that is fulfilled in Jesus Christ is not the only way to human self-awareness and human self-understanding, it is meaningless to assert that Jesus Christ is the way, the truth, and the life (cf. Jn 14:6). The struggle for the absoluteness of Christianity[13] is already a truly depraved form of the actual and true struggle for revelation. For no one can say anything about the true divinity of Jesus Christ if he does not simultaneously believe his true humanity as *an article of faith*, if the true humanity of Jesus is understood as an empirical-historical facticity.[14] Yet to believe in the true humanity of Jesus means to believe that the image of the exposed, poor, homeless [*heimatlosen*] person nailed to the stake of sin is the truth of the person that he cannot know but only believe in Jesus Christ—the counter-truth to the Adam who reaches for likeness of God, which for that reason does not lie in our blood but is brought to us by the Spirit who proceeds from Jesus Christ. "*Quia enim ascendimus in Adam ad similitudinem dei, ideo descendit ille in similitudinem nostram, ut reduceret nos ad nostri cognitionem. Atque hoc agitur sacramento incarnationis.*"[15] This is why this truth of the human

---

13. [The question of the "absoluteness of Christianity" arose out of the relativization of the history of Christian tradition in comparison to other religions. Cf. Ernst Troeltsch, *The Absoluteness of Christianity and the History of Religions* (1902), trans. David Reid (Louisville: Westminster John Knox Press, 2005). Rolf Schäfer, "Absolutheit des Christentums," in *Historisches Wörterbuch der Philosophie I*, ed. Joachim Ritter (Basel and Stuttgart: Schwabe, 1971), 31f.]

14. [Theological historicism—in view of true human existence—wanted to supplant that which the early church's Christology articulated (in the formulation of the Council of Chalcedon in 451: the belief in Jesus Christ as *Deum vere et hominem vere*, "true God and true man"; cf. Denzinger and Hünermann (ed.), *Enchiridion Symbolorum*, nr. 301. Heinrich Karpp, *Textbuch zur altkirchlichen Christologie. Theologia und Oikonomia* (Neukirchen-Vluyn: Neukirchener Verlag, 1972), 138, through the attempt to comprehend the actual humanity of Jesus as a historical fact. Here the "historical Jesus" stands for the *vere homo*.]

15. "Since we ascended to the likeness of God (namely) in Adam, he came down to be in our likeness in order to bring us once again to the knowledge of ourselves. That is the meaning of the sacrament of the incarnation." WA 5, 128,39-129,1 [translation our own]. Cf. the whole passage concerning Ps. 5:2 in WA 5, 126,25-129,16.

person is the point of Christian preaching of the law, and every action that we are commanded to do must reinforce the person's delusion about himself if this awareness is not above it. "*Adam operibus aedificatur.*"[16]

So the question is what we are doing when we preach the law: whether in doing so, we are nourishing the Adamic drive for life and activity within the person, who is from the earth (1 Cor. 15:47) and wants for precisely that reason to storm the heavens, or whether beginning with the cross, we set that truth in motion that only the church can set in motion: the destruction of the person who lives from *his own* action and inaction. For when with the preaching of the law we nurture the *praesumptio operum* (the expectation that is placed in works), whether in open or veiled form, a person develops beneath our pulpits and in the cultural (*geistig*) and spiritual atmosphere that emanates from them who necessarily sees in Jesus Christ a scandal that must be stamped out, that is embarrassing for the human race. Then we ourselves cultivate that person who can no longer coexist in the world with Jesus Christ, then we ourselves are the ones by whom the scandal comes. Every preaching of the law is thus a decision that falls to one side or the other: either it is giving in to the illusion of human self-understanding or it is an active conflict with it in the confession of the true humanity of Jesus Christ, the crucified. It is no use if we expend a lot of effort to chop a few heads off the thousand-headed Hydra of godlessness while our proclamation and teaching are the fertile ground from which it continually gains new vigor. For the true church will only ever be persecuted by the false one that has grown up with it and within it. The son of the church who is born of the flesh must persecute the one who is descended from the Spirit (cf. Gal. 4:29).

One may object—and this is the common objection of the theologian—that the proclamation of the law in its *usus theologicus* has become unfamiliar to the congregation and that a simple and moral preaching of the law is needed at least as a prep course from the perspective of praxis. But even if we were to allow this argument of praxis, which opens the door wide to the caprice of opinions, there is still the question of whether a lack of understanding and the *communis opinio* can be grounds for ceding something of the truth. The practical question of how one should proclaim is only justified, only has a point when the "what" of proclamation is firm and can no longer be altered and bent by the "how." And one can be quite confident when it comes to the "how" because it is precisely the apt preaching of the law that seizes the person obnoxiously, paradoxically, unexpectedly. How should people notice, then, that they have wandered away from right understanding if they do not come up against it again? Maybe that precisely that thing will come about that has not yet come about in spite of all psychology and existential philosophy: that people actually wake up because this collision wrests them from their slumber. Because in the end, the question of the "what" in

---

16. ["Adam is edified by works." Cf. LW 31, 35-70, 53; WA 1, 362,28f. Thesis 21: "Through the cross works are dethroned and the old Adam, who is especially edified by works, is crucified."]

the proclamation of the law and the question of the "how" are one and the same: if you have the "what," you'll find the "how" there, too. Only therein lies the crisis of our proclamation: that today, a good part of what we had up until now held to be the essential thing in the proclamation of the law has been taken from us and could be taken from us because it did not actually belong to us. The text "Render to Caesar the things that are Caesar's" (Mk 12:17) applies here, too. It is through precisely this that the heart and mouth will open up for that which is God's. It is frankly horrifying to see how the church seeks to parallel the new legislation of the nationalist (*völkisch*) state by yet again, and with increased effort, incorporating its old bourgeois proclamation of the law, which is accordingly in step with the times, in order yet again to betray the Word to morality, the law of God to morals.[17] The blind Faust, one foot in the grave, imagines that it is the sound of work that meets his ears[18] and does not suspect that it is his own grave being dug. Do we not suspect that with this turning point that we are experiencing, even that old dogma of Christendom as the religious-moral correctional institution upon which this whole endeavor of religious transformations and underpinnings is grounded will go to its grave?

Why do we not reorient the preaching of the law according to the criteria of biblical truth and Reformation teaching: that the law brings awareness (cf. Rom. 3:20, 7:7) and not action; that the law—given for life's sake—works death (Rom. 7:10); that it is holy, just, and good (Rom. 7:12) and truly the eternal will of God toward the person, and yet that it is utterly powerless and useless in the matter of making wicked people into good, sinners into righteous, blind into seeing, crooked into straight, fallen into upright? The salvific significance of the law is only comprehended by the one who knows his own limits and knows that his fulfillment does not come from himself. For this is the limit of the law: that it cannot make anything new, that it can only set in place, administer, and order what is already there. The law cannot bridge the dichotomy of life and death, sin and righteousness, wrath and grace, existence and nonexistence; it can only reveal it. It plays its role within time and within the fallen world and does not reach beyond them. It cannot make that which is not living living, and it cannot kill that which is not already undergoing death; yet everything that is hidden will be revealed when the law "comes," which is why its coming is the revelation of the mysteries of existence. Then they break open like old wounds: the mysteries of unbelief, sin, death, and eternal despair. This revelatory inbreaking of the judging Word is the preaching of the law, and "no creature is hidden from his sight, but all are naked and exposed to (his) eyes" (Heb. 4:13).

---

17. [Iwand here points to the Synod of the Old Prussian Church of the Union of September 4/5, 1933, which in accordance with National Socialist ideology introduced racial laws in ecclesial jurisdiction, pushing aside Christians of Jewish origin.]

18. [Cf. Johann Wolfgang Goethe, *Faust* II, V. 11499-11510, 11552-11556, 11559-11586.]

Or why do we not consider again the old conundrum of the correspondence and dual legality of person and cosmos? Does not the law that is sketched in the starry heavens stand in a mysterious accord with the law that is proclaimed to us as the guiding principle of life? "The stars shone in their watches and were glad; he called them, and they said, 'Here we are!' They shone with gladness for him who made them" (Bar. 3:34f.). What is man that he refuses to obey this law that the suns and worlds in their paths must serve? Why does he believe that he can only live among all created beings if he goes his own ways? "The ox knows its owner, and the donkey its master's crib, but Israel does not know, my people do not understand" (Isa. 1:3). The lilies of the field and the birds of the air preach the law of God's goodness against the worrying of people day by day (Mt. 6:25ff.). The totality of natural events exposes the person as the great disruption in the harmony of the worlds. This is why he must be bound and chained by law, order, justice, and state: he, the unfinished creation, the incarnate contradiction of his purpose whom his purpose thus befalls as the contradiction of his desire and aspiration. And thus finally even death, the law of all life that is no longer life out of the law.

Or why is it with such difficulty that we comprehend what was so commonplace for the Reformers:[19] that the law of human community, the political law, finds its reference in the *iustitia Dei*, which lives invisibly and mysteriously in all the orders of existence and must only be compelled where life is no longer lived from faith in God's Word? That *iustitia* that must be artificially and artfully built into our coexistence so that it does not totally tear apart, as a *iustitia civilis* that should exist "by nature" in matrimony, in parenthood and childhood, in brotherhood and love for neighbor, in allegiance and fidelity? Except that, as opposed to the romantic naturalism with its "*retournons à la nature*," we want to hold fast in attentive distrustfulness to the sober fact that the naturalness of life is the last thing and the unnaturalness the first thing, that the so-called natural person (1 Cor. 2:14) is precisely the person who no longer lives in the divine ordering of the world, and that the return home is a destination that we only approach in this life, that the new heavens and the new earth (Isa. 65:17, 66:22; 2 Pet. 3:13; Rev. 21:1), the end of days, and the inbreaking of the resurrection are already postulated with this returning home and the turning back of the person, that the *nomos* thus only becomes the inner law of life where the person has already been born again to a new, living hope in the gospel of cross and resurrection (cf. 1 Pet. 1:3). Only for that person will the law become a gentle protection on his way, the hearth to hold the glimmering, flickering blaze of his mortality together with light and warmth in his cabin. This is what prompted our fathers to distinguish between the *primus*

---

19. [*Iustitia civilis* ("civil righteousness," which is grounded in laws, on reason and philosophical foundations) and the righteousness of God are differentiated much as nature and grace—among other things in connection with Augustine, *De natura et gratia* 40, 47 (CSEL 60, 268, 9)—Also CA IV (BSELK 277, 18ff., KW 124, Ap IV 22ff.). In this case however, the incomparability of civil righteousness and spiritual righteousness (*iustitia spiritualis*) is at the fore; cf. Ap. XVIII (BSELK 553, 7ff., KW 232, Ap XVIII 9).]

and the *tertius usus legis*.[20] For this function of the law, to lead us home in the inner course of life, is and remains something that we approach, never something that we reach. We only see the promised land from afar (cf. Deut. 32:52). For all life under the law is the fate of Moses and even the Christian should not be under any illusions about the fact that the day is still to come when he will enter into God's rest (cf. Heb. 4:1ff.). The law daily reminds us of precisely that; it is the sting that does not allow us any rest.

The law of God has experienced a twofold interpretation in the history of salvation. It oscillates between two poles. It is the law of Sinai and the law of the Sermon on the Mount, and when we interpret it, everything depends on whether the interpretation moves in the right direction. The one cannot be without the other; the giving of the law from Sinai is not without the one who placed his "But I say to you" (Mt. 5:22, 28, 32, 34, 39, 44) above it, but also this day of fulfillment is never without the enduring-strict grappling of God with the people of his own possession (1 Pet. 2:9)—except these two revelations do not balance each other out in some fluctuating equilibrium; rather, above it all is the πολλῷ μᾶλλον of Romans 5 (:9-10, 15, 17), that incomprehensible even more of God's grace. And if that aspect of understanding the law is applicable that is found in this passage: "They tie up heavy burdens, hard to bear, and lay them on people's shoulders, but they themselves are not willing to move them with their finger" (Mt. 23:4), then right over the words of the Sermon on the Mount stands another word incomprehensible to natural reason: "My yoke is easy, and my burden is light" (Mt. 11:30). Here lies the final alternative that stands over every interpretation of the law, the continental divide between the letter that kills and the Spirit who gives life (2 Cor. 3:6).

There is an interpretation of the law that stands entirely underneath the sign from Sinai, underneath the contradictory mystery of the either-or of life and death, the decision that is still open, making reference to the uncertain future. There is certainly the nearness of God there, but this nearness of God is deadly, delimiting, unbearable. A covenant is certainly cut there, but at the same time that the prophet stands before God, his priestly brother organizes the dance around the Golden Calf (Exodus 32). There was certainly a pronouncement of God and an instruction of the Lord there, but no one beheld his face (cf. Exod. 33:20), and his

---

20. [Cf. the early Protestant teaching of the threefold (later fourfold) use of the law: FC Ep VI, Concerning the Third Use of the Law (*De tertio usu legis*): "The law has been given to people for three reasons: first, that through it external discipline may be maintained against the unruly and the disobedient [= *usus politicus*]; second, that people may be led through it to a recognition of their sins [= *usus paedagogicus*]; third, after they have been reborn—since nevertheless the flesh still clings to them—that precisely because of the flesh they may have a sure guide, according to which they can orient and conduct their entire life [= *usus didacticus*]." BSELK 1250, 29-34, KW 502, FC Ep VI 1. Supplement from the editor of *Evangelische Theologie*, Ernst Wolf.]

goodness had not shone on anyone (cf. Tit. 3:4). It was God's alien work[21] that took shape there. It was no longer Egypt, no longer the drudgery of foreign servitude, but it was also not yet the promised inheritance, the freedom of the children of God (Rom. 8:21). It was basic instruction (cf. Gal. 3:24) but not awareness, the dominion of God but not the service of God [*Gottesdienst*]. It was proclamation under the call: "God is the Lord," but the mystery of this dominion still remains: that the Lord of the world came into the world, not to be served but to serve (Mk 10:45), and that he wishes to establish his kingdom not with those who wish to serve him but with those who let themselves be served by him. That is the mystery that "the heart of man [has not yet] imagined" (1 Cor. 2:9), that is the absurdity of God's dominion in Jesus Christ, by which everyone continually is appalled. It is really not hard to call upon people to enlist in God's service. However, who remains in his service when the hour of trial comes, when it is revealed that the Christ must suffer in order to enter into his glory (cf. Lk. 24:26)? When the time of the law has come to an end and the time of grace dawns (cf. Jn 1:17)? When God sets his intention to suffer for us against our intention to fight for him?

It is a totally different image that the Scriptures place before our eyes when Jesus preaches the law in the midst of the people. Here there is no boundary and no distance; he is the blessed center of those who labor and are heavy-laden (cf. Mt. 11:28). He is the center of attention; therein lies the "total otherness"[22] of the situation. When he makes people into sinners, they are those who are saved; when he diagnoses the disease upon them, they are those who are called to healing [*Heil*]; his Word is the doctor's treatment (cf. Mk 2:17 par.), the Good Shepherd's searching (cf. Lk. 15:3ff.; Jn 10:11ff.), the healing of the lame, the giving of sight to the blind (cf. Mt. 11:5 par.), and plenty of other images. What he was talking about parabolically in those images actually takes place here, in the interpretation of the law that Jesus gives. That is the authority of his speech (cf. Mk 1:22 par.). He, the dying and risen Christ, stands behind the "But I say to you" (Mt. 5:22 etc.).

Here we do not hear, "you are a murderer and you an adulterer and you a wicked servant (cf. Mt. 18:32) and you a miser." Jesus makes no use of such vaunted *ad hominem*[23] attacks; rather, in a solemn silence and solitude, he invites each

---

21. [Luther understands God's dealing with sinners as an "alien work" (*opus alienum*), referring to Isa. 28:21 as distinct from his true and proper work (*opus proprium*), the revelation of his righteousness. Cf. Martin Luther, *Sermon for St. Thomas's Day on Ps. 19:2* (1516), WA 1, 112,24-113, 5; Martin LW 31, 44; WA 1, 357,6-8; Proof of Thesis 4; Martin Luther, *Treatise on Good Works* (1520), LW 44, 77; WA 6,248,1-15; Martin Luther, *The Roots of Reform*, ed. Timothy J. Wengert, vol. 1 (Minneapolis, MN: Fortress Press, 2015), 327.]

22. [Rudolf Otto understands the "total otherness" to be the religious mystery to which "amazement absolute" gives rise. Rudolf Otto, *The Idea of the Holy* (New York: Oxford University Press 1976), 26. Here this formulation that was in vogue in the theological parlance of the 1920s is taken up and recast.]

23. [The *argumentum ad hominem* is a classic figure of rhetoric: the conversation partner is addressed "personally" in order to confute him persuasively. The *argumentum*

and every one of us to examine himself, singles out people from the crowd, and holds before each individual the mirror of his heart. He speaks as into the wind: whoever—the one who hates his brother, he is . . . (cf. Mt. 5:22), whoever looks at a woman, he has already . . . (Mt. 5:28), when you give alms . . . (Mt. 6:2), when you pray . . . (Mt. 6:6). He speaks as if he means to speak of no one, and yet his speech hits everyone.

But who are we that we should be able to emulate him? The sword with which *we* fight is a two-edged sword (cf. Hebrews 4:12), and the judgment that we render is always a judgment of ourselves (cf. Mt. 7:1ff.). Does the church still dare to stand under the judgment of Matthew 23, where everything that the world says and can say about the "*Pastorenkirche*"[24] is anticipated and exceeded? Who could preach on any one of the commandments with the consciousness that he does not stand on the side of those who are attacked by it, judged by it? This is not an accident, nor is it the particular misfortune of some individuals; rather, it is always our situation when we are compelled to interpret the law. We have the figure, the form, the μόρφωσις of knowledge (Rom. 2:20); we know how it should be, and because of that we let ourselves be tempted all too easily by it to serve as blind guides (Mt. 15:14); we do not notice at all what the people before whom we pretend to be guides have figured out long ago, that above all such interpretations of the law, we actually needed to write the word with which Jesus warns his disciples before the scribes: "so do and observe whatever they tell you, but not the works they do" (Mt. 23:3). And what do we do when our ecstasy of self-forgetfulness eventually comes to an end, when we have reached that irrefutable conclusion: "you who teach others and do not teach yourself," (Rom. 2,21) when we realize the internal impossibility of the preaching of the law? For sure, we can interpret the law in such a way that we are spared from its anathema, but then our speech ceases to be speech from God. It is only speech from God when it drives us all to the point where we must simply fall silent (cf. Rom. 3:19) in shame and distress, fall silent in the very simple and candid realization: "what are we that we teach others?" fall silent out of obvious solidarity with everything that is flesh (cf. Rom. 3:23). For all speech that takes place *before* this point is no speech from God; rather, it is speech from one's own presumptuousness. Yet all speech that is still possible beyond this point where this mute agony is loosened is a speech that confesses, that is self-confessing before God and people. This is the mark of authentic preaching of the law in the New Covenant, that the person confesses his entire self and that God's power is mighty in his weakness (2 Cor. 12:9).

The person who is and must be first impacted by the law all on his own is the preacher of the law himself. This is the enormous *Anfechtung* of the preacher, "the

---

ad hominem is in order when one is not dealing with ascertainable facts but rather with opinions and decisions that are based on them.]

24. [*Pastorenkirche* (literally, pastors' church) was a derogatory saying alluding to the institutional nature of the church as ruled by the clergy.]

mystery of his experiential theology,"[25] that he himself is the first one who collides with the word of the law. To use an image: the preacher does not simply stand as a teacher before the class, lecturing them on what should be and what should not be, nor does he thrill his hearers like the general before the charge in order to stir up in them the ardor and the drive for prestige; rather, he, the messenger of the gospel, knows himself to be among the sinners to whom he is sent, always as the foremost, as the first. Either everyone will be impacted in him or no one will. His priesthood is a fragment of the high-priesthood of Christ, who took on flesh and blood so that he might be made like his brethren in all things (cf. Heb. 2:14ff.); for how should the preacher help the ones to whom he is sent if he does not suffer the things that they suffer along with them, or if he is not tempted along with them in the same way that they are tempted (cf. Heb. 4:15)? Here there is more than a demanding will; it is also a hand that seizes me. More than the sublimity of the categorical imperative that hangs over me,[26] it is also the appeal of the brother who is next to me. It is not only the self-evident "that" of the demand; rather, it is the "how" of the action that is evident to me, that becomes good news to me, the answer to the question, "*Quomodo bona opera fieri possint?*"[27]

25. ["Experiential theology" in the critical sense that Iwand means here is the foundation of theological knowledge on the experience of faith, as the Erlangen theologian Fr. H. R. Frank, for example, described it, as the immediate awareness of the object of faith, the "essential identity of subject and object" (H. R. Frank, *System of the Christian Certainty*, trans. Maurice Evans, 2nd ed. (Edinburgh: T & T Clark, 1886), 66, Available online: https://catalog.hathitrust.org/Record/100435950 (accessed September 1, 2021). "It is the man come to himself, come to his true self" (Ibid., 141). As opposed to that, Iwand relates the question of truth to the antithesis of revelation and knowledge. By saying that theology should be based upon experience means for Iwand—following after Luther—that "the question of truth is always the question of knowledge in which man himself becomes true, not only knowing what is true, and that for that reason all knowledge of truth is of no use if the knower does not himself become a "true man" because of it." Hans Joachim Iwand, "Die Krisis des Wissenschaftsbegriffes und die Theologie" (1935), reprinted in: Iwand, *Um den rechten Glauben*, GA I, 62–74, esp. 64, and in *Theologie als Wissenschaft*, ed. Gerhard Sauter, Theologische Bücherei (Munich: Christian Kaiser Verlag, 1970), 279–91, esp. 281—cf. also Iwand, *Glauben und Wissen*, NW I, 168, 233, 242ff.]

26. [Cf. Immanuel Kant, *Critique of Practical Reason* (1788), trans. Mary Gregor, 2nd ed. (Cambridge: Cambridge University Press, 2015), 129: "Two things fill the mind with ever new and increasing admiration and reverence, the more often and more steadily one reflects on them: *the starry heavens above me and the moral law within me*." Emphasis in the original.]

27. Ap IV 136 [BSELK 323, 8-10: "*Falso igitur calumniantur nos adversarii quod nostri non doceant bona opera, cum ea non solum requirunt, sed etiam ostendant, quomodo fieri possint.*" KW 142: "Therefore the opponents' claims are false when they charge that our people do not teach about good works since our people not only require them but also show how they can be done."]

For it is only there that the preaching of the law takes place under the banner of the New Covenant, where it is able to be an answer to this question—to *be* an answer, not just to *give* one. The interpretation of the law must come to meet the heart's ceaseless asking about the "*quomodo,*" as it were, must presuppose it, must do it justice. Then, the "*quomodo*" will no longer be inquired about as a result of the "*bona opera*" not being there. Rather, this asking about the "*quomodo*" is understood and receives a response because the "*bona opera*" are now ours. Of course, ours in such a way that the answer to the "*quomodo*" can only be: "*Sola Dei gratia*" (through the grace of God alone).

Where faith is born of the hearing of the Word, it is never without works precisely because it is the justifying faith that is certain of its God even without those works—indeed, only without these works. Where faith is, there are also works, but just the works of faith. Works that are there so that they might actually happen, not so that they might be seen. Works that are done to address a need, not to rock the person back into security. Works that come and go and have their time. For it is not the works that accompany the faith but rather the Word. But we people are so blind that we are always seeking to strengthen our weak faith by looking at great achievements, as if this were not precisely the distress of our faith, the unbelief in our faith: that we are on the lookout for works, that we have apostatized from hearing to wanting to see, from doing to knowing about doing, from the works of faith to the works of the law.

To preach the law may mean, then, to make God's will heard in such a way that wishing and accomplishing are both included within it, that God's law and the person's will are no longer enemies, that the question about the "how" of the action is answered through the bestowal of the action. Now, this would mean precisely, "you can because you should,"[28] whatever the undeterred anti-Kantians would argue against it, except the capability that is revealed here is incomprehensible to myself, a marvel to myself. To preach the law may mean, then, nothing other than to proclaim God's grace that does not leave faith without works; it would be a speech with the Third Petition (Mt. 6:10) standing at its beginning and its end. It would be an aid and not an aid to faith but rather an aid from faith, an aid to action, to doing that which is commanded out of listening to the commandment.

---

28. Cf. *Critique of Practical Reason*, 27–8; Book 1, Ch. 1, §6: "He judges, therefore, that he can do something because he is aware that he ought to do it . . ." Cf. also idem, *Groundwork of the Metaphysics of Morals* (1785), ed. and trans. Mary Gregor and Jens Timmermann (Cambridge: Cambridge University Press, 2011), 14–39, Section 1; idem, *Religion within the Boundaries of Mere Reason* (1793).

The formulation has its origin in the "Xenien" of Johann Wolfgang Goethe and Friedrich Schiller (*Goethe-Schillers Xenien*, ed. Adolf Stern (Leipzig: Philipp Reclam, 1871), 56): "Auf theoretischem Feld ist weiter nichts mehr zu finden, Aber der praktische Satz gilt doch: Du kannst, denn du sollst!"—"On the theoretical plane there is nothing further to be found, but the practical sentence still holds: 'You are able because you should!'" [Translation our own.]

For where else is the key to all of the individual words of Jesus in his interpretation of the law but in the sequence of hearing and doing? Yet in just such a way that requires believing hearing, not unbelieving hearing. If inability becomes the principle, how should he still be able to hear what is said to him? How differently do the words of the Sermon on the Mount sound if we take them "at their word"? "Everyone who looks at a woman with lustful intent has already committed adultery with her in his heart" (Mt. 5:28). This is precisely not an ethics of conviction (*Gesinnungsethik*)[29] nor is it an intensification—or it is all of this, too, but it is even more than all that. For who believes the word of Jesus: "He has already committed adultery?" Do we not say exactly the opposite: he has not committed adultery yet, he just wants to do it, he is about to, he is in the midst of temptation, he is toying with the possibility? But Jesus says, "He has." That which you determine to be your potentiality he determines to be your actuality; that which you determine to be your temptation he determines to be your fall. And while you think that you are about to give passion free rein and you seem to yourself to be easy and flexible—pouncing like a tiger on its prey, this word of Jesus turns your gaze onto yourself, and you see yourself as you see yourself in the mirror of the act committed, of the irreversible guilt. You see yourself depicted in his word about the act before it even took place. His word has planted contrition in your heart and thereby guarded you against the act. And while you are otherwise waking from your passion with the horrifying recognition: "What have I done!," you now look up out of your contrition to the one who preserved you through his word.

Or the words of anger and hatred, of ῥαχά and μωρέ (Mt. 5:22): isn't it as if the backdrops of our coexistence are clearly evident in all these words of Jesus? As if we all of a sudden had to recognize that we all bear the sign of Cain upon our brow (cf. Gen. 4:15)? Would we continue to deal with our brother the way we deal with him now if we knew how deeply indebted we were to him? If we knew that in careless words and thoughtless gestures, there are powers that break in that we will soon no longer master? And could it not be that out of our terror at these things, we begin to do what we who are evil are just barely able to do (cf. Mt. 7:11)? That we become more mindful in our dealings, kinder in our daily encounters, milder in our judgment? Not as if we were already free from those powers but in such a way that a hopeful light wafts through the darkness of our days in those small signs. Not as if we had already endured the most difficult thing but in such a way that we begin with the easiest one, like people in recovery who exercise their convalescent powers carefully and weakly but in a new hope for life.

Or when we hear the word about laying up treasures (Mt. 6:19ff.), is it not, as if Jesus wanted to say to us: take all your anxious thoughts and worries,[30] take this

---

29. [Iwand here refers to Max Weber's contrast between an "ethics of conviction" and an "ethics of responsibility."]

30. [Cf. Paul Gerhardt, "Entrust Your Days and Burdens" (1653), LSB 754, stanza 2:
No anxious thought, no worry,
No self-tormenting care
Can win your Father's favor;
His heart is moved by prayer.]

burden and go look at the lilies of the field, hear the rejoicing that fills the air, and let them be preachers, the flowers of the field and the birds of the air, and you be their hearer one time. And God will grant you what you cannot do by yourself: forgetting your worries and bearing the burdens of your cares, through the poor, miserable creature that lives much more hard-pressed and vulnerable than you do. And if people overwhelm you and you still work nonstop, go an extra mile (Mt. 5:41), and if you grow weary of their impudence (cf. Lk. 11:8), give up your cloak, too; then, you will enjoy that which brought you indignation before.

Even with the commandment to love our enemies (cf. Mt. 5:43ff.), we do not want to interrupt right away with our faithless "impossible." It is absolutely not as if Jesus said that we lived on an island of the blessed. He appeals precisely to those who live in hostility and who are each other's enemies. Jesus absolutely does not imagine that you would be someone who had no enemies, not only those who see you as their enemy but precisely those whom you see as yours. In precisely this situation he commands you: love your enemies. For as long as you see them as your enemies, you are in their hand, for your heart is bound to them in your hostility. Love your enemies; then, they are in your hand, or rather God's hand, and you will come to realize that they cannot touch a hair on your head against God's will. Into whose hand would you rather give your heart: God your Father's or your enemies'?

This is why there is more here than in Moses because the commandments of Jesus are an aid, an aid precisely because they talk to us about and into the reality in which we are living and then free us from it. Can we also do this in our preaching of the law? Do we do this, too? Or do we perhaps think that people today are waiting for this liberating Word less than people back then? When the Word takes the lead in a person's life, it also shows him the way of action. Indeed, listening to God's Word is the only way to the doing of his will. Admittedly, this way is always a way of repenting and being called back, but this repentance and reflection of the heart is not nothing; rather, it is the readiness, the openness for God's action. If the person has heard the one promise that stands over all the commandments: "I am the Lord your God" (Exod. 20:2; Deut. 5:6), and if he has recognized that Jesus Christ is not something in addition to that promise but rather the very yes of God to his promise (cf. 2 Cor. 1:20), then he also knows that God will not leave this faith all too long or all too deep in the *Anfechtung* of inaction. "*Christus non est otiosus!*"[31] Yet the most wonderful deed of faith is persevering in inaction, waiting on the time and manner of the divine action. For the Christian faith lives in activity[32] but not from activity.

---

31. [Cf. Martin Luther, *Lecture on Psalm 45* (1532), LW 12, 247; WA 40/2, 537,36f. On Ps. 45:9: "Our comfort is that we must not suppose Christ to be an idle king . . ." / "*Est autem haec nostra consolatio, ne fingamus Christum otiosum esse regem, . . .*"]

32. [Cf. Martin Luther, *Zirkulardisputation de veste nuptiali* (1537), WA 39/1, 311,8-10: "*Non fit per charitatem talis, sed confirmatur in Christo, sed tantum certificatur per opera, quia non est res otiose, sed efficax.*"]

And so once more: let us train ourselves to distinguish between the works of the law (Rom. 3:20 inter alia) and the works of faith (cf. 1 Thess. 1:3; 2 Thess. 1:11). The works of faith have their own appearance; they are not publicly exposed like those other works. Only God sees them; only the neighbor experiences them. They come and go with each passing day. Faith does not cling to them; rather, they cling to faith. As the water of a fresh spring always flows out and does not stand still, so must faith always be free from works so that they might constantly flow out. For the spring must remain clean and uncontaminated so that the water can always flow fresh and vigorous.

How do we preach the law? Now we know what this question means. It means no more and no less than this second question: How do we make the person free from all his own work so that he can once again be an unwarped and docile tool in the hand of the one who does none but good works?! Is not the preaching of the law the resurgence of the lost creation? The sound of a life that we no longer dare to acknowledge? The starting to flow of all standing waters into the river and the outbreak of every hope hidden in our soul? Do we really still find this language of promise where there is talk of the law? Is the people of God really still called the move, still called into the endless movement toward the new heavens and the new earth (cf. 2 Pet. 3:13)? Or is the spirit of the law long since fossilized and the old priestly business taken up once again: tying up burdens and loading them onto people (Mt. 23:4 par.)? Let everyone answer this question for himself, let everyone determine for himself what he has to say about the law of God as a Christian in the pulpit and what he may expect to hear about it from the pulpit—one thing should be clear: the "Christian life" does not only commence with the proclamation of grace; rather, it is already decided in the matter of whether the *nomos* governs the *logos* or the *logos* governs the *nomos*.

"If one does not know how to say anything to the Christian person but moral philosophy and human ordinances so that he is convinced he therein walks rightly before God, that is death and destruction. For in this way, it will come about that on this basis he will criticize, condemn, and persecute everything that is contrary to him, and thus he scorns the cross of Christ and utterly despises the way of God, which is best and happiest when we live without our own guidance and our own council and follow Christ in the pillar of fire, so to speak, through wilderness and waylessness."[33]

"Such [a faith] is not produced through love but is rather made strong in Christ, but it is proved by works because it is not a dormant but an efficacious thing" Translation our own.]

33. [*Proinde nihil potest Christiano homini pestilentius tradi quam philosophia moralis et decreta homium, si ita tradantur, ut credit in his se recte incedera coram deo. Nam sic fiet, ut consiliis his innixus quicquid contra se geri viderit, iudicet, damnet, persequatur, ac per hoc Crucem Christi repudiet et viam dei penitus contemnat. Quae tunc optime et prosperrime habet, quando sine ductu et consilio nostro vivimus ac velut per desertum et invium Christum in columna ignis equimur.* WA 5, 107,5-11.]

Chapter 2

THE OBJECTIVITY OF THE THEOLOGICAL TASK

First published as Hans Joachim Iwand, "Die Sachlichkeit der theologischen Arbeit," in *Gottes Herrschaft: Flugschriften für die evangelische Kirche im Osten*, vol. 1 (Königsberg: Wichern Buchhandlung, 1935), 25–40; also in Iwand, *Um den rechten Glauben*, GA I, 75–86.

In 1934, the conflicts in the East Prussian Church had reached a climax. The mainly German Christian [Deutsche Christen] church leadership had attempted to remove Iwand as director of the "Lutherheim" in June 1933, which at that time was made undone by Erich Koch, the Nazi Gauleiter in East Prussia. In 1934, however, Iwand again was dismissed and he applied for the New Testament professorship at the Herder Institute in Riga (Latvia), where pastors were trained for German-speaking congregations. He was appointed and moved with his family in October 1934 to Riga, where he presented the lecture "The Objectivity of the Theological Task" at a theological retreat in January 1935. In it, Iwand outlined what he saw as the task and claim of theological work between academic science and church practice and in confrontation with the German Christian appropriation of the church, and at the same time with Liberal theology, which he saw as the fundamental theological basis for the German Christian theology.[1] *Here Iwand's theology of the cross reveals itself in its characteristic intensification of theological existence.* (CN)

When we speak about the theological "task" as the topic that we wish to clarify, we certainly do not do so because we were empowered or even encouraged by our contemporaries or public opinion to speak in such a way.[2] According to the opinion of our time, it is sheer hubris to use the word "task" in relation to theology. Medicine, engineering, pedagogy, law, these are tasks. But theology? Where is its mandate, its benefit, its purpose, its method? Even if that which we do as theologians should be given all possible recognition, there is *one* title that must not under any circumstances be applied to the doing of theology and that is the title of

---

1. [Iwand implicitly criticizes the Liberal and the German Christian theology at the same time in this article. Fundamental ideas and proclamations of both theologies are added in the footnotes to make transparent these ideologies with which Iwand is struggling.]

2. These thoughts are based on a lecture that was presented at a theological camp in Riga [Latvia] in January 1935.

"task." And yet we must in all circumstances insist upon precisely this title if our work is not to become pointless. We must insist upon it, even if this claim should cost us all the recognition and good will that we still have.

It is naturally not a question about the word "task" itself; it is rather a question of the substance contained within that word, namely that everything that we as theologians do and say and don't do and don't say must take place with the awareness that we stand with a certain object and within a task that has been handed over to us; a task to which we are bound, for better or for worse, from the moment that we first laid our hand to the plow; a task that must be done, satisfied, attended to, maintained, and carried out to its conclusion; an object that compels the one who gets involved with it into *its* own demand (1 Cor. 9:16); an object that is not there for our sake but for whose sake we are there from now on, that is so closely bound to our life and personal being that its realization becomes the realization of our own lives, that its failure becomes the failure of our own lives. This is what we have in mind when we speak of a "task" and what applies when a true task—of any kind—becomes the content and worth of a human life. Are we theologians the only ones who are not worthy of this? Are we the only ones who have no claim to be those who work on a task? And would it not be possible that we would see and understand theology in a whole new light if we were to understand it again from this perspective?

If we were to do this, some things that we today "could understand" in the behavior and in the ways of a theologian would no longer be understandable and some things that we do not "understand" would suddenly become understandable to us. For it would be quite clear to us that the theologian, seen from this perspective, may not live to see the endangerment or even the downfall of the object of his studies without himself becoming endangered and being dragged into the same downfall right along with it, just as the disciples whom the Lord called to his task (Mt. 4:19) were dragged along in the hustle and turbulence that arose along with it. Then it would become clear to us in these same distresses and temptations that they don't constitute a danger or a downfall so long as that other object, the object that has been commended to our faithfulness, remains. Yet it would similarly become clear what we would have to say about those who think that they must preserve themselves for the sake of further life and career opportunities and for this reason will not endure the stormy ride, preferring to wait for more comfortable weather. They will, of course, continue to live and work, but their lives will be found lacking in that moment when they are to be scrutinized for their fidelity to the object[3] of

---

3. [Cf. for the "object" of theology according to the National Socialist Program: "The party as such advocates the standpoint of a positive Christianity." (The program of the NSDAP §24, in *Nazi Conspiracy and Aggression*, vol. 5, document 1708-PS, Available online: https://avalon.law.yale.edu/imt/1708-ps.asp [accessed August 16, 2022]). The German Christians specified this "object" as a return to "the heroic Jesus figure" and a fundamental renunciation "of everything un-German in worship and confession." in "Entschließung des Gaues Groß-Berlin der Glaubensbewegung 'Deutsche Christen,'" in *Die Bekenntnisse und*

their studies.[4] This is that horrible judgment, the crisis, that lies concealed whenever we are speaking of a task. The one who betrays his task salvages only an eternally doomed existence. This is why we are warned so seriously that, as we carry out our mandate, we should not fear men but should rather fear the one who can destroy both body and soul in hell (Mt. 10:28).

This is what we mean when we speak of the objectivity of the theological task. When we say this, we mean the fear and assurance of a man who knows that a certain object is on the line and with that object his very life. Only where the object of study and the human life are one in the moment of scrutiny are we faithful. For then we know that the life lost in service of the object has lost nothing; a life saved by means of betrayal to the object has saved nothing. It is at once a horrible fear and a wonderful assurance. We are like a wanderer who trudges ahead on a steep ridge, passing by chasms on the right and on the left, and yet makes confident steps, preserved even in his fear by the one who calls him to walk in this way (1 Cor. 10:12-13).[5]

From this foundation it may become clear why we cannot under any circumstances abandon the claim that we've been discussing from the beginning: that in theology we are dealing with a commanded object, with an applied task, to whose service we are called. For if we stand and do not fall, it will only be because and as long as we hear this call and follow it. Whoever doesn't want to admit this must revise the history of the church, must—with all witnesses to the contrary—deny that in the beginning a mandate was given, a sending order was issued, that an outstretched hand, visible to all times and all generations, was lifted to point the way. He must reverse and turn upside down everything that the Apostle Paul writes in Rom. 10:14ff concerning the relationship of calling, faith, obedience, proclamation, and sending. He must interpret the entire phenomenon of the evangelical church in something like the following fashion: they call on God without believing, they believe without hearing, they hear without it being proclaimed, they proclaim without being sent! At any rate, this must happen and has continued to happen again and again when one cuts the thread by which the whole thing—the object!—is held together. Then everything falls apart like the pearls on a broken necklace; the name of God is called upon but is no longer hallowed; faith exists, but the obedience of faith is no longer; one can hear all possible internal and external voices, interpreters of dreams and false prophets,

---

grundsätzlichen Äußerungen zur Kirchenfrage des Jahres 1933, ed. Kurt Dietrich Schmidt (Göttingen: Vandenhoeck & Ruprecht, 1934), 133f, 134 (art. 4f).]

4. [In many congregations of the Confessing Church, prospective pastors (vicars and, at that time, so-called assistant preachers) acted as preachers illegally and alongside the church structures, remunerated only from donations; emergency churches [*Notkirchen*] in inns and parish halls of free churches [*Freikirchen*] were used for the services.]

5. [Cf. Karl Barth, "The Word of God and the Task of Theology," in idem, *The Word of God and Theology*, trans. Amy Marga (London and New York: T&T Clark, 2011), 171-98, 196.]

but the voice that calls us by our name cannot be heard; proclamation is there, but those who proclaim speak their own stories and dreams and yet are surprised that they do not arouse the church with these stories and dreams but rather put it to sleep. This wild, frantic dissolution begins when one leaves off the fact that the church and its doctrine, theology, stands under a mandate that is valid for all time, that there is here only *one* Lord (Eph. 4:5) and all others are the servants, laborers in a vineyard that doesn't belong to them (Mt. 20:1ff).[6]

What will happen if the servants forget that they are about an alien work, that their work is the task and service of being servants who must give an account? Are we surprised when wherever this is forgotten, the servants no longer gather together but rather scatter, seeing as they are no longer held together by the "bond of peace" (Eph. 4:3)? Are we surprised when the diversity of their gifts of the spirit, intended for the purpose of complementing one another in service and displaying the richness of the spirit (1 Cor. 12:4ff), suddenly transforms into the insubordination of a thousand smaller spirits who all want to be the one great Spirit to whom all the others must submit? Are we surprised that when "*I* am the Lord, your God" no longer stands at the beginning in the church, the servants no longer devote themselves to their work but rather take control for themselves, that they only quarrel among themselves about who gets to sit in the first chair? Are we surprised when everything that is noticeable in the world as signs of decline necessarily breaks into such a church twice or three times as powerfully as it does in the world? How could it be otherwise if the "unclean spirit" returns to the house from which he was cast out? How could it be otherwise if here, in the church, the qualitative distinction between master and servant, between speaking and hearing, between mandate and implementation, is no longer taken seriously? If the spirit of man begins in arrogant freedom to correct the mandate, to make amendments and deletions, to reform the Spirit of God in accordance with his own spiritual insights and judgments—do we believe, perhaps, that the spirit who does these things is a clean spirit?

So, it is something more than a foible or a false ambition when we make the claim that theology always presupposes a mandate and that only that theology that knows itself *a posteriori*, that knows itself in its continuation, in its transmission, in its works, in the task, is worthy of the name theology. For insofar as we maintain this claim, we give the glory to God. And if some think that they can reform the church by determining the task of theology according to the times, according to their discretion and insights, that they can hitch eternity to the wagon of time,

---

6. [Cf. in contrast "Die 28 Thesen der sächsischen Volkskirche zum inneren Aufbau der Deutschen Evangelischen Kirche" (December 10, 1933), in *Die Bekenntnisse und grundsätzlichen Äußerungen zur Kirchenfrage des Jahres 1933*, ed. Kurt Dietrich Schmidt (Göttingen: Vandenhoeck & Ruprecht, 1934), 98–102, 99: "§3: A member of the Volkskirche, therefore, can only be one who, according to the rights of the state, is a member of the Volk . . .; §4: The Christian of another race is not a Christian of inferior rank, but a Christian of another kind."]

then we believe that, by once again recognizing and appreciating the appropriate ordering of theological knowledge and doctrine, we can usher in the reform that is, in fact, needful, which is to call time to a stop, that time is called to be still before eternity. For this is what Reformation theology means to us: that we have to do theology bound to a particular mandate, oriented in a particular direction, obligated to a final exclusivity, to an exclusivity that points back to God himself who tolerates no other gods beside himself. Our intolerance in the midst of all our human forbearance is nothing but the indication that the student is not greater than the teacher, nor is the servant greater than his master. We do not have to correct the one-sidedness and one-mindedness of the revelation of God in Jesus Christ in order to appear tolerant;[7] we have to do theology in such a way that the ship of the church, borne rudderless by the wind, regains its course, and the end toward which our preaching, teaching, services, and the work of the church are all driving becomes clear. Or do we want for the judgment to be spoken also over us and our work: "I have not sent them" (Jer. 27:15)? Do we understand that it will only depend, not upon the judgment or opinion of man but upon whether our work and activities have been a task and not indolence, a mission and not an arbitrary action, work and not performance?

When we speak of a task, we mean to speak of the internal relationship in which the service at the altar takes place, the relationship between calling, sending, proclamation, and witness. For it will not do only to pass on what God has instructed us; we must rather answer for this message in order to witness to it. No one has yet heard anything of the call to the task who has not at the same time become aware of the simultaneously uplifting and horrifying: "I make you this day a fortified city, an iron pillar, and bronze walls. Do not be dismayed by them, lest I dismay you before them" (Jer. 1:18.17), who has not received this accolade and has not made this oath of allegiance, which decides from now on between existence and nonexistence: "But even if we or an angel from heaven should preach to you a gospel contrary to the one we preached to you, let him be accursed. . . . If I were still trying to please man, I would not be a servant of Christ" (Gal. 1:8,10).

But does this have anything to do with the "theological task"? Does it have anything to do with one's training? Doesn't this calling happen immediately as the work of the Spirit, directly without human assistance? Since we are so accustomed to tearing apart Spirit and Word, calling and office, the theological task has become meaningless to us. It has come to the point where we "deal" with the witnesses of

---

7. [This supposedly "tolerant" approach toward the weak was taken up in the expert opinion by the Erlangen faculty about the admission of Jewish Christians into the ministry, stating that if Jewish pastors become a problem for the congregation because of their being born Jewish, they could be removed from office (cf. "Theologisches Gutachten über die Zulassung von Christen jüdischer Herkunft zu den Ämtern der Deutschen Evangelischen Kirche (Erlanger Gutachten)," in Ryan Tafilowski, *Dark, Depressing Riddle: Germans, Jews, and the Meaning of the Volk in the Theology of Paul Althaus* (Göttingen: Vandenhoeck & Ruprecht, 2019), 224–30, 230 (§7).]

the Christian faith in the same scholarly manner that we would the origins of Islam or of Buddhism, with the final goal of academic objectivity,[8] even as we are not really clear what objectivity would mean in this circumstance. In truth these are but fig leaves covering up a theology that is no longer able to claim a calling or a mission. And we know from the history of theology that its academic character has not always been used to cover up its objective characterlessness. We know that this is an abuse that touches on both theology and science, both faith and reason. It's not as if theology should first begin to become objective where it devolves into speaking in tongues, and reason, the means of understanding, is then simply switched off (1 Cor. 14:14), but preaching and teaching are the gifts of the Spirit, and we are directed toward him when we are in the pulpit or at the podium. But wherever the life-giving Spirit expounds upon the Word, this expounding will in itself be a calling and a mission. At that point it will become clear what must be proclaimed and why, and we will grasp what our life's work as theologians is.

In his 36th sermon, Bernard of Clairveaux gave a good characteristic of the various possibilities that exist in *"scientia."* Following 1 Cor. 8:2 (If anyone imagines that he knows something, he does not yet know as he ought to know), he says:

> He [i.e. Paul] does not approve of the well-read man who observes no scale of values in the knowledge he possesses. See how the fruit and usefulness of knowledge is determined by the manner in which one knows. And what does that manner imply? It implies the order, the application, that we pursue more eagerly all that strengthens love more; and the purpose, that we pursue it not through vain-glory or inquisitiveness or any base motive, but for the edification[9] of oneself or one's neighbor.
>
> For there are some who long to know for the sole purpose of knowing, and that is shameful curiosity; others who long to know in order to become known, and that is shameful vanity. [. . .] There are others still who long for knowledge in order to sell its fruits for money or honors, and this is shameful profiteering; others again who long to know in order to be of service, and this is charity. Finally, there are those who long to know in order to benefit themselves, this is prudence.[10]

---

8. [Cf. Ernst Troeltsch, *The Absoluteness of Christianity and the History of Religions* (1901), trans. David Reid (Louisville: Westminster John Knox Press, 2005).]

9. [The cited English edition of Bernard's sermon translates the word "welfare" but for Iwand's interpretation as *"Erbauung"* a translation with "edification" is more fitting.]

10. [Sancti Bernardi Opera, ed. Jean Lecercq et al., vol. 2, *Sermones super Cantica Canticorum*: 36-86 (Rome: Editiones Cistercienses, 1958), 3–8, 5, 17–26, 24; Bernard of Clairvaux, "Sermon 36: The Acquiring of Knowledge," in idem, *The Works of Bernard of Clairvaux*, vol. 3, *On the Song of Songs II*, trans. Kilian Walsh (Kalamazoo: Cistercian Publications, 1976), 173–80, 175f.]

What Bernard here calls "edification" does not have the hackneyed sense that the word often carries today. Rather, it should be understood in relationship to the Greek word (1 Cor. 8:1; 14,3; 2 Cor. 10:8), which means to build up, in contrast to destruction, and is related to the assembly, the building of God. If we are thus coworkers with God in his work, our knowledge must also be measured according to this standard: whether it builds up or destroys the assembly. Scientificity as such is no criterion of the theological task, properly speaking. The criterion does not lie in a system or in an abstract conceptualization but rather in the fact that this knowledge is acquired and utilized in order to do the work of building up that God began with the founding of his church. This is what Bernard, and Paul before him, called "love." And it is precisely at this criterion that Gnosticism took offense, at the folly of the cross for those who teach wisdom.

Yet Bernard also says something else. It is not enough only to edify others; it is also necessary to be edified oneself. We are not primarily the knowers, the givers, the teachers in the theological task. Rather, we are only those things insofar as we are "impostors, and yet are true" (2 Cor. 6:8). We are only those who pass on insofar as we are those who were once given something, teachers insofar as we were once taught. In everything, whatever we offer others as "edification" must resonate with the confession that we ourselves have experienced it to be edification in the brokenness, truth in our error, salvation in confusion, power in our weakness. This proposition has often been opposed on the grounds that the theologian must bear and suffer all weakness and all sin just as little as the doctor must endure all the illnesses that he treats. Yet this objection cannot stand because the comparison doesn't hold; we are not the doctor—not even as curates of souls [*Seelsorger*] (what a horrible, unbiblical name!)—rather, we simply have the command to point to the one who says of himself, "I am the LORD, your healer" (Exod. 15:26) and bring him into the places of need and suffering.

For this reason, only one thing can be our task: nothing will edify others that does not edify us, and nothing will help others that will not help us. There is no being finished [*Fertigsein*] for the preacher, and where there is a being finished, his preaching is only just skill [*Fertigkeit*]. Even we ourselves always remain those who have "made work for God with our sins" (cf. Isa. 43:24), and it is only as those on whom God himself is working that we can work on others. It is only as those who are in progress that we can recognize what we have to say. It is not enough to know the Scriptures; "*experientia*" must be bound to it, which is to say the [*Anfechtung*] that "teaches" us to hearken to the Word (Isa. 28:19). And it is a task of a particular kind, to cling to this Word in this hour of *Anfechtung* when nothing can comfort us, nothing internal and nothing external, when all we can hear is the echo of the accusation that bubbles up and reverberates within our hearts, the accusation toward which we also turn. It is then that God examines us to see if the "by faith *alone*" that we preach and teach is true, if we are willing to admit of ourselves what we proclaim to others to be salvation: "If I only have you . . . Seek first the kingdom of God . . . Fear not . . . Those who sow in tears shall reap with shout of joy" [Ps. 73:25f; Mt. 6:33; Lk. 2:10; Ps. 126:5]. This is the task that God accomplishes in us so that we might be skilled instruments in his hand. This is the career of the theologian, not incidentally but rather necessarily, for the object to which he has bound himself, God's object, drives him to it. And whoever cannot understand that one will quarrel with God and accuse him of having destroyed his joy, happiness, pleasure, and reputation has not yet understood anything of his calling: "O LORD, you have deceived me, and I was deceived. You are stronger than I, and you have prevailed. I have become a laughingstock all the day; everyone mocks me" (Jer. 20:7). And whoever has not yet quarreled with God, that this should be the *result* of his *mission*, has not yet grasped anything of his task. Whoever has not faced the *Anfechtung* that he should do as the lying prophets, that he should dare to sign on with the "God of Lies" and the "agreement with Sheol" (cf. Isa. 28:15): "I will not . . . speak anymore in his name" (Jer. 20:9). And whoever has not also been conscious of the burning fire in his bones, the fearful *Ananke* (1 Cor. 9:16; Amos 3:8), that it is a terrible thing to fall into the hands of the living God, that only one thing counts in such times: "Therefore do not throw away your confidence, which has a great reward" (Heb. 10:35), such a person has never quarreled with his God nor thrown his calling at his feet. For it is exactly when we taste the opposition of the world against the Word of God in our calling that we are on the right path and are walking along the way that is called Christ. This is the theology for refugees [*theologia viatorum*] and the theology of the cross [*theologia crucis*]. These are the trail markers that can make us confident that we are not "beating the air" but are rather on the track that leads to the goal (1 Cor. 9:24-27).

Do our theologians at the universities understand this? Does anyone tell them what matters? Does anyone tell them the full truth? Or are they being led with promises onto a journey that will in the hereafter prove to have been empty and false?[11] One thing is certain, at any rate: when a person knows this and recognizes it, when the Lord whom he wishes to follow tells him where this path leads and he nonetheless lays his hand on the plow and stays the course, then because of this, that against all the powers and forces, that wish to tear him away, another wonderful force counteracts them; because in this darkness of being at a loss for what to do and where to go, there is at once a bright light that shines and makes quite clear where we belong. "[T]o whom shall we go? You have the words of eternal life, and we have believed, and have come to know, that you are the Holy One of God" (Jn 6:68-69).

We have believed *and* have come to know! This is the calling with which the irrevocable decision is made. The only retreat that remains is the retreat against better insight, an action that no longer stands under the plea: "Father, forgive them, for they know not what they do." Those who "have once been enlightened, who

---

11. [Cf. on the one hand for a critique of academic liberal theology the groundbreaking essay by Friedrich Gogarten, "Zwischen den Zeiten," *Die christliche Welt* 34 (1920): 374-8. Cf. on the other hand for a classic work of the *Volkstum* theology [*people-theology*], Paul Althaus, *Kirche und Volkstum: Der völkische Wille im Lichte des Evangeliums* (Gütersloh: Bertelsmann, 1928), 11: "It is intolerable that the church has so little sense and space for the highest good, the people [*Volkheit*]."]

have tasted the heavenly gift, and have shared in the Holy Spirit, and have tasted the goodness of the word of God and the powers of the age to come" (Heb. 6:4-5) can no longer go back, for who should forgive them if they abandon the one who is forgiveness. And no theology can be properly brought forth and taught without this decision being made, for it is made with this: believed and come to know!

And there's yet another thing, a third thing! Since *vocatio* (calling) and *illuminatio* (enlightenment) actually lie in the theology that is properly carried out, since these are not things that take place adjacent to but rather in and through the theological task, the transition from scholarship into the practical office should never be what it has all too easily and all too often become: an escape into praxis. For we are not walking away from desperation about theology into the practical office; rather, we are walking into the practical office on the basis of the mandate that we have received in theology. Or who would wish to endorse such a beginning to the practical task, a beginning that is undertaken with the consciousness, not to have come to terms with theology—which is to say, with the Word of God. This faith in the redeeming power of praxis is a reliance on works and a self-redemption on one's own merits. And with such an attitude, it makes no difference whether much or little positive or negative is done; unbelief, the minus sign in front of the parenthesis by which everything else is determined, is the verdict already settled beforehand over such a performance. What benefit is zeal for the building up of the kingdom of God if the proper understanding of *how* the building must be carried out (Rom. 10:2) is missing? No, this praxis that prides itself in being untheological is a deed that no one even asked for, and it is worse than doing nothing at all. And it should probably be said at this point, in order to give all the "church builders" a heads-up, that the Reformation was undertaken not under the banner of activity but rather under that of the *iustitia passiva*. God works, and we are his instruments. God has no need for us to set his work into motion, as if he were lost without us in the world. This is exactly what we must learn again from Luther, that "God can be found only in suffering and the cross. [. . .] Therefore, the friends of the cross say that the cross is good and works are evil, for through the cross works are destroyed and the old Adam, who is especially edified by works, is crucified" (Explanation to Thesis 21 of the Heidelberg Disputation).[12]

We are continually experiencing this today, that the intrinsic worth of the theological task is opposed in the name of praxis. But this protestation, often made with the appearance of piety, is no less devoid of character and pernicious for the continuation of the church as that other protest in the name of academic objectivity. This is the crossfire in which the theological task is carried out. Both of the antagonistic brothers, the "academic" and the "practitioner," constantly fighting and despising one another, are strangely agreed when it comes to the matter of maintaining the necessary requirements of their traditional disagreement.

---

12. [Cf. Martin Luther, *Heidelberg Disputation* (1518), LW 31, 35-70, 53; WA 1, 362,28f.29-31.]

The unity of word and deed, of faith and life, of truth and reality, must not be achieved. It's almost as if Satan himself were arguing about the perpetuation of his dominion, about the perpetuation of this last and inmost discord that brings about the end of the kingdom of God. Even in the church, academia and praxis have divided between themselves the realm of their activity and have introduced the art of double-entry bookkeeping, which is to say the art of tearing apart head and heart, understanding and faith, prayer and fulfillment, heaven and earth. This is why they blame us, each from his own perspective, for the converse: the academic explains that this type of theological task belongs to churchly praxis while the practitioner tells us, to the contrary, that theology is academic and subject to the arcane discipline of scholarly work. Only when this fatal double dealing is recognized, when we begin to distrust these slogans, when we finally summon up the courage critically to reexamine the validity of these deeply entrenched prejudices will our eyes be opened to how unnatural and nebulous this appraisal actually is. What, then, should the simple Christian make of all this if he wishes to look behind these arts, behind these habitual sins of the scribes and high priests? "Surely," it is said to us, "from an academic perspective, we decide so and so . . . but on the basis of our personal conviction, we are, of course, quite certain." And now all doubts concerning the stance of the "scholar" that would be expected from academic coherence have been destroyed through a personal (i.e., noncommittal in this instance) "confession." Should that be the art that the theological youth has not yet grasped and ought to learn? Is this the maturation that comes with age now elevated to the level of method? "We have come to know and not believed. We have believed and not come to know." Should this be the last word where the skepticism of the cleric and the humanist are one?

It is in this fragmentation of the one whole truth of God's Word that we find the prerequisite for that faith in praxis which is actually nothing but unbelief, a faith which actually does nothing else but put something else at the beginning: not the Word but rather deed. We ought to be cautious and mistrusting when the enemy, whom we have perceived behind the mask of the academic, now approaches in a new disguise and seeks to lead us astray from the right path with the pathos of praxis. For the pursuit of wisdom and the doing of works are the enemy's mutually contradictory forms under which he tries to lead us astray.

So there remains one question: indeed, an uneasy question and a quite understandable helplessness: Where then is there a place in the world for our deeds? Does the world need us for its continued existence? The answer to this question is given to us in the Scriptures, where it says concerning the birth of our Lord: "[T]here was no place for them in the inn" (Lk. 2:7). And the one who entered into the world there says to those who would follow him that he would have less of a place in the world than the beasts of the field and of the air. It is as the one who is cast out that he becomes Lord of the world, as the one who is thrust to the side that he becomes its center, as the one ignored by the agenda of world history that he becomes the fullness of time. Thus he stands in the world as the one who is not of the world and thus he places his own into the world. Whether the church is dispensable to the world or to the nation—who is to say? It could just as easily be yes as no. If the world got to decide, the church would have been done away with long ago, but since God gets to decide, the world cannot get rid of it.

God makes an inn for his Word among men and gives it a place where it can be loud. And insofar as God does this, he confesses himself to the world. For this is the love of God to this world, that his Word finds a dwelling in it. In this besieged, persecuted, underestimated, despised *assembly* God holds the world, just as he had once held it, in Jesus Christ. This is the vivid image of God's love for us that even with bloody hands, derided, crushed, bound, and killed, he nevertheless does not leave the world and preserves it from its own destruction. The assembly is the body of Christ, its continuing existence in the world is the sign that God has not abandoned the world even today, and its mission in the world can thus be none other than to testify to what it is in its being: the love of God for the world in Jesus Christ, the crucified.

For this reason, these two belong together: the theology of the cross and the Church Militant.[13] Here lies the unity of truth and reality of the Word of God. This is what the reality that we evoke with this theology looks like, and there will be many who yield if this reality that is granted to this truth in the world becomes clear to them.

When the Lord gathered together with his own for the last time, he said to his companions, "One of you will betray me." And all were frightened and asked, "Is it I, LORD?"

---

13. [Cf. Hans Joachim Iwand, *Explanations to Vom unfreien Willen [On the Bondage of the Will] by Martin Luther*, in idem, *Ausgewählte Werke*, ed. Hans Heinrich Borcherdt and Georg Merz, Supplementary vol. 1 (München: Chr. Kaiser Verlag, 1939), 287–371, 331: "Precisely because the Church is *Ecclesia Dei*, she does not appear as such before the world, but is preserved by God as the precious pearl and kept pure in the hiddenness of the cross."]

Chapter 3

SED ORIGINALE PER HOMINEM UNUM[1]

A CONTRIBUTION TO THE DOCTRINE OF MAN

Originally published as Hans Joachim Iwand, "Sed originale per hominem unum: Ein Beitrag zur Lehre vom Menschen," *Evangelische Theologie* 6, no.1 (1946/47); also in Iwand, Glaubensgerechtigkeit, GA II, 171–93.

This essay originates out of the sixtieth birthday gift in 1943 for Prof. D. Julius Schniewind from his East Prussian friends and students. At that time only 700 copies were published as a publication for the members of the "Society for Evangelical Theology."

In 1943 Iwand wrote this article for the Festschrift that was presented to Julius Schniewind (1883–1948) in the honor of his sixtieth birthday. Since 1929, Schniewind had been Professor for the New Testament at the University of Königsberg and together with Iwand he dedicated himself to the Confessing Church in East Prussia. In this article Iwand focused on the theological concern and issue of the doctrine of sin in its fundamental significance for the theological anthropology. Thereby he built on his thoughts which he had explained in his earlier study, "The Righteousness of Faith According to Luther," two years earlier, inasmuch as he had demonstrated the correlation between the knowledge of sin and the knowledge of God.[2] Iwand's reflections on this defined his approach to the question of guilt and responsibility after the end of the Second World War. Schniewind played an important role in this, who considered the "Joy of Repentance" as the "Basic Question" of the Bible.[3] In the 1920s and 1930s, theological anthropology belonged to those topics which

---

1. [Martin Luther, *Lectures on Romans* (1515/16), LW 25, 297; WA 56, 310,3f: "[B]ut original sin came through this one man."]

2. [Cf. Hans Joachim Iwand, *The Righteousness of Faith According to Luther* (1941), ed. Virgil F. Thompson, trans. Randi H. Lundell (Eugene, OR: Wipf & Stock and Lutheran Quarterly, 2008).]

3. [Julius Schniewind, *Die Freude der Buße. Zur Grundfrage der Bibel*, ed. Ernst Kähler Göttingen: Vandenhoeck&Ruprecht, 1956.]

were controversial in Protestant theology and led to a breach within the so-called Dialectical Theology.[4] [MB]

I. *The Theological Concern*

Our goal in the following pages is to ascertain the theological concern contained in the doctrine of original sin. Thus, we are trying to determine the intention that has led to the establishment of this doctrine, the differentiation of *"peccatum originale"* and *"peccatum actuale."* Insofar as this can only become evident as we continue to clarify the concept at issue, our goal cannot be reached thematically. Yet if this little proposition precedes Luther's lectures on Romans, this is because the following reflections were set in motion precisely through this statement from Luther and because the topic around which this analysis revolves is implied in these few words: the relationship between *sin* and *man*, understood in such a way that the origin of this relationship becomes comprehensible.

At any rate, this discussion should begin from the outset with a misunderstanding so commonly encountered that it is appropriate for us to illuminate the goal of our investigation—even if it is oriented toward a different direction—by delineating against it. This misunderstanding is the way of thinking that manifestly embraces a variety of possibilities: considering the "phenomenon" of original sin in such a way that the theological formulation would stand alongside other formulations and would only earn its place in connection with those "facts" given as metaphysical or biological or medicinal.[5] Then, this theological doctrine is merely an "interpretation" of a phenomenon that can be "interpreted" in various ways, and one will probably and enthusiastically and thankfully declare that "echoes" of this doctrine can be found in many places that are best utilized "apologetically." We mean to say that with such an unexplained "linking,"[6] one runs the risk of making the actual theological sense of the expression *"peccatum originale"* inaccessible from the outset. It must first be clear what is meant *theologically* by this expression before one attempts to look for "analogies."

That certain analogies naturally suggest themselves is a fact that, for its part, only needs to be clarified and understood from the present state of affairs. The existence of this fact can be endlessly more problematic than it appears at first glance. The similarities can be based on delusion. It certainly cannot be denied that the concept of "original sin" taken in its broadest and thus most unclarified sense ends up in many and various manifestations, roughly in the Buddhist doctrine of "karma," certainly in the profound metaphysical formulation of this

---

4. [Cf. Wilhelm Link, "'Anknüpfung,' 'Vorverständnis' und die Frage der 'Theologischen Anthropologie,'" *Theologische Rundschau Neue Folge* 7 (1935): 205–54.]

5. [Cf. Emil Brunner, *Man in Revolt: A Christian Anthropology* (1937), trans. Olive Wyon (Philadelphia: Westminster Press, 1947).]

6. [Cf. Link, "Anknüpfung."]

idea,[7] but also in the ideas of reward and punishment found in all religions even down to the modern theories of heredity, which represent a novelty insofar as the *Ur*-idea of all their original religious and ethical principles expresses itself unbound in a naked materialism. Such a tenacious life inhabits this idea, originally of metaphysical origins, that it maintains itself even into the crassest Materialism. All of these theories have this one thing in common: they represent their ideas of original sin as a *causal nexus* between fault and fate. They differ depending on how they understand the ratio of the two entities, and they find their end at the extremes, where either the component of fate vanishes entirely since everything is understood as fault because of the absolute freedom of the will—as in Idealism— or where every kind of fault seems merely to be determined by the sociological, biological, or psychological manner of human existence. Accordingly, the theological grounds for the doctrine of original sin in the nineteenth century sought to understand this from the relationship of individual sin to the common fate of mankind. One can readily speak of a discovery of the "sociological aspect" in the entity of sin.[8]

Yet we are asking at this point whether the doctrine of original sin even belongs in the framework of such a way of thinking that takes for granted this causal nexus. We doubt that the origin and the meaning of our article of doctrine can be found here. Rather, we mean to say that this "schema," even when pervaded and reshaped by theological ideas, conceals the true meaning of this doctrine more than it reveals it. There admittedly remains a certain "similarity" that cannot be denied. And one will need to demonstrate somehow, even if one maintains an absolute distinction in the genesis of the theological and the philosophical methods of teaching, how it was possible for this confusion to come about and what the term "original," which is to say *propagatio* (Augustine),[9] means when used in connection with "sin."

II. What Is Man?

We understand the theological point at issue in this article of doctrine to be something totally different: not the theological interpretation of a phenomenon that exists per se but rather an original insight, one that only has meaning in the context of theology. We contend that this article of doctrine will unfold the theological view of man, that theological anthropology can be found concealed behind the unassuming title of this doctrine of *peccatum originale*. And we should

---

7. [Karl Heim notably disagreed intensively with Buddhism: (cf. Karl Heim, "Der Zen-Buddhismus in Japan," *Zeitschrift für Theologie und Kirche Neue Folge* 4 (1923): 245-59).]

8. [Cf. Paul Althaus, "Zur Lehre von der Sünde" (1923), in idem, *Theologische Aufsätze (I)* Gütersloh: Bertelsmann, 1929, (51-73) 62; Walter Künneth, *Die Lehre von der Sünde, dargestellt an dem Verhältnis der Lehre Sören Kierkegaards zur neuesten Theologie* (Gütersloh: Bertelsmann, 1927, 146.]

9. [Cf. Augustin, *De nuptiis et concupiscentia II*, 27 (PL 44, 461-463; CSEL 42, 297-298).]

certainly ask if it is advisable to exchange these two titles and to replace the doctrine of "*peccatum originale*" with a "theological anthropology," as sometimes happens today.[10] That we find no such thing in the history of theology but rather find a very thorough doctrine of sin—one that contains a fertile problem insofar as it often differs—should make us suspicious. The anthropology that theology has to offer is manifestly rooted in the doctrine of the "*peccatum originale*," not the other way around. There is no anthropology behind this concept nor can one be produced apart from it. Scholasticism is the large-scale effort to unite Greek anthropology and Augustinian teaching on sin. This attempt at a synthesis broke down during the Reformation, and the doctrine of "*peccatum originale*" regained its biblical, Augustinian status. Later, in German Idealism, we encounter the attempt to develop a doctrine of man that does not "originally" begin with the sinfulness of man. But in joining in this approach, theology put itself in danger of abolishing itself. For the verdict on whether theology is theology is determined not solely by its concept of God. Rather, it is determined at least as much by its doctrine of man and his capabilities. Yes, this is precisely the point where the actual verdict is reached, whether we understand man in his essence to be determined by God and his revelation or we understand God and the concept of God as the manifestation of each human self-understanding.[11]

In his introduction to the 51st Psalm, Luther gives the following noteworthy definition of theology: "The proper subject of theology is man guilty of sin and condemned, and God the Justifier and Savior of man the sinner. Whatever is asked or discussed in theology outside this subject, is error and poison."[12] Luther speaks here about the foundation of theology, that which underlies it as a science [*Wissenschaft*] and simultaneously as an object to be delved into. "*Subiectum*" is to be understood here in the sense of "υποκειμενον." Indeed, it is the *homo peccator* and the *deus salvator*. And just as little as one can reach behind this *deus iustificans*, which is to say *salvator*, to some "God in himself," so little is it possible to reach behind sin to find "man as such." This is what Luther means when he says, "that the natural powers are corrupt in the extreme."[13] The "natural man" exists where man appears in light of the God who is judging him, no longer a real entity. He is not the starting point of theological thought. In this respect, one could say that

---

10. [Cf. Friedrich Gogarten, "Das Problem einer theologischen Anthropologie," *Zwischen den Zeiten* 7 (1929): 493–511; Link, "Anknüpfung."]

11. [Cf. H. J. Iwand, "Der Prinzipienstreit innerhalb der protestantischen Theologie" (1958), in idem, *Um den rechten Glauben* GA I (222–46), 231–6.]

12. Martin Luther, *Lectures on the Psalms* (1532), LW 12, 311; WA 40/II, 328,17-20, on Ps. 51:2. ["The proper subject of theology is man guilty of sin and condemned, and God the Justifier and Savior of man the sinner. Whatever is asked or discussed in theology outside this subject, is error and poison."]

Cf. The Introduction by the editors of the "Evangelischen Theologie," *Evangelische Theologie* 1 (1934–35): 4f.

13. [LW 12, 308; WA 40/II, 323,30.]

theology as a science is soteriology if it is clear that by this we are warding off not only the reaching back to God "as such" but also the reaching back to man "as such," that both a *cognitio hominis theologica* [theological knowledge of man] and a *cognitio Dei etiam theologica* [theological knowledge of God] are required simultaneously. This simultaneous connection of God and man to one another in the actuality of sin and righteousness is the actual foundation of theology. Sin is virtually "the essence of man in theology."[14]

All of this becomes clearer when we see how Luther highlights precisely from this point the peculiarity of theological knowledge in comparison to the other scientific fields. They all have to do with the question "What is man?" Yet "[A] theologian discusses man as a SINNER,"[15] even as the philosopher starts out from the stipulation of man as "*animal rationale*,"[16] the jurist speaks of man in his capacity as "owner and master of property,"[17] and the physician makes the sick or the healthy man into the object of his science. In this way and none other is the *homo peccator* the object of theology. Everything that is studied and disputed in theology outside of this "*subiectum*" should be regarded as "error and poison."[18] "Such things are for natural science to discuss, not for theology."[19]

III. Self-Knowledge and Revelation

Insofar as theology answers the question "What is man?" [Ps. 8:5] with the phrase "*homo peccator*," theology and theology alone makes the demand, "*ut homo se cognoscat*" (for man to know himself). Theology thus bears a certain likeness to philosophy, which commences with the demand to "Know yourself."[20] The difference, however, is that the answer that theology gives with its designation of man as sinner will never be found in philosophy. This is crucial, that the sinfulness that is obviously known as such to the philosophers—how could it not be!—is not the answer to this question. Yet the *cognitio theologica hominis* (theological knowledge of man) confirms precisely this, and in so doing, it meets the qualifications to be theology.

Of course, it will be necessary to ask if the knowledge of sin was initially meant to be the answer to the question of the knowledge of self. There is no question that the knowledge of self plays a role, but is the endeavor of knowing oneself the necessary condition of the knowledge of sin? It is precisely at this point that great

---

14. [LW 12, 310; WA 40/II, 327,21 (The structure of the English phrase was altered by the editor).]
15. [LW 12, 310; WA 40/II, 327,20f (LW omits the emphasis from the original Latin).]
16. [LW 12, 310; WA 40/II, 327,18.]
17. [LW 12, 310; WA 40/II, 327,19.]
18. [LW 12, 311; WA 40/II, 328,19f.]
19. [LW 12, 310; WA 40/II, 327,18.]
20. [Plato, *Protagoras* 343a.]

and difficult questions burst forth in our time. If we see it correctly, the relationship of that philosophical demand for self-knowledge to this answer given in Christian revelation is the *theological-historical* achievement of *Augustine*. The *cognitio sui* [self-knowledge] is the *terminus a quo* [limit from which, i.e., earliest], the knowledge of *peccatum originale* the *terminus ad quem* [limit to which, i.e., latest] of his method,[21] which determined the entire Middle Ages and has continued to have an effect beyond that (Pascal,[22] Tholuck[23]!). That *this* answer is given to *this* question marks the break with Antiquity. Namely, that the man who is summoned by the "γνῶθι σαυτόν" (know yourself) to knowledge could find the truth of himself in the confession of his sinfulness is an inconceivable idea to the Greeks. In the moment that this takes place, Antiquity ends and the Middle Ages begin.

What if philosophy were now to make the attempt to answer the question "What is man?" by itself, which is to say to rediscover its actual origin in keeping itself open to this question in principle? If it were to reclaim this, its "Christianized" original question? If theology disconnected from the fundamental answering of this question were to be rejected as irrelevant? If that ancient attempt to highlight this question simply from man's being-in-the-world and more or less to answer it were repeated yet again? Thus to explain the whole enquiry from a God-less understanding of the world, as is clearly taking place in modern existential philosophy?[24] Does theology in this way lose the right to insist upon the *cognitio sui* on its own? Is this only the heritage of philosophy? Or does the determination of man, independent from the philosophical formulation of the problem, lie within the limits of *revelation*? Yet how should this be understood? Am I as a "Christian the actual object of my theology?"[25] Do the testimonies of theology only have validity over man insofar as we keep ourselves under the spell of Christian self-awareness? Or is Christ truly the second Adam [cf. 1 Cor. 15:45] and Adam now

---

21. [Cf. Augustin, Confessiones X, 10, 17 (PL 32, 786; CSEL 33, 238, 39).]

22. [Blaise Pascal (1623–62) was a French mathematician, physicist, and philosopher. Cf. Blaise Pascal, *Pensées*, Fragm. 66, ed. Léon Brunschvicg (Paris: Classiques Garnier, 1961, 86).]

23. [August Tholuck (1799–1877) was an evangelical theologian who taught at the University of Halle and also influenced many students from the United States. Cf. August Tholuck, *Die Lehre von der Sünde und vom Versöhner oder: Die wahre Weihe des Zweiflers* 7th ed., (Hamburg: Friedrich Perthes, 1851), 173.]

24. [Cf. Martin Heidegger, *Being and Time* (1927), trans. Joan Stambaugh (Albany: State of New York University Press, 2010), 53f.]

25. [Johann Christian Konrad von Hofmann, *Der Schriftbeweis. Ein theologischer Versuch* (1852), vol. 1, 2nd ed. (Nördlingen: C.H. Beck'sche Buchhandlung, 1857), 10; cf. idem, Theologische Ethik. *Abdruck einer im Sommer 1878 gehaltenen Vorlesung* (Nördlingen: C.H. Beck'sche Buchhandlung, 1878), 17.— Iwand referred to this quote in his lecture on the history of nineteenth-century theology in light of the difference between Schleiermacher and Lutheran Confessionalism (cf. Iwand, *Theologiegeschichte*, NWN III, 91f.)]

the τύπος τοῦ μέλλοντος [type of the one to come, Rom. 5:14]? Is the "ἄνθρωπος" [person] of Rom. 3:28 only a universalizing representation of the life experience of a particular type of person, namely the pious Jew under the Law? Or is what is said there intended in such a way that in this "logic of the gospel," in this "judgment" (from the revelation of God), a statement is being made about man per se, about man in his essence before God—for this is precisely what is meant by the expression *iustificare* [to justify]? Yet, we ask further, if the gospel justifies "without the works of the law" [Rom. 3:28; Gal. 2:16], must we not identify along with the "being under the law" [cf. Romans 7] an existence that comprehends all men, an existence that identifies even the existence of man qua man apart from the gospel, even if man is not conscious of it? For precisely this was likely the bias of our theological "Cartesianism,"[26] in which a good portion of Augustinianism yet remains, namely that we equate being and consciousness. Revelation means precisely the opposite. Revelation assumes that being and consciousness do not correspond, that man lives in an *ignorantia invincibilis* [ignorance of the invincible][27] in relation to himself, that for this reason man's being before God, his "*esse coram Deo*," does not naturally coincide with his "self-awareness" and thus that the true *cognitio sui* is the consequence of the encounter with the revealed God. "Nor is there any hope that man in his principal part [which refers to the philosophical designation of man as *anima*] can himself know what he is until he sees himself in his origin which is God."[28]

And so we see that the doctrine of *peccatum originale* designates the theological knowledge of man as primarily theological, that it occurs with the claim of a universal validity and should not only be considered the expression of a Christian self-awareness, that it is for this reason on a collision course with a philosophical-existential self-understanding that will, for its part, never stop taking up the old question: What is man? That self-understanding, however, that just as emphatically asserted—and, we think, correctly—that this question does not necessarily lead to the consequence of "*peccator sum*" ["I am a sinner"]. The philosophical enquiry does not end with the *Confessio* [confession], but the theological enquiry begins precisely at that point. Who knows if in theology, the two are really related to one another as question and answer! Who knows if the confession of sinfulness is really the answer to this question! After all, this question could only arise from that confession. It could be a calling into question of man, a calling into question of all that man intends to be, his self-awareness, and that not only in ontic sense but also precisely in an axiological sense, in which, however and whatever he

---

26. [A theological way of thinking determined by the philosophy of René Descartes (1596–1650), whereby self-confidence is established by "I consciousness" (*cogito ergo sum*, "I think, therefore I am").]

27. [Cf. Thomas Aquinas, *Summa Theologica*, trans. Fathers of the English Dominican Province, 2nd ed. (New York: Benzinger Brothers, 1920), I-II q 76 a 3.]

28. Martin Luther, *Disputation Concerning Man* (1536), LW 34, 133-144, 138; WA 39/I, 175,36f, thesis 17.

"judges," a calling into question of man, who intends to know about himself, who seeks to make out of the *ignorantia invincibilis* [ignorance of the invincible] a *docta ignorantia* [scholar of ignorance]²⁹ and to make a virtue out of need. Here, in theology, the question first arises out of the answer, the judgment—and this is even more than a "question"—concerning man and what he believes himself to be arises out of the knowledge of sin.

At any rate, it has probably become clear from all of that that the doctrine of *peccatum originale* only has meaning when and insofar as it comprehends—said in general terms—a doctrine of man in light of revelation, which is to say in light of justification.

IV. Luther's Interpretation of Rom. 5:12

We are attempting to develop this article of doctrine through isolated analyses by seeking, at the same time as this theological analysis, to arrive at a criterion for testing the appropriateness of individual definitions. We are starting out from a proposition of Luther on Rom. 5:12, the classic passage for the doctrine of original sin. Luther says here, "*Actualia enim omnia per diabolum intrant et intraverunt in mundum, sed originale per hominem unum.* [For all actual (sins) enter and have entered into the world through the devil, but originally through one man.]"³⁰ At this point, between Paul and Luther stands, as a stage of theological interpretation, the interpretation of this passage by *Augustine*, who introduces in his dispute with Pelagius the distinction between *imitatio* and *propagatio* in order to make clear the two forms of "the source of sin" and accordingly its "*intrare in mundum*."³¹ According to Augustine, the sin about which Paul is speaking here does not come upon us from outside as the seductive power of the Evil One ("*imitatio*") but rather because we share Adam's nature ("*propagatio*"). Luther takes up this distinction by simply making a succinct compilation, omitting the thought of *imitatio* or *propagatio*: "actual sins [. . .] through the devil, but original sin came through this one man."³² He is concerned here with a particular situation, with the "entry of sin into the cosmos," with the intraworldly, or as Luther quickly adds, human-historical possibility. This question is actually totally out of place in talking about actual sins, for "no actual sin enters the world."³³ Of course this is true because the question's proper place is with what it does ("remains on each person").³⁴ For this reason, the idea of "enters the world" is only meaningful in view of the

---

29. [Nicolaus von Cues, *De docta ignorantia*, Opera omnia, vol. I, ed. Ernst Hoffmann (Leipzig: Raymond Klibanski, 1932).]
30. [LW 25, 297; WA 56, 310,2-4.]
31. [Augustin, *De nuptiis et concupiscentia I*, 1, 1 (PL 44, 413; CSEL 42, 211).]
32. [LW 25, 297; WA 56, 310,2-4.]
33. [LW 25, 297; WA 56, 310,13f.]
34. [LW 25, 297; WA 56, 310,16.]

peccatum originale, since this is universal, and its entry into the world means "the world becomes guilty and sinful because of one man."[35] *World* in this context will always be understood as "men in the world."[36] In all this, Luther remains in the usual interpretation; it is only substantial—and illuminating of the dissimilarity between how he and we speak of sin—that he speaks directly of the devil where we would expect him to speak of man, his freedom and responsibility—namely of actual sin—and then speaks of man where we would expect him to speak of the devil. Man and *peccatum originale* belong together—likewise with the devil and the *peccata actualia*. In this interpretation, Luther has certainly gone beyond Paul, after his forbear Augustine, but doesn't every true interpretation do that? Only now does the Pauline δι' ἑνὸς ἀνθρώπου ["through one man," Rom. 5:12] receive its proper sound and color.

V. Sin of "Commission" as Suffering

We can take two things from this: first, an entirely new view of the so-called actual sin or sin of "commission." Is it necessary for the doctrine of the freedom of the will to be the only possible starting point for understanding the *peccata actualia*? First, let's be clear what it would mean if Luther had seen the matter correctly! In that case, the "acts" of sin would originate with two wills, the will of Satan and the will of man, and certainly in such a way that man's will is too weak to prevail against the purposes of Satan. Thus, man is not in any way the "actor" in "actual" sin. These sins are the acts of an alien will, a will that man suffers but suffers in such a way that this frailty is sin, and this sin is at once an indication of an ultimate human weakness.[37] Or if we go one step further: actual sin always includes at the same time a deception of man, an ἀπάτη, a trick; in the act of sin, man is tricked in such a way that man in the very act of sin suffers at the same time a deception, a cruel disillusion. For man does not will sin in the sense that it is then against his will: "Just as a sinner does not want to sin for sin's sake—he would prefer that sin did not exist at all—but for the sake of the good that seems to be in it."[38] The good that man initially has in mind but does not come to fruition identifies sin as the deception of man. For this reason, sin is an act, an irreparable occurrence, a *perfectum*, for man and for the actuality of his life, an evil (*malum*) and a punishment (*poena*) and is thus willed by God as "*ignominia hominis*."[39] "Therefore God wills that sin be done not for its own sake but for the sake of penalty and punishment."[40]

---

35. [LW 25, 297; WA 56, 310,24.]
36. [LW 25, 297; WA 56, 310,17.]
37. [Cf. "The Freedom of the Christian and the Bondage of the Will" in this volume.]
38. [LW 25, 161; WA 56, 180,30-32.]
39. [Cf. LW 25, 162; WA 56, 181,17-22: "Shame of man."]
40. [LW 25, 161; WA 56, 180,28f.]

Luther doesn't avoid the fact of sin in the conversation of God's permission, for actual sin is more than just an "act" of man, whose freedom must somehow be coordinated with the divine predetermination. Rather, he recognizes the phenomenon of sin as necessary in order to make man see his own shame. Precisely in the act of sin, man grasps that he is not free. He is the victim of a deception—and this deception makes him see for himself, precisely in view of his act, if instead of doing the good that he wanted to do, he has done the evil that he did not want [Rom. 7:15]. Insofar as the act of sin deceives man, who thinks himself to be great and exalted, it is the will of God and the punishment that comes upon man. In the sin of commission, man is in a certain sense the one who suffers: the sin reveals the strength of those powers that blind and seduce men, the powers that must first be revealed to man in that place where sin, by becoming an action, reveals man's shame. Of course, sin reveals nothing to the one who believes in the freedom of the will. Rather, sin only obscures that which he believes himself to possess: the good will! It would, however, reveal something, namely the previously concealed "*per diabolum.*" With that we recognize in whose hands we are and at the same time the one who promises to free us from it. How it comes about that not every sinful act reveals this "*per diabolum*" to man, that not every sin makes man disappointed and sober to his salvation is a question that comes up at this point, a question that we cannot yet answer here, as the knowledge of sin can never be developed from the notion of actual sin alone.

Yet something else should be said here. In Luther's theology, we continue to encounter his wonderful ability to comfort the believer and to guard him against despair. He can do this because he doesn't speak to man in his sin from the perspective of morals, and thus not from the premise of a "free man," but rather as one who suffers under that sin. One single passage should make it clear for us: incidentally, Luther takes up this state of affairs in Rom. 9:19 ("*Why does he still find fault?*")[41]—it has to do with God's inscrutable guidance—and speaks to those who for this reason fall into blasphemies and rebellion against God:

> Now it surely is no sin if a man out of fear and humility and piety says to God: "Why did You make me thus?" Even if he would commit blasphemy because of the overwhelming violence of his temptation, he would not therefore perish. For our God is not a God of impatience and cruelty, even toward the ungodly. I am saying this for the comfort of those who are perpetually troubled by thoughts of blasphemies and are in great anxiety; since such blasphemies, *because they are violently extorted from men by the devil against their will*, they sometimes sound more pleasant in the ear of God than a hallelujah or some kind of hymn of praise. For the more horrible and foul the blasphemy, the more agreeable it is to God, *if the heart knows that it does not will this, because the heart did not produce it or choose it*. But it is a sign that a man did not will it from his heart and that

---

41. [LW 25, 390; WA 56, 400,13.]

he is really innocent of it, if he is truly afraid and terrified that he has done such thing. For the clearest sign of a good heart is the fear of doing evil.[42]

The blasphemies into which men fall in their deception are "violently extorted from men by the devil." Since they must think such thoughts and such feelings mustarise in them, they themselves suffer under them. The suffering of men under the extreme pain of such thoughts that impose themselves upon them is the true praise of God. Their current inability to praise God will one day stand as a pure alleluia before God, for it is born in the suffering of the agonizing struggle [*Anfechtung*]—inaudible and imperceptible. It is only in the "*sentire se illam nolle* [sensing by oneself that unwillingness]," in the "*pavor mali* [terror of evil]," in the terror before the Evil One which settles as a burden over the soul. And yet it is precisely here that the praise of God is heard in such a way that man is seen not as himself but as one who has been delivered from the agonizing struggles and assaults of Satan. This is only one example, but one can clearly gather from it the fruitful possibilities for paranesis that open up precisely in the treatment of actual sin when we know: "*actualia per diabolum intrant in mundum et intraverunt.*"[43]

VI. *The Distinction between* peccatum actuale *and* peccatum originale

The other thing that we can take from all this will have become clear over the course of this analysis of the notion of actual sin: that the opinion of them—and of the knowledge of sin that emerges from them—is totally indivisible from one's attitude toward *peccatum originale*. The notion of sin points beyond the act as such. For this reason, the matter is also decided of how we regard the sin that manifests itself in acts beyond its actuality. The judgment is reached precisely where sin in its essence is confessed and recognized: before God! This is, first of all, the profound meaning of the theological distinction between *peccatum originale* and *actuale*, that the question of the essence of sin is oriented beyond actions and the relationship of man to the world and instead toward the forum of God. This (forum of God) is called "*Coram Deo*" time and again by the Reformers. That which qualifies a deed as *peccatum* lies beyond the act itself; it is only recognizable in its essence and source where the person, the man, is known before God.[44] In this way, the distinction between *peccata actualia* and *peccatum originale* (which can only be spoken of in the singular) always points us away from actions and teaches us to inquire about the origin, the *origo peccati*. Thus the proper understanding of this distinction must emphasize the *peccatum originale*, not as if this were something different—abstractable, if you will—from the *peccata actualia*, but in such a way

---

42. LW 25, 390f.; WA 56, 401,7-19 [emphasis added by Iwand]. Cf. Martin Luther, Lectures on the Psalms (1519-21), WA 5, 170,10-26, on Ps. 5:12.
43. [Cf. Section "Luther's Interpretation of Rom. 5:12" for the translation.]
44. [Cf. Iwand, GA II; see Fn. 2 in this chapter.]

that it becomes clear that one can gain no explanation of the essence of sin from the sinful act as such: "the works of sin are the fruits of this sin."[45] It is precisely for this reason that the overcoming of sin cannot take place on the plane of mere deeds, for we do not reach the root in this way. The *"radix peccati,"* however, is *"incredulitas* (unbelief)."[46] It is about recognizing sin itself in the actual sin, the sin that manifests itself within the actual sin and yet still conceals itself—sin in its proper essence. This is essential when the discussion has to do with *peccatum originale*.

Since this internal connection between *peccata actualia* and *peccatum originale* is revealed, we see that *sin* can only be comprehended *by means of itself*. At this point, sins will no longer be accounted for with "something" that is not sin, somewhat like how evil finds its expression in not-knowing according to Socrates.[47] This theological doctrine constitutes a circle and asserts that only the one who moves within this circle will comprehend the essence of sin. Should we ask about the "whence" of the *peccata actualia*, we will be directed to the *peccatum originale*. In other words, the origin of the sinful deed is sin itself. In this way, sin remains in the strict sense something undeductible, inexplicable. It remains a mystery that will be solved in a different way, from which man must be rescued in some other way—as through explication, which is to say through speculative knowledge. However, if we were to remove that pointing from the *peccata actualia* to the *peccatum originale*, the way is open to all possible paths, which is to say false paths, toward encouraging the "education of the human race" through "enlightenment"[48] and moving down the path to the utopian heights of a new and better time. It belongs to the essential characteristics of Reformation theology that it tackles the question of sin yet again at the notion of *peccatum originale*—in direct contrast to scholasticism!—and thus carefully fenced itself off from all those, who "have deflected the discussion of sin to the matter of good works only."[49]

VII. Origo peccati

While it was said of *peccata actualia* that they come into the world *"per diabolum* (by the devil)," it was said of *peccatum originale*, both with reference to and as an interpretation of the Pauline phrase: *"sed originale per hominem unum* (but originally by one man)"! What does this juxtaposition mean? First, it means that sin's entry into the world is inconceivable—without man. That the presence of sin

---

45. LW 25, 259; WA 56, 271,14f., on Rom. 4:7.

46. [Martin Luther, *Lectures on Genesis* (1535), LW 1, 162; WA 42,122, 12: "the root and source of sin is unbelief and turning away from God."]

47. [Cf. Plato, *Apology* 21d.]

48. [Gotthold Ephraim Lessing, *The Education of the Human Race* (1780) (London: Smith, Elder and Co., 1858), 67f (§ 80f).]

49. LW 25, 263; WA 56, 276,6f, on Rom. 4:7.

in the world is thus not to be traced back to Satan but rather to men. Looking to a satanic power will not enable one to comprehend sin in its origin. Rather, sin will be properly understood from the humanity of man. If we ask about the origin of sin, we may not skip over man or attempt to look behind him. Rather, man must all the more "*in se introire*," or go within himself.[50] The answer to the *origo peccati* lies in man himself, not in the devil.[51]

In this respect, that place where the *origo peccati* is understood in the biblical sense, the sinfulness of man cannot be understood as a tragedy, as the state that fate assigned to him according to the way that the world is. The existence of sin in the world is not a given into which the man, who is in himself guiltless, is hurled. Rather, it is much more a reflection of the fact that man and his history cause the world to appear the way that it does. The presence of sin in the world tells of an event between man and God that is decisive for the history of man and the world. This is where the dividing line to myth lies. The "myth of the fall into sin" [Genesis 3] does not say directly: *originale per hominem unum* (originally by one man). Rather, it says: *originale per diabolum* (originally by the devil)! This is why man's salvation "from the fallen world" is something entirely different from the forgiveness of sins, the contents of the *promissio Dei* [promise of God] and the gospel of Jesus Christ.[52] The conflict between history and myth is in our opinion not an ultimate conflict, further not a conflict that is relevant for faith.[53] We must first be critical of myth where it "dehumanizes" sin and *thus* "de-sin-izes" man.

It may be said at this point that the doctrine of the fall into sin and the proliferation of this "*nativa propensio in omnem posteritatem* (inborn propensity in all posterity)"[54] stands close to a mythical idea, and this is why we can only speak of the origin of existence—exactly as we can only speak of its end—in this manner. At this point, we come to the limit of history as such. This limit is referred to by the term "myth." But it is for precisely this reason that the notion of the fall

---

50. [Cf. LW 25, 213; WA 56, 229,21, on Rom. 3:5: "enter into ourselves."]

51. [Cf. LW 25, 300; WA 56, 313,4-16, on Rom. 5:14.]

52. [The understanding of sin stood in the middle of the debates regarding theological ethics in the 1930s (cf. Emmanuel Hirsch, *Schöpfung und Sünde in der natürlich-geschichtlichen Wirklichkeit des einzelnen Menschen* (Beiträge zur systematischen Theologie 1) (Tübingen: J.C.B. Mohr, 1931); idem, "Brief an Karl Barth vom 27. February 1932," in Karl Barth, *Offene Briefe 1935–42*, ed. Diether Koch, Karl Barth-Gesamtausgabe, vol. 36 (Zürich: Theologischer Verlag Zürich, 2001), 191; Dietrich Bonhoeffer, *Creation and Fall: A Theological Exposition of Genesis 1-3*, Dietrich Bonhoeffer Works vol. 3, (Minneapolis: Fortress, 2004).]

53. [Iwand hereby separates himself from the program of "demythologization" of Rudolf Bultmann (1884–1976), which Bultmann first put forth in the 1941 essay "New Testament and Mythology," in *Kerygma and Myth: A Theological Debate*, ed. Hans Werner Bartsch (New York/Evanston: Harper and Row Publishers, 1953), 1–44.]

54. [Philip Melanchthon, *Commonplaces: Loci communes 1521*, trans. Christian Preus (St. Louis: Concordia Publishing House, 2014), 37.]

into sin may not be taken on its own and thus turned into a history alongside other histories. It is telling that the Scriptures do not do this. Adam figures into them as a type; his history is our history. Thus we may say initially: the addendum "*per hominem*" resists the attempt to respond to the mystery of sin in myth.

But what does the expression "*per hominem*" mean in the positive sense? Here we are facing the question, if we may flip our thinking around: Does humanity mean sinfulness? Precisely that would not be correct. Not only because Adam is at once the type of the man to come [Rom. 5:14] and in Jesus Christ we run into the man "tempted in all things as we are but without sin" [Hebrews 4:15] but rather because sinfulness is understood according to this definition as a determination of fate. When man confesses "I am a sinful man" [Lk. 5:8], this "I am" means something other than when he says, "I find myself in a situation that is defined thus and so."

The confession of sin has to do with an *essence*, but what sort of essence is it? The Middle Ages attempted to interpret the sinfulness of man with the term "*concupiscentia*"[55] [concupiscence] with the result that it became the expression of the interconnectedness of man in the "*vanitas mundi*" [futility of the world, cf. Rom: 8:20]. The Reformers liked to speak of "*affectus*" [feeling], "*motus cordis*" [the movement of the heart], "*sensus*" [perception], "*cogitatio*" [awareness] with the result that the confession of sins subsequently degenerated into a psychological datum, an awareness of sin. Luther, properly recognizing the difficulty that is present here, said that sinfulness should be believed just as the state of righteousness: "by faith alone we must believe that we are sinners, for it is not manifest to us, indeed, we often do not seem to ourselves to be aware of that fact."[56] This is why this essence is also best described as the *esse coram Deo*. The relationship in which we comprehend our sinfulness is neither our being-in-the-world nor our being by ourselves; rather, we come to this through God meeting men with his Word. This essence is identified by the encounter between God and man. "Therefore we have to stand under the judgement of God and believe His words."[57] This is to say, to be revealed as a sinner, which is why Luther preferred to use the term "*fieri*" [becoming] to the term "*esse*" [being] in describing this event. "But we have to say something about the way in which a man must spiritually become a sinner. It is not a natural way. For that way every does not become a sinner but is one."[58] The recognition of sin is thus a spiritual event. It should not be thought of at all as a monolog. Rather, it is the realization of man standing before God.

---

55. [Cf. Thomas Aquinas, *Summa Theologica*, I-II q 30; Rudolf Hermann, *Luthers These "Gerecht und Sünder zugleich." Eine systematische Untersuchung* (Gütersloh: Bertelsmann, 1930), 39.48.]
56. LW 25, 215; WA 56, 231,9-11, on Rom. 3:5.
57. LW 25, 215; WA 56, 231,11f., on Rom. 3:5.
58. LW 25, 217; WA 56, 233,5-7, on Rom. 3:5.

VIII. Humanity as a Positive Determination of Sin

Nevertheless, humanity remains a positive determination of sin. Whenever we wish to speak properly of sin—and here we ought to think also of our preaching—we must speak of it in a manner that is human, not "inhuman." Only in this way can sin in its origin be revealed. One must speak of sin in such a way that man knows how to understand it according to the potentialities that lie within him and for that very reason does not operate with imputed and constructed potentialities. "God the Father [. . .] does not save imaginary, but rather, real sinners."[59] Man in himself must be revealed to be the origin of sin. For sin is not "something" about man, something adopted, a cloudiness upon the unspotted mirror of our souls, a depravation of human nature that intrudes from the outside. Precisely this is to speak inhumanly about sin, to forget that the origin of sin lies within man himself. Considered in this way, man and sin remain in a more or less accidental, fatal, at any rate incomprehensible relationship with each other. This is the moral perspective; "*naturalia post peccatum permanserunt integra* (natural things after sin remained whole)"[60] applies to it; it clings to an "*inclinatio naturalis ad virtutem* (inclination of nature toward virtue)" (Thomas)[61]. Yet it is precisely for these reasons that this is not the biblical-Reformation view. This view does not understand the meaning of the confession of sin and will more or less relate this confession to "thoughts, words, and deeds."[62] Something else entirely happens in a true confession of sin: here the tongue of man, once mute in his opposition to God, is loosed by the Spirit of God. In his very core, inaccessible, closed-off man finds his way back to the Word—precisely to that place whence he had fallen. In the confession of sin, he recognized God's truth concerning man within himself and to himself. In such a confession itself, he again becomes a partaker in the Word of truth [cf. Jas 1:18]; he thinks God's thoughts concerning himself and gives him his due. In this way, the fellowship of man with God is restored. "This acknowledgement or confession is the truth, not a philosophical truth which reason hears and sees, but a theological and hidden truth which only the Spirit sees and hears."[63]

It will also be noted at this point that the realization of man standing before God in this way is not a *meritum* [wage]—indeed, the content of this truth prohibits such a thought. For in confessing myself to be a sinner before him, I am delivering myself over to God's punishment. When, in spite of this, fellowship with God still comes about, this is right now and right here the wonder of his grace,

---

59. [Martin Luther, *Heidelberg Disputation* (1518), LW 31, 63; WA 1, 370,9f.]

60. [Cf. Thomas Aquinas, *Scriptum super libros Sententiarum* III d. 20 qu. 1 a. 1 qc. 1 arg. 1; Gottfried Thomasius, *Die christliche Dogmengeschichte als Entwicklungs-Geschichte des kirchlichen Lehrbegriffs*, vol. 2: Die Dogmengeschichte des Mittelalters und der Neuzeit (Erlangen and Leipzig: Andreas Deichert, 1889), 150.]

61. [Thomas Aquinas, *Summa Theologica*, I-II qu. 85 a. 2 ad 3.]

62. [Cf. WA 50, 228,21-27.]

63. LW 12, 356; WA 40/II, 391,34-36, on Ps. 51:8.

which bespeaks the sinner righteous and always remains wonderful in view of man's confession of sin.

IX. *The Universal Significance of the Knowledge of Sin*

The question remains: What does it mean, if we are continuing to speak of "man," that "man" should come to *cognitio sui* [knowledge of self] and *veritas* [truth] in the confession of sin? Is this the knowledge of myself in my individual situation, my strengths, weaknesses, lusts, mistakes, wishes, passions, and so on? In this case, I would certainly not be recognizing and coming to know the *peccatum originale*. The *peccatum originale* has much more to do with a knowledge of the whole man and the whole of humanity, with the general sense of sin in its totality,[64] which can only become clear to man in certain individual cases—like how David arrived at the profound understanding of the 51st Psalm on the occasion of a specific sin [cf. 2 Sam. 12:13]—which, however, always means a situation in which the whole human race feels affected and understood.

This is why the proposition of man's sinfulness is simply not a logical conclusion that could be drawn from the sum of various individual cases. Rather, this recognition is "*divinitus*," from God.[65] "If I were without the Word, I could not have the knowledge to talk this way about myself and all men."[66] The theological testimony concerning the *peccatum originale* is decidedly the confession of an individual, but it transcends the individual, the particular, and reveals individually the common essence of man before God. In God's Word we find the condition for such a recognition concerning man per se, a recognition that is corroborated in the experience of the individual but cannot be derived from it.

X. *The True Man*

What about that *veritas* [truth], though, toward which the revelation of God aids man? To what extent is it a *veritas* that concerns man as man? To what extent does it mean exactly *veritas* for the *homo* [man] in his essence as *homo* when he recognizes himself to be a sinner? Luther assists us at this point, as well. First, he says in view of the cross and suffering of Christ that God makes through it "out of unhappy and proud gods true people, that is wretched and sinners."[67] The likeness unto God, the desire to play God, is that from which man must be freed. It is his untruth, his inhumanity. Man ascribes things to himself that belong only

---

64. [Cf. LW 12, 338; WA 40/II, 367,26-28.]
65. LW 12, 339; WA 40/II, 369,28.
66. LW 12, 340; WA 40/II, 369,37f.
67. *ex infoelicibus et superbis diis homines veros, idest miseros et peccatores* [WA 5, 128,38f.]

to God: life, righteousness, wisdom, omnipotence. To become a true man means to recognize God and what belongs to him, to let God be God, to fulfill the First Commandment and thus to see oneself as poor and bare and reliant upon God for all things we are as humans. The truth that has to do with this recognition lies somewhere in the fact that we rediscover the lost boundary between God and man so that we respect it again. Now it becomes clear to what extent the phrase "originally by one man [*originale per hominem unum*]" is justifiable, for this sort of deification, this hero-worship of man is only comprehensible as the elevation of human existence.

It is the hallmark of true humanity that it is only conceivable to us as sinfulness in which no true humanity can be found. In this respect, no man—even as we are all sinners—can find in himself the truth of that which God intends with humanity. Even this truth lies *extra nos* [outside of us]. Jesus Christ alone stands among us as true man, and this is the meaning of his incarnation: "For because we ascended in Adam to the likeness of God, God therefore descended to our likeness, in order to lead us back to the recognition of ourselves."[68] Luther calls this the sacrament of the Incarnation.[69] The Incarnation of Christ is thus the exact opposite of Adam's attempt to become God, and the crucified one stands as "true man" in the midst of a world whose humanity has abandoned its own truth, the truth of its humanity, and thus robbed itself of the knowledge of God. In this way, he stands as true man in the midst of "deplorable and proud gods;" by placing him among us in this way, God calls humanity back to the *cognitio sui*. This will only be obtained, however, so that every individual can have his old Adam called out of untruth to truth (i.e., through death to life) in his encounter with the Word of God become flesh.

---

68. *Quia enim ascendimus in Adam ad similitudinem dei, ideo descendit ille in similitudinem nostram, ut reduceret nos ad nostri cognitionem.* WA 5, 128,39-129,1, on Ps. 5:2f.

69. [WA 5, 129,1.]

Chapter 4

LOVE AS THE FOUNDATION AND LIMIT OF FREEDOM

Originally published as Hans Joachim Iwand, "Die Liebe als Grund und Grenze der Freiheit," *Frankfurter Hefte* 6 (1951): 81-9; also in Hans Joachim Iwand, *Kirche und Gesellschaft*, Nachgelassene Werke Neue Folge Vol. I, ed. Ekkehard Börsch (Gütersloh: Gütersloher Verlagshaus, 1998), 194-205.

Iwand published this article in Frankfurter Hefte, *a periodical of critical Roman Catholic intellectuals. After the Second World War he had become acquainted with one of the editors, Eugen Kogon, a Jewish Christian who had survived six years of imprisonment in a concentration camp at Buchenwald. Based on his own experience, Kogon published his book* The SS-State: The System of the German Concentration Camp *shortly after the war. Iwand wrote an impressive review ("Ecce homo: Ein Wort zu Eugen Kogon, Der SS-Staat," Die Zeit 14. August 1947), which was one of the first public writings by a Protestant theologian concerning the Nazi crimes. He concluded this review by quoting 1 Jn 3:14: "We know that we have passed out of death into life, because we love the brothers." This Bible verse is the very essence of this article, in which Iwand elaborates on what love implies in a "state of exception" like Nazi Germany. Love is framed here not as a natural human characteristic or a virtue but rather as the incarnation of faith. It is the power of faith that does not recoil from the invisible boundaries that the state has established in society. This love that has death behind itself renounces the foundation of the state on a friend-enemy principle (Carl Schmitt) and so cannot but help people in need. In other publications from this period—examples in this volume are "The Bible and the Social Issue" and "Church and Society"—Iwand explains how the parables of the New Testament, like the "Good Samaritan," which is essential to this article, expose the reality of God's liberating presence in society.* (GdH)

I.

The cultural [*geistige*] situation in Germany today,[1] perhaps in all of Europe, differs from the situation after the First World War in a noteworthy, and one could even say frightening, way.

---

1. Cf. the excellent article by Alain Clement, "Aufstieg oder Niedergang Deutschlands," *Frankfurter Hefte* 5 (1950): 10: 34-47.

The First World War brought about a cultural [*geistig*] awakening such as we had not experienced for some time. Perhaps it came down to the fact that this conflict forced a particularly problem-rich and receptive young generation that was accustomed to prolonged peace to live quite close to death, or maybe it was the fact that it shook the whole world for the first time and involved all the civilized nations in the war and thus under the paradox of war made the question of a mutuality among all nations a topic of discussion; or was it the fact that, in the face of this upheaval of nations, the actuality of the kingdom of God and the meaning of the Christian command to love proved anew to be something otherworldly and yet obligatory? At any rate, it is a fact: as the weapons fell silent, a revision of the foundations of our moral, religious, pedagogical, and social life had gotten underway, a revision to which we owe highly fruitful accomplishments that are poignant on a human level.

In a short period of renewal, hardly lasting ten years, works of enduring worth came into being. This generation longed not so much for specialized knowledge [*Fachwissen*]; rather, it pursued with a Greek zeal, so to speak, the knowledge of knowledge. It asked about the purpose of everything, the purpose of the university and the purpose of a cultural [*geistig*] life on the whole. Since 1918, we have been experiencing in all fields of study a revolt against pure knowledge of a subject [*Stoffwissen*]. The issue runs like a deep plow through fields that have been meticulously delineated over against one another and provokes the indignation of those who only cultivate their own parcel of land. There is no other way. The perplexity is too great, the terror too mighty, the feeling that the preceding generation has failed too fundamental for any thinker to be able to escape this radical question. And where there is danger, the rescue also grows.[2] Perhaps not always, but that is how it was after 1918. It burst forth like spring in theology and philosophy. A new conception of history came to the fore; the image of history (of Leopold von Ranke) as an objective, one could almost say spectator-like reproduction of the past, gives way to the attempt to bring the past truly into the present. In revolutionary assaults on classical pedagogy, an educational model develops that involves community and eros as active forces. Until the day then comes the historical necessity (if there is such a thing) of which is not yet appreciated, the day when the counterrevolution will come to power from a fateful interplay of power-political circumstances, this resistance of lethargy and gloom, of vitality and brutality, which draws its aimless instinct from enmity against culture [*geist*]. Counterrevolutions do not live off on an idea that is powerful or has become fundamental in itself. Rather, they live off the contempt for ideas; how peculiar that Christians were also repeatedly seen marching in line who shared this idea-hating stance. Let us hope that they did not know what they were doing.

If the European history of the last 200 years is understood as an interplay between revolution and counterrevolution, then Hitler, along with the societal factors that stood behind him, was the most adept and disastrous master of his field. This

---

2. [Friedrich Hölderlin, "Patmos," in *Poems & Fragments*, ed. and trans. Michael Hamburger, 3rd ed. (London: Anvil Press Poetry, 1994), 483–97, 483.]

explains the wasteland that prevails in our cultural [*geistig*] life today in contrast to the period after 1918. The discovery of friend and enemy[3] as relative political possibilities has enriched political theory and made it more true; however, it has injected the absolute "friend-foe thinking," thus the generalization of mistrust and hate, into the whole of the common public and legal life, into the interior life of the nation like a sickness of the culture [*geist*] that can only be eradicated with great difficulty. Ever since, the vapors of this counterrevolutionary fog hang over the landscape, and we are all threatening to suffocate on them. Human groups are grouped together on the grounds of the ideologies that they embody or represent and are deprived of their rights within the society, and one attempts to annihilate the ideas that these groups represent through the annihilation or at least the practical elimination of the groups themselves: one applies the anti-Semitic schema to all kinds of inconvenient groups.

Today we stand before the question of how we can escape this paralysis, indeed, this cultural [*geistig*] death that is growing among us. This question includes the more limited question of whether there is yet a way to find a connection to the fruitful approaches from the years following 1918. To give a few names: Who is continuing what Max Scheler and Edmund Husserl, Ernst Cassirer and—the great initiator behind them all—Wilhelm Dilthey began?[4] Where is the movement that once emerged from Barth's *Romans*[5] and Thurneysen's *Dostoevsky*?[6] Who knows about Ferdinand Ebner[7] anymore? Who knows Eugen Rosenstock?[8] What did

---

3. [Iwand refers here to the German legal philosopher Carl Schmitt (1888–1985), who in 1922 in his *Political Theology: Four Chapters on the Concept of Sovereignty* (1922), trans. George Schwab (Chicago: University of Chicago Press, 2006) asserted that the sovereign has the right to distinguish between friend and enemy as the principle of authority. In 1933, he joined the National Socialist Party and presented his theories as an ideological foundation of the Nazi dictatorship and a justification of the authoritarian state in terms of legal philosophy.]

4. [Iwand here refers to a line of inquiry in philosophy, which started with Wilhelm Dilthey (1833–1911), the inaugurator of the Lebensphilosophie. He mentions the names of diverse thinkers like the Jewish father of phenomenology Edmund Husserl (1859–1938), Roman Catholic Max Scheler (1874–1928), and Jewish philosopher Ernst Cassirer (1874–1945), but obviously does not intend to go deep into the ideas and the significance of these diverse philosophers. He just wants to point at a common drive and interest in philosophy, phenomenology, and hermeneutics.]

5. [Karl Barth, *The Epistle to the Romans*, Second edition, London 1933 (German: *Der Römerbrief*. Zweite Fassung, Munich 1922).]

6. [Eduard Thurneysen, *Dostoevsky* (Richmond: John Knox Press, 1964).]

7. [Ferdinand Ebner (1882–1931) was an Austrian elementary school teacher, but also a philosopher who was one of the "founders" of the I-Thou philosophy.]

8. [Eugen Rosenstock-Huessy (1888–1973), a Jewish Christian philosopher, represented a specific sociology.]

the students of Karl Holl[9] make out of his fire, which may be under much ash but nevertheless glows? And what is the deal with Eberhard Grisebach[10] and Theodor Haecker[11] and—likewise—with Stefan George[12] and his school? These names hint at something new that came into existence all of a sudden, over a few years, without anything being "made" of it. Just as something that sprang up out of nowhere, it was there, with similarities among all fields. And in just as short a time, it was trampled by the boots of marching lifeforms, having thoroughly and methodically given up on thought. There are not often times that are so palpably and visibly shaped as ours by decisions that took place in the cultural [*geistig*] realm prior to taking place in the visible realm. What came thereafter were all just consequences. The choice had been made; what followed from it fits with the slogan: "Now you have what you wanted."

When a piece of history as the past lays before our eyes, an unprocessed, unapprehended burden is molded to that extent by our actions and omissions, then the truth gains an actual meaning, which Max Scheler has impressed upon us: the teaching that the past, with its specific dimension, stands in an insoluble relationship with the present. Max Scheler wanted to say in his famous essay "Repentance and Rebirth"[13] that the past only blocks off the way into the future for a generation, where this generation does not "abrogate" the past in the power of repentance, by destroying it with its "it is the way it is." We can compel the past to release for us the way into the future, but the only one who will find this way is the one who is able not only to understand the past but to judge it, who is thus able to affirm the character of guilt in its occurrences. It is precisely here where the hidden approaches of a new life lie, a life which God preserves for the one turning back, for the one who is sincerely and bitterly repenting, here (at the location of his action) as a gift of his rich mercy. If a generation finds the way to this site of its own failure, then it is saved; then is the true cultural [*geistig*] continuity recovered in the power of repentance. For cultural [*geistig*] life takes place according to different laws from that of natural reproduction, which stands under that of ever further development.

---

9. [Karl Holl (1866–1926) was the founding father of the "Luther renaissance." When his articles on Luther appeared bundled in 1921, it highly inspired Luther research.]

10. [Eberhard Grisebach (1880–1945), philosopher, cofounder of the I-Thou philosophy, a close friend of Friedrich Gogarten.]

11. [Theodor Haecker (1879–1945), German writer, translator, and cultural critic, opponent of the Nazi regime.]

12. [Stefan George (1868–1933), German author, poet, translator. After the First World War, he criticized the German culture, opposing bourgeois mentality. He was in search of a new, noble German culture. His longing for "the thousand year Reich" made him attractive for the Nazis; George, however, kept distance and went to Switzerland in 1933, in order to avoid being imprisoned. His ideal of a society ruled by a hierarchical spiritual aristocracy inspired Claus Graf von Stauffenberg, who placed the bomb in Hitler's headquarters on July 20, 1944.]

13. [Max Scheler, "Repentance and Rebirth," in *On the Eternal in Man*, trans. Bernard Noble (New York: Harper, 1960).]

Cultural [*geistig*] existence, and the historical existence that is effected by it, stands under the law of repentance.

My past accompanies me as long as I live in a particular awareness that is only accessible to me, that is certainly also manifest through me, in confession. No one can take away from me the means of knowing and saying how it is with me, how I relate to my fully accomplished life. Only in dealing with my past can I gain my future. Where we attempt to extinguish our past, we only extinguish ourselves and become masks. There are doors to the past that are locked by such heavy guilt that we wish to give up hope in our attempts to open them. And it is precisely there that such moments of "I" are included, moments that—if they are not freed from this prison—can tear apart our lives forever and turn our existence into a lie. Thus, no historical unity of life can be gained without forgiveness before God and men. Forgiveness means that all the stations of our way are absorbed into the consciousness, that we now live with a free face turned toward them, and that that cowardness is removed from us in which we attempt to obtain the future by avoiding the past. Yet, we will not get rid of the past by turning our back on it. This is what Augustine called "*memoria*" and where he recast the platonic concept of "remembering" (*anamnesis*) in a Christian way. For his *memoria* coincided with the *Confessio* of his life. It can only be obtained on this way of "confession," a confession before the eyes of the one who scrutinizes the heart and kidneys [Jer. 11:20, 17:10, 20:12; Ps. 7:10 a.o.]. It is no coincidence that it is in his "Confessions"[14] that Augustine introduces that unity of interiority and the historical existence of men and nations without which our Western consciousness would not be what it is. Only when we succeed in accepting our past, in turning our face toward it, in waiting so long before its locked doors that they open for us in the great, redemptive yes of truth and forgiveness, only then will we find our way home to historical existence, in Germany, in Europe, in the whole world, menaced as it is by the naked law of technology and natural life processes. For the law of nature is perishability, and man as a natural being is subject to it. It is a Greek myth to declare the spirit as such, as a substance, to be immortal. The Christian understanding tells us that life is only obtained in rebirth and also the history of nations is inconceivable without rebirth, without repentance and restoration right in the midst of their historical development. We may quietly risk the analogy to the individual, for a nation is not a biological whole but rather an association of a people which can renew itself as such in their renewal.

II.

It is about the relationship between love and freedom.

The eighteenth century established freedom with the autonomy of the thinking individual, who seeks to develop and preserve himself in opposition to tradition,

---

14. [Augustine, "The Confessions," in *The Works of Saint Augustine: A Translation for the 21st Century*, vol. 1, trans. Maria Boulding (Brooklyn: New City Press, 2002).]

dogma, and the positive realities in the state and the church. Are we dealing with this kind of freedom when we speak today about it being under threat? Do we have to defend the individual against orthodox or absolutist entities that are raising their heads again? We often hear our situation described in this way. Freedom of the individual versus the total state! This contrast contains hardly a reminder of what we were lacking. Have we somehow offended against this freedom of the individual? Couldn't that thing that is so flippantly called the "total state" be a much more complicated phenomenon? Couldn't it contain the pronouncement of judgment against a liberalism that delights in and confesses only a certain freedom without love for neighbor, thus not as a gift or sacrifice but rather as a degrading element of the community? Does not this "freedom" that reaches to the very core of thought, this monadic "in-and-for-the-self" beg for such a state as its inevitable consequence? One hears in the realms of "freedom" the roaring of the waves that roll in from the east and threaten to burst all the dams. Thus the trembling all around. But who can do away with this nexus put in place by a higher authority between guilt and atonement?

We know Jesus' parable of the Good Samaritan (Lk. 10:29ff.). There will be few to whom it does not relate. It is necessary only once to see such a poor man who has fallen in among robbers. His hardship only needs to have sufficient time and potency to pervade our heart, and we will help. Couldn't we be in the same position tomorrow? Of course, there may be people who are so heartless as to pass by this sort of thing, but they are thankfully not so common. Not every priest and Levite wanders on down the road. But a moment has come along that complicates the matter tremendously. Something new that we have not seen as of yet. Even in the preaching of this text, it was hardly brought up. The nineteenth century made the matter too simple. Our fathers have said nothing to us about the possibility that awaits us here. They have allowed us to wander into this fray unwarned and unfortified. They have not shown us the background of the whole, the abyss, and the dread that is hidden behind this so easy- and lovely sounding responsibility, namely that there is all of a sudden a hand above this poor man who fell in among robbers, a hand that says: this man belongs to me! It does not always need to be only a single unfortunate person; it could be hundreds, thousands of them! Around them there is a visible or an invisible fence. A loaded wire. It says: compassion is forbidden here; at any rate, active compassion, acts of love coming to fruition are forbidden. Here it is proclaimed from "above"—and this voice will presume to be the voice of "authority"—that love is a crime in this place and that whoever practices love here is a child of the same death that is already written on this face of this miserable one. "Whoever loves his life shall pass by" is the invisible inscription that is nevertheless known to all, the inscription that stands over men and places where love is forbidden. And so these spaces devoid of rights arise in the midst of our modern society, spaces that cause this theme of freedom to break through in an entirely new, totally unsentimental sense.

Moreover, in this kind of society (and that which concerns us here is not primarily a problem of the state but rather a problem of the society and the righteousness that is applicable within it), this bondage of mercy becomes law, becomes a slogan to which everything tacitly conforms: the Church, mission (internal as well as external), ethics and pedagogues, teachers in the schools, and even morality within the family. This sinister hand that brings fear, mercilessness, and with it crime right into the middle of our action and inaction, our buying and selling, our marrying and getting married this hand that wishes for us all to give in before the barrier that it has set up reaches into the innermost depths of our being. It hardens the hearts of the people who must live in this society that is so crisscrossed with the wires of death. Because it is not as if it did not matter to us if we pass by the poor and violated. It is precisely this—that it does not matter—of which someone wants to persuade us with this public voice, but in reality, this passing by is a piece of personal history for me. Perhaps it waits for me in the recollection at a place that is still unfamiliar to me. "I was in prison and you did not visit me" (Mt. 25:43)! By passing this person, I have lost my freedom. Then and there! In this way, through abandoning the act of love, we all become unfree.

The more zones of silence arise within our society and the more dangerous it becomes to live in it because of the invisible wires of death that crisscross the whole of it, the more this attitude becomes a general atmosphere. It threatens to become the "law of life," the grave of freedom. To this cowardice below can then only correspond the tyranny above. And so that which happens in the dark dungeons of violence and in the blocked-off zones of those deprived of their rights becomes the history of a whole people or even of an epoch. There will still be freedom, but there will no longer be freedom to do what the Good Samaritan did: "When he saw him, he had compassion. He went to him and bound up his wounds, pouring on oil and wine. Then he set him on his own animal and brought him to an inn and took care of him" (Lk. 10:33f.). As if there were for him not the hand that says, "That will cost you your life!" As if there were not the inscription that read, "Whoever cares for his life, let him pass by." Or none of the wires of death stretched out between us and that poor person. Everything is free! He had compassion on him, and he went to him! That is love as the foundation and basis of freedom. Nothing, no limit, no power from above, no abyss opening up behind the beggar. He is saved because someone dared to go pick him up and act as if there were only one thing: the commandment to love. But since none of us does this, not because he does not have compassion or because he cannot part with his possessions but because the step to the poor person costs him his life, because there is fear in his love [cf. 1 Jn 4:18], we cease to be neighbors to one another. That distance comes between us that makes all nearness even more unbearable. We know about one another: when push comes to shove and I should see you lying under this hand, I must (even with a bad conscience) pass you by—and I beg you already to understand me. This horrible future as a possibility, as *the* possibility, of the already lost freedom of love lives in the midst of our society and that is its deepest fragility.

Something has obviously been forgotten in sermons about our parable: the actual danger and difficulty of action has been hidden from us. Society determines, or those in power at the time determine, where you are allowed to love and where you are allowed to show mercy. If you should "have compassion" on someone who does not belong to the objects of love approved by the society, watch out. At least let no one notice it. Order stands above love. Keep to this order, or else your act will turn into support for the society's enemies.

At this point, a question comes up that has so recently arisen for our whole generation. Yet it is such a simple question: if we are ready, if it should be necessary, to lay down our lives for love. If we are ready with action to smash this Babylonian captivity[15] that forbids us from being neighbors to one another in time of need and in this way to regain the freedom that we are all—one externally, the other internally—in danger of losing. It should be noted that it is about freedom in human society, about the healing of its mortal illness. This freedom is not born out of this same society and its rational legality, as the last two centuries thought; it is born out of the act of love, indeed from such a love that knows no limits, that cannot transgress any law because it is the fulfillment of the law. To this alone do we in the society owe that which we call freedom.

III.

In every act of this kind of love—love that loves the other as the self and thus even more than one's own life, love that for that reason pays no attention to the strong hand of the tyrant—a twofold thing takes place: as an action in the face of public life, it is a rally for the universality of love, and at the same time, it is *per se* bounded by one person and his need.

Thus a connection is made [*gesetzt*] (not presupposed [*vorausgesetzt*]!) here that embraces everything that bears a human face. All limits and barriers are broken open here and only in that place where these are ought to be broken open does love occur in this sense as an act of freedom. But although this act is universal according to its intention so that no limit—even no ethical limit—is conceivable that could make it seem unwarranted, wrong, or reprehensible, yet in its implementation it is directed toward one particular person in one particular situation. It concentrates totally, as it were, on the fact that it is this action. It comes to an end there. In these times that have been so rocked and torn apart by war and revolution, there has continually been such a breaking open of limits, individual acts of such a broadly radiating purity and dignity that shine as a light in the darkness. In view of the deadly seriousness of love for neighbor, wherever it has to do with removing this barrier set around this poor person, actively breaking it open, this is precisely the precondition that arises for me: in this other person lies my own life. God's love is stronger than the hate of the tyrant. In this way, the brother is laid upon our path so that the praise of God may be manifest toward him. In the liberating action of love towards him, it becomes manifest that God is greater than our heart (1 Jn 3:20; cf. Ezek. 11:19).

---

15. [Iwand here refers to Luther's *De captivitate Babylonica/The Babylon Captivity of the Church* (1520), LW 36, 3-126; WA 6, 497-573.]

In this way the individual person, that is, the one who "fell in among robbers," becomes for us a call to witness to the freedom of the children of God. We do not find a principle that we can establish but a person whom we can love! This means a correction of our ethical approach that has been conventional up to this point. According to this approach, ethical precepts are the first thing, and the love for neighbor belongs "naturally" to these precepts. Precepts seem prudent, reasonable, and clear in themselves. The hard thing is merely the "instance" of their application. Every person who becomes the object of love is thus a priori an "instance." The extraordinary part, the unforeseen part of the encounter with him—that he helps me toward freedom by his need and abandonment that move my heart and lay a claim on me, that it is precisely in the action that freedom is won—this is all overlooked. Rather, a societal freedom is presupposed that enables without risk the practice of love. Only within these freedoms granted beforehand do these "instances" now come to the fore. We see others just as little as the priest and the Levite see the brother on the way. This is why we concern ourselves first and foremost with the "instances" in which love, compassion, and self-sacrifice are "allowed," not commanded—"allowed" by a pronouncement of "society" that originates from a wholly different domain. This is why these actions are now losing everything extraordinary, unprecedented, irritating, and exemplary. One cannot feel anymore that the kingdom of God is breaking in here, that our narrowness is burst open and our self-righteousness is condemned here; rather, God and the current society with its conventions collapse into one. God has become a guarantee of the morality and morals of a particular societal configuration. He has relinquished the right to his free, unlimited grace toward us people, and we now set limits to it, be they political, confessional, or even ethical. The name of God is misused in order to cover up injustice that a group of people—no matter what kind—sets barriers around love because it perceives the free expression and action of love as an overthrow of its orders.

Wherever the forces of people—the steering of the love for neighbor, as it were—are bastardized in this sense into "orders," the "regular" actions of love that we perform in compliance with the limits that we have set up no longer mean anything. The fact that nothing "forbidden" takes place in them anymore makes everything vapid and empty. They only mean something quantitative anymore; even here the tally starts to obscure the internal hollowness. That an action of love exists, to an individual, that the whole structure of mercilessness can be burst in a single place will neither be believed nor seen. For believing and seeing are one thing in this case. These actions of love that are "exempted" for us do not change the world's appearance anymore, either. For this appearance does not change through an accumulation of "instances" or through an ever-increasing statistic of "loving activity." Rather, it changes in that place where the actions of love remove the distance between individuals, peoples, and classes. Our society continues to live from such revolutionary actions of love that are not to be recorded but are effective in themselves; through them it is made visible to the society that its putative freedom is a deception. For its salvation [*Heil*], it is reminded of the nearness of another kingdom, which is always "on the way," unlike its own "being."

Society is reminded that there is only freedom in the constant elimination of its limits through the action of love that extends out over it. By love expanding the range of the same right ever more broadly in the society in this way, its speaking and doing is the expansive power within the society that will not stop coming into conflict with the limiting of the state and its organization. All "civic" freedoms are born from these conflicts. For this reason, they still have here and there the scent of a flower that does not originate in our garden.

IV.

We bring our reflection to a close by following the consequences of this insight in a different direction. What was, we ask, the error of the previous generation? Where is the shift of thinking that will be necessary for us? Why does repentance in this case simultaneously mean rethinking and thus the revision of a doctrinal position that we have held? It is difficult to formulate here. Because by asking about the formula, we ask about a point out from which the repentance of the whole would be made perceptible. If, however, through the formation of those "lawless" spaces in which the love for neighbor is labeled as crime, a whole epoch threatens to become ethically powerless, then it must also be possible theoretically to apprehend the point at which the illness lies. Just as those dark powers have their "methods" to eliminate the freedom of love and with it love itself—precisely by forbidding us to love the victims of their lawlessness—there must also be an insight into the reversal that is culturally [*geistig*] required by our entire epoch. It is clear that love—love from person to person and brother to brother—is only possible in freedom in that place where death has lost its power. Only in this world that has been liberated in the power of the Lord's resurrection is love possible. Only there is everything so clear and plain and simple as we hear in the parable. No hand can be seen there that says, "the wretched one belongs to me." All the ghosts of the night have disappeared there. It is there that the way of love runs unhindered to the location of anguish and crime. But if we first allow death its justice that is contrary to God again, it will make a mockery of love.

But what does that mean? It means that perhaps the most profound error of our epoch lies in the fact that we think that ethics can subsist off itself. That we only today are beginning to comprehend what our fathers did as they degraded dogmatics to a specialized theological knowledge in the course of an optimistic rationalization and forgot that it was originally the first, the confession, with which Christianity called the world to repentance and action. But then came the age when it was thought that dogmatics belong more or less to the mythical epoch of mankind.[16] This time was thought to have come to an end. Dogma was also to

---

16. [In the nineteenth century, under the influence of Georg Wilhelm Friedrich Hegel dogmatics was seen as a highly speculative product of the human mind (e.g., Ferdinand Christian Baur), with hardly any implication for ethics. In the second half of the nineteenth

have fallen with this mythical worldview [*Weltbild*].¹⁷ By contrast, the Christian ethic was to be serious, tangible, eternally binding. The more it was detached from dogmatics, the more universally valid it could be. That God is love and that he demands love is something that even the twentieth century is not yet willing to let go. Rather it thereby only finishes that which was already dreamed by former generations, while it is time to wake from sleep (Rom. 13:11) and to apprehend that faith and love are a whole and that we will strive in vain to keep love alive where faith dies away. Love—and with it freedom—will not remain with us if we perceive this world of death as the final reality but only when we live out of the new reality of the kingdom of God that has entered into society and history with Jesus and is "on the way" (Mk 1:15, 11:10; Mt. 11:3).

From here it would also become understandable what our fathers have concealed in the interpretation of the parable of the Good Samaritan. They have concealed from us that it is solely a parable. That its meaning, its relationship to reality, is not simply the issue of application, of "praxis." This story is a parable because the one who tells it is *in praxi* the Good Samaritan and because one must already know something of the story of his life and death in order to apprehend the parable: "When he saw him, he had compassion and went to him." That is the story of this life that came to us by eliminating the boundary between heaven and earth, between God and humanity—here, the boundary is the law. For the law is given so that we respect the boundary. We all stand on this side of the law, we have all—through the law—become lawless before God. That which we see growing within our own ranks is only the progression of the sickness.¹⁸ But that is not the whole story. From the story of the one who tells the story of the Good Samaritan and thus tells his own story, we also know the price that breaking through the strictly guarded boundary of the law cost him. (And it was precisely the pious people who were on guard!) We know that the way of the Samaritan to the one "who had fallen in among robbers" was successful only at the cost of his death. But it did succeed. The shackle is shattered. On Easter, love's victory was manifest in the power of the resurrection. Here God's righteousness triumphed. And since Easter, the hand stretched out over the wretched one is disempowered so that we no longer need to fear it. Since Easter, the door of freedom is open to the action of love. Since the resurrection of Jesus Christ from the dead, another hand is stretched out over all

---

century, Richard Rothe and Albrecht Ritschl stressed the ethical relevance of Christian theology, subordinating dogmatics under ethics. Iwand had the strong conviction that understood fully that dogmatics had ethics already within it (cf. Iwand, *Theologiegeschichte*, NWN III).]

17. [While the concept of *Weltbild* is only a conception of the world (cf. for example the Copernican *Weltbild*), the term *Weltanschauung* denotes a normative idea which is the basis of sense and meaning in this world and thus, in contrast to the term *Weltbild*, very philosophically loaded. Cf. in this volume "Church and Society," n 13.]

18. [Iwand here alludes to the idea of Nietzsche that the traditional Christian teaching had made men "sick."]

the disenfranchised and the lost—the hand of the one who sits at the right hand of God. The resurrected one guarantees that unity of love and freedom that applies to all men and yet always seeks the individual.

If the bars of the prison that has become the tomb of love and freedom together are to come down, we will need to get used to letting the resurrection of Jesus Christ from the dead again be considered as a message intended for the whole world.

Chapter 5

THE BIBLE AND THE SOCIAL QUESTION

Originally published as Hans Joachim Iwand, "Die Bibel und die soziale Frage," *Junge Kirche* 13 (1952): 65–75 and 113–23; also in Hans Joachim Iwand, *Kirche und Gesellschaft*, Nachgelassene Werke Neue Folge Band Vol. I, ed. Ekkehard Börsch (Gütersloh: Gütersloher Verlagshaus, 1998), 231–61.

In the early 1950s, Hans Joachim Iwand lectured at several meetings and conferences in Germany and abroad on topics connected to the relationship between church and society. He had realized during the Nazi period that the fact that Protestant social ethics had been fixated on the relationship between church and state was one of the main reasons that the evil of a totalitarian state could have occurred. During that time, both church and theology—including Iwand himself!—mainly shared the idea that the proper distinction between church and state was Protestantism's crucial contribution in the field of politics. Socialism was rejected by this dominant school of thought precisely because it took a critical stance with regard to the state. Consequently, mainline Lutheran Protestantism had rendered itself unable to resist effectively the Nazi ideology which had conquered the state. The underlying error was that society was neglected as the realm wherein an exchange of thoughts concerning the structure and content of political life takes place. Soon after the war Iwand participated in a number of meetings between Christians and socialists in Germany—and also in the Netherlands and England—thus seeking and contributing to the discussion on society and politics. In the vein of these efforts of bringing together Christians and socialists, the English Anglican priest and prominent Christian socialist Father John Groser (1890–1966) organized a small conference in St. Catherine's Foundation Stepney (East London) from November 16 to 21, 1951, where Iwand delivered the presentation "The Bible and the Social Issue." In early 1952, he published his paper in the periodical Junge Kirche, *mentioning that it was an "enlarged" text. (GdH)*

I.

Many people today still hold the opinion that the topic of "church and state" constitutes the epicenter of all the controversies that Christianity has to endure in its relationship with the extra-Christian world. On the other side, there are certain political tendencies, liberal and socialist groups and parties who see things a similar way. The one side wants for state authority to be limited by the church; the other side conversely fears the church's influence, particularly in the cultural sphere, and consequently transfers these functions to the state.[1] Here lies the root of the question of the "confessional school" that is currently stirring all of Western Europe—not only in West Germany. Starting from this schema, one interprets all manner of church struggle [*Kirchenkampf*], the German struggle that lies behind us in no different manner than the current controversies in [communist] Eastern Europe; in short, here one has the formula from which the phenomenon on the whole can be judged, here one finds "tried and true" solutions that can easily be applied to newly arising problems and tasks. For me, the question is whether it is right, whether it is wise, whether one is doing justice to the extraordinary thing that the catastrophe which has befallen us revealed. One could go even further and examine the New Testament with regard to this state of affairs. Is the topic of "church and state" really the essential issue for the church's relationship to the extra-Christian world in the New Testament? How is it, then, that this question is simply missing from a letter so essential as Ephesians? The doctrines regarding the church rather flow into the table of duties [*Haustafeln*],[2] which is to say not into the "*politeia*" but rather into the "*oikonomia*." Not the "*polis*" (state) but rather the "*oikos*" (house) is the original building block upon which the all-encompassing structure of the church rests. We predominantly encounter societal issues and topics insofar as the New Testament church exerts itself for the sake of its witness to the world. For this church, it is about—if it can be described with a buzzword—the "de-deification" or even the "dis-enchantment" of public life, about its cleansing from the political mythos and, in this respect, about an act that reaches out far beyond the domain of the congregation as such. Because the true, living God reveals himself and views the congregation as the dwelling-place and workplace of his Spirit, the false gods must give way. In this way, freedom and responsibility within societal life will become possible for the very first time. Starting from this point, even the state will now be newly constituted insofar as Christians are called upon, on the basis of their freedom and responsibility, to subject themselves to its authority and to cooperate with that authority so that even the state in its "position of service" will be seen with respect to God. And so church and state are in a unique relationship to one another, a relationship where the collapse of the service of God [*Gottesdienst*] into idolatry [*Götzendienst*] must

---

1. One should compare Wilhelm von Humboldt, *On the Limits of State Action* (1792), ed. John Wyon Burrow (Cambridge: Cambridge University Press, 1969), published anonymously in 1792, officially in 1821, with Friedrich Schleiermacher, *Über den Beruf des Staates zur Erziehung* [On the Educational Mission of the State] (1814), in: idem, *Kritische Gesamtausgabe*, section 1, Vol. 11: Akademievorträge (Berlin: de Gruyter, 2002), 127–46.

2. [Haustafeln is translated as "table of duties" in Luther's Small Catechism. In New Testament scholarship, it is typically translated as "household code" or "domestic code."]

also result in the perversion of the state. The state cannot remain what it was—in paganism—if the gods that were once "its" gods have diminished.

Conversely, this state will do whatever it takes to defend the pagan cult and its corresponding societal structure with its power and arrogated majesty as long as it is able to do so. It was not only in the first centuries of the church that the "state" joined together with the "pagan mythos" in order to preserve the hierarchical order and the authority that rests within it; it happened just as much in the Reformation. Yet the Reformers did not see their actual adversary in the state but rather in that religious institution that manifested itself as a hybrid of state and church. The decisive transformation brought about by the Reformation in the concept of "saint"—as the "justified sinner" who can be found in every station and walk of life and who finds his duty in the "home," in the "world," and so on—resulted in a "dis-enchantment"[3] of the society which had profoundly declined into the mythos that was similar to the one that Christianity once brought upon the ancient world. Gods tumble again and again when God himself is found, worshipped, and proclaimed. This movement toward the "dis-enchantment of the world" is that which is distinctively Protestant, that which first revealed its power that collides with the church and society in the proclamation of the Old Testament prophets. Correspondingly, it would have been imperative for German Protestantism to resist altogether the attempt to create a new state mythos and from there to transform the ethos of the society. That its resistance was so weak, that it included only a fraction of the pastors and an even more negligible fraction of the "Protestant" laity, could make it clear to the sober observer how watered down the Protestant heritage had become.[4]

II.

In its essential components, National Socialism was the large-scale attempt—that was, in a sense, set up in our culture development—to solve modern societal problems (including the problems of marriage and family) from the point of view of a new paganism that broke radically with Christianity. Among us it was thought, as an English author from Mexico once described it:[5] Christ is tired. He just needs to "sleep" again, and the old gods who have rested long enough must rise again in order to stir up a tired generation to strength and power again!

It was the horrible fallacy of the military and the leaders of industry that the "worldview" [*Weltanschauung*] should be surrendered to the party, fatally thinking

---

3. [Max Weber sketched the process of modernization as an ongoing "dis-enchantment" of the world, in which step-by-step, thanks to progress in science, realms of life and nature are reduced to understandable processes, to be handled and controlled by man.]

4. This comes clearly to the fore in Paul Tillich, *The Protestant Era* (Chicago: University of Chicago Press, 1948).

5. David H. Lawrence, *The Plumed Serpent* (Toronto: MacMillan, 1926).

it would "only" be something cultural or even something totally "fantastical," even while putatively reserving to themselves the "key positions" in the state. In reality, the state was surrendered by doing this, for it consequently became the "executive power of the party,"[6] a development that the bourgeois collaborators of the "movement" never grasped.[7] In the end, frankly even the most simple-minded noticed it as not only the racially "foreign" but also the incurably ill were "exterminated," as the institution of ancient slave labor camps [Ergasterien] took root among us, as the family was regarded only from the standpoint of procreation and a "biology" that was raised to the level of dogma was taken in all domains as the point of departure for a restructuring of the society. But why was it only after such a long time that all of this first came to be understood? Why were people frightened only when the most basic tenets of Christian civilization were infringed upon? Why were they silent regarding the proclamation of new dogmas and thought that they would only need to begin their protest when the transformation of ethics began to work its way out from them? Why did they hold on frantically

---

6. Authentic saying of Hitler on a "Parteitag" (mass assembly of the Nazi Party) in Nuremberg. If we had still been Protestants, then we should have appealed against it. [In Nazi ideology the "people" (Volk) is the foundation of the state, since "the people" is the living organism, represented and led by its "Führer." The state is therefore no longer a safe haven of rights, since the party establishes what right is.]

7. This is the shocking thing, in several memories of military and civilian members of the Nazi administration, that those who write about those days obviously still haven't understood—which cultural direction the train was headed upon which they had boarded. Just one man in Hitler's first cabinet apparently noticed, the Baron Eltz von Rübenach. I had the privilege to hear from his own mouth the story of his resigning the cabinet, which I searched in vain in the memoirs of his fellow ministers. Baron Eltz von Rübenach declared at the end of the meeting of the cabinet on January 31, 1937, at the time the Golden Party badges were distributed and Hitler wanted to hand one over to him, that he did not regard himself in the position to accept it, if the Führer were not to insure him that the war on the Christian churches of both confessions would end. (Eltz von Rübenach was a Roman Catholic.) Adolf Hitler said, "I cannot except the conditions being set up for this honor." Hitler leaves the room, the Minister of State Otto Meissner appears, who suggests von Rübenach to offer his request for withdrawal immediately. Baron Eltz von Rübenach was dismissed without a pension. None of the other members of the cabinet stands up for him. They all already had accepted the Golden Party badge. Baron Eltz von Rübenach was the last one in this line. What Dr. Hjalmar Schacht (Minister of Economics, August 1934–November 1937) and Baron Johann Ludwig von Schwerin-Krosigk (Minister of Finance, 1932–45) may have commented, these gentlemen will know more authentically than I do. Why is this not reported? What would have happened if the former "national German" ministers on this cabinet meeting had stood up like Baron Eltz von Rübenach and would have made the acceptance of their honoring dependent of the fulfilment of this condition? Probably then the saying that this system could have only been thrown down from outside should have to be revised.

to the positions of the state without grasping that we had already long ago been sitting on the short arm of the lever? Why did they believe that they could despise the cultural cells of resistance even as they were demonstrably the only ones who were standing firm and among whom one could still "breathe freely."[8] All of this is because, I would say, our education [*Erziehung*] in Germany looks upon the role of society and its capabilities, issues, ideologies, and responsible ordering as a secondary thing just as it has been taught in theology and philosophy (also in history!) since the middle of the nineteenth century, and setting the society prior to the state is considered to be nothing less than one of the most terrible theological heresies. This is why Christians—and perhaps also socialists—were so blind when the danger of the total state broke onto the scene. The socialists also trusted that they had the state in their hands and did not grasp at all—which they themselves could have known best—how easily the state can become a function of the prevailing societal powers and authorities.

And yet for me, it is not now a matter of pursuing further the question of the breakdown of Christianity and socialism vis-à-vis the modern totalitarian systems. Rather, it is about a fact that refers to our own present: that—at least with us in Germany—after a tragedy occurs, there is a return to the former cultural, particularly the doctrinal, structures to begin the "reconstruction" from there. Everything that has happened was not enough to make us call for a revision of the cultural presuppositions with which we entered into the catastrophe of 1933. We want to avoid the fatal surface-level consequences, but will we be able to avoid them if we are not ready at the same time to examine our presuppositions? In historical relationships, too, there is something like cause and effect. Without an abrogation and transformation of the cause, it will scarcely be possible to escape the inevitability of the effect. But how do we arrive at a revision of the cause within a historical process? Not only through recognition but rather through repentance. Only being prepared to repent brings about the recognition of which we would otherwise be deprived.

III.

The prominent Italian historian Guglielmo Fererro once said that for 150 years, the back and forth between revolution and counterrevolution—as France experienced in 1789 and 1799, for example—became the consistent theme of European politics.

> There are two French revolutions, each the negation of the other: the first and the second, the great and the small, the revolution of 1789 and the revolution of 1799: the revolution of the rights of man and the revolution of the Constitution of the Year VIII, the liberal revolution of representative regime and the

---

8. Cf. the latest novel of Ernst Jünger, *The Forest Passage* (1951), trans. Thomas Friese (Candor, NY: Telos Press Publishing, 2013).

dictatorial revolution of the totalitarian state, the revolution that is the daughter of the eighteenth century and the revolution that was spawned by the great panic after the storming of the Bastille. As long as this dualism is not understood, the history of the West will remain an incomprehensible enigma.[9]

As a matter of fact, we find ourselves in the middle of this maelstrom, and there are few indications that we are able to escape from the "mechanism" of worn-out repetitions.

Today it is very possible to realize this in light of the resurgence of the old schema of state and church. Following the furthest reaches of state omnipotence under Hitler's dictatorship, a situation came about that was similarly advantageous for the proponents of the ecclesiastical prerogative as was the situation under the Bourbons following the overthrow of Napoleon. The church—indeed, the church as an institution—is needed in order to support the authority of the state, weakened and hollowed out as it is by revolution and counterrevolution. Conversely, the church also wishes to see its rights—extensively limited and, in the time of persecution, abrogated—restored and secured. This relationship of *do-ut-des* [I give so that you might give] results in the state and church being characteristically bound together in the times and among the projects of the Restoration. But that which seems to be a sign of progress is only a flame that is bright yet again but rapidly burning out. Even while institutions are strengthened, the people become alienated from the content of the message. One of these days, it will need to be said that an apostasy has arisen behind the façade, an apostasy such as has never been seen even in the worst times of persecution. The church has made the connection between it and the state that is protected by it as intimate as possible, but in doing so, it lost the infinitely more important influence on the society and the courage for the reforms that are necessary within it. In its structure, the church itself has not emerged unchanged from the age of dictatorship. Some things have "hung on." Listen to another great historian, Hippolyte Taine, on the effects of the Restoration in France on the church:

> Directly or indirectly, Napoleon made his mark on all secular and military entities—hence the tyranny of the episcopate. Absolutism is even more pronounced in the church than it is in the state. For this absolutism corresponds to the essential nature of the catholic ecclesia.... Today (he means the era circa 1870),[10] the bishop in France is de facto and de jure a general while his pastors are de jure and de facto nothing more than sergeants and corporals.

He submits a nice proof for this assertion. During the senate session on March 11, 1865, Cardinal Bonnechose said,

---

9. Guglielmo Ferrero, *The Principles of Power: The Great Political Crises of History*, trans. Theodore Jaeckel (New York: G. G. Putnam's Sons, 1942), 211.

10. [Explanation by Iwand.]

It is an offensive presumption that we are not masters in our own house, that we do not understand how to lead our ministerium or that we are directed by it [that is, by the lower clergy!]. No general will put up with the accusation that he cannot keep his soldiers in order. Each of us has a regiment to command, and we are the ones who make it march.[11]

Taine encapsulates the outcome of this epoch of Restoration in this striking passage:

In the middle of the most tremendous revolutionary movements, the whole populace—shopkeepers, workmen, the women in the market, etc.—was pious.... And today? Nothing is so unpopular among today's shopkeepers, workers, and minor officials as the Catholic Church, because it united itself with regressive governments under the Restoration and the Second Empire and because, in both cases, the clergy was the effective tool and the mainstay of oppression.[12]

Taine recounts that in the two years following the events of 1830 (the July Revolution), no priest in Paris dared "to show himself in public in a cassock."[13] That age saw the development of that "counter-church" in France, the anticlerical parties that were not merely a product of the Revolution but rather a product of the Revolution and the Restoration all at once. Flowing out of their oppositional thinking, they have no other program than the total separation of church and state. France's legislation of 1905[14] concerning the church, which the Bolsheviks then followed in 1917, constitutes a significant consequence of this development in the aftermath of the Restoration in post-Napoleonic France.

IV.

What is confusing is that even though we know all of this and have outstanding depictions of the history and development of the nineteenth century from the

---

11. [Translation here and in the following two quotes are our own from Iwand's German citations which appear to be from a different edition than the following English translation: Hippolyte Taine, *The Origins of Contemporary France* (New York: Holt, 1878–88).]

12. [Taine, *The Origins of Contemporary France*.]

13. [Ibid.]

14. [Law Concerning the Separation of the Churches and the State, December 9, 1905, Art. 2: "The Republic does not recognize, pay, or subsidize any religion. Consequently, as of January 1. following the promulgation of this law, all expanses related to the exercise of religion shall be removed from state budgets, departments and municipalities." https://www.legifrance.gouv.fr/loda/id/JORFTEXT000000508749/ (accessed August 16. 2022) Translation from the French our own.]

pens of the best historians and philosophers,[15] we cannot actually get out of the rut. Until after automatic repetitions, deteriorations, progressive coarsening of the methods, only a little pile of ash will remain of this once-so-impressive Europe! Why do we not go right to the heart of things and examine the presuppositions of these theoretical bottlenecks in which we have gotten stuck! Is this lack of cultural [*geistiger*] flexibility grounded in the affect of the masses, both churchly and otherwise? Why is there an insurmountable antisocialist and antidemocratic complex in almost all of the continental churches? Why can socialists and liberals who "have nothing against religion" but have everything against the church not be converted? Has no one among us wondered, then, if the internal and external development of Germany would not have been totally different if Christians and socialists had stood up together after 1918 against the totalitarian and fascist movements? For they were both the real victims because, according to Nietzsche's prognosis, Christians and socialists together make up the "Chandala-apostles"[16] must be exterminated if one intends to realize the will to power and create the man of tomorrow, the "Superman" (*Übermenschen*). How has it come about that we have not seen this nor are we ready to take it seriously today?

But let me ask further: Why does one not, or why do we not, allow some time for reflection in order to investigate the particular catastrophe for its deeper causes? Are there still too many living among us who are not interested at all in the success of such an investigation? Europe has neither time nor the opportunity to realize from a higher vantage point the unity of processes that are moving it. Encapsulated in national "cells," it lives in the belief that that which takes place in this or that region represents something quite exceptional. It resembles a sinking ship where the passengers lock themselves in their cabins instead of understanding that even if they are in distinct situations for the moment, their situation is dictated by a single greater destiny. The churches have long taken part in the narrowness of this nation-state thinking as well. They have lost their sense of the unity of the cultural [*geistigen*] phenomena on our continent. They think that whatever happens in Poland or Czechoslovakia with regard to legislation concerning the church has pretty much nothing to do with us in Holland or in the Rhineland. These are all the most precarious mistakes. Because we have lost sight of the societal processes that, inasmuch as they are revolutionary, represent a unified movement, the national churches and confessions jealously keep watch over the canonical and the confessionally bound borders. The gospel no longer "works;" rather, the various state churches have dug their cisterns in which they wish to collect water.

All of this makes up part of the topic: church and state. It does not allow any third factor to stand alongside these two; no neutral element that could then, in a

---

15. Cf. Benedetto Croce, *History of Europe in the Nineteenth Century* (1931) (London: Allen and Unwin, 1934).

16. [Friedrich Nietzsche, *The Anti-Christ* (1888), in idem, *The Anti-Christ, Ecce Homo, Twilight of the Idols: And Other Writings*, ed. Aaron Ridley and Judith Norman (Cambridge: Cambridge University Press, 2005), 1–68, 60 aphorism 57.]

sense, be the thing that includes them both and—again, in a sense—be the thing that binds them both; the society as a third entity, independent with regard to both church and state. It corresponds either totally to the state or likewise "perfectly"— at least in theory, but that is what matters here—to the church. This is why the societal element does not operate in a relativizing way with us; society cannot exercise its benevolent and instructive influence in the way that it does in the classical lands of democracy. Instead of a true and lively relationship between the church and society as two independent partners with each being "free" in its own way, we now observe a phenomenon that can pretty much be described in the following way:

The state that has already been weakened and hollowed by dictatorship is degraded into an instrument, not quite of "welfare" but rather of "order." But the meaning of order is no longer to be gathered from the political functions of the citizens and their rights; rather, it is defined from the metaphysical Christian sphere. As a result, in order that it might "only" keep order, the state must be cleansed of all ideologies, which is to say all of the cultural [*geistigen*] tendencies that are inherent to it. In doing so, however, it simultaneously becomes estranged from the society because its becoming at home in the state is based on an act of cultural [*geistiger*] freedom. Meanwhile, the cultural [*geistige*] and religious [*geistliche*] leadership is supposed to be handed over to the church because this church as a divine institution, as the mixture of supernatural and natural powers, has at its disposal the proper insight into the entirety of order, which the person threatened with destruction craves.

To this end, something further steps in. This church that is called to "internal" leadership—to the interpretation of the content of order—that understands itself to be responsible for the cultural, social, and ideological [*weltanschauliche*] direction within the state again, for its part, requires this state as an ordering authority in order to protect this cultural [*geistige*] structure. Even the military structure is included in this protection, which is why these churches stand up—which is entirely necessary from the perspective of their basic approach— positively for rearmament.[17] But the gospel is not sufficient to justify this "system." It is no longer possible to start out "purely" from the gospel. Because when seen from the perspective of the gospel, the church no longer looks like the partner of the state. Here, its power is not analogous or adequate to the power exercised by the authorities; rather, it is "power" or "authority" in a subversive and paradoxical sense. It is the power that indwells the kingdom of God that is breaking into and breaking out among us with his Word, the kingdom of the world "to come," while when dealing with the state, we are dealing with an entity "of this age." Seen from the perspective of the gospel, the schema of the relationship between state and

---

17. [In the 1950s, Iwand was deeply engaged in the discussion about rearmament of Western Germany, not only because he feared the catastrophe of a nuclear war, but also because he foresaw that it would bring about conditions in which the German people would remain divided for an infinite period.]

church would need to be rejected because of its "timelessness"—thus because of its missing eschatological component. Seen from the perspective of the gospel, the power of God's Word will correspond to the visible powerlessness of the witnesses that is perceptible even to them. The church does not increase with its "increasing" Lord; It must rather decrease that he might increase. This is the law according to which it operates. This is the *theologia crucis* [theology of the cross] contained within the Protestant conception of the church, which makes space for God and reckons with his wondrous works in the manner of Psalm 46. The gospel proves to be an insufficient point of departure if one wants to operate as a partner of the state and its power and to be able to share leadership with it. For this, a certain confessionalism must assume the place of the "pure gospel," a confessionalism that is in itself a mixture of faith and tradition and thus combines the doctrine of the church with particular, indeed conservative, antirevolutionary and estate-distinguishing [ständischen] societal doctrines. Only through confessionalism (the more profound sense of which will be the subject of the controversy of our day) do the churches become fitting allies for the state powers.

V.

What have we said, then, in all of this, in this somewhat drawn-out and cumbersome introduction? I mean to say this: that the free and responsible society, which makes up people's existence in their public life, is a third thing alongside church and state and that the independence and "relative" autonomy of this third thing is one of the inviolable components of Protestantism. If we should abandon the society to one of these two other components, state or church, then Protestantism has ceased to be a constitutive and productive phenomenon. For it is only in society that the Word "works." Eduard Heimann[18] once conveyed to me an insight that has always stuck with me. He said to me as if in passing: the state will not allow itself to be "evangelized," but society will. The society is the manifestation of the universal. It is the womb where all cultural movements are formed, and it is in society where the controversy first comes about between the gospel and the cultural driving forces from which we try to build up this society, to reform it, and to bring it to ever new configurations.[19]

---

18. Here I would like to point especially to Eduard Heimann, former professor in Hamburg (economist and philosopher) and currently theologian and sociologist at Union Theological Seminary in New York. In his personal life he has travelled the entire course from Marxism to a theologically grounded understanding of society. He thus could have great significance in furthering the questions which press us in Europe today. Cf. Eduard Heimann, *Freedom and Order: Lessons from the War* (New York: Charles Scribner's Son, 1947).

19. Society is a product of cultural forces. This is largely what Dilthey put forth in his life's work and again Max Weber in a different vein. However, a book in which this insight with the great reflections of a philosophically trained historian has achieved, one might almost

In the nineteenth century, it was liberal theology that especially concerned itself with societal issues, but it knew too little about the church to develop the proper distinction between church and state, that is "Christian Community and Civil Community."[20] It is only a logical consequence that Richard Rothe describes the dissolution of the church into the state as the subject of the generally recognized Christian ethos as the end goal of this development.[21]

These "liberal" theories, born of a fundamental optimism, theories in which the boundary between time and eternity is blurred much as in certain socialist systems and neither death nor sin is taken entirely seriously, resolved themselves somewhat naturally in the days of the church struggle [*Kirchenkampf*]. They were "weighed in the balances and found wanting" (Dan. 5:27). Besides, it had come about that long before the church struggle, as a theological presupposition and an unforeseen "foreshadowing," the principles of liberal theology were shaken. The concept of "religion" ceased to be the reference point of dogmatics, real theology again took the place of religious studies, and—last but not least[22]— in the church struggle, we actually discovered the church, amid suffering and acts of confession. We discovered it just as newly as we had once discovered theology in our encounter with the Reformers and the eschatological character of the New Testament. But where was Protestantism, that Protestantism that had had the protection of liberalism for a century? Moreover, according to a commonplace formulation "Neo-protestantism"[23] had become the epicenter

---

say, a perfect presentation might be Benedetto Croce's *History of Europe in the 19th Century*. The following recognition deserves more attention than previously given: "Communism was not an immediate consequence of the workmen's sufferings; it wasn't the workmen but the thinkers standing before new economic and moral tasks that produced communism as they have produced every other political system." (Our translation from Benedetto Croce, *Geschichte Europas im 19. Jahrhundert* (1931), 2nd ed. (Stuttgart: Kohlhammer, 1947), 147. Cf. idem, *History of Europe in the Nineteenth Century*, trans. Henry Furst (London: Unwin University Press, 2019), 138. The English translation of Furst carries quite a different meaning than the German: "[B]ut they [i.e. the workmen] set before thinkers [...] economic and moral problems..."

20. The famous essay of Karl Barth from 1946. [In 1946, Barth published "The Christian Community and the Civil Community," in *Community, State, and Church*. (Garden City, NY: Anchor Books/Doubleday, 1960), in which he gave a blueprint for the relation between church and society in a democratic context].

21. [Richard Rothe (1799–1867) can be seen as the founder of "cultural Protestantism" in nineteenth-century Germany. His idea was that the visible realization of the kingdom of God which had its starting point in the church is about to find its fulfilment in the Christian state, framed as an overarching organ of all national states.]

22. [English in Iwand's original.]

23. [Neo-Protestantism is the name of the liberal Protestantism that arose in the nineteenth century. Important representatives were a.o. Albrecht Ritschl (1822–89), Adolf von Harnack (1851–1930), and Ernst Troeltsch (1865–1923).]

of all heresies, was it any wonder when it was thought that Protestantism as a whole could be looked on as suspect? And yet it had long been on the scene and forms even today the actual epicenter of unrest in the churchly and also the political life of Germany. If Protestantism is connected to the fact that a church that is awoken to confession must loudly and clearly say no before "emperor and empire,"[24] if God's yes in Jesus Christ may otherwise be authentically heard again, then—at least in certain times—a Protestantism has been on the scene in the Confessing Church that was only recognized and acknowledged as such to the slightest extent by its neo-Protestant namesake,[25] a Protestantism that was conversely most suspicious of the confessional person in spite of his new "orthodoxy,"[26] a Protestantism that did not fit into any of the available schemata and yet was true Protestantism because it carried out the present-day witness of the gospel over against the myths and enchantments of public and churchly life. It had to bear witness to the one and only God and his singular incarnation in Jesus Christ over against all alleged incarnations of ideas and myths. It had the sobriety to stand the test, the sobriety that behooves those who go out to meet the morrow. Sobriety is an eschatological concept. It is the timbre of Protestant preaching, which appears as "doctrine."

But how will this encounter with society take place from this basis—from the rediscovered basis of God's revelation in Jesus Christ (in the sense of the first thesis of the Barmen Declaration[27])? That must be clarified if we wish to sort through and comprehend anew the renowned "social issue," which some assert does not exist. For we must not make the mistake of taking hold of it from the presuppositions of the (liberal!) nineteenth century, which have since become obsolete. Without the church—that is to say, the church that confesses *in actu* Jesus Christ, the incarnate

---

24. ["Vor Kaiser und Reich" ("before emperor and empire") is a reference to Martin Luther at the "Reichstag" in Worms 1521.]

25. One should, however, take into account the attitude of Hans von Soden and Rudolf Bultmann to the Confessing Church! [Bultmann and von Soden were professors in Marburg, who were engaged in the Confessing Church and who managed to refrain their faculty from the "German Christian" domination.]

26. [Iwand here alludes to the conservative—mainly Lutheran—Protestant churches, which during the church struggle had their objections against the stand of the Confessing Church in the line of Barmen (May 1934) and Dahlem (October 1934).]

27. ["I am the way, and the truth, and the life; no one comes to the Father, but by me" (Jn 14:6). "Truly, truly, I say to you, he who does not enter the sheepfold by the door, but climbs in by another way, that man is a thief and a robber . . . I am the door; if anyone enters by me, he will be saved" (Jn 10:1,9).

Jesus Christ, as he is attested for us in Holy Scripture, is the one Word of God which we have to hear and which we have to trust and obey in life and in death.

We reject the false doctrine, as though the church could and would have to acknowledge as a source of its proclamation, apart from and besides this one Word of God, still other events and powers, figures and truths, as God's revelation.]

Son of God, the crucified and risen Lord—the "social problem" probably cannot—at any rate, not in its biblical understanding—be seen correctly and set in motion at all. The reform of the church is connected most closely with the reform of society and vice versa—the reform, not the eradication of the church as was unfortunately intended by the policies of the revolutions in the nineteenth century.[28] For that which we read in the Bible concerning righteousness and peace, concerning the great coming kingdom of peace and the impending judgment: when you see the axe swung that is laid right at the roots of every tall tree [Mt. 3:10], when you see the fire burning in which all bloody clothes will be burned (Isa. 9:4), when you see the great equality of all people rising because every valley is exalted and every hill brought low (Isa. 40:4), when at the Lord's birth you hear that song of praise of his virgin mother that now the mighty are cast down from their seat and the hungry are filled with good things (Lk. 1:52f.), when the veil is torn apart for just a moment that divides this world (our world!) from the world to come (God's world) and we see poor Lazarus and the rich man in their traded places (all revolutions practice something of Lk. 16:19ff.)—all this, the glad tidings to the poor and the promise of coming judgment, is nonexistent without the covenant of grace that God has made with people, that is to say with particular people in Jesus Christ. The liberalism of the nineteenth century has crafted a social policy from the Bible, especially from the Sermon on the Mount, that seemed "transportable" and timeless. It divided Jesus (as a historical figure) and his gospel (as a timeless truth). And thus on the one side stands Jesus—that is to say, Jesus the way the liberals see him, the truly human person, not the one who was numbered among the sinners (Isa. 53:12)—and on the other side stands a programmatic, but relationless, gospel that is doctrinaire and in that sense "social." One without the other, Jesus without his gospel and his "glad tidings" to the poor without this Jesus Christ: that is the absurdity and the calamity of our time.

VI.

This is why we will have to look around for a new way now that liberalism has come to its end. We will not be able simply to join in the rejoicing of the "orthodox," who think that the end of liberalism signals their ascent, their "comeback."[29] In this perception they will be mistaken. Liberalism—I am thinking roughly of Ernst Troeltsch's comprehensive examination of social doctrines[30]—at least saw the problem; it did not merely disregard it in order to define the church simply from the perspective of dogma, as if the congregation did not belong to the gospel, as if

---

28. Cf. the books of Eugen Rosenstock-Huessy (1888–1973), esp. *Out of Revolution: Autobiography of Western Man* (New York: William Morrow & Co., 1938).

29. [English in Iwand's original.]

30. [Ernst Troeltsch, *The Social Teaching of the Christian Churches* (1912), trans. Olive Wyon, 2 vols. (Louisville and London: Westminster John Knox Press, 1992).]

a particular "*societas*" did not belong to the Word of God. Perhaps it understood the meaning of dogmatics better than its orthodox opponents in this regard because it still knew that dogmatics is always simultaneously ethics, that there is no justification that does not include sanctification within it.

But what should be done? Who should take up the good and enduring heritage of Protestantism, even that of its "neo-Protestant" age, and develop it? Orthodoxy is simply not in a position to separate the wheat from the chaff, and it does not see sufficiently well the precariousness of its own doctrinal legalism and its "symbolic legalism."[31] On the other side, we actually confront an extraordinary difficulty that concerns societal doctrines. For these were developed in the eighteenth and nineteenth centuries almost entirely in the absence of the church. The fact that church and world make up God's creation in their opposition and connectedness to each other remained hidden to them. They were conceptualized from the perspective of a nonexistent church. No wonder that, over the course of their actualization, liberals and socialists, democrats and revolutionaries, had to arrive at the idea that the church would disappear "on its own" through successful societal transition. The *credo in ecclesiam in perpetuum mansuram*[32] was forgotten. No wonder, moreover, that where this did not take place on its own and the theory did not seem to coincide with reality, people proceeded to help with violence and to "make" the forecast "fit." The main problem lies in the theory, in this point from which our societal doctrines depart. It must be revised. We will need to ask if the eschatological reference of the church has been sufficiently taken into consideration, if this eschatological reference does not signify a foundational transformation in the relationship of church and society. For the two do not both lie on one and the same level. Both do not fall within one and the same time. Both do not stand under one and the same law. A new, bright light shines down from the gospel over everything that happens in society, over its institutions and customs, written and unwritten laws. Now we recognize "their time," their validity that is relative and for this reason also changeable. They must be changeable, or else they would not be relative. They do not reach up to the heavens nor are they an expression of an "eternal" order. The significance of time must be recovered, the imminent character of these societal doctrines must be abolished, the "hole" in the middle of them must become visible again.

Yet it is precisely this that the church has not done. Rather the churches, particularly the theories of church law in this epoch that lays behind us, beset as it was by revolutionary theories and practices, have moved anew toward

---

31. [Martin Kähler coined the word "Symbollegalismus," indicating the way of dealing with the symbols of the church in a legalistic manner (cf. Martin Kähler, *Die starken Wurzeln unserer Kraft: Betrachtungen über die Begründung des Deutschen Kaiserreiches und seine erste Krise* (Gotha: Perthe, 1872), 207.]

32. ["The doctrine that the church will remain forever" cf. CA VII; KW 42; BSELK 103,5.]

5. The Bible and the Social Question

the medieval models.³³ They thought that they could content themselves with charitably oriented and estate-based [*ständisch angelegten*] social doctrines. They ultimately sought the true order of society in the church itself. That which diverges infinitely widely there in the rationalistic societal doctrines so that there is no more connection, no more relationship, is moved so closely together here. Even here, time is "passed by," the "not yet" is no longer taken seriously. Becoming and passing away has ceased and been replaced with a legal stasis. There, it looks as if the last things simply blow up and abolish the penultimate (this is the "utopian" character that inheres in all democratic societal theories as long as they are still revolutionary and transformative), here, as if we finally content ourselves with the penultimate without asking about the last things (this is the embarrassing thing about the doctrine of the two realms as it emerges already with Melanchthon and analogously in the post-Tridentine theology of the Catholic Church³⁴).

If we want to avoid these two errors, on the left and on the right, then we will need to treat and develop the relationship between church and society as an open relationship. Because of this openness, there will be a cooperation of Christians in total freedom on the issues of society, and conversely, even the society will not be able simply to declare itself disinterested in the existence of the church in its midst. It needs to understand that this also portends something for it. The light that emanates from here, or at least could emanate from here, shines on everyone in the house (Mt. 5:15), not only the Christians but also those who are not yet Christians and those who will never be. God makes the sun shine over good and evil [Mt. 5:45]; the mercy of the God who preserves the world and bears it in ineffable fidelity knows no "iron curtains."³⁵

---

33. [Iwand here refers to the Romanticism of the early nineteenth century, with figures like Novalis (Georg Friedrich Philipp Freiherr von Hardenberg [1772–1801]), who dreamt of a Christian Europe, and to conservative Lutherans like Friedrich Julius Stahl (1802–61), who advocated an episcopal constitution of the Lutheran Church and a Christian state. Cf. Hans Joachim Iwand, "Warum 'Protestantische Monatshefte'?," *Junge Kirche* 13 (1952): 354–61; idem, "Von Ordnung und Revolution: Das Thema in der ersten Hälfte des 19. Jahrhunderts," in idem, *Vorträge und Aufsätze*, NW II, 153–92.]

34. [In the time Iwand writes this text, he intensively deals with Melanchthon's ideas about Law and Gospel and the realms of Church and State. He does so in his lectures "Law and Gospel" (winter semester 1950/1951 in Göttingen) in Iwand, *Gesetz und Evangelium*, NW IV, 231–401 (on Melanchthon, 309–58) and "Das Widerstandsrecht der Christen nach der Lehre der Reformatoren," in *Vorträge und Aufsätze*, NW II, 193–229 (on Melanchthon, 199–217). Iwand reproaches Melanchthon for assigning the Law to the government, since it implies that the Church and its proclamation of the Gospel has vanished from society. Politics is just about maintaining the existing order of society in a rational and legitimate way, the Gospel of the death and resurrection of Jesus Christ has no significance whatsoever for society and political order.]

35. [Iwand alludes here to the so-called iron curtain after the Second World War, which separated the "free Western world" and the communist countries of Eastern Europe. Cf. Iwand, *Frieden mit dem Osten*.]

To set up such a curtain remains reserved to the Pharisees. In the community of God, there lives a fellowship which could even protect society from becoming hostile towards members. On the other hand, this openness also signifies freedom and limit. There must be the morally justified, institutionally recognized possibility of Christians refusing their cooperation in certain circumstances, not only tacitly and silently but rather openly and confessionally. Only in this way can they make God's Law heard to the society; only in this way can they remind it that there is one Lord who will come again to judge—that is, to judge all people. There must also conversely be this freedom for the member of the society with regard to the church. Because membership in the church is grace and must be recognizable as such. This is carried out in the freedom of faith, which will only have power in this way as a testimony. The church can do nothing more than implore, "Be reconciled to God" (2 Cor. 5:20)! Under no circumstances may it approve the *cogite intrare* (compel them to come in! cf. Lk. 14:23), even when it is exercised in an ever milder and more tolerant form. In doing so, it would obscure what a joyful message it has to bring, what a great good it has to offer. The freedom of society with respect to the church makes it possible for the church to stand there offering, promoting, with the testimony of the Holy Spirit winning over people by the truth of its message in the midst of an unredeemed and lost generation. Society simply requires a voice that directs it to its lost estate, not an "unconscious Christianity," an "*anima naturaliter Christiana*"[36] hidden mysteriously within it. Otherwise, the person who lives within it cannot come to faith.

There is a positive relationship of these two to one another, a relationship within which the freedom of God's grace, in which he calls us to him and receives us, encounters the freedom that acknowledges the church with its proclamation and cooperation in society as such. For this reciprocal relationship of church and society in which even the relationship to the state would be incorporated (society will soon need to defend the sovereignty of the state against a church that does not maintain its own boundaries; the church will soon need to defend the state's servitude to God against a "party" that degrades and depraves the state into its mere executive power), I find no other word than that of openness. I also find in it the prerequisite for everything that should be said about the relationship to socialism. This openness corresponds to that which God's revelation signifies on another and higher level. We will have to ask if there is an openness of the church toward the society and *vice versa*, if there is such an openness of the society toward the church. In the fundamental openness of both of these toward each other, I see the promise that is given to us for the renewal of the church and the reordering of society.

---

36. "A soul which is Christian by nature." [Cf. Tertullian, *Apologeticum* 17.6. Cf. also idem, *A Treatise on the Soul*, which was written to explain this phrase further, in *Ante-Nicene Fathers*, vol. 3, *Latin Christianity: Its Founder, Tertullian*, ed. Alexander Roberts and James Donaldson (Buffalo: The Christian Literature Publishing Company, 1887), 181–235.]

VII.

With the words "the church's openness" I mean the reality of reform—the reform that is a given with the church itself and embedded in its character as church under the Word. Karl Barth is right when he places the *ecclesia perpetuo reformanda* [the always in need of Reformation church] next to the *ecclesia perpetuo mansura* [the always remaining Church]. This is really nothing other than what Luther says in the first of his "95 Theses": that Christ, when he preaches repentance, desires "the entire life of believers to be one of repentance."[37] The church, in the Old Testament just as in the New, is a church continually judged and pardoned by God and his Word. It is only through this act of "killing and making alive" (1 Pet. 3:18), which is the power of the Holy Spirit, that the church "lives." Only in such a way that it lets the judgment of God which stands over the world be manifest over itself, that is to say, in such a way that this righteousness of God is not to be feared but rather to be loved because it is life-creating even in death, does the church remain open for the society. The church that justifies itself, that presents itself in "its own" righteousness and holiness, that offers itself to the world as an example and leader ("blind leading the blind!" Mt. 15:14), has extinguished its openness and mission to the world. It has to testify not to its own righteousness but to a foreign righteousness, the "*aliena justitia*" [alien righteousness] (Luther) with its "*poenitentia*" (repentance).

This results, as far as I can see, in a threefold state of openness of the church toward the society.

(a) [Pentecost: the Permanent Criticism of the Church]

As it is confessed in the church's creed, faith in the Holy Spirit and his work precedes the confession of the "*una sancta catholica ecclesia.*" These two do not coincide. Pentecost permanently wants to remind the church that the Holy Spirit is poured out "over all flesh" (Acts 2:17), that the limits of the extant ecclesial community are not the limits of the Spirit of God. For he is sent to glorify Jesus, which means to convict the world and the people who live in it of the fact that all their sin consists of only one thing: not believing in Jesus [Jn 16:9]; that all their righteousness lies in only one thing: that Jesus has gone back to the Father and represents us (Jn 16:10) and that the judgment that was rendered over the world has been executed. For Satan is overthrown. Our sin no longer reaches up to the throne of God.

---

37. [Martin Luther, *Ninety-Five Theses* (1517), LW 31, 17-33, 25; WA 1, 233,10f. That Luther thus deliberately wanted to turn repentance from an ecclesiastical institution into an act of Christians in the world is quite clear from the resolutions: "Christ must teach a repentance, I say, which can be done in every walk of life, a repentance which the king in purple robes, the priest in his purity, and the princes in their dignity can do just as well a the monk in his rituals and the mendicant in his poverty." Martin Luther, *Explanations of the Ninety-Five Theses* (1518), LW 31, 77-252, 84; WA 1, 531,8-11.]

That is the action of God that precedes the church as God's people and that prepares the way for him, for the Holy Spirit is the *praesentia Dei* itself, God's presence that is bound to the congregation and to which the congregation is bound—the former by grace, the latter by obedience. Before the Holy Spirit is bestowed upon the disciples, they sit "behind locked doors" (Jn 20:19, 26); they are not the open church, the church that engages, the church that confronts the world with its sin and calls it to repentance. The Holy Spirit opens up the gate to the world by testifying to Jesus as the Lord of this whole world. Sitting behind locked doors is the "ghetto existence" of the church that is not simply found wherever there are persecutions or obstacles to free proclamation. The earliest Christian church was genuinely persecuted and amply obstructed. It did not encounter a world that would make it easy to convey its testimony publically, yet its existence was anything but a "ghetto existence." Conversely, today in the midst of the mild air of tolerant conditions, we see churches and congregations that "are quite content with themselves," that regard "their" ways of life and customs as the truly godly ones, that preach of conversion, which they understand as conversion to their "rules" and "regulations." The ghetto existence of the church always has its origin at that place where we try to add certain "additives and attachments" to the free grace of God.

Pentecost with the gift of the Holy Spirit is the judgment over this little faith. Now the curse of the confusion of speech will be lifted, a new language will be bestowed upon the people of God in which all people will understand each other again, the language that "tells the mighty works of God" (Acts 2:11). In this language, the sermon penetrates into the alleys and the marketplaces, into the great cities and the heathen lands, right into the middle of the old world's "Babylon the great" (Rev. 14:8). And everywhere it finds ears that hear, hearts that believe, and lips that confess. The praise of God becomes loud in all the world. It is heard among sinners and the lost, in the "lower regions of the earth" (Eph. 4:9); it is heard in the songs of praise coming from liberated prisoners whose bars are burst and who emerge free from their bondage. The actual, visible church—as organized in its congregations—follows after all of this. The Holy Spirit goes on ahead, he "blows" (Jn 3:8) like a squall over the valleys of dry bones in this world [cf. Ez. 37:1-10], and the congregation follows. It does not create itself nor does it order itself, and it especially does not live from the thrice-cursed "self-understanding,"[38] which is only the treacherous expression of seclusion in its own righteousness. This church that is subject to the Holy Spirit and delivered over to him in judgment and grace, in shattering and restoration—and every Divine Service is such an act of purification and reassessment!—knows no "self-understanding," nor does it "order" itself according to the spirit or the letter of "its" confessions. Rather, through the Spirit

---

38. [Iwand refers here to the tendency in German theology of his days, without mentioning the names of Rudolf Bultmann and Friedrich Gogarten and others, which he, however, explicitly does in his "Against the Misuse of the *pro me* as a Methodological Principle in Theology."]

who has been given to it, this church aims in all things to understand God, to do his will, and not to lag behind in its hope. It is in fact—thanks to the leading of the Holy Spirit—the "wandering people of God" (Ernst Käsemann[39]) that is now assigned "to discern what is the good, acceptable and perfect will of God" (Rom. 12:2). It does not stand still, the whole world is its "parish" (John Wesley), and it can literally be studied in the breathless run of the Apostle to the Gentiles, how he finds no rest until his message leads him to the boundaries of the ecumenism (*Ökumene*) of his day. In that respect, he is its prisoner.

Thus the priority of the Holy Spirit continually shatters the church's limits. He abolishes these limits in the way God abolishes things: by shattering them and replacing them, by taking that which is "not a people" and making it God's people (Rom. 9:25) yet also truly establishing it anew. The Spirit of God does not dissolve the church's limits into limitlessness and nebulousness; rather, he dissolves them in such a way that he sets the preservative and protecting commandment of God into the place of its legal and coercive regulations. Our holiness is repugnant, our righteousness hypocritical and embarrassing to "sinners" who are "outside" (1 Cor. 5:13), our piety affects the "poor in spirit" (Mt. 5:3) just as the possessions of the rich affect those who have nothing. But God's holiness makes the unholy holy, and his righteousness is loveable because it does not eschew the society of sinners and the godless but rather "resides" in their midst and "brings them all home." This very movement takes place within it, thanks to the *praesentia Dei* (presence of God) itself, this movement that Jesus once—that is to say, once and for all, as *exemplum* [example] and *sacramentum* [sacrament]—accomplished as he entered the realm of humanity. As opposed to the exclusionary regulations of the Pharisees, the grace of God is a dominion that includes, preserves, and protects the lost person and protects him from the sin that is constantly reaching out for him. People will flee to it in the time of *Anfechtung*; here they will learn anew to walk according to God's good pleasure and not to grow weary. If the church would truly be the church of the Holy Spirit, it must be so open that its doors are stood wide open for salvation in the midst of a society marked by the judgments of God. To belong to this church is not an accomplishment nor a thing of worth nor a merit; rather, it is a protective and preservative act of God.

As the Spirit is the subject, the creator of his "*creatura*" church, since in him and through him God proves to be the Lord who with his presence is the only one who constitutes the joy and power of the assemblies of his saints, no one in this fellowship belongs to anyone else. The priest does not guide and lead the congregation; rather, if he assumes that the Spirit of God has long since worked in and on the hearts that are open to his Word, only then can he speak and hope to be understood. Principally, he preaches to those already elected in the grace of God. The opinion that when we are dealing with people who live outside the church, we are dealing with godless people to whom we must bring the gospel, is easily misinterpreted and aligns neither with

---

39. [Iwand refers here to Ernst Käsemann, *The Wandering People of God: An Investigation of the Letter to Hebrews* (1939) (Minneapolis: Augsburg, 1984).]

the content of the message nor with the form of its proclamation. For the message goes out to those people who were elected from eternity, thanks to the grace of God. What a hope will thus be spread throughout the entire society, hope like a dawn that breaks forth in the middle of their night of doubt and sin!

One thing still needs to be added onto this. In every church—whether it be so small and limited, whether it lie in a corner of the earth, whether it be hidden and undercover in an underground congregation in the midst of persecutions or in a small mission congregation on the "dark" continent, whether it make an appearance in a "world council" or even in a meeting that is transmitted out from this very ecumene—the unity of humanity is real no matter what. Here there is "neither Jew nor Greek, neither slave nor free, neither male nor female" (Gal. 3:28). All borders, barriers, limits of morals or race, sex, or estate that exist in society are leapt over as an anticipation, as a hope and promise of a great, final, coming possibility of God! This is because the very end of ages has come with the gospel of Jesus Christ. This is why the world as a whole comes into our view at this point. In the congregation, we see the hopeful and great fact prefigured that it is neither the "struggle of all against all" nor the devastating hatred of the sexes nor the class-struggle born out of the disparity between mine and yours nor the war of the great against the small or the strong against the weak that stands at the end of all things; rather, it is the unity of humanity and peace. This one humanity exists only in the action of a church that has been opened up by the Holy Spirit. If the church should be extinguished or should the action within it be prevented which is born from God's turning towards us (by submitting it to human direction), then the unity of humanity will become an illusion. It will collapse in that same moment where it seems to be "there." Society cannot of itself produce the unity of humanity, for this is an eschatological event. Should faith in the mission of the church be ignored, should its mission be transferred directly to the society, it will cease to be promise and favor and turn into force and pestilence. Society will experience itself—in its own bodily existence—what it has done by doing this, that it has stolen the unity of humanity, the "fire of this unity," from the altar. Either we will then need to slaughter ourselves because this unity of all has turned into an opposition of all to all, or we will need to become humble and grasp that the unity of humanity belongs to the great mysteries of the Third Article and ecclesiology.

(b) [Jesus Christ: Lord and Head]

I find the second law of the church's openness to the world—and this always simultaneously means openness to society—in the observation that Jesus Christ has two different names and titles. He is called the head of the church (Eph. 1:22, 4:15; Col. 1:18, 2:10, the head of any power and authority), and he is called the Lord = *Kyrios* (both of the congregation and of the cosmos). In congregational life, Jesus Christ is called upon and prayed to as the Lord but is never, as far as I can see, designated as "head of the world." (Gnosticism did this first, and it has that in common with all phenomena that reshape Christianity into a worldview [*Weltanschauung*], all the way up to Schelling's concept of the organism.) The title

5. The Bible and the Social Question

of "head" is reserved, however, for the body, that is, to the church, and the cosmos is not the body nor is it the emergent body that is growing into him, the body that is "incorporating" into him and in that regard the presumptive body, the "head" of which would be Christ. "Do not be conformed to this age" (Rom. 12:2) applies even and precisely here. For incorporation into the body of Christ is an act of rebirth and is not possible from the standpoint of my nature and world. This is why church and society can never be collapsed into one, yet they are subject to the same Lord, only so that his dominion appears in the world in such a way that he is witnessed as the head of the church. Thus the church will need to guard itself against wishing to make this dominion that is hidden under powerlessness and suffering into one that is overt over the society. Conversely, however, it must not dismiss the society from the clandestine dominion of and proximity to Jesus Christ. In the church, this Lord is confessed, he is prayed to, his name is called upon for the forgiveness of sins and salvation from death; the church lives openly under his governance while the society stands under it in a covert way. This means that the dominion of Jesus Christ in the church as in his body already encompasses the ones who "are not of this fold" (Jn 10:16). The church must always expect that the limits that it has drawn, limits that will often be also of a societal nature, will be overturned by him. For he stands within the church and yet outside of it. He is the door, (Jn 10:9) both to the outside and from the outside to the inside. An everlasting movement takes place in him; he brings in the lost and judges over the righteous.

Perhaps one more thing can be said in order to disconnect the image of head and body from the "concept of the organism," which is so present to us. When it is said that Christ is the head of the congregation, we are intending first of all to say that the Lord of the congregation is invisible and does not require a vicariate in any form. The Incarnation of the Word in Jesus does not continue to progress in the church! The church does not have the head at its disposal; rather, the head has the body at his disposal. The body—on its own—is but a frame, a torso without a head; in this isolation, it is a downright anti-Christian figure. By applying it to the relationship between Christ and the congregation, the image of head and body in its original understanding is burst open and voided. The content bursts the image open. It transforms it into new meanings. Only "to those outside" does everything take place in "figures" (Mk 4:11) so that they can see and yet not perceive, hear and yet not understand.

In other words, where the head is in this sense "incorporated" anew into the body, no longer by having the visible body directed by the invisible head but rather the other way around—this is where the anti-Christian tendency sets in!—starting from the visible church, transforming the invisibility of the head into visibility; at this point the openness of the church toward the society comes to an end. For now the church must identify itself with the functions of its head. It will not allow him, Jesus Christ, to be the clandestine Lord and master among his subjects who are still estranged from him; rather, it will understand itself and the expansion of its dominion over the society as the growth of the body towards the head and the coming of his dominion. Only as long as the church differentiates between itself as the body (which is precisely not the head) and the head, as long as it sees the unity between itself and the society in this head—but not in itself—as long as this unity remains a promise yet does not become an actual fact, this openness is preserved. The dependence of the body on the head is not reciprocal in the case of Jesus and his congregation. This head does not live from his body like the body lives from him. And so the church remains *creatura* [creature], and in it creation arises anew; this is why its doors open wide to everything that is created because it is all created for Jesus—for the church's own head.

(c) [Jesus Christ: Crucified outside the Gate]

We have already said: the fact that Jesus' title is twofold brings along with it the fact that Christ is within the church and yet is ever outside of it. The church witnesses this through the confession. And at this point, something sets in that will frankly shock all liberals and even socialists, insofar as they have not yet been able to separate themselves from this "liberal" leaven, something that includes within itself the entire shift in theology and church into which "Protestantism" today has entered. By confessing Jesus Christ as the crucified and risen one, the church confesses that it found him in the fellowship of sinners and not among the righteous. With that, it confesses where he has taken his place, thanks to the grace and provision of God, his place that is so vexing not only for the society but even also for the church.

It is first with the advent of the liberal impression of Jesus—and here is the point where Albert Schweitzer in his influential book *The Quest of the Historical Jesus*[40] does not quite totally break through—that the church's doors close to the "masses," to the "people." For now the "historical" Jesus is severed from the dogma that was added on later, as it is said. Now the attempt is made, an attempt the significance of which has long not been appraised but an attempt which has a profound impact even in societal terms, to purify and separate the human Jesus from what the theologians have made of him. Now the doors of the church close before the godless and sinners, and it produces an ethic itself that no longer speaks to people who live in this world, no longer calls upon them, brings them home, protects and guards them; rather—Adolf Schlatter[41] always excepted—it almost appears as if the ethic of this peculiar church was only there to make people's guilty conscience even guiltier than it already is. This is called the "*secundus usus legis*."[42] This is the most horrible thing that has happened and could happen. The confession of the crucified and risen one was seen as "theology," as something that

---

40. [Albert Schweitzer, *The Quest of the Historical Jesus: A Critical Study of Its Progress from Reimarus to Wrede* (London: A. and C. Black, 1910).]

41. [Adolf Schlatter (1852–1938) was a Protestant professor of the New Testament and Systematic Theology at Greifswald, Berlin, and Tübingen. From a theological perspective, he was a conservative Christian theologian, but he was also open minded for new insights and had a huge influence on his numerous students.]

42. [The second use of the Law. By this is meant the function of the Law in bringing sin into consciousness.]

"comes in" (Rom. 5:20), and it is for this that Jesus fell "into the hands of men" (cf. Mk 9:31, 14:41). This handing over of the human Jesus to the "society"—today still bourgeois, tomorrow perhaps socialist—means that now the church and its confession will be handed over to all the antagonisms and passions, all the sins and self-righteousnesses of a society that is disintegrating into itself. In socialism, the church will no longer be open for the "evil" capitalists. In capitalism, it will no longer be open for the "evil" communists. The "crucified and died, buried and raised" is removed from the head of Jesus Christ, and now the children of the world trifle with his name.

As strange as it sounds, it is dogma (indeed, in the sense of the divine determination and distinction of this very name) that has kept the church's doors open to the godless. With this dogma it is proclaimed that there are no more godless. For God is in the midst of sinners! With his nearness he puts an end to their "self-understanding," their existence. He invalidates the word of the godless person. "There is no greater sin than not to believe in the forgiveness of sins" (Luther).[43] The church's closed-off-ness in relationship to the masses follows from the apostacy of its proclamation from the witness to the Jesus who was crucified for our sin. He can only live among sinners. He cannot be taken away from this place; it is in this place that God wanted him to be displayed for the whole world, made visible to all eyes like the serpent that was lifted up (Jn 3:14). We do not owe it to the theologians, even Paul the "theologian," that Jesus is proclaimed in the world as the crucified and risen one; rather, God himself has accomplished this in his gospel. But the moralists have hijacked the subject and made out of Jesus a "saint"—naturally a modern, a bourgeois-humane, or even a socialist-revolutionary or a pacifist-philanthropic saint—in any event, a saint who represents the worth and life ideals of a group, a class of "righteous people." As long as Jesus Christ is confessed as the crucified and risen one and his place in the midst of sinners—where God placed him—is maintained, this cannot but have the most significant consequences for people's life in society. For all ethical differences are put into perspective from there; it no longer works for the good to form a party and in so doing to degrade the putatively evil ones, the outcasts and the lost. God has reserved it to himself to distinguish between good and evil, and within the political and social controversies of society, there can only be the comparatively better or worse. With that, good and evil—insofar as we are dealing here with norms of societal ethics—will always be understood as a value, and every incision that Kant's rigorism makes between duty and inclination will not last. In the social morality eudaemonism is justified. Here, it must be about well-being and the greater utility; here, one can ask for the happiness of the masses and will need to take care not to end up in the quest for the "*summa justitia*" (the greatest righteousness)

---

43. [There is no greater sin than not to believe this article of 'the forgiveness of sins' which we pray daily in the Creed." Martin Luther, *Sermon on the Sacrament of Penance* (1519) LW 35, 14.]

with the most terrible injustice (*"summa justitia summa injustitia"*).[44] As long as the church with its confession of Jesus Christ is on the scene, it cannot and may not come to pass that moralistic pharisaism should take hold within society unchecked and unopposed. And it is precisely the democrats who must recognize how great this danger has become for them because of their historical origins.

VIII.

In these three points—the fundamental priority of the gift of the Holy Spirit before the existence of the church, the differentiation between head and Lord in the titles of the exalted Christ, and finally the inseparability of the name and history of Jesus from the predicate of the one who was crucified for sin—I would see the theological determination upon which the openness or the closed-off-ness of the church with regard to society depends. The question should be asked if there is not also a similar openness of the society, but now not with respect to the church but rather with respect to the coming kingdom of God, even because this kingdom has already come to us. Society's association to the church will always be an indirect one; it is mediated through the nearness of the kingdom of God, through the promise and threat that are given with it, without which our society would not be what it is. Only from there is that movement explained that the human society of our day is making, the movement that will soon make us hope for the impossible and fear for the worst. This is why this society moves like a tempestuous sea, as if it could not find any rest in itself. Society has become for us what untamed and unexplored nature was to the primitive: something sinister and enigmatic that we would like to control and that yet continually eludes our ordering and organization. Indeed, we hardly fear the unforeseen outbursts of nature; we have learned to subject its powers to our spirit [*Geist*]. But simultaneously with humanity's dominion over nature there emerges modern society, a natural phenomenon of a higher degree. No one can say where that will lead. Insofar as they were not later remodeled and domesticated in either an ecclesial or a civil fashion, the societal reforms that came about in modernity, reforms that have had constitutive effects, are all aimed at the goal of taking the kingdom of God by force (Mt. 11:12). Therein lies their power and their allure. And it seems to me as if there is also here a threefold openness: an openness of society and of the people within it toward the dominion of God.

(a) [The Nearness of God's Kingdom in Jesus' Parables]

First, the parabolic openness about which Karl Barth can speak so convincingly in his still unsurpassed Tambach lecture "The Christian in Society."[45] People's

---

44. [The greatest righteousness results in the greatest injustice. Cf. for example Martin Luther, *Fastenpostille*, WA 17/2, 92,11.]

45. [In 1919 Karl Barth gave a lecture at a gathering of religious socialists in Tambach (Thüringen), in which he uttered radical and profound criticism of the idea of a bond

coexistence with one another and also their relationship to the nature that surrounds them are not as trivial, as empty and indifferent in view of the eternal as they seem. Quite the contrary, these must provide the images in which God's nearness to us is reflected, as if everything only existed to be a stage, decorations, material, a secret code meant, when the hour should come, to represent and proclaim something totally different: that which no eye has seen nor ear heard (Isa. 64:3f.). The Kingdom of God is not as far away as we think. When it rises up before us, we sense how everything that is created becomes transparent in order to testify his presence to us: "for in him we live and move and have our being" (Acts 17:28). As members of the society in which we live, we are not so abandoned, not totally fallen out of his hand. He still makes his sun to rise over the good and the evil (Mt. 5:45) and surrounds us with the signs of his mercy, even where we wish to judge and divide people into those who deserve to live and those who are not worthy of life. The very life that surrounds us is the divine protest against this. The totally other is near to us in him: God's goodness and mercy, God's forgiveness and God's peace. Yet it is always near to us only in a parabolic way; that is to say, it has a nearness that first fully and completely reveals our remoteness. The birds that sing God's praise reveal, even in so doing, the judgment over our worrying, and the lilies of the field could put a person to shame if he only understood the language they speak [cf. Mt. 6:26-29]. This is no accident; rather, it is grounded in the principle of liberal theology when it does not recognize the link between the parabolic character of the proclamation of Jesus Christ and the word of hardening (Mk 4:12).[46] This theology supposes that the parables of Jesus would thereby become meaningless; as a matter of fact, they can only be understood from this perspective. The way in which the kingdom of God comes near in parables simply expresses its nearness to us and never our nearness to it. No matter how transparent societal processes may be for the laws of the Kingdom of God, the transparent glass wall between it and us only becomes much more painfully perceptible in this way. You can torment all the wealthy people in the world and deliver all the poor to Abraham's bosom [cf. Lk. 16:22f.], you can make the chasm between here and there as deep as possible, you can dream of revolutions that will start world history over again—the new age will not be ushered in by any of that. The end of days does not come when we would wish or compel it to. And it is no different with those parables that come across as paternalistic, that at first read in such a way that

---

between Christianity and socialism. Barth criticized this bond so fundamentally and convincingly that his lecture caused a deep crisis of the religious socialists (Karl Barth, "The Christian in Society," in *The Word of God and Theology*, trans. Amy Marga (London and New York: T&T Clark, 2011), 31-70.]

46. [Iwand here refers to what Jesus answers his disciples, when they ask Him why he starts to preach with parables. Jesus then stresses that the coming near of God's kingdom in the parables according to Jesus' words won't lead to an easier understanding and a moral improvement but to a "hardening," a closure with respect to God's kingdom, only to be resolved by the Holy Spirit. Liberal theology in its reading the parables of Jesus as "timeless" illustrations misses this point.]

everyone says to himself, "I know that; I understand that." But where is the father who gives his son his share of the inheritance and lets him run around in self-selected freedom, only to take the returning heir, broken in body and soul, into his arms in a joy so great that it moves heaven and earth (Lk. 15:11ff.)? Where is the king who throws a wedding feast and brings in the poor and the crippled from the streets and alleys (Lk. 14:16ff.)? Where is the supper to which the good and the evil come to sit together and cast off the ideas that divide them as if they were false masks fabricated by an evil spirit to divide the children of the one God from each other? Where is the shepherd who leaves the ninety-nine sheep in the wilderness and then goes to find the one sheep who is lost (Lk. 15:4ff.)? Where is the farmer who sows the seeds on the path and among thorns (Mk 4:1ff.)—wherein, as is well known, Goethe saw a crooked trail?[47]

All of these parables are expressionistic. The images and figures that they employ are distorted. Using everyday circumstances and experiences common to everyone, they are supposed to express something that is absolutely not common or everyday: that with Jesus Christ and only in him, the kingdom of God has entered into our midst. When one begins from there, these images and parables start to speak in a new and different way. All of our actions and thoughts become parabolic, seen from Christ outward. They encompass everyone, whether he is a child or a father, whether he sows seed in the soil or she is a woman searching for her lost coin (Lk. 15:8ff.), whether she waits for her bridegroom night after night (Mt. 25:1ff.) or he is a moneylender who successfully speculates on the stock market (Mt. 25:14ff.). Nearness to and distance from the kingdom of God is summarized here in the parable; no one will be able to make excuses, saying that its speech is too lofty for him, its concepts too mystical, its reality too fantastical. The age to come has drawn near, and the age in which we are living must bear witness to it. But we do not notice a bit of it. We buy and sell, we eat and drink, we plant and build until fire and brimstone rain down from the heavens and our evil flesh perishes (Lk 17:28f.).

(b) [The Distance of the Kingdom as God's Judgment]

Yet it is not only the nearness of the kingdom of God to us that contains an openness; our distance from it also contains an openness. Society's distance from God is the impending judgment within itself. Having abandoned itself, it is delivered over to its sins and atrocities that lie within it like a restlessness, that want to be "confessed" and yet find no mouth to do the confessing. "Therefore, God gave them up," we find in the first chapter of Romans (Rom. 1:24), and therein lies the key to the obstinacy and decay that is described there. Why did God do this? For no other reason than that they did not give him the glory. Because they transformed God, the invisible and immortal one, into images of perishable creatures. It is not true that it was

---

47. [Iwand refers here to the last stanza of Johann Wolfgang von Goethe's poem "Ilmenau," which references the wavering sower of the parable.]

only the transgression of the Second Table of the Decalogue (Exod. 20:12-17) that had a destructive effect on the existence of modern society. Society carries another secret in its bosom: the wrathful judgment of God. This means that it cannot do anything else but itself become a disgrace and an abomination in transgressions of its own order. In terms of the kingdom of God, the substantive thing is that which takes place and has taken place between people and God on the level of the First Table (Exod. 20:2-11). That divine giving-up takes place where people put together their own religion and their own ethics, where they proclaim their own worth and pray to their gods. Everything else is punishment. On the level of the Second Table—which is to say, within that which we call morality—all that takes place is the rightful act of judgment in which the wrath of God envelops everyone that takes his glory from him. Because with the images and symbols that people make out of God, images and symbols that function demonically and powerfully within society, those destructive powers burst forth from below and destroy every bond, the bond between man and woman, between parents and children, between those who govern and those who are governed, all the way to the perversions and blasphemies that dissolve and disintegrate the cultural [geistigen] and physical organism of the society like a sort of toxin. Society becomes a prison in which God incarcerates his rebels until they annihilate themselves. They must disgrace themselves. But precisely in this sin that surges like flood waters and penetrates every nook and cranny, their having been abandoned is in relation to God, to the God whom they do not know—and who is yet near to them with his judgment.

This is why this "dis-enchantment of the world,"[48] this intrinsically Protestant legacy, means infinitely more than previously supposed from the vantage point of mere religious studies. It is not only an act of the Enlightenment—even the Enlightenment will one day give way to a new mythos—rather, it is the establishment of true worship, the liberation of the person from his inescapable fate. Only then will ethics starting with the First Commandment be possible again. Only then, starting with faith in the gospel, can these people, once marked with the seal of condemnation, begin to live out a new and gracious calling. God must open up the prison. The knowledge of God must sweep over the whole people like a vast river [Hab. 2:14], every person must know him, great and small must know what he has done in order to quench the wrath and take away sin, so that we can emerge born again into the redeemed world. It is indeed a fact that modern society has almost entirely lost its grasp on the significance that the knowledge of God has and could have for it. But why should the day not come when society comprehends what the church is there for, the church that to this day stands waiting in its midst proclaiming and praying?

This is not yet everything that could be said about the idea of distance. There is the restlessness that lies within the society, the question of righteousness that always arises out of itself anew. There is the voice of the brother Abel [Gen. 4] that never falls silent even when the bearer of this name is long since unable to accuse.

---

48. [Cf. Fn. 3.]

There is the difference between mine and yours that does not allow the relationship between I and you to be sorted out properly; there is luxury and there is want; there is the hungry person who is not satisfied, and there is the satiated person who no longer hungers and thirsts for righteousness. One day, there will be no more of "the headbands and anklets, the bracelets and head scarves;" one day, the "heads of the daughters of Zion will be stricken with a scab." Then, it will stink of rottenness where it once smelled of perfume; there, one will wear "instead of a belt, a rope . . . and instead of a rich robe, a shirt of sackcloth" (Isa. 3:16ff.); one day, the day will come when the "Lord will enter into judgment with the elders and princes of his people" (Isa. 3:14), in whose houses there is the spoil of the poor. And this day will be darkness and not light (Amos 5,18.20). For the afflicted are his people; whoever mistreats them needs to know that he is violating the property of God. It will be of little use to stage divine woship service after divine worship service [*Gottesdienste über Gottesdienste*] to try with processions and churchly festivals to throw a veil over this unrighteous behavior that so displeases heaven. "Seek justice, correct oppression; bring justice to the fatherless, plead the widow's cause" (Isa. 1:17). That is the wisdom of the prophets, born of the fear of God. Just as useless as this empty worship is the secret politics with which the princes and leaders wish to save themselves from this state of affairs. "Ah, you who hide deep from the Lord your counsel, whose deeds are in the dark, and who say, 'Who sees us? Who knows us?'" (Isa. 29:15). For the "boiling pot, facing away from the north" is a sign from the Lord, behind which is "the fierce anger of the Lord" (Jer. 1:13, 4:8).

Now war appears to be God's last resort on the horizon of a society that has the audacity to bend justice. That society will realize that righteousness is a factor that it cannot abrogate and recast. It will not succeed in reinterpreting and distorting light into darkness and darkness into light, to make good into evil and evil into good. The limit of its capabilities lies within itself.

Yet the churches are mistaken if they think they would be in the situation to fight back against the disorder that is breaking out within society. This disorder is a punishment, and no one will escape the punishment without turning back and repenting before the living God. What is required is not order but repentance. We do not need to fear when the sea roars and foams if we know where the city of God has its fortress and peace (Psalm 46).

(c) [Waiting for the New Man]

Then—and this is the third thing—it seems to me that the society is always moved by the expectation of the new man. That is where society is ahead of nature. Society is the place where this new man is expected. It is in the big city, precisely where society is most estranged from nature, where the question of the man becomes the only question, a burning wound[49] that society bears on its body. It is no use to

---

49. [Iwand here alludes to Friedrich Nietzsche, who in his *On the Genealogy of Morals* (1887) framed the people of the European Christian civilization of his times, the

try to heal this wound by reverting to naïve and primitive ways of life. Immature primitivism as we experience it today turns into barbarism and magnifies the suffering. Society is drifting toward a situation that tears nature and spirit [*Geist*] far apart from one another, a situation in which physics and ethics almost entirely lose the knowledge of their common origin. But precisely this is the third openness of the society toward the kingdom of God. In society, the creation—all of creation with us, as it were—awaits the birth of the new man.[50]

> But there are moments when we realize this: then the clouds are rent asunder, and we see that, in common with all nature, we are pressing towards man as towards something that stands high above us. In this sudden illumination we gaze around us and behind us with a shudder: we behold the more subtle beasts of prey and there we are in the midst of them. The tremendous coming and going of men on the great wilderness of the earth, their founding of cities and states, their wars, their restless assembling and scattering again, their confused mingling, mutual imitation, mutual outwitting and downtreading, their wailing in distress, their howls of joy in victory—all this is a continuation of animality: as though man was to be deliberately retrogressed and defrauded of his metaphysical disposition, indeed as though nature, after having desired and worked at man for so long, now drew back from him in fear and preferred to return to the unconsciousness of instinct. (Nietzsche[51])

Is this not the same thing that resounds in the eighth chapter of Romans about the groaning of the creation that awaits the new man who would deliver it from its futility? Here we find the third and final openness that we would have to discuss. Here the recognition arises that neither principles nor ideas nor laws nor rules can deliver us, that it is absolutely not in these "cultural" [*geistigen*] realms where the final decision that we await is made—but rather in the place where God becomes man, where God meets us just as we are, as a person among people. God's kingdom must come to us, if it is truly to come to us, in a human being like us, in a life that our eyes can see and our hands can touch (Jn 20:24ff.). In this "final" man, ethics and physics will again become one; that is to say, his nature will be his goodness, and his goodness will be his nature.

second half of the nineteenth century, as animals, who bear the "brand" of conscience on themselves. Friedrich Wilhelm Nietzsche, "On the Genealogy of Morals: A Polemic by Way of Clarification and Supplement to My Last Book," *Beyond Good and Evil*, trans. Douglas Smith (Oxford: Oxford University Press, 1996). Nietzsche regarded traditional culture with its norms and values as a hindrance that delays the birth of the new man.]

50. [Cf. Max Weber, "Religious Rejections of the World and Their Directions," in *From Max Weber: Essays in Sociology*, ed. H. H. Gerth and C. Wright Mills (Milton Park, Abingdon, Oxon and New York: Routledge, 2009), 323–59.]

51. [Friedrich Wilhelm Nietzsche, *Untimely Meditations* (1873-6), trans. R. J. Hollingdale (Cambridge: Cambridge University Press, 1997), 158.]

Three moments: the parabolic character, the place of judgment, and the birthplace of the new man constitute, analogously to what was first mentioned, the points where society is open to the kingdom of God. In such an openness to one another, church and society could meet one another, yet they can also get rid of this openness and violate one another. But in the middle, between the two is the kingdom of God, belonging to neither of them, manifested and evident in the one man Jesus Christ, to whom the church—in spite of it all and everything that happens within it—bears witness and whom society—in spite of it all and everything that happens within it—still awaits.

Chapter 6

CHURCH AND SOCIETY

Originally published as Hans Joachim Iwand, "Kirche und Gesellschaft," in *Bekennende Kirche: Martin Niemöller zum 60. Geburtstag*, ed. Joachim Beckmann and Herbert Mochalski (München: Christian Kaiser Verlag, 1952), 101–17; also in Iwand, *Kirche und Gesellschaft*, NWN I, 262–80. Original manuscript in the Iwand-Archive, Bundesarchiv Koblenz: A 1/2.

In the aftermath of the Second World War Iwand became convinced that a fatal error of church and theology was to focus social and political ethics on the relation of church and state, thereby ignoring society as the field of cultural exchange of ideas. From 1950 till 1952 Iwand held lectures at the Göttingen University and at several other platforms on the subject of "church and society." One of these texts is the here translated contribution to the Niemöller Festschrift.[1]

With the founding of the FRG and the GDR, the Korean War, and the rearmament of Germany, the East-West conflict had come to a threatening head. In view of this world-political situation Iwand asked to what extent church and society are (still) open for each other, to what extent there could be an aura of the church toward society.

With the paradigm "church and society" Iwand related two discoveries to each other: the rediscovery of the church as a living figure, as creatura verbi, *as it had newly opened up to him in the church struggle,*[2] *and the discovery of society in the course of the philosophy of Enlightenment as the living together of free individuals interacting with each other. Iwand thus replaced the static scheme, founded in the nineteenth century, of "church and state" including its antirevolutionary, authoritarian theory of society and a strict separation between the religious and political spheres. Instead, Iwand looked for the points of contact where church and society are related to each*

---

1. [Martin Niemöller (1892–1984), one of the main representatives of the Confessing Church, was imprisoned in the Sachsenhausen concentration camp. After 1945, he played a leading role in the reorganization of the evangelical church in Germany and engaged in many social issues.]

2. [Cf. Hans Joachim Iwand, "The Bible and the Social Issue," in chapter 5 of this volume: "We discovered it (i.e., the church) just as newly as we had once discovered theology in our encounter with the Reformers and the eschatological character of the New Testament."]

other and open to each other. He understood the kingdom of God in the living presence of the Holy Spirit as the third dimension that can be distinguished from both church and society. Toward the kingdom of God church and society will be kept open by God, so that the faith and witness of the church and the need and hope of the society will remain related to each other. (CN)

I.

During the last hundred years, the topic of "church and society" has receded more and more in Protestant theology. And yet it really could have been the most interesting, the most exciting, and the most challenging portion of any ethic in this era, which has seen so much transformation and foundational collapse in the societal realm. What a difference stands between the theological textbooks of the Wilhelmine era[3] and what the poets at the turn of the century—Ibsen and Strindberg, Gerhard Hauptmann, and Arno Holz—cried out and put forth in writing as the deep distress of this seemingly-so-intact society![4] In France it is Zola, in Russia Tolstoy, who could no longer endure a world that bears so thoroughly the traces of demise. They realize that a terrible catastrophe looms within and across society. They see the thunder clouds that gather threateningly on the horizon of a humanity so highly developed in both industry and culture. They are the apocalyptics of their time. However, in the church, in its official textbooks and institutions, in colleges and examination offices, in sermons and official announcements, it has barely been detected. Friedrich Naumann[5] and his circle could not hold on within the church; such a formidable writer as Hermann Kutter[6] in Basel is actually being read and understood for the first time only after the first Great War in Germany. Congregations are not accustomed to the prophetic word resounding *within* the church; where this takes place, it ends mostly with a circle

---

3. [The Wilhelmine era, named after the German emperor Wilhelm II, is the phase between 1890, the year Reich chancellor von Bismarck was dismissed by the emperor, and 1918, the end of the First World War and the resignation of Wilhelm II. Its main characteristic was a conservative, imperialistic, and militaristic culture and politics which also influenced architecture, art, and other fields.]

4. [Henrik Ibsen (1828–1906), August Strindberg (1849–1912), Émile Zola (1840–1902), Lev Nikolayevich Tolstoy (1828–1910) and in Germany Gerhard Hauptmann (1862–1946) and Arno Holz (1863–1929) are among the most important authors of naturalism, who strove for a realistic reflection of the social hardships and conflicts that were increasingly breaking out in their time.]

5. [Friedrich Naumann (1860–1919) was a pastor in Langenburg and Frankfurt. His interest in questions concerning the Industrial Revolution and its effects on society led him to leave the ministry and become an organizer, writer, and politician.]

6. [Hermann Kutter (1863–1931) was a pastor and theologian who preceded Barth and Brunner in dialectical theology and wrote on the topic of socialism and theology.]

of leaders' victory over the "idiosyncratic" pastor.[7] A critical history of this era of our church has not yet been written, though it would be extraordinarily useful to us today. For in this second half of the nineteenth century, we see the beginnings of the catastrophe that threatens to bury us under itself today. It is not enough that we are critical of ourselves; we must in this regard also be just as critical of those things that our fathers and grandfathers have done and not done.

In the nineteenth century, it is actually only Schleiermacher who sees these societal questions and pursues them theoretically. Along with him one could name Richard Rothe[8] and—the fully forgotten but highly interesting and unique— Alexander von Oettingen. The latter has done something within theological ethics that the French moralists had begun to do in view of the looming modern urban distress: he has written on the statistics of morality.[9] In this work he examined, with greatest judiciousness and expertise, what meaning the milieu and fate has for ethics along with what influence the fate of institutions has on the field of ethics. He thereby conquered its merely imperative and categorical character and sought to make clear that, in the ethical process, it is a matter of the plight of real people, a plight which has remained a certain inevitability and regularity through society. The plight of the individual is subsequently even more closely and ominously linked with that of a totality, a collective, a group, party, or other such thing, such that any ethic speaking to private existence functions as an empty concept.

Yet this is precisely what Schleiermacher thought. To him, the abstractness of the categorical imperative was profoundly repugnant. He saw in ethical formation a life process corresponding to the historical maturity of an era. He thought that one would not be able to direct his course without analysis of the moments determining this process. He saw—as did none of the theologians after him—that the chasm between spirit and nature postulated by idealism is inimical to life. He suspected that an ultimate connection must exist between physics and ethics and that neither of these two forms of knowing about life could be developed more highly than the

---

7. Cf. the biography of Adolf von Harnack on the "Jatho" case: Agnes von Zahn-Harnack, *Adolf von Harnack*, 2nd ed. (Berlin: Hans Bott Verlag, 1951), 303–12, also Carl Jatho and Adolf von Harnack, *Jatho und Harnack: Ihr Briefwechsel, mit einem Geleitwort von Martin Rade* (Tübingen: Mohr Siebeck, 1911).

[Carl Wilhelm Jatho (1851–1913) was a Protestant pastor in Cologne who was removed from office for his heretical positions. He tried to defend himself referring to Adolf von Harnack's position in the "*Apostolikumsstreit.*" But von Harnack supported the church authorities to remove the pastor writing to Jatho: "Sure, every pastor should be allowed to say freely and openly what he experienced and realized; but not every pastor can demand that the state church has to endure him under all circumstances." Carl Jatho, ed., *Briefe* (Jena: Eugen Dietrichs, 1914), 316.]

8. [Richard Rothe (1799–1867) was a professor of theology in Heidelberg and Bonn and advocated the idea of moralizing the society through the spirit of Christendom.]

9. Alexander von Oettingen, *Die Moralstatistik und die christliche Sittenlehre: Versuch einer Socialethik auf empirischer Grundlage* (Erlangen: Deichert, 1868).

other.[10] It is probably this very opposition between humanities and the natural sciences [*Geistes- und Naturwissenschaft*] that has subsequently prevented both philosophy and theology from mastering the societal questions that are increasing in a colossal way. Insofar as the natural sciences have been eliminated from the complex of ethical questions, the societal questions had already been negated from the beginning. Schleiermacher's misfortune was that exactly that which he had sought to hinder with all his theological work promptly entered into the field of theology: the inbreaking of ethical dualism in Christendom, which came about through the reception of Kantianism and belongs today to the fundamental articles of confessional theology under the pseudo-Reformation formula of "Law and Gospel" or the teaching about the "two realms," which are unfortunately defended with particular fervor.[11]

Ernst Troeltsch[12] recognized much about this calamity that crippled both theology and church in German Protestantism for the past hundred years and caused them to seek refuge in the intellectual arsenal of the Restoration in every present-day question. Despite great and grotesque errors, which have to do mostly with his conception of early Christianity, he was correct in his overall evaluation of the path of this development and with his warnings of the conservative Christian alliance across the board. The means by which he intended to avert the catastrophe do not in any way inspire confidence. In this respect he was too much a son of the prevailing liberalism, even in things theological. Yet he felt the problem of modern society and the tensions and antitheses arising from it for the church with every fiber of his being; it gnawed at him. He saw—and this is the merit of "historicism," at any rate—that the church today is no longer allowed to consider itself as the straightforward continuation of the early church, which invited its assault on the world as arising out of its eschatological and, in that respect, revolutionary basis. The original distinction and opposition between church and world has been, so

---

10. [Cf. In this volume "Against the Misuse of the *pro me*."]

11. [Cf. as a formidable example Werner Elert, *The Christian Ethos*, trans. Carl J. Schindler (Philadelphia: Fortress Press, 1957), which is solely based on a radicalization of these distinctions. For the problematic consequences of these supposedly Lutheran ideas, cf. the *Ansbach Ratschlag*, an answer to the Barmen Declaration by Bavarian theologians including Elert and Paul Althaus ("Der 'Ansbacher Ratschlag' zu der Barmer 'Theologischen Erklärung,'" in *Dark, Depressing Riddle: Germans, Jews, and the Meaning of the Volk in the Theology of Paul Althaus*, ed. Ryan Tafilowski [Göttingen: Vandenhoeck & Ruprecht, 2019], 231–4).]

12. Especially in Ernst Troeltsch, *The Social Teachings of the Christian Churches*, 2 vols., trans. Olive Wyon (Louisville and London: Westminster John Knox Press, 1992), and Ernst Troeltsch, "Protestantisches Christentum und Kirche in der Neuzeit," in *Die Kultur der Gegenwart: Ihre Entwicklung und ihre Ziele*, ed. Paul Hinneberg, vol. 1, 4, 1, *Die christliche Religion: Mit Einschluss der israelitisch-jüdischen Religion* (Leipzig and Berlin: B. G. Teubner, 1906), 431–792. [Troeltsch (1865–1923) was one of the most important representatives of the school of history of religions and of liberal theology.]

he thought, toned down more and more over the course of time. Only the sects have retained something of this authentic spirit of the original, world-denying Christianity of the Sermon on the Mount—they have therefore remained the salt of the earth and have again and again changed and reformed society anew—while the more or less secularized state church has diluted the Christian ethic with the help of natural theology and then made these into the foundation of a conservative order.

Apart from these few great attempts to make the understanding of church and society within Protestantism into the object of theological knowledge, our topic soon had to give way to another, the topic "church and state," which would for a long time be the dominating topic within which societal questions would be dealt with (whereby one mostly came out on the State of Estates ["*Ständestaat*"]). This transformation took place with the alliance that entered the continental European state churches—incidentally, with all three confessions, the same took place even in Russia—after the fall of Napoleon with the antirevolutionaries and, in this regard (namely, a fundamentally antirevolutionary *Weltanschauung*[13]), conservative powers and ideas. We have experienced the effects of the last—hopefully the last!—phase of this alliance, as eyewitnesses, victims, and accomplices. We have experienced the effects that made the church blind and impotent, and we remain in the midst of them until now. If one reads today the relevant literature of the time 100 years ago—when the fundamental ideas of the Restoration were formulated[14] (I'm thinking roughly about the first years of the *Historisch-politische Blätter*[15] or the introductory words that Friedrich Julius Stahl set forth for his legal philosophy;[16] Johann Hinrich Wichern's speech to the church assembly at Wittenberg[17] also belongs in this context)—it is noticeable that we have been moving around in a circle since then and know how to encounter the ongoing

---

13. [The German term "Weltanschauung" has a rich philosophical-historical background. It denotes a fundamental spiritual-cultural orientation and encompasses the whole of ideas and values concerning the interpretation of the world, the role of the individual in it, the view of society, and, to some extent, the meaning of life. Of great importance were Wilhelm Dilthey, "The Types of World-View and Their Development in Metaphysical Systems (1911)," in Wilhelm Dilthey, *Selected Works*, vol. 7, ed. Rudolf A. Makkreel and Frithjof Rodi (Princeton: Princeton University Press, 2019), 249–94, and Karl Jaspers, *Psychologie der Weltanschauungen* (Berlin: Springer, 1919).]

14. Franz Schnabel, *Deutsche Geschichte im 19. Jahrhundert*, 2nd ed., vol. 4 (Freiburg: Herder Verlag, 1955), esp. 143ff: "Die christlich-konservative Solidarität und ihr Ende."

15. [G. Phillips and G. Görres, eds., *Historisch-politische Blätter für das katholische Deutschland*, 1838ff.]

16. [Friedrich Julius Stahl, *Die Philosophie des Rechts*, 5th ed., vol. 1 and 2 (Heidelberg: J. C. B. Mohr, 1878). Stahl (1802–61) was a lawyer, conservative politician, and philosopher of law.]

17. [Johann Hinrich Wichern, "Rede auf dem Kirchentag zu Wittenberg, 1848," in *Johann Hinrich Wichern, Sämtliche Werke*, ed. Peter Meinhold, vol. 1 (Hannover: Lutherisches

revolutionary shocks of modern society through nothing other than an ever nearer partnership with the counterrevolutionary powers. It was for this reason that Christians of both confessions in Germany were so blind regarding nihilism as it appeared in the slogans of the political "right." They were trained to expect the enemy to come from the left. What the romantic historical perspective had taught first—that Enlightenment, political, and social revolution all have their roots in the movements begun by the Reformation—becomes a political statement of faith of the ruling, patriotic circles in the middle of the nineteenth century. On the Lutheran side, the anti-Catholic stance of the Book of Concord is now consciously and deliberately corrected insofar as it assaults the ecclesiastical order. For it is now valid, over against the decay of a society seized by democracy and revolution, to posit the church as a force for order [*Ordnungsmacht*].[18] Thus emerges modern "Lutheranism," which still sets itself apart from Catholicism in doctrine but no longer in its concept of church. On the contrary, one seeks here to restore the connection to the Middle Ages after its rehabilitation in the consciousness of the educated people (which Novalis initiated)[19] has made such great strides.

The most significant teacher of this restorative era on the Protestant side— equally important as politician, legal philosopher, and ecclesiastical leader—is Friedrich Julius Stahl, who teaches that revolution is the original sin and then evaluates the societal theories of his time from that starting point. In this he also finds the important and consequential difference between the Lutherans and the Reformed. The latter, due to their notion of church that simply emanates from the congregation understood as a sociological quantity, are not in a position effectively to take part in defending against the evil of the revolution, a defense in which the Lutheran Church knows itself to be agreed with the Catholic Church on account of their doctrine of office. So it is first and foremost the societal teachings, which make the barrier between the two Protestant confessions appear essential for Stahl (notwithstanding the fact that Stahl had come to faith due to the preaching of a Reformed preacher in Erlangen named Krafft[20] and that later, when he was

Verlagshaus, 1962), 155–71. Wichern (1808–81) was a pioneer in the establishment of inner mission and the church social services in Germany.]

18. This reemerges repeatedly, especially in August Friedrich Christian Vilmar, *Über die Lehre von den drei Ständen der menschlichen Gesellschaft hinsichtlicher der Verwendung dieser Lehre in der Lehre von der Kirche*, Pastoraltheologische Blätter 3 (Stuttgart: Liesching, 1862).

19. Georg Philipp Friedrich Freiherr von Hardenberg (Novalis), *Die Christenheit oder Europa* (1799), in Novalis, *Schriften*, ed. Ludwig Tieck and Friedrich von Schlegel, 4th ed., vol. 1 (Berlin: Reimer, 1826), 187–208, 189: "Those were beautiful and bright times, when Europe was a Christian land, when *one* Christendom inhabited this humanly shaped part of the world; a great common interest united the most remote provinces of this vast spiritual empire."

20. [Johann Christian Gottlob Ludwig Krafft (1784–1845) came from the Lower Rhine revivalist movement and had been a preacher at the Reformed congregation in Erlangen since 1817.]

the leader of Confessional Lutheranism in Prussia, he didn't shy away from recognizing that he owed his Christian existence to a man "who always carried the Heidelberg Catechism around with him"). Friedrich Julius Stahl could go so far—and in this he betrays himself—as to declare against Christian Karl Josias Bunsen: "Synodalism is the *contrat social* in the Church."[21] It is Rousseauism that shall be excluded in all circumstances by restoring the Confessionalism of the post-Reformation era. Those things which had been valid first and foremost in relation to *dogmatic* questions are now seen, evaluated, and newly developed based upon their meaning for *societal* questions. So this rediscovered Confessionalism stands as godfather for the antirevolutionary alliance, which the ruling estates together with the state form against the revolutionary ideas and movements in modern society.

What has been arranged, however, through this establishment of the church upon a specific societal ordering in the middle of the preceding century can hardly be expressed with words in light of the crisis that has still in no way come to an end. Even the wars occurring in this era must probably be seen in this context. They are based on certain ideologies, in terms of both domestic and foreign politics. They remain closely related to feared or subdued revolutions and are anything but isolated "fates" which have to be fatalistically accepted. Rather, they much more depict exceptionally devastating and intense explosions of a public spirit that is reshaping all ethical and historical judgments, a spirit that long ago threw the usual distinction between foreign and domestic political phenomena out the window. Likewise, the wars of the last hundred years are culturally linked [*geistiger Zusammenhang*][22]—or better: "ideologically" linked—with the revolutions and counterrevolutions on the continent, which follow one after the other as push and pushback, mutually causing and triggering one another.[23]

II.

The distress that is moving us is still widely seen in the relation of a person to the "total state"; however, it could be that this form of government is secondary and that societal processes and ideas stand behind it. It could be that the justifiably feared "total state" is not a problem of constitutional law but rather a "societal"

---

21. [Friedrich Julius Stahl, *Wider Bunsen* (Berlin: Hertz, 1856), 16.]

22. [Iwand is convinced that political realities are not accidental but result from the fundamental theological-philosophical convictions of an epoch. By this Iwand is echoing Hegels' philosophy of mind. Cf. Hans Joachim Iwand, "Geistige Entscheidungen und die Politik," *Blätter für deutsche und internationale Politik* 3 (1958): 56–64. On a discussion with Hegel, cf. Iwand, *Glauben und Wissen*, NW I, 211–18.]

23. Cf. Guglielmo Ferrero, *Macht* (Bern: A. Francke, 1940).

problem, a problem connected to certain ideas,[24] particularly when one considers that the concept of totality at issue here originates from organic political thought, was discovered by Plato, and found its first German herald and philosophical advocate in Immanuel Hermann Fichte.[25] Even the measures and objectives of the "Third Reich," which brought about such distress for us, were essentially societal transformations and processes (though not with revolutionary but with antirevolutionary objectives), for which the authoritarian reconstruction of the political apparatus was only a means to attain the objective of societal reform as completely and rapidly as possible. Since the advent of Parliamentarianism, the state becomes the executive of the party in power at the moment—a party defined by societal objectives—just as the state was once considered to be the executive of the church.

All of that to make clear that we are merely treating symptoms when we suppose that we must see the political problem of our day in the relationship of people to the "total state"; that is not the issue at hand for us. The Confessing Church in its constitution, more compelled by its circumstances than resolved through clear reflection, must have been on the right path—at least during the time of the Third Reich and in its apt ordering of itself at the Dahlem Synod,[26] which was never implemented but more of an anticipation of things to come. For here the evangelical church, as a community ordered under the Word, was poised to be given that corresponding form that empowered it to confront the society that was forming the "total state." The fact that the forms of ecclesiastical order, newly emerged at that time, which arose in the midst of confession and suffering, in true historical distress and exigency, were dismantled and removed after 1945—among others the apparatus of the "Councils of Brethren" [*Bruderräte*][27]—brought about the fact that today we neither feel nor recognize the real problems of our ecclesiastical and Christian existence. These problems will come from ongoing societal reforms—whatever we say and how we delude ourselves so that we might not see the trial that approaches us! During the church struggle [*Kirchenkampf*], we already aborted the conflict offered to us, a conflict that began as a true crisis of the church with the rise of the Third Reich—and it was not the fault of the man to whom these pages are dedicated with grateful memory[28] that it was aborted. If we would see the church struggle not as a triumph but—seen on the whole—as a

---

24. I would intend this in contrast to Brunner, who regards the total state as a consequence of centralism in Emil Brunner, *Justice and Social Order* (1943), trans. Mary Hottinger, 2nd ed. (Cambridge: Lutterworth Press, 2003).

25. [Immanuel Hermann Fichte (1796–1879) taught as a philosopher in Tübingen and was the son of Johann Gottlieb Fichte.]

26. [The second synod of the Confessing Church met in Berlin-Dahlem on October 19–20, 1934. It adopted the so-called ecclesiastical emergency law (*Notrecht*) and declared the rule of the German Christian church leadership unlawful.]

27. [*Bruderräte* were the collegial governing bodies in the Confessing Church.]

28. [Cf. Fn. 1.]

defeat, then synods like Dahlem would appear in a much more favorable light, as pointing the way forward. It was then that a lofty height became visible; it cropped up before us as a demand too lofty for our little faith, a demand before which we admittedly recoiled, but somehow and some day we will have to scale it if the church of Jesus Christ within the society of today and tomorrow should be what its name implies. Everything that we have done and "organized" since 1945 moves about below this lofty height. We find ourselves in the valleys of anxiety and longing for security but no more on the assault. The gospel, however, is an assault.

Perhaps one could even say that the coming apart of the Confessing Church that was becoming visible at the Synod of Oeynhausen (1936) into the Confessing Church led by the "Councils of Brethren" and the "confessing Confessional Church" (Ernst Wolf)[29] which remained in its old forms both with regard to state law and ecclesiastical law and was therefore in a position to compromise with the state is connected with our question: the so-called intact churches, which were at the same time the confessional churches—and of both Protestant lines, to be sure—remained primarily oriented toward their relationship with the state, with which they hoped to reach a compromise, a modus vivendi after the mode of a "concordat."[30] For them it was and is decisive to limit the omnipotent state. They see in the church as a public institution such a state-limiting entity. For us, in the meantime, it was not the state in which we saw our true adversary but rather the cult that was connected with it and that fundamentally alienated the state from its actual purpose, that made it into a quasi-ecclesiastical, liturgical, and sacramental

---

29. [Ernst Wolf, "Bekennende Kirche oder bekennende Bekenntniskirche?" in *Dialektische Theologie in Scheidung und Bewährung 1933–1936: Aufsätze, Gutachten und Erklärungen*, ed. Walther Fürst (München: Christian Kaiser Verlag, 1966), 284–302.]

[At the fourth and last synod of the Confessing Church in Bad Oeynhausen from February 18 to 22, 1936, the Confessing Church split over the question of state-church relations into the Evangelical Lutheran Church in Germany (usually called the Luther Council [*Lutherrat*]), to which the so-called intact Lutheran state churches belonged on the one side, and the Dahlemite wing, the Councils of Brethren [*Bruderräte*] on the other. The Luther Council, which emphasized its Lutheran confessional commitment against supposed unionist tendencies within the Confessing Church designating itself as a "Federation of confessionally determined Confessional Churches" [*Bund bekenntnisbestimmter Bekenntniskirchen*], did not evade cooperation with the Reich Church Ministry. The Councils of Brethren on the other hand formed the Dahlemite wing of the Confessing Church, which increasingly fell into illegality by declaring the German Christian church regiment to be heretic and was persecuted for its positions. Dietrich Bonhoeffer, Martin Niemöller, Ernst Wolf, and Iwand, for example, belonged to this wing.]

30. [The allusion is to the *Reichskonkordat*, a state-church treaty concluded between the Holy See and the German Reich, July 20, 1933, which regulated the relationship between the Reich and the Roman Catholic Church.]

entity in order to spiritually inspire the process of transforming the society.[31] We were and are of the opinion that the state must be restored much more to its original function and that the church forfeits its existence as church when it tolerates that the state, deprived of its dignity, becomes the "executive" of a *worldview*, be it a pagan or even a "Christian" *worldview*.

III.

But what is society, then, this typical product of a new time molded by the Enlightenment and natural science?[32] One should never overlook that the entity that we call "society" today would never exist without the modern control of nature. It is inextricably bound with technology, with the shrinking of space and time, with the formation of ideological parties as bearers of the political will, with the press and the direction of the masses enabled thereby, with capitalism just as with the socialism that has at the same time sprung up with and become inseparable from it.

"Society" has become so significant that, mysteriously and powerfully, it will sometimes emerge as a monstrosity, sometimes as the location of the greatest hope for men and their future. What is this society, then? And what does the church have to do with it? Are they right who simplify the problem saying that the church is addressed as a *societas perfecta*[33] and that its antecedents lie in the "natural" society? In that case, church and society would relate to one another as the true essence and its mere reflection, broken through the shadow of the perishable and sin. Then the church as socially significant would stand in the middle of society as its true image and essential revelation. It would be here, then, that marriage, authority, justice, political order, and society all first find their true meaning. It is just as reasonable as it is alluring to think this way, chiefly because this construction theoretically works out so easily. But we find in the Scriptures nothing pointing to this idea which is in itself oriented more toward the restoration of the cosmos (*restauratio*) than toward redemption (*redemptio*) and related more to institutions than to people and life.

---

31. [Cf. Hermann Sasse, "Die Kirche und die politischen Mächte der Zeit (1932)," *Kirchliches Jahrbuch für die evangelischen Landeskirchen in Deutschland* 59 (1932): 30–113; also in *In Statu Confessionis: Gesammelte Aufsätze von Hermann Sasse*, vol. 1, ed. Friedrich Wilhelm Hopf (Berlin and Schleswig-Holstein: Die Spur, 1975), 251–64, esp. 252 Fn. 1 and 255–6.]

32. Cf. Wilhelm Dilthey, "Über das Studium der Geschichte der Wissenschaften vom Menschen, der Gesellschaft und dem Staat (1875)," in idem, *Gesammelte Schriften*, vol. 5/1, 8th ed. (Göttingen: Vandenhoeck & Ruprecht, 1990), 31–73.

33. Cf. Karl Gerhard Steck, *Politischer Katholizismus als theologisches Problem* (München: Christian Kaiser Verlag, 1951).

Just as simple and consequently no less plausible is the other way—to leave church and society as two sociologically significant things separated from one another, two entities that exist harmoniously [*schiedlich-friedlich*] with one another under the same roof of the "constitutional state." This is the view of all those who utilize the doctrine of the "Two Realms" as their point of departure in this question. By this they mean that this distinction between the two is to be carried out harmoniously [*schiedlich-friedlich*]. The realm of the church is a spiritual realm, therefore also internal, even as society shapes public existence where man lives and behaves outwardly. As a result, the church, as a matter of principle, dispenses with every exertion of influence that does not have to do with "inwardness" and thus with "personal Christian matters" [*christliche Persönlichkeiten*]. Only in the realm of the irrational are there connections left between church and the public sphere.[34] By occupying offices with "Christian personalities," one believes that he has become master of the fatality that exists in principle. This "new Protestant" solution to our question would presuppose that faith in the New Testament is a "Christianity of personal matters" [*Persönlichkeitschristentum*], a presupposition that cannot be substantiated by means of biblical theology or dogmatics. Such a fundamental coexistence—as if the church were in no way aimed at the society nor was the society aimed at the church—is truly the manifestation of a profound resignation and hopelessness, which in principle, in basic theological approach, dispenses with changing the world through the gospel. In this conception "world" refers to the forms of life and existence within which the life of society moves. Change is limited to individual people, to "attitudes;" that is, it has retreated fully into the subjective.

Yet that totally contradicts the gospel and the sending of the congregation into the world. For in Jesus Christ, it is not only the confined realm of the "inward" but rather everything that has been made new. The existence of the church in the world—since Pentecost—is the invasion and the disruption of this independent life of society, the powerful assault of God on its secured and ever-newly-barricaded realm of life in which man seeks to fashion his existence within this world according to his own laws. The gospel of Jesus Christ is—as a result of the history received in him, namely the history of the Incarnation, Crucifixion, and Resurrection of Jesus Christ in Jerusalem—totally different from a confirmation of supposed orders. It is affirmation, the yes and amen of God that was spoken to us and to the whole world in Jesus Christ, but just as a "negation of the negation," a *theologia negativa*—and only in this respect a *theologia affirmativa*—a yes in a no. And whoever does not hear the no, to whomever it appears too bitter, too hollow, too hard, too unmerciful, that person cannot understand the yes hidden within it. "Be saved[35] from this crooked generation" (Acts 2:40). So says the gospel. It

---

34. [Cf. Hans Joachim Iwand, "Kirche und Öffentlichkeit" (1948), in Iwand, *Vorträge und Aufsätze*, NW II, 11–45.]

35. [Although many English translations render the verb σώθητε with a middle active sense "save yourselves," Iwand's German is, however, clearly passive, "*lasst euch erretten.*"]

does not think at all about glorifying what is present in the so-called orders in this society and mourning their rupture. It knows that "what falleth, that shall one also push!"[36] (Romans 1). The orders or the bonds in which people live, be it marriage or the state, be it property or family, can naturally be nothing but "godless fetters."[37] In these "orders" the crookedness of this age is fixed and elevated to a rule. In this way people's bondage and slavery to the powers and forces of this age are pronounced to be inevitable fate, the prison falsely said to be the "home condition" of man. Here death is set up as the final entity, and man, cooped up between birth and death, is handed over to the "elementary principles of the cosmos." No matter how ideal the cultural [*geistig*] structure of the society may be, if we do not come any further than a religious adoration of orders and bonds, its true existence remains bound up in matter, hunger, and desire.

For this reason, the structures of the society in which we live all bear something of this abysmal crookedness. Whether we say state or law, whether money or wage, family or marriage, whether it is a matter of the supervision of the governing over the governed, the relationship of husband and wife, or parents and children—it is said a thousand times how it should be, but how is it in reality? How is it possible that the images of how it should be hover so empty and powerless over all this reality—as the Spirit of God over the chaos? Does it not depend on the fact that we do not have the courage to smash the old magic spells with which the imprisoned are held in their cells, the magic spells of a divinely established order—one that is established without and outside of Jesus Christ and his gospel? There is only one divinely established order: the gospel of the forgiveness of sins in Jesus Christ. And there is only one way to live in the "divinely established" order: faith, which receives life new and transformed from the hand of God. In faith we know the Lord of all and know that he is our brother, the man Jesus Christ. Behind the magic spells of the orders of this world lies not this Lord but "the prince of this world" (Jn 12:31), who wished for all to remain as it is, the Not-God who adorns himself only too gladly with the name of God, behind which, however, nothing stands—as sure as God stands with everything that he truly is, with his whole power and all his mercy, with all his activity and each of his promises, behind the one name of Jesus Christ. As soon as the tyrant is overthrown and has been exposed in his powerlessness and lies, should not the message spread through the whole prison, to those above and those below, to those who are the hammer and to those who are the anvil,[38] to those who violate and to those who are violated: that the hour of liberation, of deliverance is here, that the chains fall if we only have the courage to

---

36. [Friedrich Nietzsche, *Thus Spake Zarathustra* (1883–5), Part 3, ch. 56, §20, trans. Thomas Common (New York: Random House, 1954), 233.]

37. "Through him befalls us a joyful deliverance from the godless fetters of this world for a free, grateful service to his creatures" (from Thesis 2 of the Barmen Declaration).

38. [Citation of a poem of Johann Wolfgang von Goethe, "Ein anderes": "Du mußt . . . leiden oder triumphieren, Amboß oder Hammer sein." "You must . . . suffer or triumph, be an anvil or a hammer."]

cast them off ("to rise together!"), that doors will open before us if we only have the faith to move them. Not only is Christ risen, but we are risen with him (Col. 2:12; 3:1)! The magic spells lose their power, the lame walk, the blind see, and good news is given to the poor (Mt. 11:5).

That is the gospel, and flowing from this gospel the dos and don'ts, the action and expectation of the congregation of God, must be understood. It must work within every society like an uprising, indeed such an uprising where also the most radical revolutionaries will always prove themselves to be "backwards." What will become of society if someone rises up out of the grave and—as Lazarus who was called out of decomposition into life (Jn 11:1ff)[39]—with death behind him (that's what it means to be baptized!) returns to society as one born again? What will become of all these idols competing with the living God, idols that are still worshipped and taken seriously there, if at once it became perceptible what only God can do and what the idols are not able to do? They cannot deliver man, they cannot bury death and guilt for him and set life and grace—nothing but grace—before his eyes. They can only—in the best case—dedicate themselves to keeping the prison in order, but to break the bars and to rob the master of death's realm of his prey, that they cannot do, for they themselves owe their power and their magic to this Not-God and to his presumed power. Man himself is the master of all things, so as one freed through God's grace who has learned to get over death, he enters once again—thanks to and in Jesus Christ—the scene of this world with eyes open to him who has become his Lord, full of thankfulness to him who made him free with his blood and life. That is what Christians are within society: Do they not stand within it as its singular and greatest hope and possibility? Can it—the society—then manage without this throng of men who have "come from death into life" (Jn 5:24)? Does it not mean anything for society that a light shines out from here over everything, that a movement is dawning that is gripping, has gripped, and will grip society again?

What will happen when the false masters of this world, its usurpers, are suddenly faced with these free people, since through the action of God in Jesus Christ they have been freed from sin and death? Will they not set new tablets for that which counted as good and evil during the age of slavery? Will they not be masters in the breaking of the old tablets that stood as that death order of the prison? Won't the new tablets and laws in truth be the old ones, which reach back to God himself and his righteousness, which were painted over and bastardized through the opinions and laws of men? What, then, will become of that which we today call the state or of that which currently counts as property? Will not family and marriage gain a new face if we no longer bear them as the "inevitable" orders of the world that are laid on us but instead know that these are the "good works that God prepared beforehand, that we should walk in them" (Eph. 2:10)? It could indeed be that the command of God is no longer a burden to us and his instruction

---

39. This is what Fyodor Dostoevsky intended with his "Raskolnikov" in *Crime and Punishment* (1866).

no longer a yoke that presses hard (1 Jn 5:3) but rather the hand that straightens us and the mouth that comforts us that we should "run and not become faint, walk and not become tired" (Isa. 40:31). What—we thus ask—happens with and in the world, with and in society, if their false masters would face such free people who have been spoken free by God?

This is the question of ethics. It will only be able to answer that question if it knows that it is entirely founded upon "hope." Then it will not speak in its usual perplexity, with fatal evasion in the *Gesinnungsethik* (ethics of conviction)—the internal "emigration" of Protestantism—with evasion in the "art of living in tension." Rather it will speak in such a way that its speech is again yes, yes and no, no (Mt. 5:37). *Fides non stat cum peccato mortali!*[40] our fathers have testified. That is to say, faith cannot live wall-to-wall with the sin that brings death. God and Not-God cannot dwell together in one heart nor consequently in one world. What has become of the state under the dominion of tyrants and the mob is crooked. Crooked also, what we made out of marriage when we subjected it to the expediencies of the walk of life, society, or even the biological propagation of the nation. The relationship between husband and wife is crooked as long as God is not recovered and believed.[41] For as people lost him, that deep and heavy shadow fell between these two, husband and wife, and they no longer comprehended that they are there of each other and for each other. Crooked also the absolute obedience that people demand of others and give to one another—as it is starting to crack more and more in political and also in ecclesiastical life—for man belongs to God, bought with his blood; for this reason we must not be servants of others (1 Cor. 7:23) nor bring or entice others into being or remaining such. Some—if not much—of what we have made out of property, out of honor, out of death is crooked. People and their welfare should count for us as more than all "material assets" [*Sachwerte*]. And as far as honor is concerned, all honor begins with the fact that we render honor to God and let him be Lord—where this is no longer the case, all our "taking honor from one another" is *vanitas vanitatum* (the vanity of vanities of Song of Solomon 1:2; 12:8). And death? One should not hold it in contempt, "*ut milites solent*"[42] who have made out of it a heroic death.

It's no wonder that such crookedness brings forth fruit—indeed, fruits that we can only remember with the most profound shame. No wonder that the world is sick, sick unto death, for a belief hangs over it like a curse that it is not able to alter this crookedness. Its unbelief is its sin—only its unbelief, the rest is just

---

40. ["Faith does not coexist with mortal sin." Cf. AC IV, 64; KW 131; BSELK 295,14-16.]

41. Cf. Karl Barth, *Church Dogmatics*, vol. 3/4, ed. Thomas Forsyth Torrance et al. (London and New York: T&T Clark, 2004), §54.1: "Freedom in Fellowship," 116–240.

42. "As soldiers are used to."

["Nor does one overcome death by disregarding it and by following the example of street bandits and soldiers"; "Soldiers engage in such reasoning and therefore scorn death." From Martin Luther, *Lectures on the Psalms* (1534/35), LW 13, 76 and 96; WA 40/3, 485,22f and 517,20f, on Psalm 90.]

punishment. Breaking its unbelief, that is the mission of the church to and within the society. Everything else—also the abysmal sins and evils by which society is haunted today—deserves compassion and mercy, but its unbelief deserves no mercy. Whoever would leave a prisoner to his dreams or his resignation since he has grown accustomed to loving his chains and seeing his prison as unbreakable, such a person would be no liberator. He would be no herald and witness of the Risen One in the world. A church who does not "castigate" the world that they "do not believe in me" speaks no longer out of the power and authority of the Spirit by whom the Exalted One testifies of himself to his own (Jn 16:8f).

IV.

On the other hand, however, because of this, the church is asked—and actually by society—whether it wishes so to stand in the midst of society and spread its message that it actually stands caught in the middle, without citizenship in the society, as a complete foreigner, at once wonderful and vexing, as the mouth of its message upon whose acceptance or rejection hangs also its own existence in the society, its toleration and legal protection, but also its persecution and loss of rights. It is evident that these two demeanors are not without profound consequences for the society, the state, and the law. They bring with them blessing and curse. But in order for this to take place, in order for this decision-packed opposition between church and society to come about at all—how often do forces from both camps wish to evade this decision and come to a sort of ceasefire for the kingdom of God!—the church must know one thing: it must not wish to be or even be considered to be more than the Word it brings. Its testimony, with which it bears the gospel of Jesus Christ within society, must become its destiny and thus the destiny of the society. It must be able to believe and to hope that, for the sake of this testimony, the society will love and bear, desire and at least tolerate it. Where that which it represents is despised and trampled underfoot (exalted though it may be by empty platitudes), it is there that the church must bear the humiliation of its Lord and distance itself neither from the humiliation nor from its Lord. Sadly, there is an attitude in society that one considers Jesus Christ to be a myth but his church to be an essential reality, essential for the sake of public morals and governing a people.[43] Hopefully, the church will say no to such a "toleration." Indeed, a hard, clear no! Only with such a no can it fulfill its obligation to such a society.

---

43. [Especially the monograph *Century of a Church* by Otto Dibelius was influential after the First and again the Second World War for its emphasis on the sociopolitical impact of the church. He believed that the church could function as "a power for social and national reconciliation" (Otto Dibelius, *Das Jahrhundert der Kirche: Geschichte, Betrachtung, Umschau und Ziele* [Berlin: Furche-Verlag, 1926], 241.) being "the educators of the German people to moral seriousness, to moral strength, to moral responsibility. They can do it.

The church is asked further if it is prepared to shoulder the reversal of the supposed societal order brought about by the gospel of Jesus Christ, that the first should be last (Mk. 10:31), that the blind should see and the lame should walk (Mt. 11:5) even as those who see should be exposed as blind and the healthy and the strong do not wish to give up their strength and righteousness. Hopefully, the church will not be ashamed if the poor and miserable, the sinners and the godless, offer it asylum. The fact that, in the days of the Reformation, the gospel of the justification of sinners that had become homeless in the church found asylum among the people—indeed in the first instance among the German people—from the minions of Caiaphas and Pilate and that neither pope nor emperor succeeded in maintaining this Babylonian captivity of the church has remained an unforgettable memorial in the history of our evangelical church. The gospel that had become homeless and without rights in the apostatized church finds a reception in the territory of the "Not-Church" of the "heathen" and makes those who are Not-God's-People (Hos. 2:23) into God's-People. The church must then take it upon itself to bear the offense of the gospel as a "social" offense. The church must content itself with believing that the weakness of God is stronger than the strength of men and that the folly of God is wiser than our wisdom (1 Cor. 1:27). Thus the church is asked if it knows how to differentiate between itself and the society and its supposed prevailing judgments—God sees the heart (1 Sam. 16:7)!—whether it knows itself to be free as opposed to the society, as it relates not only to the decaying society but also to the ordered society, as it relates not only to the nihilistic but also to the conservative, it must fundamentally differentiate itself from all such entities. It is also *societas*, but it is not inherently *societas*. It must not forget for a moment that God according to his own will has entrusted to it the mystery of the redemption of the world in Jesus Christ, a secret hidden from eternity, veiled even before the angels in heaven (1 Pet. 1:12), a mystery that is now in it—in the church—made known to all the world.

Precisely here it is necessary to pay attention to one thing: when we read the New Testament message, we realize the reckless certainty that the people of that time had who bore this testimony to the world, testifying to the now and today of this revelation and bringing it into focus. They have a message that carries with it knowledge, but not a message, like that of the Gnostics, that becomes expendable through knowledge. The gospel is no timeless truth. The Apostles do not find the message to which they testified before the whole world already present and formed in the hearts or the spirit of people, so that they only had to remind them of something that had been forgotten in the sense of a platonic anamnesis, in order to lead people from the inauthenticity [*Uneigentlichkeit*] of their manifest existence to the authenticity [*Eigentlichkeit*] of an eternal truth present within

---

They must" (Otto Dibelius, *Nachspiel: Eine Aussprache mit den Freunden und Kritikern des 'Jahrhunderts der Kirche'* [Berlin: Furche-Verlag, 1928], 20).]

them.⁴⁴ Rather, truth was made manifest in one person for all people and has spoken to all people in one person (cf. Rom. 5:15). And this message now has a hearing; this word has now been heard through the one man Jesus Christ. Now will men also know him by whom they are known (1 Cor. 13:12). For this reason, the preaching of the church is not merely a pedagogical beginning beyond which the mature and the advanced then pass. Rather, it is the abiding center of its existence; in the proclamation a wonderful and singular today comes about, a today that characterizes the gospel of God's grace.

With preaching the church brings a new element, an element not previously extant—the "today" of God's grace—into the other, manifold speaking and listening to one another in society, into its all-encompassing conversation. With preaching, the expectation and hope is demonstrated that God, God himself, has intervened in this conversation, even in a way that he has never and nowhere done before—not mediated by a creaturely essence, not as one who is speaking or suspected within us, not as one who can be perceived or interpreted in the storms of world history, not as a God who treats us like the creation and its two-faced nature which is sometimes nasty and at other times pleasant, but rather as the God who has become his own mouth and witness, as the God who has formed his own Organon in order to speak with men that he might be the one who, entirely he himself, who speaks here—the ultimate contrast to all people who are subject to sin and death. Only because this has happened, because there was a time where the sun and moon stood still, as it were, and God's Word stepped into our midst—free, in service of no man, at the pleasure of no authority—because this has happened as *factum* and *faciendum*, as a phenomenon that the society can no longer get rid of— only for this reason is there still preaching. It reminds us that we are not alone, that our speech must not remain a human and thus psychological "monologue" but rather that, whether we know it or not, it is theological existence!⁴⁵ An existence in the midst of which the Word of God is present and joins in the conversation! This is the life of all people through the preaching of the church.

What could preaching mean within society? Does the church even know that it stands within society as the message-bringing, "evangelizing" entity in the grand

---

44. This is always "philosophy," even when in the guise of theology. [Iwand alludes to Rudolf Bultmann's existential interpretation here, which is strongly in debt to Martin Heidegger's philosophical conceptualization. On the discussion with Bultmann cf. Iwand, *Theologiegeschichte*, NWN III, 246–53.]

45. [Iwand refers to Karl Barth's important paper "Theological Existence, To-Day" from 1933: "We are agreed about this too, that alongside of this first business [e.g., the preaching of the Word], as the meaning of our labour and our rest, our diligence and relaxation, our love and our scorn, we brook no second as a rival. But we regard every second or third thing that may and should incite us as included and taken up in this first concern, and condemned or blessed thereby. On these things we agree or we are not preachers and teachers of the Church." Karl Barth, *Theological Existence To-Day! (A Plea for Theological Freedom)*, trans. R. Birch Hoyle (Lexington: American Theological Library Association, 1962), 13.]

course of divine election, which has come about "today" to us and to this world? Does it know that preaching is decisive for its existence, for its obedience before God and its service to humanity? The Word of God that is made known in preaching—one need to think only of Romans 10—is neither a call to be conservative (though it can also be this from time to time) nor a call to be progressive (though it can also appear now and again to be evolutionary and optimistic), but it is essentially and always the call into the today of God's grace. The grace of God in Jesus Christ has in store a particular today that is specifically for us, a day in which we may live, live and die, increase and decrease (Jn 3:20). It is not such a today as our natural and historical life carries in itself, a today that is only the hairy edge between what was and what is coming, a today that we can only ever but touch, only to lose it again, this symbol of passing time that hangs on like a bitter tear in all our joy and all our enjoyment and that is thus sought for, lusted after, and lamented in the societal existence of humanity as the present that can never quite be grasped. The today of God's grace in Jesus Christ is a today that stands still, a today that waits for us, watches over us, and preserves us. It is not subject to the law of the age but rather brings that which is enduring, brings truth and peace in the age. It moves with us without changing. It remains young and new each day, even when our life grows old and we grow weary of its repetitions. It rises over us as a lofty, primordial star when our young active life steps for the first time into its splendor. It is old when we are young and young as we age. It never changes in itself, but because we are always moving along our course from birth to death, it manifests itself to us in ever new form and splendor.

Such an encounter exists within the life of humanity, such a coexistence (Luther's *simul*!) between the temporal "today"—with all that this "today" embodies—and the eternal "today" of God's grace—again with all the abundance and fullness that lies settled within it—just as one "today" blends into another and finds its peace and stability therein. In the same way, could not the "today" of society, with all of its need and guilt, submerge itself in just such a way under the "today" of the kingdom of God and there for the first time be alright again? Everything that we experience today has a peculiar tendency within it. In the deepest hopelessness of our day, something of a hope breaks forth, so great and sweeping as has not been perceptible for such a long time. Both "todays," the great, grace-filled "today" of the gospel—"Today, if you hear his voice" (Heb. 3:7, 15)—and the lesser, transitory "today" of our human society, filled up with so much worry and guilt, with perishable vitality and incessant movement, must become related to one another so that a spark bursts forth and we may once more "walk in the light" (1 Jn 1:7). They must not coincide; that is to say, the church must not give up its inheritance and confuse the "today" of God with our human "today." But they also must not be so far removed from one another that there is no longer any tension or contact between one and the other. The one extreme would rightly merit the accusation of enthusiasm [*Schwärmerei*],[46]

---

46. [This seems to be said in light of the Wolf article as well, for that answers a critique by Hermann Sasse that the Confessing Church are enthusiasts. Cf. Wolf, "Bekennende Kirche oder bekennende Bekenntniskirche," 284f.]

as it believes in a kingdom of God that would come visibly and tangibly. Yet the other extreme leads to unbelief and satiety, as it places a division between the "two realms" so that their limits run as two parallel lines that make contact only in infinity. At this point the proclamation of the church ceases to be the occurrence of God's Word in the "today." At this point the proclamation begins to keep quiet where God wills us to speak: on war and peace, on social justice and human freedom, on marriage and work, on money and property. Then, a church that has become tired and dull drags itself back into its own corner and leaves society to its own devices. Yet this society left to its own devices will soon need to recognize that it is exposed to the laws of nature (and we with it) and thus to the bondage and drudgery of the elementary principles of this world (Gal. 4:3).

Both church and society are related to one another by God; they remain open to each other and must be open to one another "until he comes" (1 Cor. 4:5). That is the evangelical rule for the relationship of the two entities to one another. The church neither coincides with the kingdom of God, in which case it would itself cease to be open to a reformation from the outside in, nor does it coincide with society or some conceivable reform thereof. Otherwise, the kingdom of God would become tangible by means of "outward observation" (Lk. 17:20), and new forms of messianism and false prophets would step into the place of the one Jesus of Nazareth to lead the masses astray and snatch them into the abyss. The man to whom these pages are dedicated[47] stood and fought against both of these errors, both in exemplary fashion for many and in brotherly fashion with many of us, both with his testimony and with his life. He ensured that society heard the message of God's grace as it sought to seal itself off from it. Afterwards, he fought for the church to remain open to the need and the hope of the society, as the church was in danger of closing its doors and depriving those outside of the "today" of God's grace.

It was and is about freedom. Then, it was about the freedom of the proclamation, which the society wished to deny the church. Now, it is about the freedom of the acceptance of this proclamation, which grants to man the freedom of his mind and of his judgment. For both, the church (as organization) and society (as organization) must remain open to each other, and it is worth fighting for such an openness. They must be open to one another until the kingdom of God comes. For the age in which they are related to one another, so full of tension and full of hope, so full of conflicts and full of commonalities, is the age between the first and second Advent. In this age, the history of humanity will always be, at its most profound level, the history of the church, which is to say the history of mission.

---

47. [Cf. Fn 1.]

Chapter 7

TOWARD A THEOLOGICAL RATIONALE FOR PROTEST AGAINST THE GOVERNMENT

Originally published as Hans Joachim Iwand, "Zur theologischen Begründung des Widerstandes gegen die Staatsgewalt," in Hans Joachim Iwand, *Vorträge und Aufsätze*, Nachgelassene Werke Vol. II, ed. Dieter Schellong and Karl Gerhard Steck (Munich: Christian Kaiser Verlag, 1966), 230–42.

In 1951, Hans Joachim Iwand was summoned to testify in the trial of Major General Ernst Otto Remer, who had been promoted rather rapidly in the last year of the Second World War due to his role in preventing the attempted assassination of Hitler on July 20, 1944. On several occasions after the war, Remer accused the members of the resistance—among them Dietrich Bonhoeffer—of high treason, for which in his view there was no justification whatsoever on moral-religious grounds. The court therefore invited Iwand together with some other Roman Catholic and Protestant theologians to deliver an assessment of this issue. The question at issue was: "Does a citizen have the right under specific circumstances to be disobedient to the government, even to the extent that one may try to overthrow it and replace it with another government?" This presentation, which is dated in 1952, belongs in the context of this trial (GdH).

I.

As I was preparing for this presentation, I read some literature published during those first years after the fall (of the Third Reich), literature written in the clarity of consciousness that was around in those days.[1] I believe that this literature will end up belonging to the most impressive discourse that our century has to offer, even if

---

1. [Iwand here refers to the period immediately after the defeat of Nazi Germany in 1945, when the reality of Nazi terror in the concentration camps, especially the Shoah, and the treatment of the Slavic people in Eastern Europe came to light. However, recent research into letters and diaries of that time has produced the acknowledgment that there was not a common "clarity of consciousness" among the German population.]

it has not yet resulted in a new attitude of the collective spirit [*Gesamtgeistes*]. But it is the seed that was sown and from which the fruit of a new cultural orientation will emerge—if it is to emerge at all. Seen on the basis of our inquiry, one can detect a striking dissimilarity between the starting position of that literature and what we observe among us today.

In those days, the collective Christian consciousness was full of the guilt with which the Christians had burdened themselves, not merely because they had not carried out resistance adequately and resolutely enough against the totalitarian ideological state (*Weltanschauungsstaat*), but even more because they had by and large offered incense to the Caesars and because in so doing they supported the development of that instrument of annihilation into an entity that knew no more limits and only maintained the emblems and functions of a state without any longer possessing its moral essence. At that time, it was clear to us that even the state can be corrupted into its antithesis, that it can go from being the institution of God indicated in Romans 13 to being the beast from the abyss described in Revelation 13[2]—emerging out of the abyss with false prophets at its side. Not only did we experience the reality of a perversion on such a scale as was hardly known before so that we became its contemporaries, but we also knew that this development, at least at its inception, in its "principles," was not merely fate. Rather, the way in which all of these things developed was more likely illustration of the phrase: now you have what you want! In what took place here, we experienced the manifestation of a cultural decision or maybe we should say a process that chose power and not justice, a process that had long been primed among us, a process toward which we had been marching as if blindfolded and that we only really recognized in its full horror after it was too late, after the gates of freedom whose vision we had long since betrayed had shut behind us. The burning down of the German Parliament in Berlin[3] was something like the squashing of a parliamentary vision that was no longer at home in the bourgeois world of the outbound nineteenth century—and in no other nation could this act of the "revolution from the right" be passed off with the simple phrase that the communists had done it! One first had to be estranged from the institution of this bourgeois freedom to accept that signal in the kind of passively mute way that just occurred in our essential estates and

---

2. [In the margin of his manuscript Iwand refers to Heinrich Schlier, "Vom Antichrist: Zum 13. Kapitel der Offenbarung Johannis," in: *Theologische Aufsätze: Karl Barth zum 50. Geburtstag*, ed. Ernst Wolf and Albert Lempp (Munich: Chr. Kaiser Verlag 1936), 110–23.]

3. [Immediately after the coming to power of Adolf Hitler's National Socialist Party on January 30, 1933, opponents were arrested as communists and social democrats and their parties forbidden. Measures were also taken to "muzzle" and "align" the press (*Gleichschaltung*). On February 27, 1933, the German parliament (*Reichstag*), was set alight by the Dutch communist Marinus van der Lubbe and burnt down, which was a blessing in disguise for the Nazis, who took the advantage of this to close the parliament and declare a state of emergency [*Notstandgesetzgebung*] which gave them almost absolute power to restrict media, parties and citizen rights.]

ecclesial leadership. Similar things could be said about the enforced conformity of the press and the ban of the left-wing parties. We did not grasp—we did not even grasp this from the perspective of the roots of our Christian conviction—that just as soon as the freedom of conscience in public life is threatened, our individual freedom is lost. This is why we were so powerless when we tried to act out against laws of injustice, laws of the very murder that was legalized by them, from this point of our embattled conscience. Resistance remained limited to the private, personal sphere. We had allowed this tool to be taken out of our hand, a tool that a responsible society needs so that the voice of conscience and consideration of human rights could be effective in the activity of public life, so that we could protect the state against its descent into the abyss of tyranny. The fact that we lacked this insight, not because it would not have been there to be found and not because it was not advocated by significant men and statesmen but rather that this insight was not demanding for us, that it was covered up by other values and judgments, by reactionary powers and romantic conceptions of the rebirth of the Wilhelmine empire,[4] and by the worry that the threat could come from the left—this fact came to be recognized more and more in those terrible years as our fault. And proceeding from this recognition, the resistance that Christians and non-Christians together carried out in suffering and finally in action against the usurpers of the state needs to be understood. It cannot be an accident that so many noble men attempted *as Christians* to remove Hitler by force on the 20th of July.[5] It was more than a conspiracy, they were not staging a coup for the sake of having the power in their own hands; rather, it was the Christian conscience rearing up against something appalling! Behind their action was an awareness of the nameless injustice with which the human face, which is exalted by God in Jesus Christ to the likeness of himself, was dishonored and disfigured to the very end—not only in the horrors of prisons and concentration camps but just as much in the horrors of the unnecessary war machine wielded in pure greed for spoils and power. For everything—from the initial days of the usurpation of the state until the annihilation of Poland[6] and with it the initiation of the Second World War, which shattered all order in Europe—stood under one and the same law. Behind all of it stood the enabling of the total war[7] of revenge and retaliation. In this way, an unbroken line runs from the Reichstag going up in flames in Berlin to

---

4. ["Wilhelmine empire" is the name for the German Reich in the period of the reign of Kaiser Wilhelm II, from 1888 through 1918.]

5. [Among the conspirators for the attack on Hitler of July 20, 1944, was a high number of Christians, both in the military ranks like the Abwehr and the Wehrmacht and in the civilian circles like the "Freiburger Kreis" and the "Kreisauer Kreis."]

6. [On September 1, 1939, Germany invaded Poland and thereby started the Second World War.]

7. [In the Second World War Nazi minister of Propaganda Joseph Goebbels famously took up this idea and called for precisely this, in theory unrealistic, total war in his speech in the Berlin Sportpalast on February 18, 1943.]

the annihilation of press freedom and the parties to the gagging of the churches and legal institutions to the atrocities of a lawless warfare, where murder is only exchanged for murder and savagery for savagery and the mentality of friend or foe is made into an absolute.[8]

The fact that we no longer make this image clear in its logical consistency, as it once stood before the soul simultaneously clear and accusatory, may be connected to the fact that remorse is an internal, cultural [*geistiger*] process that cannot be brought into common awareness by means of modern technology, propaganda, or training sessions. It will always arise individually out of the depths of the accusing conscience. It arises, as Max Scheler showed after the First World War in an unforgettably beautiful essay, as the internal purification that must take place if I want to strive for new goals.[9] Yet, as Scheler shows, it also stirs up the past that is otherwise so bitterly and immovably static and makes a blessing out of the seemingly unbearable. We stand again today in a similar struggle between on the one hand coming to terms superficially with the past, wherein one can hear those nationalistic demands and blustering expressions of the "strong men" all over again who threaten everyone who does not join in with them with charges of treason and on the other hand of that profound Christian renewal born out of internal reflection.[10] This renewal knows that the way forward must be enabled by God and that the tomorrow that we approach in this kind of repentance and hope must have and will have a totally different face, even culturally [*geistig*], than the yesterday from which we have come. And the shift in the Christian's posture toward the state is precisely a part of this renewal.

II.

This shift begins principally at two significant points. The first point pertains to the divine ordinance of the state, its *ordinatio* sanctioned by God. Here Rom. 13:2 has become a text of primary importance: "Whoever resists the authorities resists God's ordinance (διαταγή), and those who resist will incur judgment."[11] Along with that text, there are still the well-known passages from 1 Peter: "Be subject for the Lord's sake to every human institution, whether it be to the emperor as supreme, or to governors as sent by him" (2:13-14). In 1 Timothy, then, there is again that well-known passage where Christians are called upon to make "supplications,

---

8. [See in this volume "Love as the Foundation and Limit of Freedom," introduction.]

9. [Max Scheler, "Repentance and Rebirth," in: *On the Eternal in Man*, trans. Bernard Noble (New York: Harper, 1960).]

10. [As to the "strong men" Iwand obviously refers to Major General Ernst Otto Remer and his allies. When he speaks of "Christian renewal born out of internal reflection," he gestures to some articles Max Scheler wrote after the First World War (see in this volume "Love as the Foundation and Limit of Freedom").]

11. Translation our own because Iwand's translation differs from the ESV.

prayers, intercessions, and thanksgivings (εὐχαριστία) for all people, for kings and all who are in high positions, that we may lead a peaceful and quiet life, godly and dignified in every way" (2:1-2). This resulted—essentially through the law of reason interposing at this point—in an identification of state and divine manifestation that left no place for a Christian duty—that is, a duty gained from faith in God—of resistance against state authority. The state itself had become the organ of divine revelation, but that is only if we do not want to state the issue directly. To put it more bluntly, it had become God. The sole law that stood above it was its own law, the *"raison d'état"* itself. The legacy left to the West—as opposed to the Eastern Church—since *Augustine's* fundamental differentiation between *"civitas coelestis"* and *"civitas terrena"*[12]—a legacy without which we will understand neither state nor church in their relationship to one another—was substantially threatened. Out of the real juxtaposition of state and church as the two methods with which one and the same God, that is the triune God, the Father of our Lord Jesus Christ, rules the world, something totally new emerged: the juxtaposition of the external and the internal, of reality and spirituality. This is why the relationship of the two entities to one another was so readily compared with the relationship of body and soul, and the church was seen as the interior of the state but not in such a way that it would be the "ruling" element of the state. Rather, the church is merely interiority limited entirely to the subjective realm. Even though the Catholic doctrine of the state never went through this kind of development because it cannot allow the church to be absorbed into interiority, the development in Germany and perhaps of all Europe is defined by a modern notion of the state, which has monopolized the notion of the absolute for itself. The divine was detached entirely from the original basis of Christian revelation, and in this detachment—in this in-and-of-itself-ness—it was accepted as an expression of state authority. Service to the state took the place of the service to God.

With the recognition that was granted to us over the course of our sorrowful history, nothing would be more appealing than to take note today—of that view of the state that Hegel championed in 1821 in his *Philosophy of Right*, a view that—whether in positivistic form or in the dialectic form of Marx, freed from the "opium" of religion—probably was of greatest significance for our further development in the nineteenth century. In that writing, the thesis that the state is the *"ordinatio Dei"* is taken to its zenith. The state, even in its most depraved form, remains the divinity as it appears outwardly.

> The state is the march of God in the world; its ground or cause is the power of reason realizing itself as will. When thinking of the idea of the state, we must not have in our mind any particular state, or particular institution, but must rather contemplate the idea, this actual God, by itself. Although a state may be declared to violate right principles and to be defective in various ways, it always

---

12. [In his *De civitate Dei* Augustine operates with the distinction between the "celestial city" and the "earthly city."]

contains the essential moments of its existence, if, that is to say, it belongs to the full formed states of our own time. . . .. The state is not a work of art. It is in the world, in the sphere of caprice, accident, and error. Evil behaviour can doubtless disfigure it in many ways, but the ugliest man, the criminal, the invalid, the cripple, are living men. The positive thing, the life, is present in spite of defects, and it is with this affirmative that we have here to deal.[13]

"The state is the divine will as a present spirit, which unfolds itself in the actual shape of an organized world."[14] It is the historical concretum of that which is moral to which religion is related as the relationship with God that lingers in the subjective. Hegel counters the objection that the state is still finite and temporal with the proposition that a "bad state is indeed purely finite and worldly, but the rational state is in itself infinite." Further, "the content of religion is and remains veiled; feeling, sensibility, and fancy are the ground on which it is built, and on this ground everything has the form of subjectivity. The state, on the other hand, actualizes itself, and gives its phases a solid reality." "Piety, when it replaces the state, cannot tolerate that which is definitely constituted and destroys it."[15] It could be demonstrated how, when one begins with this theory of the state, even the oath and the existence of civil servants are bound indissolubly to the state with a bond that is subject to no higher norm than the very one that is the actualization of the moral in the world. The possibility of saying "no" to the state, the possibility of proclaiming that "no" from a true moral commitment and putting that "no" into practice, has disappeared. All countermovements fall under the verdict of the negative, of "fanaticism" as Hegel says, and are still seen in the subjective from the perspective of the raison d'état at precisely that point where they are grounded in the religious. It is strange that this view has persisted in people's consciousness even to the present day. It is also strange how when seen from that perspective, resistance against state authority, insofar as it is brought about by Christian responsibility, is still considered something "subjective" that as such stands outside of the course of world history in the way that Hegel—particularly at the end of his *Philosophy of Right*—sets forth in a grizzly image. "In world-history, which lies beyond this range of vision, the idea of the world-spirit, in that necessary phase of it which constitutes at any time its actual stage, is given its absolute right. The nation, then really flourishing, attains to happiness and renown, and its deeds receive completion."

> In the history of the world this nation is for a given epoch dominant, although it can make an epoch but once. In contrast with the absolute right of this nation to be the bearer of the current phase in the development of the world-spirit,

---

13. [Georg Wilhelm Friedrich, *Philosophy of Right*, trans. Samuel Dyde (London: G. Bell and Sons, 1896), par. 258, 247.]
14. [Ibid., par. 270, 260.]
15. [Ibid., par. 270, 271–3.]

the spirits of other existing nations are void of right, and they, like those whose epochs are gone, count no longer in the history of the world.[16]

It is sufficient to keep this image in all its cohesion and savagery in mind, if we are to grasp what the Christian's resistance in the struggle against the state is aimed at: this image became a reality—probably mostly unbeknownst to those who had to bring it about—and as this delusion became history in all its magnitude and horror, the question of resistance against state authority was grasped anew from the depths of faith in God and Jesus Christ. For example, it is striking that even in Luther, of whom it seemed until now to be a settled fact that he condemned active resistance against state authority in principle—a putative fact that is still taught today by most Lutherans[17]—one discovers that he approves of the killing of tyrants, indeed commands it as Christian. Admittedly, this is only as a last resort when the tyrant sets himself up as the norm of all laws, whereby the "*anomos*," the lawless person, usurps the power of the state. The jurist Johannes Heckel, who has recently done particularly good work with the question of ecclesiastical law in the Reformation tradition, has come out against Hans von Schubert and others with the thesis that Luther differentiated between lesser and greater tyrants and that in the case of the latter, the "monster" who places his "I will" in the place of God's command, he sees assassination [*Totschlag*] as the sole salvation of the people in the face of this monstrosity.[18]

The murder of tyrants is always—even for the medieval theologians who taught it—a last resort, *ultima ratio*;[19] it will not be justifiable when it comes to matters of faith. Yet that there is a point in the progress of the demonization of power where the whole can be saved with the removal of the one and thus, as Prof. Angermeier explained in the Remer trial,[20] the common good is at stake in the radicality of

---

16. [Ibid., par. 345–47, 343.]

17. [After the Second World War not only conservative Lutheran theologians but even theologians of the Confessing Church regarded the conspirators, such as Dietrich Bonhoeffer, as contradicting the ethical paraeneses of the Reformation and especially Luther. That is also the reason why Iwand and Wolf were explicitly summoned to elaborate on Luther.]

18. [Johannes Heckel, *Lex Charitatis: A Juristic Disquisition on Law in the Theology of Martin Luther*, trans. Gottfried Krodel (Grand Rapids, MI: Eerdmans, 2010; German original 1953). For the right to resistance, see Appendix 1, "Luther's Doctrine of the Right of Resistance to the Emperor," 133–9.]

19. [Cf. Hans Joachim Iwand, "Das Widerstandsrecht der Christen nach der Lehre der Reformatoren," in Iwand, *Vorträge und Aufsätze*, NW II, 193–229; Iwand, "Estate and Sacrament," in this volume.]

20. [Cf. Rupert Angermeier, "Moraltheologisches Gutachten über das Widerstandrecht nach katholischer Lehre," in *Die im Braunschweiger Remerprozeß erstatteten moraltheologischen und historischen Gutachten nebst Urteil*, ed. Herbert Kraus (Hamburg: Girardet, 1953), 33–6 (29–39).]

existence and nonexistence—that is something of which we will not be permitted to lose sight in Christian civic doctrine in the future. Thus, I see that 20th of July, a day in which an event almost unprecedented in the history of Germany and of Christianity among us illumined at the same time our failure and our hope in a flash, as the end of an era that leads to a radical reconsideration in view of the Christian's duty of resistance with regard to state authority—and has already led to this reconsideration in many testimonies and deliberations. As one example out of many, I cite a document that cannot be considered official but that was circulated in anonymous and illegal form in Holland during the occupation and exercised great influence in the church struggle [*Kirchenkampf*] in Holland.[21] It was drawn up in 1941 by a group of pastors and parishioners. There we find among other things concerning the state:

> We believe that the authorities in their turn are subject to the Lord of all things, Jesus Christ, by whose grace they exercise power. We believe that the authorities, too, owe obedience to Him, and that therefore in certain cases obedience to Christ may mean for the subject disobedience to the authorities. For we should obey God rather than men.

Therefore, we do not believe but reject as a deadly error, which may turn numberless people away from the Lord Jesus Christ, the idea that the authorities may ever have absolute power over their subjects. We do not believe that the authorities have the power and the right to ask for things which are against the laws of Christ, the Lord of the world. We believe that in such cases the authorities not only go beyond the limits of their office but also turn into their very opposite-anarchical tyrants. *Disobedience to such authorities in things forbidden to us by the Word of God is a glorification of God, to whom above all things we owe obedience. Christians have to accept for the Gospel's sake the suffering which will follow.*[22]

---

21. [From 1937 till winter 1940, a group of Dutch theologians initiated by Rev. Dr. Jan Koopmans formulated a number of theses in close connection with the Barmen Declaration of May 1934 but with an explicit rejection of anti-Semitism. In 1941, during the Nazi German occupation of the Netherlands, the pastors Dr. Jan Koopmans, Dr. Kornelis Heiko Miskotte, and Kleijs Hendrik Kroon wrote a kind of Confession of Faith "Wat wij wel en wat wij niet gelooven" ("What we believe and what we do not believe"), which says: "We believe it [= anti-Semitism] to be one of the most stubborn and most deadly forms of rebellion against the holy and merciful God whose name we confess," in *The Struggle of the Dutch Church for the Maintenance of the Commandments of God in the Life of the State: Church Documents*, ed. and collected W.A. Visser 't Hooft (London: S.C.M. Press, 1944), 81. This was in line with Karl Barth's dictum that anti-Semitism is "sin against the Holy Spirit" (Karl Barth, "Die Kirche und die politische Frage von heute" [December 5, 1938], in idem, *Eine Schweizer Stimme. 1938–1945* [Zürich: Theologischer Verlag Zürich, 1945], 90).]

22. [*The Struggle of the Dutch Church*, 85f (italics in the original).]

III.

It is quite striking that there is an almost universal condemnation of *tyrants* in the tradition of Christian theology. This is still the case in the scriptural interpretation of the Reformation. As far as I can see, this condemnation first begins to recede with the advent of the enlightened state after the wars of religion. Here, the Christians found themselves in agreement with the best of the pagans, with Plato, Aristotle, Cicero, and Quintilian. In dealing with the Roman pagans, Augustine, for example, relies precisely on these witnesses from their own midst to testify to the just state. But these Christians also found countless proofs in the Old Testament, beginning with Jotham's fable in Judges 9, where the trees wished to anoint a king over themselves, and all the noble trees, the olive tree, the fig tree, and the vine, refuse the honor because they serve God and people far more with their fruits than they would as king, until the honor falls on the bramble—up to the idol that King Nebuchadnezzar beheld, made of gold, silver, bronze, and iron, which was then broken in pieces by the "stone." "But the stone that struck the image became a great mountain and filled the whole earth" (Dan. 2:35). And Daniel gives the king of Babel the prophetic interpretation: "And in the days of those kings the God of heaven will set up a kingdom that shall never be destroyed. . . . It shall break in pieces all these kingdoms and bring them to an end, and it shall stand forever" (Dan. 2:44). It is understandable that this interpretation of Daniel is then seen as fulfilled in Jesus for Christians in the new covenant and thus that promise meets us anew in the book of Revelation (11:15) and in 1 Corinthians in the renowned chapter of the resurrection (15:24). Compared to the kingdom of God, all the other kingdoms of this world are temporal, and if Jesus is called *kyrios*, he is thereby the "Lord of all lords." That means that even the powers and authorities that rule here are already subject to him—whether they know it or not, whether they want it or not—from the perspective of their eschatological destiny. They are limited in him; they are sanctified in him. This is why the tyrant is the godless one who has no backing, for he rises up against his own creator.

Thus the Christian doctrinal tradition continues to differentiate between state and state. It did not allow the state as such to impose the concept of *justitia* upon itself; rather, the proposition that Augustine formed in *De Civitate* applies: "True justice, however, exists only in the republic whose founder and ruler is Christ. . . . But if this use of the term, which is ordinarily employed in other contexts with other meanings, is too remote from our usual way of speaking, true justice certainly exists in the city of which the Holy Scripture says, *Glorious things are spoken of you, O city of God* (Ps. 87:3)" (emphasis original).[23] This is precisely what the Protestant theologian Karl Barth meant to say when he entitled his small

---

23. [Italics in the original. Augustine, *The City of God* (*De Civitate Dei*), trans. William Babcock (New York: New City Press, 2012), Book II, Chapter 21, 59. "*Vera autem iustitia non est nisi in ea re publica, cuius conditor rectorque Christus est . . . Si autem hoc nomen,*

study on the doctrine of the state "Righteousness and Justice" [*Rechtfertigung und Recht*].[24]

Our earthly justice must mirror something of that righteousness, that righteousness of faith where grace is justice and justice is grace, which reigns in the kingdom of Christ and which is a truly human, humanitarian righteousness that also guards and judges people. The law of reason must not be made absolute; rather, it must be the speculum, the mirror of a higher justice and kingdom. But the concept of tyranny does not only concern justice; it also concerns the person. And here it is Thomas in his mirror for princes *de regimine principum*, which he wrote for a king in Cyprus, who conceives of the person as servant of the common good and brings that idea of service to bear in mapping the depiction of Christ the king, who put his majesty into service and thus turns *justitia* into life and peace and well-being for the people entrusted to him, onto the prince.[25] Even here, the notion of the tyrant comes up on its own: precisely because of the fact that the prince is only the liege lord of a divine office, the one who usurps power to himself forfeits justice. The tyrant on the throne is a contradiction in itself. This view persisted even in the *Reformation*, and even the proposition that the king is the servant of his state still emerged out of that view, only here the state and the raison d'état have taken the place of the people who carry them out.

It is frankly striking and most instructive that with the proclamation of human rights as a true, equivalent *être de raison*, some things that are not actually tyrannies seem now to be tyrannies that ought to be done away with. And so a new difficulty arises out of the new natural law emancipated from Christianity, a difficulty that pushes the churches entirely too much to the side of the conservatives and their restorations. But this is a topic in itself—the tyrant is something different in the ecclesial-biblical tradition than it is in the sight of the egalitarian state. And here lies perhaps a peculiar source for the profound crippling of the right of resistance that has taken place in the church, as no one wants to be suspected of a rebellion that unravels regulations.

---

quod alibi aliterque vulgatum est, ab usu nostrae locutionis est forte remotius, in ea certe civitate est vera iustitia, de qua scriptura sancta dicit: Gloriosa dicta sunt de te, civitas Dei!]

24. [The original title of this work in German "Rechtfertigung und Recht" could be most literally translated as "Justification and Justice." Here and in the following sentence Iwand depends on the German word play of "Rechtfertigung" (justification or being made/declared righteous), "Gerechtigkeit" (the state of being justified or righteousness), and "Recht" (justice or legal right). English is not able to retain this word play. The English translation of Barth's work bears the title "Church and State" to denote its general topic. Karl Barth, *Church and State*, trans. G. Ronald Howe (Greenville, SC: Smyth & Helwys, 1991).]

25. [Cf. Thomas Aquinas and Ptolymy of Lucca, *On the Government of Rulers—de regimine principum*, trans. James M. Blythe (Philadelphia: University of Pennsylvania, 1997).]

Thus, I might be able to summarize the critical points of the justification of resistance against state authority in this way:

1. Every true Christian resistance against state authority follows from a high and positive appraisal of the state. Christians are jointly responsible that the state, which should be a power in the service of justice and peace, is not perverted into its antithesis. The proposition that all power is evil must lead to power being surrendered to the evil. This is why Christians' participation in the state must all be in view of the fact that they are not afraid of this kind of ἐξουσία either, but rather that in it they perceive [*erkennen*]—that is, they recognize [*wiedererkennen*]—a "servant" of the God who is the Father of Jesus Christ. The word "You would have no authority over me at all unless it had been given you from above" (Jn 19:11) marks the power that bears Jesus to the cross as an innocent man to be a perversion. And yet through his witness and his suffering, it is given back to God, won back for him. This is why the resistance of the Christian—whether passive or active—is always aimed toward the goal of making the perverted state into what it is by nature, according to its purpose: *power* that serves *justice*.

2. Resistance against state authority cannot, insofar as it originates from Christians, disregard the difference between good and evil. That word in Rom. 13:2 is spoken against those who work against the authorities without regard to conscience. These will not only receive the judgment in themselves; rather, they will receive it here—this can also certainly be called "in themselves"—in the course of history. For resistance against the authorities is exactly not a mere dispute with people; rather, these people are in fact—even when they are not Christians but serve justice—protected by an authority that stands above them. They are indeed something like the masks of God.[26] And it is not in anyone's hand (this is the error of all modern revolutions) to transfer this authority—arbitrarily—to himself. In the end, this authority originates in the fact that the authorities are not beyond but rather within the bounds of good and evil. They are constituted as the authorities precisely by their making sure that this dichotomy does not become an arbitrary both-and.

3. Where the state no longer bears its sword to protect and reward the good and to punish the wicked, when on the contrary the wicked protect themselves with the sword and the good must appear to be villains—when Christ is numbered with the transgressors—then it is time to take the sword out of its hand. The sword does not belong in those hands. This means at the same time, however, that the state cannot determine of its own accord who or what is good and what is evil. Morality is not relinquished to the state but rather to the *society*. This is the mediating third party between church and state, and all Christian resistance against tyranny should have the positive

---

26. [Cf. LW 14, 114; 24, 37; 26, 95; WA 40/1, 174,12f.]

goal of being the salt with which a responsible society is conducted to its own civic responsibility and freedom—just as probably everything that we once procured for freedoms within the modern world cannot be thought of without sacrifice, which is rendered in resistance against unrighteousness and tyranny—whether these emanated from the improperly used power of the state or—the mind turns to Caiaphas—from the church that has apostatized from its Lord. In this sense, the time that we look back on and that is still in no way over for many Christians in their oppression by state authority is the time of a great planting. Even if we will not see the harvest here, it might still ripen internally, precisely in this Christian resistance, in the witness of the many who know themselves to be called to it, into the thing that we are hoping for: the state, which will always admittedly stand at the left hand of God but that stands at the left hand of *God*, not at the right hand of the devil.

Chapter 8

AGAINST THE MISUSE OF THE *PRO ME* AS A METHODOLOGICAL PRINCIPLE IN THEOLOGY

Originally published as Hans Joachim Iwand, "Wider den Mißbrauch des 'pro me' als methodisches Prinzip in der Theologie," *Theologische Literaturzeitung* 79 (1954): 454–8, also in *Evangelische Theologie* 14 (1954): 120–5.

*The theologians' meeting [*Theologentag*] from January 3 to 6, 1954, at the Johannesstift in Berlin gathered 150 professors and lecturers from the entire German-speaking area in East and West. In a short lecture, Iwand critically examined the neo-Protestant methodology up to Rudolf Bultmann's existential hermeneutics. Iwand wanted to show that for Luther the "pro me" is included in the "is-statements" (assertions) of theology, which should not be framed as mere matters of fact but as the promises of the gospel of Jesus Christ. Therefore, all statements about Christ are at the same time statements about his being "for me" and that the "pro me" belongs in the gospel.*

With Kant and in his wake, the "pro me" had acquired a completely different meaning, insofar as man now posits the unprovable existence of God in practical freedom "for himself." This restriction of the truth and relevance of the "pro me" to the epistemological realm implies that the statements about God's existence show a purely formal character and that a whole field of theological exploration of God's presence and working remains bare. In his postdoc thesis in 1927, "Rechtfertigungslehre und Christusglaube," Iwand had already shown that the doctrine of justification is an implication of faith in Christ and that the believer finds and grasps his life in Him.[1]
(CN)

I do not intend to give a polished presentation here.[2] Rather, I will be content if I can draw up a thesis that is not insignificant with regard to the principles of theological knowledge. I hope to do this by attempting to illustrate the recognition

---

1. [Cf. Hans Joachim Iwand, *Rechtfertigungslehre und Christusglaube: Untersuchung zur Systematik der Rechtfertigungslehre Luthers in ihren Anfängen*, 3rd ed. (München: Kaiser-Verlag, 1966).]

2. This chapter is based on a short presentation held at a theologians' meeting [*Theologentag*] in Berlin in 1954.

and the role that the *"pro me"* has played within Protestant theology *before* and *after* Kant and then comparing these two roles to one another. The thing about which I am concerned is showing that a fundamental transition has occurred in the theological meaning and the scholarly use of the *"pro me."* What I mean is that, to begin with, the Reformation *"pro me"* has a certain meaning with regard to its content and is an inseparable part of the gospel of Jesus Christ, "who was delivered up for our trespasses and raised for our justification" (Rom. 4:25), even as the expression later gained a formal significance and indicated the methodological distinction between two *kinds of knowledge*, one of which does not concern "me" as a person and is thus called objective and metaphysical knowledge, while the other impacts the existence of the person and presents me in the subjective sense as the subject of myself with the question of whether or not I wish to accept the existence of a supreme being as a religious union between the laws of nature and the laws of morality. In this formal or even existential sense, the *"pro me"* has been raised to the level of a methodological principle, which stands in the anteroom of revelation and decides broadly between two methods of knowledge: the tangible and the intangible, the objective and the "subjective," the uninterested and the interested knowledge. The *"pro me"* now comes to rest in the realm of *practical* reason or, we should rather say, it is included in the realm of *reason*, even if only in its practical aspect, and this methodological use of it henceforth distinguishes the knowledge of God from the knowledge of the world; it shifts the form of knowledge of all theological propositions—even before the content of the revelation has found its way to speech—into the realm of the subjective, which is to say of the practical. Perhaps it may be said that, at least from Albrecht Ritschl[3] through Wilhelm Herrmann[4] and up to Rudolf Bultmann[5] and Friedrich Gogarten,[6] this methodological use of the *"pro me"* is practiced and made out to be typically Protestant and that, beginning from there, they accomplish that

---

3. [Cf. Albrecht Ritschl, "Theology and Metaphysics," (1887) in idem, *Three Essays*, ed. Philip Hefner (Eugene: Wipf and Stock Publishers, 2005), 149–218. Albrecht Ritschl (1822–89) was the main representative of cultural Protestantism [*Kulturprotestantismus*], emphasizing the worldliness of the kingdom of God.]

4. [Cf. Wilhelm Herrmann, *The Communion of the Christian with God: A Discussion in Agreement with the View of Luther* (1886), ed. J. Sandys Stanyon (London, Edinburgh and Oxford: Williams and Norgate, 1895), esp. 173–7. Hermann (1826–1922) was a pupil of Ritschl who continued his thoughts and emphasized the heart as the place of the encounter and knowledge of God.]

5. [Cf. Rudolf Bultmann, "New Testament and Mythology," in *Kerygma and Myth: A Theological Debate*, ed. Hans Werner Bartsch (New York and Evanston: Harper and Row Publishers, 1953), 1–44. Bultmann (1884–1976) was a member of the dialectical theologians, who later advocated for a demythologization of the New Testament.]

6. [Cf. Friedrich Gogarten, "Conclusion," in *Demythologizing and History*, trans. Neville Horton Smith (New York: Scribner, 1955), 82–90. As Bultmann, Gogarten (1887–1967) was a member of the dialectical theologians until his split with Karl Barth. For a short time, he

identification of dogmatic = metaphysical propositions, which is set in front of the free development of theological-dogmatic conceptualization like a barrier that is not to be transgressed. What matters to me is to investigate whether this lock is the sort that the theologian only pushes back out of speculative willfulness because faith in God dictates that he should stop at the line that is drawn by it or whether it is a pseudo-limit that must be overcome and moved to a different location, which is the task of a theology of revelation. I might add that I think the latter and that, for this reason, a vast, long-neglected field of dogmatic knowledge and judgment opens up for us anew. For one does not simply feel compelled to establish such a thesis that breaks with a significant tradition in Protestantism without a good cause and only for the sake of breaking with a custom that was familiar up until now.

My thesis is intended to say that that "*pro me,*" if we wish to grasp it and comprehend it in its biblical-Reformation understanding, is an inseparable part of the election and justification that happens to us by God in Jesus Christ, that the "I" who is addressed here is not the same "I" that we come across in the realm of practical reason but rather the "I" of God's election that, hidden and determined in the story of Jesus Christ, expects to be taken hold of by me and made into the center of my self in faith. This is something like what Augustine expresses in his *Confessions*: "*ecce intus eras et ego foris . . . mecum eras et tecum non eram.*"[7] Or as we recognize it from Paul Gerhardt's passion hymn: "*Ach möcht ich, o mein Leben, an deinem Kreuze hier, mein Leben von mir geben, wie wohl geschähe mir.*"[8] Whenever the "*pro me*" cannot be harmonized with the other Reformation formula of "*extra me = in Christo*,"[9] then it is deprived of its theological, or perhaps one could say of

became a member of the German Christians [*Deutsche Christen*]. One of his major interests was the role of Christianity in secularization.]

In the original version in *Theologische Literaturzeitung* 79 (1954) it says: "up to Rudolf Bultmann and Friedrich Gogarten," while in *Evangelische Theologie* it only says "up to our days." Probably the editor at the time, Ernst Wolf, proposed this correction.

7. [Augustine, *Confessiones*, 10, 27.38, CCSL 27, 175, 11f; idem, *Confessions*, trans. Henry Chadwick, Oxford's World Classics (Oxford: Oxford University Press, 2009), 201: "And see, you were within and I was in the external world. . . . You were with me and I was not with you."]

8. ["Oh I wish, O my life, on thy cross here, I would give up my life, what good would happen to me." The word *mein* is highlighted in Iwand's quote.]

9. [Cf. Martin Luther, *Lectures on Romans* (1515/16), LW 25, 136; WA 56, 158,9: "[E]verything that is outside of us and is in Christ." Iwand interprets this *simul* in idem, *Rechtfertigung und Christusglaube*, 29, as identification and thus comes to his formula. Cf. also LW 25, 267; WA 56, 280,2-4; on Rom. 4:7: "For if the confessions of the saints are to be understood as only of past sins and that in the present they show themselves pure, why then do they confess not only their past but also their present sins? Is it not that they know that there is sin in them but that for the sake of Christ it is covered and is not imputed to them, so that they may declare that their good is outside of them, in Christ, who yet through

its Christological, content. The "*pro me*" does not belong to the *fides qua* but rather to the *fides quae creditur*,[10] or to say it better, beginning with the proper theological understanding of the same, this distinction of a twofold *fides* no longer matters.[11] All Christological propositions are *pro-me* propositions and vice versa, all *pro-me* propositions in theology must be interpreted Christologically.

The whole thing looks totally different if we understand the "*pro me*" as a methodological principle for the kind of propositions that have *God* as their object. Then, it is transformed into the form of a subjective knowledge, the kind that has the character of a decision in which, by my decision to say yes to the existence of a supreme being, the same decision falls "simultaneously" over my existence. In the "Dialectic of Pure Practical Reason," in his discussion of the "greatest good," Kant expressed himself more precisely concerning that which he calls the "subjective condition of reason,"[12] "the only way in which it is theoretically possible for it to think the exact harmony of the realm of nature with the realm of morals as the condition of the possibility of the highest good."[13] He speaks of a restriction of this judgment to the "subjective conditions of our reason"[14] and understands the manner of "its assent" [*ihres Fürwahrhaltens*][15] to be one of them. "[I]t follows that the principle that determines our judgment about it, though it is *subjective* as a need, is yet, as the means of promoting what is *objectively* (practically) necessary, the ground of a maxim of assent for moral purposes, that is, *a pure practical rational belief*."[16] For this reason,

> The upright man may well say: I *will* that there be a God, that my existence in this world be also an existence in a pure world of the understanding beyond natural connections, and finally that my duration be endless; I stand by this [. . .] and I will not let this belief be taken from me; for this is the only case in which

faith is also in them?" Luther names the scholastic alternative in thesis 27 of his *Disputation Concerning Man* (1536), LW 34, 133-44, 139; WA 39/1, 178,22f: "[T]hose say that a man 'in doing what is in him' is able to merit the grace of God and life."]

10. [Cf. Augustine, *De Trinitate*, 13.2.5, CCSL 50A; 26-31. Augustin differentiates the act of faith (*fides qua creditur*) and the object of faith (*fides quae creditor*).]

11. [Cf. Rudolf Bultmann, "What Sense Is There to Speak of God," *The Christian Scholar* 43 (1960): 213-22, 218f.]

12. [Immanuel Kant, *Critique of Practical Reason* (1788), trans. and ed. Mary Gregor (Cambridge: Cambridge University Press, 2015), Part 1.2, *Dialectic of Pure Practical Reason*, 87-118, here 116. Iwand eliminates the emphasis from the original.]

13. [Ibid.]
14. [Ibid.]
15. [Ibid.]
16. [Ibid., 117. Iwand eliminates the emphasis from the original.]

my interest, because I *may* not give up anything of it, unavoidably determines my judgment.[17]

And so this now is the decision of faith at which we arrive in our pursuit of practical reason, that because conviction [*Gesinnung*]—as Kant says—cannot be commanded, and thus is not an obligation, the person here on a *higher* level places the existence of God in practical freedom "for himself." For this is the only way to ensure the final unity between physics and ethics, and with it the reality of ethical principles in view of the world as such.[18] This is a faith in which *I* choose, in which I rise up in the last sense that is still comprehensible to reason to become a person in the sense of an "endless duration." If Kant speaks here of the realm of the "subjective," then he has left the concept of willfulness far behind. He has in mind a subjectivity that is not accidentally but rather necessarily the form of all propositions concerning God and his existence. This subjectivity is not underneath but rather over the kingdom of the objective and thus cannot be set loose from it or challenged by it. On the contrary, it is the highest peak of practical reason, in which it proves itself to be the epitome of an order encompassing nature and ethics in the sense of the greatest good.

It is obvious that the fundamental position of biblical-Reformation thought has been abandoned with this reinterpretation of the "*pro me*." Kant can say, "I will that there be a God" because by positing the existence of God, his own existence is also validated in the sense of a higher intelligible order. This is the new meaning that the "*pro me*" has now obtained and that Albrecht Ritschl later introduced to theology under the concept of the value verdict [*Werturteil*] as opposed to an existence verdict [*Seinsurteil*].[19] He believed that in so doing, he was able to rely upon Luther and Melanchthon and their rejection of "speculative" theology, as if following after them in a straight line.[20] Ritschl had a precursor in

---

17. [Ibid., 115. The omission is due to a sentence rearrangement in the English translation.]

18. [Cf. in this volume "Church and Society."]

19. [Cf. Albrecht Ritschl, *The Christian Doctrine of Justification and Reconciliation: The Positive Development of the Doctrine* (1874), ed. Hugh R. Mackintosh (Eugene: Wipf & Stock, 2004), 205: "But independent value-judgments are all perceptions of moral ends or moral hindrances, in so far as they excite moral pleasure or pain, or it may be, set in motion the will to appropriate what is good or repel the opposite." Ritschl, *The Christian Doctrine of Justification and Reconciliation*, 207: "In Christianity, religious knowledge consists in independent value-judgments, inasmuch as it deals with the relation between the blessedness which is assured by God and sought by man, and the whole of the world which God has created and rules in harmony with His final end" (emphasis in the original).]

20. [Cf. Hermann, *The Communion of the Christian With God*.]

Christian Ferdinand Baur,[21] who as a student of Hegel had already anticipated this interpretation of the Reformation faith as a faith of the principle of subjectivity.

It will not be possible to apprehend in its full significance the scale of the transformation that had thereby taken place without accepting that the question "*an Deus sit?*"[22] that determines Kant's whole thinking on this issue did not exist at all for the Reformers and for good reason. Luther formulates: "*homo non potest velle Deum esse Deum!*"[23] When he speaks of the existence of God, he speaks of God in this form. *Deum esse Deum!* Denying the existence of God is not-wanting for God to be God (*annihilatio Dei*).[24] Behind this stands the First Commandment. Luther comes to the opposite conclusion: the person cannot want God to be God. If he could want this, then he would have to recognize that even for him—thus "*pro me*"—God is God in the same way that he is in himself = in Christ. This is why for Luther, the "*pro me*" can be the victory and triumph of faith, because in faith I let God be my God in the way that he is by himself—*intrinsece*. That God is God is the epitome of his righteousness, which has been revealed in Jesus Christ "without the law." In the "*pro me*," this divine righteousness, the *justitia coelestis*, will be victorious and come to be recognized even in me, just as it has already been victorious over sin and death in itself—in Jesus Christ. This is why "my righteousness" in Christ precedes my existence. The person cannot want this naturally because in so doing, he is hindered to make himself into a moral being—as with Kant—but on the contrary, he must give up his ethical presumption in order to live in a foreign righteousness.

With Kant and the theological methodology inaugurated by him, the "*pro me*" becomes an epistemological principle in the sense of subjectivity, of the I that is always turned in (reflected) on its own existence. This seems to lead to a general

---

21. [Cf. Ferdinand Christian Baur, *History of Christian Dogma* (1858), ed. Peter C. Hodgson (Oxford: Oxford University Press, 2014), 354–60. Baur (1792–1860), Ritschl's tutor, was part of the Tübingen School and a pioneer of the historical-critical method in the New Testament.]

22. ["Does God exist?" The Latin word "an" introduces a question expecting a negative answer.]

23. ["Man is unable to want God to be God." Cf. Martin Luther, *Disputation Against Scholastic Theology* (1517), LW 31, 3-16,10; WA 1, 225,1f: "Man is by nature unable to want God to be God. Indeed, he himself wants to be God, and does not want Got to be God."]

24. [Cf. LW 25, 359; WA 56, 369,15-20: "Or is this not cursing—to think in our hearts that God is an enemy and adversary, to oppose Him in feeling and will, and, if possible, to take a stand against Him with all of our powers, indeed, of trying to destroy God and His will and change His will to be like ours, that is making it nothing? For to wish that someone be turned into nothing is the worst curse, which all the damned and those who have the prudence of the flesh hope for God."]

[The Latin addition within parentheses (*annihilatio Dei*) is added in the *Theologische Literaturzeitung* version only and means for Iwand the assimilation of God to human desires and ideas.]

distinction between faith verdicts [*Glaubensurteilen*] and existence verdicts. Yet in reality, this is the victory of natural theology and the formalism (*an Deus sit?*) that dwells within it, a victory gained by using the Reformation sign that was originally intended to mean something entirely different. The question of certainty of faith as a proposition concerning a supernatural reality pushes to the foreground and cuts itself off from specific dogmatics, to which the equally impossible and no longer decisive task falls of incorporating the revelation of God in Jesus Christ into a predetermined system of the non-objectifiable. It was unavoidable that this activity would only find success by means of reinterpreting the Christian doctrines as propositions about the human existence as such. In reality, dogmatics (faith and doctrine) is thereby deprived of its factual content in favor of reflection (faith and understanding),[25] something which no less than Hegel saw and said with great pain and an awareness of his powerlessness, in so doing making a change as a philosopher.[26]

Yet what is the "*pro me*" in its Reformation understanding and use? This is not the place to develop that in detail; it may suffice to cite a few theses from Luther's disputation "*de fide*".[27] There we find among other things:

Thesis 18: "*[Sed] vera fides dicit: Credo quidem filium Dei passum et resuscitatum, sed hoc totum pro me, pro peccatis meis, de quo certus sum.*"[28]

This could still be understood in the sense of the "value verdict." But the rationale that follows does not speak at all of a "detachment from the world;" rather, it applies Christ's action precisely to the world and its lost estate:

Thesis 19: "*Est enim pro totius mundi peccatis mortuus. At certissimum est, me esse partem aliquam mundi, ergo certissimum est, pro meis quoque peccatis mortuum esse.*"[29]

The "*pro me*" bears witness to the relationship of my existence to the world and thus becomes the mark of true faith:

Thesis 24: "*Igitur illud, pro Me, seu pro Nobis, si creditur, facit istam veram fidem et secernit ab omni alia fide, quae res tantum gestas audit.*"[30]

---

25. ["Faith and Understanding" is the title of a collection of essays by Bultmann in four volumes of which only the first one has been translated: Rudolf Bultmann, *Faith and Understanding*, vol. 1, trans. Louise Pettibone Smith (New York: Harper & Row, 1969).]

26. [Cf. Georg Friedrich Wilhelm Hegel, *Lectures of the Philosophy of Religion*, ed. Peter C. Hodson, vol. 3, The Consummate Religion (Oxford: Clarendon Press, 2007), 160f.]

27. [The following theses are taken from Martin Luther, *Theses Concerning Faith and Law* (1535), LW 34, 105-32, 109-14; WA 39/1, 44-8.]

28. ["But true faith says, 'I certainly believe that the Son of God suffered and arose, but he did this all for me, for my sins, of that I am certain.'"]

29. ["For he died for the sins of the whole world. But it is most certain that I am some part of the world, therefore, it is most certain that he died also for my sins."]

30. ["Accordingly, that 'for me' or 'for us,' if it is believed, creates that true faith and distinguishes it from all other faith, which merely hears the things done."]

With the declaration that he died "for the sins of the whole world" and for me as a "portion" of the world, a *decision* is made, an either-or that separates the true faith from all false paths to salvation:

Thesis 26: "*Pugnant enim ista duo, Christum pro nostris peccatis traditum satisfacere, Et nos ipsos per legem a peccatis iustificari.*"[31]

Thesis 27: "*Aut enim ille non est traditus pro peccatis nostris, Aut nos non iustificamur per legem a peccatis nostris.*"[32]

The *aut-aut* exposes two paths which in our modern understanding have *both* flowed into one. The one is the evangelical path that is apprehended from the obedience of faith, that bears witness to the sinner's solidarity with the world even as the other sets himself apart from the world, that is private,[33] that declares God's action "*for me*" and in so doing is "self-righteous." But that this *aut-aut* is not based on experience:

Thesis 28: "Scriptura *autem clamat, omnium nostrum peccata in ipsum esse posita, Et pro peccatis populi Dei est percussus, Et Livore eius sanati sumus.*"[34]

So what is that "*pro me*" of Thesis 24 that differentiates false faith from true? *In this "pro me," I take hold of God's predestination by recognizing and seeing myself as the one who I already am according to God's will revealed in Jesus Christ. In his history, I take hold of myself in my own story.* In this "*pro me*," the "upright" one does not opt for the existence of God as the guarantor of the reality of the moral idea; rather, I as a sinner[35] take hold of the decision of forgiveness that has fallen upon me from God. Only on the precondition of God's predestination in Jesus Christ is the "*pro me*" theologically meaningful. The "*pro me*" finds its permanent place where we allow the righteousness of God to apply to ourselves and work on ourselves apart from ourselves. The "*pro me*" belongs in the gospel. By making the content, *doctrine*, determinative for the method of knowledge again, that doctrine accomplishes the liberation of dogmatics from the shackles with which epistemic formalism has bound it by its misuse of the "*pro me*."

---

31. ["For these two propositions battle each other: Christ was delivered to make satisfaction for our sins; and, we ourselves are justified from our sins through the law."]

32. ["For either he was not delivered for our sins or we are not justified from our sins through the law."]

33. [The *Theologische Literaturzeitung* writes "personalistic" instead of "private."]

34. ["Scriptura" is highlighted by Iwand. "The Scriptures, however, proclaim that the transgressions of us all have been laid on him and he was smitten for the sins of God's people and by his bruise we are healed."]

35. [The words "as a sinner" are missing in the version in the *Theologische Literaturzeitung.*]

Chapter 9

ESTATE AND SACRAMENT

Originally published as Hans Joachim Iwand, "Stand und Sakrament," in idem, *Verantwortung für den Menschen: Beiträge zur gesellschaftlichen Problematik der Gegenwart*, ed. Friedrich Karrenberg and Joachim Beckmann (Stuttgart: Kreuz Verlag, 1957), 37–53.

After the Second World War, Iwand sought ways of conversion and renewal in church and society, which was an important impetus of his theology. He was driven by the question of theological co-responsibility for the rise of National Socialism in Germany and found the answer especially in the common modern Lutheran doctrine of the state. Iwand wondered how it was possible to abuse Luther to justify authoritarian regimes and if Luther himself could provide inspiration against the temptation of authoritarian political ideas.

In "Estate and Sacrament," Iwand first shows how Luther, in substantiating the sacrament in a similar way as the worldly authorities, is concerned with the fact that we are faced with God's action in both the one and the other. Just as the unity of word and element in the sacrament of baptism is the original (which cannot be separated into "sign" and "thing"), so too is the unity of God's Word and officials to be understood in his doctrine of estates. In the concrete "outside" of the visible event of baptism or the "action of office," the human being experiences God's salvific attention and care.

For Iwand, the problem with this analogy of Luther's lies in the fact that, in contrast to the element, human beings can abuse their divine commission. Iwand shows how Luther takes this problem into account by emphasizing the commandment character of God's Word, which shifts the emphasis to the right use: where God's Word is abstracted from, the order is no longer what it is, just as baptism is then no longer what it is. But God's commandment is the form for worldly life, which God has prepared beforehand, so that people can walk in them (Eph. 2:10). Therefore, the preaching of the law, critically related to public life, takes on such great significance as a force for the preservation of this very life. [CN]

In the section on baptism in Luther's Large Catechism, there is a highly curious commentary that, on closer inspection, raises a myriad of questions yet simultaneously—as we would also presume because of the didactic position that

Luther gave it—has had a significant impact on the question of church and society as it has been developed in Germany. The passage reads:

> Therefore, we constantly teach that we should see the sacraments and all external things ordained and instituted by God not according to the crude, external man (as we see the shell of a nut) but as that in which God's Word is enclosed. In the same way we speak about fatherhood and motherhood and governmental authority. If we regard these people with reference to their noses, eyes, skin, and hair, flesh and bones, they look no different from Turks and heathen, and someone might come and ask, "Why should I think more of this person than of others?" But because the commandment is added, "You shall honor father and mother," I see another person, adorned and clothed with the majesty and glory of God. The commandment, I say, is the golden chain around the neck, yes, the crown on the head, which shows me how and why I should honor this particular flesh and blood. In the same manner, and to an even greater extent, you should give honor and glory to baptism on account of the Word, for God himself has honored it by both words and deeds and has confirmed it by miracles from heaven.[1]
>
> I therefore admonish you again that these two, the Word and the water, must by no means be separated from each other. For where the Word is separated from the water, the water is no different from the water that the maid uses for cooking and could indeed be called a bath-keeper's baptism. But when the Word is with it according to God's ordinance, baptism is a sacrament, and it is called Christ's baptism.[2]

It is evident from the structure of this excerpt that Luther establishes and analyzes the "estate" [*Stand*] and the sacramental character of baptism in an analogous fashion. He proceeds according to the method of abstraction; he imagines father and mother, that is the particular bearers of the ruling authority, undressed, naked, apart from the command of God, and he finds there only "flesh and blood."[3] Here Luther runs into the principle of universal equality as the principle of pure abstraction, and he sees the dissolution of all ordinances, not only the proscription but also the annihilation of *authority*, emerge from there. I have spoken intentionally of the method of "abstraction." The concept that one reaches in this way, the concept of the mere person in his in-and-for-himself is for him not the true, historical person because that person is always in a particular relationship to the other through God's command. Luther regards the existence of the person in this case, in his being-in-the-world, not as if it existed for itself; rather, that existence is embedded in particular "institutions," "estates." Yet he does not perceive this embeddedness in a positivistic way as a natural relationship. Rather, he perceives it in such a way that "the commandment is added." The *commandment* is the "golden chain," "yes, the crown on the head." For the sake of the commandment, father and mother, even the governmental authorities can

---

1. [LC IV 19-21; KW 459; BSELK 1114,24-1116,2.]
2. [LC IV 22; KW 459; BSELK 1116,4-9.]
3. [Cf. LC IV 38; KW 461; BSELK 1120,13f.]

require *honor* from me; for the sake of the commandment, not simply for the sake of their own existence, do I honor them.⁴

Luther proceeds according to the same method in establishing *baptism* as "Christ's baptism," which is to say, a sacrament. Here, too, what matters for him is *honoring* baptism. Of course, as a sacrament he elevates it over above the estate and says that "in the same manner, and to an even greater extent, you should give honor . . . to baptism." But in the juxtaposition of "in the same manner" and "to an even greater extent" lies the problem of this method of operation. With baptism, too,

---

4. In his writing *Wider die Ächtung der Autorität: Eine politische Kampfschrift* (Jena: Diedrichs, 1930) and later in his *Politische Ethik: Versuch einer Grundlegung* (Jena: Diedrichs, 1932), Friedrich Gogarten transformed these thoughts of Luther in his own way into modernity. But with him the relation of a human being to the other, also the relation of the human being in his "estate" to the other, becomes a kind of divine *order*, very similar to Friedrich Julius Stahl [1802–61], who lived and worked a hundred years ago. The freedom of *God's Word*, which establishes or abolishes this order, falls away, and rather this order is understood from the antithesis to the modern concept of freedom politically, but no longer theologically. "The first here is to be attentive [*Hörigsein*] to the other" [Gogarten, *Politische Ethik*, 184], this freedom only has its meaning from being an attendant [*Hörigkeit*], from the responsible bondage to the other person. It is, so to speak, enclosed by this bondage" [Ibid.]. Gogarten wants to differentiate between a "freedom of being-in-and-for-oneself [*Freiheit des An-und-für-sich-Seins*]" and a "freedom of ever-being-for-the-other [*Freiheit des je Für-den-Anderen-seins*], the ever-being-from-the-other [*des je Vom-Andern-her-seins*]" [Ibid.]. Even from a purely philosophical point of view, one will hardly be able to justify these determinations, especially since they are based on a strict demarcation of the relation to nature and the relation to persons. Who would claim a freedom of being-in-and-for-oneself? Who has ever advocated it? Maybe Max Stirner, *The Ego and Its Own* (1845), ed. David Leopold (Cambridge: Cambridge University Press, 1995)—but neither Kant nor Fichte. And what about authority or what Gogarten calls "being an attendant [*Hörigkeit*]"? If I follow God's Word, which regulates the relationship of people to each other, this is a different "being attentive [*Hörigsein*]" than if I understand myself as being from the other! For God's Word creates *faith* in me and to that extent it is "author" of my being. But it is never the other to whom I am ever related to through the Word. For Gogarten, the commandment and the existence of man "from the other" coincide in such a way that the commandment is completely absorbed in this relation. Therefore, he can no longer critically *superordinate freedom* to bondage but must subordinate social or personal freedom to bondage. "This very bondage is the 'unassailable treasure of non-freedom,' without which freedom cannot be at all" (Gogarten, *Politische Ethik*, 184). This is in line with Gogarten's subordination of society to the state, cf. the chapter "Sozial oder politisch; Gesellschaft oder Staat" (147–52). It is true that the direction indicated here has suffered terrible shipwreck and has widely contributed to the delusion of Christians to follow this—false!—either-or, but I do not see where a *fundamental* correction of this whole terminology has taken place so far and where its origin from Luther or the Lutheranism of the nineteenth century has been examined as *critically* as these terms deserve in light of the catastrophe that has occurred. It is not done with the fact that we behave well "democratically" today.

Luther stands firm against the danger of separation: the enthusiasts [*Schwärmer*] take the external element, the water, in its being-in-and-for-itself. For them, the baptismal water is nothing other than the water "that the maid uses for cooking" or "water in the pot;"⁵ regardless of its divine establishment and institution, the baptismal event is regarded as a "symbolic" activity, the significance of which lies in the subjective, in "faith." Consequently, the problem of infant baptism arises for them. As a "problem," this is all foreign to Luther.⁶ For him, it is a matter of a divine *activity* that is taking place here and now, as it once took place by way of example in the baptism of Christ. For him, baptism is not a "churchly" activity, but rather— this corresponded to his anti-Roman view of the sacrament—our baptizing is *God's* deed, archetypically depicted in the baptism of Jesus when God opened the heavens and the Holy Spirit descended. This can be seen, moreover, in Luther's baptismal hymn.⁷ For him, the conflict concerning baptism must have become all the more significant. It must be understood as God's *action*:⁸ God in his majesty, as the triune Lord, is the one who baptizes, the one who dips the child into the font; the person who collaborates alongside God only provides his hands and his mouth, holds the child, and speaks the words. But God himself has baptized me! That is the only reason why the person can hold on to baptism, that is, to the divine promise. That is the Reformation view.⁹ That is why the water that God employs in baptism is something other than "plain water."¹⁰

   5. [Cf. LC IV 61; KW 464; BSELK 1126,29: "water in the creek or in the pot."]
   6. [Cf. LC IV 52; KW 463; BSELK 1124,8-10.]
   7. ["To Jordan Came the Christ, Our Lord"; LSB 406 and 407.]
   8. [Cf. LC IV 10; KW 457; BSELK 1112,15-17: "To be baptized in God's name is to be baptized not by human beings but by God himself. Although it is performed by human hands, it is nevertheless truly God's own act." LC IV 35; KW 460f; BSELK 1118,31f: "Baptism, however, is not our work, but God's work."]
   9. Martin Luther, *First Sermon on Baptism* (1538), WA 46, 145-151, 148,16-20: "For not the one who baptizes baptizes, . . . it is God's true and own doing. But because he wanted a manifest sign to be there, which could be seen and heard by the five senses, and because he himself cannot be seen." WA 46, 149,26-29: "I baptize you is not said about the baptizer but about the Trinity: *It baptizes* through a medium. The monks have neglected these signs, they thought that God would give them a special sign in the [churches'] corner, so they bind God to their devotion and special places. That is why there are so many orders" [emphasis added by Iwand.]
   Luther invokes baptism as a sign of the common priesthood against a special clerical estate. In his writing *The Babylon Captivity of the Church* (1520), LW 36, 3-126; WA 6, 497-573, Luther sets the freedom of baptism (LW 36, 74; WA 6, 538,28f: "supremely religious and most rich in works—the freedom of baptism") against all special vows (*vota*) (LW 36, 74; WA 6, 538,27f: "whether [. . .] religious orders, or [. . .] pilgrimages or [. . .] any works whatsoever") and substantiates with *it* as a sacrament that belongs to all Christians the *freedom* of the Christian to all worldly activities; LW 36, 74-81; WA 6, 538,35-543,3.
   10. [LC IV 14; KW 458; BSELK 1112,32-1114, 3: "Now you can understand how to formulate a proper answer to the question, What is baptism? Namely, that it is not simply

Here lies the parallel to the governing authorities, to the estates of fathers and mothers, whom God employs as "hands, channels, and means,"[11] much as he does with the water. "Therefore, we should not spurn even this way of receiving such things through God's *creatures*, nor are we through arrogance to seek other methods and ways" (on the First Commandment).[12] Luther manifestly believed that God employs a creaturely "thing" in the sacrament, just as in estate and vocation, in order to make out of it something totally different than our earthly senses perceive in it, namely a "divine, heavenly, holy, and blessed water."[13] These are the shocking words that make it look on first glace as if, in *baptism*, Luther teaches something like a transubstantiation of the water. The mere thought of such a "transformation" causes us to realize that we are on the wrong track here. If he were speaking of such a transformation, Luther would have been sliding far behind everything that he had taught earlier about baptism as *Testamentum Dei*.[14] Even here, for Luther it is first of all a matter of guarding against separation. Whoever says that the "water is water"[15] is *making a separation*. That is why Luther "admonishes" the catechism's readers "that these two, the Word and the water, must by no means be separated from each other."[16] In another passage, he understands this separation in such a way that when we separate these two, we "rip out his most precious jewel, in which God has fastened and enclosed his ordinance."[17] This means that *we* construct with our rational mind a "something" that does not exist at all, that is only constituted because of our "separating," that is to say, because of our mode of thinking that tears apart Word and creaturely means. Whoever would say that here—in baptism—we have before us only "bath water" or a "dog bath,"[18] "*balneum caninum*," that is the one who would no longer be operating in the reality of God's institution but rather in an abstraction fabricated by the "spirit."[19] The unity of *Word* and *Element* in the

plain water, but water placed in the setting of God's Word and commandment and made holy by them. It is nothing else than God's water, not that the water itself is nobler than other water but that God's Word and commandment are added to it."]

11. [LC I 26; KW 389; BSELK 938,32f: "Creatures are only the hands, channels and means through which God bestows all blessings."]

12. [LC I 27; KW 389; BSELK 940,1-4. Emphasis added by Iwand.]

13. [LC IV 17; KW 458; BSELK 1114,17.]

14. [Cf. Martin Luther, *The Holy Sacrament of Baptism* (1519), LW 35, 23-43, 33; WA 2, 730,20-22: "This blessed sacrament of baptism helps you because in it God allies himself with you and becomes one with you in a gracious covenant of comfort."]

15. [LC IV 16; KW 458; BSELK 1114,7f.]

16. [LC IV 21; KW 459; BSELK 1116,4-6.]

17. [LC IV 16; KW 458; BSELK 1114,9f.]

18. [Martin Luther, *Sermons on Holy Baptism* (1534), LW 57, 139-98, 157; WA 37, 642,17f.]

19. Luther regarded the concept of "spirit" coined by the enthusiasts as something diabolic. This comes out particularly clearly in the writing: Martin Luther, *Against the Heavenly Prophets in the Matter of Images and Sacraments* (1525), LW 40, 73-223; WA 18, 62-214. I quote only one passage for many others (LW 40, 147; WA 18, 137,11-19): "Do you

sacrament of baptism[20] is the *original thing*. It is not that there is a sensory sign given that *indicates* something or would become efficacious as a bearer of grace in a spiritual sense through the addition of the Word—that would be the scholastic classification of *signum* and *res* [sign and actuality] as it has defined the medieval doctrine of the Lord's Supper up until the modern day ever since the groundwork was laid by the Lombard.[21] In that scheme, the creaturely element is a visible *sign* that refers to an invisible, spiritual *res*, ultimately to the actuality of the *Christus praesens* in the Sacrament of the Altar. Here, the "outward" thing is understood spiritually. Wherever we may stand with regard to the *Quaestio juris* in this matter, we must first state that that is not Luther's view of the sacrament *in genere*; he had fundamentally broken with this view by his *Babylonian Captivity* at the very latest.[22] We have already indicated earlier that for Luther, the sacrament is the *action of God* himself, that the concept of the mystery in the sense of a "holy action" performed by men perceptibly fades away and the platonic scheme of visible and invisible, sensory and intelligible, world is eliminated from the foundation of the

---

not see here the devil, the enemy of God's order? With all his mouthing of the words 'Spirit, Spirit, Spirit,' he tears down the bridge, the path, the way, the ladder, and all the means by which the Spirit comes to you. Instead of the outward order of God in the material sign of baptism and the oral proclamation of the Word of God he wants to teach, not how the Spirit comes to you but how you come to the Spirit. They would have you learn how to journey on the clouds and ride on the wind. They do not tell you how or when, whether or what, but you are to experience what they do." For Luther this "Spirit" is here also associated with the dissolution of the civil order "that we may not have images, churches, or altars, that we may not use the word 'mass,' speak of a sacrament and its elevation, or wear chasuble instead of grey coats, and we ought to address one another as neighbor 'dear.' They advocate the murder of godless rulers . . . O wonderful saints! If you ask who directs them to teach and act in this way, they point upward and reply, 'Ah, God tells me so, and the Spirit says so.' Indeed, all idle dreams are nothing but God's Word. What do you think of these fellows? Do you fully grasp what kind of a spirit this is?" (LW 40, 147-48; WA 18, 137,23-138,1.138,6-9 [omission made by Iwand]).

20. [LC IV 18; KW 458; BSELK 1114,20-23: "This, too, is where it derives its nature so that it is called a sacrament, as St. Augustine taught, '*Accedat verbum ad elementum et fit sacramentum*,' which means that 'when the Word is added to the element or the natural substance, it becomes a sacrament,' that is, a holy, divine thing and sign."—Augustine writes: "*Accedit . . .* " (*In Iohannis evangelium tractatus* 80,3; Pl 35, 1840 = CCSL 36,529,5f).]

21. Cf. Mathias Joseph Scheeben, "Die Mysterien des Christentums: Wesen, Bedeutung und Zusammenhang derselben nach der in ihrem übernatürlichen Charakter gegebenen Perspektive dargestellt," in idem, *Gesammelte Schriften II*, ed. Josef Höfer, 12th ed. (Freiburg im Breisgau: Herder, 1951), 472–4.

22. [Cf. LW 36, 124; WA 6, 572,10-22. Ernst Bizer has recently made it likely that Luther's break with the Catholic teaching of the sacraments already happened in his lecture on Hebrews [1517/18]; Ernst Bizer, "Die Entdeckung des Sakraments durch Luther," *Evangelische Theologie* 17 (1957): 64–90.]

concept of the sacrament. As a result, the earthly givenness of creation receives a new formulation. It loses the metaphysic that stands behind it. It becomes a true "outside." Indeed, precisely *through* the Word of God, it becomes this indissoluble and indestructible "outward thing."[23]

And so—in order to do justice to what Luther was really trying to say—I wish to assert that the set of issues that has arisen around the concept of "outward thing" with Luther, just like his campaign against the dissolution of the "external world" that he waged against the enthusiasts and the modernity that arose with them, must be understood from the perspective of his dissolution of the established medieval metaphysic of *signum* and *res*. In the Middle Ages the *sacrament*, rather the overall sacramental character of life, determines the *doctrine of creation*. Things are inherently transparent, so to speak. They are according to their true essence "intelligible," culturally [*geistig*] speaking. The transposition of seeming existence into the spiritual real world is the great and comprehensive achievement of the Middle Ages, regardless of the misfortune that lies within it. It was the era of "Catholic idealism," behind which stood the rediscovery of Greek philosophy and its worldview [*Weltbild*],[24] which similarly stood behind Protestant idealism. Luther breaks with this traditional understanding of "thing," which is to say "*res*." Yet the "earthly *res*" are not accepted by him—somewhat in the sense of the later sensualism—as "things in themselves." Rather, they are the "means" through which God's outward-objective *dealing* with us is made possible. Of course, God deals differently here than where he deals with us immediately with his *Word*. These are, expressed Thomistically, the "*causae secundae*,"[25] that are the point of this "outward thing." Except that in Thomas, the doctrine of the Word as the "*prima causa*" is

---

23. [LC IV 7f; KW 547; BSELK 1112,3-6: "It is the chief cause of our contentions and battles because the world is now full of sects who scream that baptism is an external thing and that external things are of no use. But no matter how external it may be, here stand God's Word and command that have instituted, established, and confirmed baptism."]

LW 40, 148; WA 18, 136,17f: "For he wants to give no one the Spirit or faith outside of the outward Word and sign instituted by him."

Cf. Franz Lau, *"Äußere Ordnung" und "Weltlich Ding" in Luthers Theologie* (Göttingen: Vandenhoeck und Ruprecht, 1933). This writing is about the relation of the rational order (under God's Word) to the order of salvation, not that much about the special relation of outside and inside. One would like to hear more about this from the author.

24. [While the concept of *Weltbild* is only the reception of the world (cf. the Copernican *Weltbild*), the term *Weltanschauung* denotes a normative idea which is the basis of sense and meaning in this world and thus other than the term *Weltbild* very philosophically loaded. Cf. in this volume "Church and Society," Fn. 14.]

25. [The scholastic differentiation of a prime cause (of action) (*causa prima* or *primum movens*) and a secondary cause (*causa secunda*) recognizes the cooperation of God (*causa prima*) in the works of his creatures (*causae secundae*). Not only do the creatures need the help of God in the single works—that is what the teaching of "*concursus Dei*" (cooperation of God) means—but can only work on the basis of their being that they owe the creator.]

missing.²⁶ In short, the fact that the *"res"* means something different, something new for Luther, that there is a true *outside* for him, may properly be connected with his rediscovery of the *Verbum Dei*.²⁷ The Word qualifies the instrument of which God makes use.²⁸ In contrast to all the defenses of Luther's teaching on the sacraments that refer back to psychological sensualism, defenses that begin with the idea that man is hard-wired to be sensual and that for that reason he needs a "sign" that can be comprehended with the senses,²⁹ it is necessary to begin with the unity of the Word of God and *res* (in the doctrine of the sacraments) and the same unity of the Word of God and the person in an office [*Amtsperson*] (in the doctrine of the estates). The other interpretation, if followed consistently, would force Luther back into the same medieval view of the sacrament that he just overcame.

Regardless of this, it must be maintained that Luther sees the God-established relationship of the Word to the thing in the element of the sacrament or to the

---

26. Here the problem of "*concursus Dei*" is foreshadowed, which Karl Barth pointed out in such a splendidly new and essential way in his *Church Dogmatics*, vol. 3/3, ed. Thomas Forsyth Torrance et al. (London and New York: T&T Clark, 2004), under §49.2: "The Divine Accompanying."

27. [LW 36, 44; WA 6, 518,12f: "And so in baptism, to the words of promise he adds the sign of immersion in water."]

28. LW 36, 62; WA 6, 530,27-31: "Therefore beware of making any distinction in baptism by ascribing the outward part to man and the inward part to God. Ascribe both to God alone, and look upon the person administering it as simply the vicarious instrument of God, by which the Lord sitting in heaven thrusts you under the water with his own hands, and promises you forgiveness of your sins, speaking to you upon earth with a human voice by the mouth of his minister."

29. [This view is approached, for example, by Hans Lassen Martensen, when he understands baptism as a "visible sign" for God's covenant with mankind (idem, *Christian Dogmatics: Compendium of the Doctrines of Christianity*, trans. and ed. William Urwick (Edinburgh: T&T Clark, 1866), 423, [§252]). Erich Seeberg, *Luthers Theologie*, vol. 2, *Christus: Wirklichkeit und Urbild* (Stuttgart: Kohlhammer Verlag, 1937), understands "signs" as "indications that something is really there" and sees the difference to the Catholic view on sacraments in the fact that "Luther is determined by a dynamic metaphysics in his theology, whereas Catholic theologians mostly follow a substantial metaphysics" (318). Adolf von Harnack drew the consequence that Iwand feared, accusing Luther of a relapse into the Middle Ages because of his doctrine of the sacraments as means of grace and especially because of infant baptism, which could only be an *opus operatum* (cf. Adolf Harnack, *History of Dogma*, vol. 7, trans. William M'Gilchrist [Eugene: Wipf and Stock Publishers, 2020], 250f).]

For Luther's view, cf. LC IV 30; KW 460; BSELK 1118,4-8: "Now, these people [i.e. the enthusiasts] are so foolish as to separate faith from the object to which faith is attached and secured, all on the grounds that the object is something external. Yes, it must be external so that it can be perceived and grasped by the senses and thus brought into the heart, just as the entire gospel is an external, oral proclamation."

person in the estate as analogous. Whoever tears the "golden chain" off the *person* makes a division between that which is *one* before God just as sacrilegiously as the one who tears apart the *verbum* and the *elementum* in baptism. Whoever does the one, in so doing, also *eo ipso* does the other as an intellectual consequence. Through this "taking apart from one another"—through this process of abstraction that could be designated "rationalism"—man in his absolutization of man against God does something, accomplishes something, "works" something that Luther perceives as an indescribable horrible and that he designates *diabolical* in contrast to other *Anfechtungen* of faith and transgressions of man. Here he could no longer see man himself at work but rather a spirit "who is without flesh and blood," which "is the devil."[30] One could say unreservedly that in his doctrine of the sacrament, Luther campaigns against the "abasement of the external world." He knew that if it is lost, even the Word of God can no longer be the Word of God for us.[31]

Another question is *whether* he was correct in coupling the doctrine of the estates and the doctrine of the sacraments together as he has unscrupulously done in this battle. This is already a problem insofar as with the "estates" it is a matter of persons, whereas with the sacrament it is a matter of tangible things, what Augustine calls the "element."[32] The persons can abuse their divine "*ordinatio*," as the tyrant, the priest, the pope, and so on, do. The "element" can do no such thing. And yet in one regard I would like to contend along with Luther *for* the concurrence of the two phenomena. Luther saw *correctly* that here just as there— particularly in his campaign against Karlstadt and the Orlamünders[33]—the issue is one and the same phenomenon of "separation." It is possible to remove the Word of God from the estates of fathers and mothers, from the authorities, and so on, just as it is possible in the sacrament to strip the promise from the material of the sacrament in order to see what is "underneath." Nothing but water! Nothing but bread! Nothing but an ordinary person! All over the place for the "enthusiasts,"

---

30. [Martin Luther, *That These Words of Christ, "This Is My Body," Still Stand Firm Against the Fanatics* (1527), LW 37, 64-283, 136; WA 23, 261,35f: "But they want nothing but spirit; and indeed, this is what they do have: the devil, who has neither flesh nor bone."]

31. To Friedrich Julius Stahl, *Die lutherische Kirche und die Union: Eine wissenschaftliche Erörterung der Zeitfrage* (Berlin: Verlag von Wilhelm Hertz, 1859) is to be said in this point that the distinction of "divine and creaturely forces" does not have to be "abstractness." "Abstractness is precisely the complete divorce of the divine and the creaturely" (73). [With this Stahl characterizes the Reformed theology and sets in opposition to it "the interpenetration and interaction of divine and creative forces, the germination growth, the confident hope and trembling and trepidation" (Ibid.).]

32. [Cf. Fn. 22.]

33. [Andreas Bodenstein, called Karlstadt (1486–1541), first a companion, then an adversary of Luther, had become pastor in Orlamünde in 1523, where he developed a strong left-wing reformatory activity and was also in contact with Thomas Müntzer. During Luther's visitation journey through Thuringia, after he had expelled Karlstadt from the church, a sharp dispute arose between Luther and the congregation there.]

there is nothing underneath. Their own "spiritual existence" is the only thing that they leave untouched. That is what Luther fears; in this critical principle of abstraction he sees something looming that threatens to destroy church and society, family and state. In this comparison in which the later Luther—just escaped from the papacy—sees himself entangled, it is not a matter of blurring the distinction of human person and impersonal materiality like water or wine. No, this distinction that later became so important is, in view of the question with which Luther is dealing here, subordinated to a higher polarity. The Anabaptists are doing exactly the same thing with baptism, with their rejection of divine authority, as they are with the "estates," with their rejection of human authority. I admit that it is not easy for us to carry out such a conclusion by analogy along with Luther in our personalistic thinking, and yet for Luther, this conclusion seems to have arisen self-evidently out of his position against spiritualism. His thesis also arrives at the matter itself. Something of what he saw was really there among his opponents. Naturally, he magnified the germ that provoked this sickness as if under a microscope and, as was his way, transformed into his view on things. His spirit was simply "the battlefield of two ages" (Conrad Ferdinand Meyer).[34] Is it not part of the essence of *thinking* and of *doctrine* that intellectual aberrations are scrutinized in due time so that it may become apparent what is going on with such seemingly correct, harmless, clearly sophistic theses? Often even the proponents of such heresies themselves are hardly aware of this. If one wants to deny this sort of working out of the antitheses of theology and only leave that part of God's truth that is most easily accessible to us, world history and church history would soon progress only according to the law of pressure and impact. That this did not take place in the Reformation we attribute to the unfaltering insight of its most significant leaders.

But—and this "but" cannot be subdued—is Luther also correct when he draws out the consequences, positive consequences in his opinion, of his insight of this danger of "separation" and then lays them out in his Large Catechism, this textbook for church and state officials? Because of course, behind the draft of the Large Catechism there is something of a vivid picture of the Protestant understanding of the world. Our "but" begins at the point where Luther unscrupulously couples his doctrine of estate with the doctrine of the sacrament in such a way that the doctrine of the estates receives a sacramental dignity and, conversely, the questioning of baptism as a sacrament becomes a political issue. This coupling of sacramental and political argumentation extends further here than with the Lord's Supper. Whoever does not accept baptism is politically disreputable is the sort of person who is manifestly capable of wresting the crown from the head of the authorities. This is the *very* interconnection of throne and altar that Lutheranism

---

34. [Conrad Ferdinand Meyer, *Huttens letzte Tage* [Hutten's Last Days] (1871), Ch. 32: "Luther"
Sein Geist ist zweier Zeiten Schlachtgebiet — His spirit is the battlefield of two ages —
Mich wundert's nicht, daß er Dämonen sieht. I am not surprised that he sees demons.]

inherits. It does not reside in the place where one would commonly expect. It must be emphasized clearly over against all those who say that with the overthrow of the reigning Protestant polity in Germany and its ruling house, the harm had been eliminated from which the continuation of the Reformation suffered, in particular the "Lutheran Church" alienated by the "Prussian Union."[35] How is it even possible after these occurrences to say that one has arrived at the final word on the subject? Little or nothing is changed culturally through historical catastrophes that, taken in and of themselves, only appear to be negative. Something can only be changed at the point where in the face of such occurrences, real *insight* and *conversion* are brought about and we have the courage to apply our criticism at the point where it substantially belongs but not draw a shoddy conclusion from the collapse of a polity or the downfall of a dynasty. The defect that is intended with the interconnection of throne and altar may lie in the coupling of estate and sacrament. The bourgeois "estate" and "baptism" must not be fit into each other in such a way that the doctrine of the estates seems to be secured "sacramentally" and that an assault on baptism is conversely tantamount to an act of political revolution that the church—in service of the public order—needs to fend off.[36]

When Luther concludes in the course of his analysis of this "separation":

> But these fanatics are so blinded that they do not see God's Word and commandment, and they regard *baptism* as nothing but water in the creek or in the pot, and a *magistrate* as just another person. And because they see neither faith nor obedience, they believe that these things also have no validity (*et baptismus et magistratus nihil esse cogitur*). Here lurks a sneaky, seditious devil (*hic vero clandestinus*—white, shimmering, bright glowing!—*et seditiosus latitat diabolus*), who would like to snatch the crown from the rulers and trample it underfoot and would, in addition, pervert and nullify all God's work and ordinances. Therefore, we must be alert and well-armed (*advigilandum est!*) and not allow ourselves to be turned aside from the Word (*abstrahi!*), by regarding baptism merely as an empty sign (*non nudum et solum signum*).[37]

—a theological thesis thereby becomes so inextricably identified with a political one, determined to be fundamentally "diabolical and insubordinate" that the concept of *revolution* henceforth includes both at once: estate and sacrament.[38]

---

35. [For example, Friedrich Julius Stahl laments this alienation (Stahl, *Die lutherische Kirche und die Union*, 493ff [Book 2, ch. 2]): "On the Irreconcilability of the Prussian Union with the Lutheran Confessions."]

36. [For the consequences, see Hans Joachim Iwand, "Von Ordnung und Revolution: Das Thema in der ersten Hälfte des 19. Jahrhunderts," in Iwand, *Vorträge und Aufsätze*, NW II, 153–92.]

37. [LC IV 61-63; KW 464; BSELK 1126, 27-1128, 2. Emphasis added by Iwand.]

38. This is also the point where Ernst Troeltsch's criticism, which has not yet been answered satisfactorily, set in (Ernst Troeltsch, *The Social Teaching of the Christian Churches*

The concept of the "enthusiasts" is "dogmatically" determined, and Luther himself abandons the distinction of the two kingdoms at this point.[39]

In the sermons that Luther preached on "Holy Baptism" in 1534,[40] we find a curious reversal that is important for our inquiry. The vehemence against "the anti-Christian ancient archanabaptists, who have baptized themselves with their own works (here he means the subjective act of faith) and are still doing so"[41] has still increased. They are "desperate traitors and rogues indeed, who knowingly tear apart baptism, sever and cut off the two best parts of it—namely, God's Word and command."[42] Here Luther progresses further with his illustration of "separating" insofar as he implicates Christ in it. "Who could not say, 'How can Christ deliver me from sin, death, and the devil's power, if as you yourself say, He is a man like any other man?' Likewise: 'Why should I obey and submit to this man (such as my father, lord, or prince)? How is he different from me?' etc."[43] And here again it says:

> This crowd does the same thing with the most worthy Sacrament of Baptism when they regard only the water, as if God's Word and order were not present. To use a crude example, they act exactly as if you were to see the elector of Saxony walking in a black cloak after you had already seen the same cloak being beaten and dusted off in some tailor's shop, and accordingly you now decided,

---

(1912), trans. Olive Wyon, vol. 2 [Louisville and London: Westminster John Knox Press, 1992], 515): "Thus the conception of a State Church still remains the centre of the social doctrines of Lutheranism." "In Lutheranism this idea was not simply part of its religious and ethical ideal; it was essential to its very existence. Lutheranism realized that it could not stand alone; it was like some frail sapling which needed the robust support of a Christian State or a Christian Society if its pure spirituality were ever to bear good fruit."

39. If recently high ecclesiastical and political authorities devoted to them—see Harald Oldag in *Rheinischer Merkur* [a newspaper owned by multiple German Catholic dioceses]—again and again use the term "enthusiast" against the ecclesiastical-theological opposition, this is probably due to this uncritically accepted copula. For them, the church and the corporative state are *one* sacred thing. Cf. to this again Friedrich Julius Stahl, *Die lutherische Kirche und die Union*, X: "I hope to have shown that this unionism is nothing else than an ecclesiastical natural law after the manner of Rousseau's contract social, which lifts all positive and lawful elements of the church out of their foundation, and that it preserves the confession which it pretends to preserve just as constitutionalism preserves the monarchy and as pantheism preserves Christianity." This is the lasting accusation against the tendencies of the "enthusiasts" who are destroying the state and the church. It is only striking that these "enthusiasts" of today were almost the only ones across the board who did not fall for the enthusiasm of the "revolution from the right."

40. [LW 57, 139-89; WA 37, 627-672.]

41. [LW 57, 141; WA 37, 627,19f. The explanation between the brackets is added by Iwand.]

42. [LW 57, 146; WA 37, 632,3-5.]

43. [LW 57, 146; WA 37, 632,12-16.]

without another thought, to beat and slap it, and then said, "How is this cloth better than any other cloth?" Then you would certainly see what you had caused. They would promptly take you by the head and beat your rags to a pulp in turn, and maybe in addition cut off your button, as a malicious despiser of his royal person. It would not help for you to keep on saying, "I was not hitting the prince but the cloth" ... It is then no longer referred to as mere empty clothing or cloth, but both coat and man are together; indeed, it is a lordly, princely coat, since it is honored and worn by the prince himself.[44]

In this way, Luther wishes here also to expose those who "separate and sever the Word from the water."[45] Whoever blasphemes baptism and calls it a "dog's bath"[46] analogously makes himself guilty of *lèse-majesté*. For God has said that it should be regarded "as my (that is, God's) water,"

> [f]or my Word and command are in and with the water. . . . From this you ought to see what *person* this water has put on, and who is in it and with it—namely, the name of the Father, Son, and Holy Spirit—so that it is called the water of the divine Majesty. It must no longer be described as the kind of water that a cow drinks, for God clearly does not appoint His water (which contains His name and majesty) for the purpose of cows drinking it or pigs bathing in it, since it is not the creature or *person* that can be baptized and sanctified.[47]

We see: Luther wishes to avoid this equation of persons and things as it was present in the Large Catechism. Here what he means is more clearly and distinctly expressed. It is not the water itself that is venerated; it is not the water in itself that is holy.[48] Rather it is the majesty of the triune *God* who has chosen the water as "his" means and sign, not to give someone a drink or to wash something, but rather to choose the *person* for the salvific work of his divine majesty. But the question is still open if it is really permissible to transfer the image of the unremarkable cloth of the "princely majesty"[49] in Saxony to the baptismal water as the vesture of the divine majesty. Does the fundamental concept of state authority not thereby precede God's authority? Indeed, Luther knows that this image is somewhat dubious and so he gives only a "crude example." Since the enthusiasts have the masses on their side, he must also use vivid language regardless of the resulting conceptual difficulty. But the analogy as such is simply fatal. The authority of the "elector of Saxony" is not as unfailing as the authority of God in his promise. Further, we see that for Luther it is not about the "element" but about us not

---

44. [LW 57, 146f; WA 37, 632,25-633,3.]
45. [LW 57, 147; WA 37, 633,5.]
46. [LW 57, 147; WA 37, 633,11.]
47. [LW 57, 147; WA 37, 633,12-14, 15-22. Emphasis added by Iwand.]
48. [Cf. SA III.5.2; KW 319-320; BSELK 766,9-12.]
49. [Cf. "royal person" LW 57, 146; WA 37, 632,35.]

despising and blaspheming the action and *presence* of God under this sign just as the proposition that "Jesus is just a man (like us)" can be the greatest blasphemy of God even though the proposition as such is true. Wherever it should thereby be denied that God is in the midst of us in Jesus Christ, the allusion to the "mere man" becomes heresy. The manner of speaking of the "mere water" and the "mere man" in this case of the father's estate, which is to say that of the prince, affects Luther similarly. Both seem to him to be an expression of a profoundly godless approach. God is present all over in his Word, but we inspect the signs of his presence, and insofar as they are "outward," be it in sacrament, estate, or office, we declare: there is nothing underneath! "In the third place, the Epicureans are making incursions with a special mode of baptizing (*which amounts to nothing*)."[50]

Moreover, in this sermon there is a certain correction of his earlier illustrations that we perhaps already noticed when Luther says that the enthusiasts "sever and cut off the *two* best parts from it."[51] Previously he had spoken of the *one* part, the Word of God. What, then, are the "two" parts, and why did he not remain with the simple distinction of word and element? For him now, the two pieces are the sacramental Word and the baptismal command. Luther comprehends—as far as I can see, this is a crucial point—that the word that he had valued up until this point, the "*Accedit verbum ad elementum*" that Augustine had formulated in light of Jn 15:3 ("Already you are clean because of the word that I have spoken to you"), was not sufficient. Indeed, this dictum is in no way typical even for Augustine's doctrine of the sacraments; it had simply helped Luther quite a lot at the beginning of his campaign against the Roman doctrine of the sacraments. Why is the quotation from Augustine not sufficient in the face of the enthusiasts? Because even Augustine devalues the outward occurrence of the sacrament, particularly with the clause that he appends: "*non quia dicitur, set quia creditur.*"[52] Luther has to defend himself against the supposition that "the Word with the water is not efficacious for *producing* a Baptism *until* our faith is added to it; thus God's Word and work would first have to receive its power and effect from us."[53]

But this is not yet the most significant thing. Rather, the most significant thing is as follows: the mere addition of the Word to the element cannot clearly distinguish the occurrence that we are dealing with in baptism from other human-sacral consecrations. God must be unambiguously emphasized as the *subject* of the *baptizing*. We baptize on his *command*. God *makes* the baptism into what it is; that is why it is called a sacrament. The words of institution are spoken; they stand before us as a sort of earthly givenness. But they are more than that. The "scriptural Word" *presupposes* the "living" Word, the "command." The *command* of God stands over every single baptism specifically. This is how Luther distinguishes between word of institution and divine command; only the two together now provide him

---

50. [LW 57, 141; WA 37, 627,20f. Emphasis here and in the following added by Iwand.]
51. [LW 57, 146; WA 37, 632,4.]
52. [See Fn. 22. "not because it is given, but because it's believed."]
53. [LW 57, 148; WA 37, 634,26-28.]

with the proper position for substantiating baptism. Word and sacrament might "combine" elsewhere, all false sorceries and consecratory actions result from this interpenetration. "Why do we not make a sacrament out of holy water and salt, all monks' and nuns' cowls, and the candles of Saints Blaise and Agatha—indeed, from every manner of blessing and incantation?"[54] Now the *Verbum* in the sacrament is doubled for him. God himself must speak it—his *command* must be present—or else the "word" is given over into the hands and willfulness of men.

> If you can add in the fact that the divine Majesty in *heaven says* (present tense)[55], 'I have ordered and commanded it (perfect tense),' those two parts conclude and make valid what is called *a Sacrament*. Otherwise (as I have said) anything a man might imagine could be a Sacrament. There is no one too simple to take God's Word into his mouth, apply it to a created thing, and *make* something with it.[56]

Here it becomes clear that Luther is not speaking of a magical transformation of the creature, thus of the element, in baptism. Baptism is not a "consecratory action," and its meaning is not to be deduced from the interpenetration of Word and creature (element). Even more becomes clear: Luther rejects the severing of the enthusiasts. But what was the *unifying* thing that is abolished with this severing? What was that living unity out from which people were abstracting? Evidently the one Word of God in the form of the "command." Herein lies the key that helps us along in our inquiry. In the parallelizing of sacrament and estate, Luther was not thinking about the sacramental word that the priest speaks; he did not wish to make out of governing authorities and the household a sort of profane sacrament for the purposes of the bourgeois world—even though it did come to that—rather, he wanted to emphasize the *command character* of the Word of God, or even more precisely, its *present-tense* form. God's command—as what that remains to be seen—stands over church and society, that is to say over its "order," at the same time! It stands over them as the great promise of *life*, under which all men live out their existence according to his finite and eternal determination at the same time. With this parallelizing of sacrament and estate, Luther probably meant to say that—wherever one abstracts out from God's Word—the creature is no longer what it is; then all that remains is the theorem: water is water and man is man. Luther's peculiar and ambiguous thesis begs to be understood neither as law nor as positivistic supposition but rather as promise, as the promise of God's presence and his good pleasure over the actions of men in church, state, and home.

But what is the deal with Luther's doctrine of the *estate*? It has more often been the case that this position, continually discussed with both favor and

---

54. [LW 57, 150f; WA 37, 636,23-26.]
55. [This and the very next bracket within the quotation are added by Iwand.]
56. [LW 57, 151; WA 37, 636,34-637,2.]

disfavor, has been the subject of value judgments[57] than that someone has striven to do an *analysis* of its provenance and genesis with Luther.[58] Often it appears as if he had borrowed the medieval doctrine of the estates and carried it on in secularized form. Whoever thinks in this way may well go astray. Admittedly, the positivistic movement of the order of the estates prevailed in the wake of Luther's development, but this was not the case in the beginning. It could be the case here that an originally *true* approach was bent and driven in a perverse direction through the subsequent struggles, through the fact of the unsuccessful joint-German Reformation. Only the one who considers the Reformation to have been rectilinear according to its historical course will derive its final social organization from "pure doctrine." That does not correspond to the historical state of affairs.

57. Cf. John Neville Figgis, *Studies of Political Thought: From Gerson to Grotius: 1414-1625* (Cambridge: Cambridge University Press, 1907). Figgis, one of the most astute critics and best experts of the theories of the state in the late Middle Ages, parallels Luther with Machiavelli (62ff). Similarly, the comment by Troeltsch, *The Social Teachings*, 552: "Even at the present time the followers of Darwin, despotic politicians, and masterful men get on better with Lutheran conservatives than with the representatives of Liberal ethical individualism. The main features of the conservative doctrine of the State and of Society have been foreshadowed in Luther's theory, and the 'Christian worldview' of our Conservatives in its most important political and social sections is based upon Luther's positivist and realistic conception of Natural Law."

Karl Holl's attempt to refute this view by his investigations of Luther himself [Karl Holl, "Der Neubau der Sittlichkeit," in idem, *Gesammelte Aufsätze zur Kirchengeschichte*, vol. 1, *Luther*, 7th ed. (Tübingen: J. C. B. Mohr, 1948), 155–287] is only partially successful, especially since Holl did not include in his investigations the older Luther enough and Lutheranism and its social teachings at all. This may also explain why Holl's students—with a few exceptions—stood on the wrong side in 1933.

For the doctrine of vocation and estate, cf. Christoph Ernst Luthardt, *Geschichte der christlichen Ethik*, vol. 2 (Leipzig: Dörffling und Franke, 1889), 28ff, where we find the scheme of inside-outside carried out in purity [see also 15ff]. Further Karl Holl, "The History of the Word Vocation (Beruf)," trans. Heber F. *Peacock, Review & Expositor* 55 (April 1958): 126–54. He provides a good presentation of the doctrine of the medieval doctrine of society determined by the monasticism. Recently Gustav Wingren, *Luther on Vocation* (1952), trans. Carl. C. Rasmussen (Eugene: Wipf and Stock Publishers, 2004) has given his account of this doctrine, however, limited to Luther, with abundant source material.

58. Although Ernst Troeltsch (and after him Georg Wünsch [cf. idem, *Die Bergpredigt bei Luther: Eine Studie zum Verhältnis von Christentum und Welt* (Tübingen: J. C. B. Mohr, 1920), 99; idem, *Evangelische Wirtschaftsethik* (Tübingen: J. C. B. Mohr, 1927, 546)]) saw that the Decalogue plays a decisive role in the development of this doctrine of the estate for Luther, as well as the influence of the Old Testament, the deeper meaning of this fact is not clear in Troeltsch. It [i.e., the meaning] is probably connected with the exceptional position of the Old Testament to the world, which, unlike all other religions of salvation, does not know asceticism and monasticism.

Precisely the early form of Luther's doctrine of the estate is the best critique of its later conservative vulcanization. Luther's doctrine of the "estate" is inextricably bound to his interpretation of the *Decalogue*. In this Errnst Troeltsch[59] is correct. But Troeltsch did not take into account the motivation, the creative interpretation that Luther brings to fruition in it.

The beginning may be found in the *sermons* on the Ten Commandments that "Luther preached from the end of June 1516 until Carnival 1517 amid great crowds of people."[60] Here we find already the beginning of his later doctrine of the estate. Indeed, in this first attempt at a "practical theology" of "justification by faith alone," we still find old mixed with new. Luther proceeds gently. He wants to display the transgressions of the commandments as sin against *God* and place the *remissio peccatorum* first and foremost. It is a preaching of the law starting from the gospel. But everything is still comprehended in a process of reconstitution. The saints and their stories are still valid—even if they recede into second place—as ethical examples, and the medieval catalog of virtues and vices is likewise interpreted positively and casuistically as he still frequently does in that era. Something is taking shape that emerges in the first interpretation of *The Seven Penitential Psalms*[61] in the German language and with a totally new attitude toward life and the world with profound religious force and poignant power of speech. The breakthrough prepared by German mysticism from the realm of a detached religious existence into the real world and practical life is taken up by Luther and incorporated into the work of his Reformation. "God is equally near in all creatures," preaches Meister Eckhardt.[62] "For a man to have a peaceful life—lived in God—[63] is good, but for a man to have a life of pain in patience is better; but that a man should have peace in a life of pain is best."[64] And, "Now, all reasonable people, take heed! The fastest beast that will carry you to your perfection is suffering."[65] Luther sees the actuality of the world in precisely this way; for him, it exists under the sign of the unpredictable, of the cross, and of the coming-into-being-formed-from-somew here-else while the monastic way of life into which he placed himself seemed to be

---

59. [Troeltsch (1865-1923) was one of the most important theologians of the school of history of religions and liberal theology.]

60. Joachim Karl Friedrich Knaake, "Einführung" *Decem praecepta Wittenbergensi praedicata populo* (1518), by Martin Luther, WA 1, 394.

61. Martin Luther, *The Seven Penitential Psalms* (1517), WA 1, 154-220.

62. ["Sermon 69: *Scitote, quia prope est regnum dei* (Luke 21:31)," in Meister Eckhart, *The Complete Mystical Works of Meister Eckhart*, trans. and ed. Maurice O'C. Walshe (New York: The Crossroad Publishing Company, 2009), 352-6, 353.]

63. [This qualification is added by Iwand.]

64. [Meister Eckhart, Sermon 69, 353.]

65. [Treatise, "Detachment," in Meister Eckhart, *The Essential Sermons, Commentaries, Treatises and Defense*, trans. Edmund College and Bernard McGinn, The Classics of Western Spirituality (New York: Paulist Press, 1981), 294.]

"self-selected holiness."[66] The self-selected part of this is intolerable to him. It is the world of *man*, even if of the pious, the spiritual man, in which he is moving about. But the Decalogue calls him out into God's world to the "good works" that are not possible in the present way of life. The "self-selected" estate conceals for him the actuality into which *God* has called and elected him, where man must follow him and God will become his master on the unknown path of his life.

> Behold, that is the path of the cross, you cannot find it, but I must lead you as one who is blind. Therefore not you, not a man, not a creature, but I myself will instruct you in the way wherein you shall walk. Not the work that you choose, not the suffering that you dream for, but what befalls you against your choosing, thinking, desire, then follow, then I call, then be a disciple, then it is time, your master has now come.[67]

It is the "unsecured" and, as such, the true life into which God's *vocatio* calls the man [cf. 1 Cor. 7:17f]. The new understanding of the command of God, the command understood as promise, helps Luther to overcome the separation of the kingdom of God and the world; he thereby overcomes the distinction between ideality and reality, and he overcomes it because it is only in that way that the *doing* of good works becomes possible. The dualistic distinction of the two realms thereby becomes void that marks off a particular domain of the world because the realization of the will of God is not possible within it. The Decalogue works like an outstretched arm that points the pious person into the world as the site where the good works of God *should* take place and *can* take place! If Luther later attacks the enthusiasts so passionately, it is because they also want to create particular preconditions for the kingdom of God to be able to come into the world. They are yearning to go back to the "gray garb"[68] and the "camel's hair" from the baptist's vesture [Mt. 3:4 par.].

The Decalogue, however, references "works, which God prepared beforehand, that we should walk in them" (Eph. 2:10). Luther offers the classic depiction of these "good works" in 1520 in his writing of the same name, in which he sketches the *ethic* of the Reformation on a foundational level for the first time in a way that is for the people and also truly reformatory for the whole understanding of marriage, society, and state.[69] The dreadful thing about this simple and straightforward writing is this: everyone now finds the fullness and multiplicity of good works quite near to himself. All he needs to do is reach out his hand; they are there! They

---

66. [LW 40, 83; WA 18, 65,28-30: "For they do not accept what God gives them, but what they themselves choose. They wear gray garb, would be as peasants, and carry on with similar foolish nonsense." See also LW 40, 148; WA 18, 138,1f.]

67. WA 1, 172,1-7, on Ps. 32:10.

68. [Cf. LW 40, 81; WA 18, 64,6 et al. The gray garb is the peasant's robe as a symbol of the simple life.]

69. Martin Luther, *Treatise on Good Works* (1520), LW 44, 15-114; WA 6, 202-276.

can take place and they do take place! They are nothing special. Good works have no name.

But the *estate* is the *form* that is not created by man but rather predefined from God, the form within which these good works take place.[70] This is why it must be so strictly delineated over against the "holy" estates established by men because these are the form and expression of a self-selected pious life. In contrast to this, the "estate" established by God is common to all men, Christians *and* heathens. By Christians "undergoing" such a life, by the monk entering into marriage and by the one who is so called shouldering the agonizing struggles and sufferings of governance and public service, they live *incognito*, seemingly equal to the world; they have no *specific* holiness in comportment or way of life because the estate in which they live and work is not a specifically Christian way of existence but rather one that is designated for all men by virtue of the creation and the command. If we do *not* undergo this, then "good works" are not possible in the sense in which God has commanded and promised them. Then our being-pious will aspire to express itself in exceptional deeds and actions and be aligned with an isolated, special holiness—which must always lead to the most people separating themselves off and the men of this world, entangled in their tasks, sufferings, and struggles, saying: if I could live in such a religiously protected realm, then I could also be "pious," but as a man of this world, I cannot do it. This difference between the pious people separated off from the world and the men of the world falls with this new understanding of the "good work."

Here the *estate* receives its profound authorization—not in the sense of the "corporate state *[Ständestaat]*" but rather in the sense of a predefined *form* within which the good works take place that are common to Christians *and* to heathens. The practical life and work of Christians in the world thereby become *meaningful speech* that even the heathens understand. Of course, there is still one difference: for the Christian, God's Word stands *over* his estate and calling and transforms the "natural" judgment through which the heathens miss the proper application of their estate, its happiness and its honor. This is nowhere clearer than with the "estate of marriage." It is not a matter of the consummation of marriage; rather, it is a matter of the proper *recognition* of what it means in grace. Reason and faith have a totally different *valuation*.

---

70. [Luther emphasizes the foundational nature of the estates, which is grounded in God's commandments; cf. Martin Luther, *Confession Concerning Christ's Supper* (1528), LW 37, 261-509, 365; WA 26, 505,7-13: "For these three religious institutions or orders are found in God's Word and commandment; and whatever is contained in God's Word must be holy, for God's Word is holy and sanctifies everything connected with it and involved in it. Above these three institutions and orders is the common order of Christian love, in which one serves not only the three orders, but also serves every needy person in general with all kinds of benevolent deeds."]

> [W]hen that clever harlot, our natural reason (which the pagans followed in trying to be most clever), takes a look at married life, she turns up her nose and says, "Alas, must I rock the baby, wash its diapers, make its bed, smell its stench, stay up nights with it, take care of it when it cries, heal its rashes and sores, and on top of that care for my wife, provide for her, labor at my trade, take care of this and take care of that, do this and do that, endure this and endure that, and whatever else of bitterness and drudgery married life involves? What, should I make such a prisoner of myself?"[71]

Over against that Luther lays out the Christian faith:

> It opens its eyes, looks upon all these insignificant, distasteful, and despised duties in the Spirit, and is aware that they are all adorned with divine approval as with the costliest gold and jewels. It says, "O God, because I am certain that thou hast created me as a man and hast from my body begotten this child, I also know for a certainty that it meets with thy perfect pleasure. I confess to thee that *I am not worthy* to rock the little babe or wash its diapers or to be entrusted with the care of the child and its mother."[72]

The heathens, however, "are blind." They "fail to see that their life and conduct with their wives is the work of God and pleasing in his sight."[73] If they saw *this*, "that it is good pleasure of their beloved Lord, they would be able to have peace in grief, joy in the midst of bitterness, happiness in the midst of tribulations, as the martyrs have in suffering."[74] Luther calls this "correctly recognizing and regarding God's work and creature."[75] This can only mean that the estate in its true essence will only be discovered through a particular recognition and a *life* that is in conformity to it, that it will only be emphasized in its divine determination, that we will not be able to "grasp" what we are dealing with here by "reason" but only by faith. Such a person sees God's *good pleasure* over his estate and lives out of that confidence. "We err in that we judge the work of God according to our own feelings, and regard not his will but our own desire."[76] By virtue of the commands, God's good pleasure stands over the estate of marriage, over the earthly authorities just as over all the estates that serve the formation of men and labor. "I say these things in order that we may learn how honorable a thing it is to live in that estate which God

---

71. [Martin Luther, *The Estate of Marriage* (1522), LW 45, 11-49, 39; WA 10/2, 295,16-23.]

72. [LW 45, 39; WA 10/2, 295,27-296,6. Emphasis here and in the following added by Iwand.]

73. [LW 45, 38; WA 10/2, 295,1f.]

74. [LW 45, 38f; WA 10/2, 295,6-8.]

75. [LW 45, 41; WA 10/2, 297,8-10: "There was a true Christian, who correctly recognized and regarded God's work and creature."]

76. [LW 45, 39; WA 10/2, 295,9f.]

has ordained. In it we find God's word and good pleasure, by which all the works, conduct, and sufferings of that estate become holy, godly, and precious."[77]

From all this the following become clear:

1. That Luther does not abandon the monastic life because he did not attain to the perfection of a "saint" that was set up there as the aim but rather because he recognizes that this aim of perfection is pointing in the wrong direction. The command of God points the Christian into the earthly estate and calling. *Only* there are good works possible. He does not resign from the [monastic] order; rather, he abolishes the order as a Christian lifestyle. This is why it is not an accident that alongside his writing *"On Good Works"* there is the renunciation of the "godless" estates in *"De votis monasticis,"*[78] a writing bearing significance as a counterpart to the doctrine of the estates that must not be undervalued.
2. That the estates are "used" in the same way by heathens and Christians, that there is no "Christian" society, no "Christian" state; rather, Christians and heathens fulfill their callings and perform their work in the same way of life. But for faith the *good pleasure* of God nevertheless stands over that way of life. Thus, here commandment is not primarily to be understood as law and task but rather as *gift*, as *happiness* and *joy*. "Nothing is so bad, not even death itself, but what it becomes sweet and tolerable if only I know and am certain that it is pleasing to God."[79] God's good pleasure stands over the estate like the star of Bethlehem over the cradle. What I do in faith in this estate is a *good* work, even if it seems so banal and ordinary from outside.
3. That there remains nevertheless a crucial difference between the one who *believes* and the heathens who judge the estate and the deeds that they are to perform according to their "feeling" and are not able to recognize the same work of God in the lowly and despised things, in the sufferings and tribulations. Only faith in God's Word and command brings out the mystery that is stored within the "estate," discovers it and displays it in thankfulness. Thus, even here we still encounter a bit of that *Theologia crucis*, according to which the gift and power that God has placed in lowliness is still concealed from human eyes and the selfish mind. And so the "estate" proves to be a gift that is not measured according to the *Lex naturalis*[80] but rather according to

---

77. [LW 45, 41; WA 10/2, 297,16-19.]

78. [Martin Luther, *The Judgment of Martin Luther on Monastic Vows* (1521), LW 44, 243-400; WA 8, 573-669. Cf. LW 44, 294; WA 8, 603,40f: "It appears, however, that God in his mercy works against them to keep them from attaining their goal of perfection, that is, the peak of godlessness."]

79. [LW 45, 39; WA 10/2, 295,12-14.]

80. [Melanchthon adopted this view of natural law (*lex naturalis*); cf. Werner Elert, *Morphologie des Luthertums*, vol. 2, *Soziallehren und Sozialwirkungen des Luthertums* (München: Beck'sche Vertragsbuchhandlung, 1932), 32.]

God's yes, that is, according to his unquestioned good pleasure established with the commandment as it is recognized and properly used by faith.

But who determines the proper use? That is the task of the "preaching of the estates," if you will—at any rate, of preaching in its living use that relates to praxis and man's life in state and society. The Word of God never coincides with the estate in such a way that it could not—or further, did not need to—be directed against the bearer of the estate. Herein lies the difference between the estate and the sacrament. With the sacrament there is no such conflict.

Since the Word of God and the estate do not simply coincide, one can understand the sharp societal critique that runs through all of Luther's sermons. One only has to look at his preaching on the Sermon on the Mount! The estate demands—seen both from God's commandment and from his command—something more and often something totally different from what we make out of it in our "estate consciousness." Herein lies the significance of the sermon that relates to public life. In such preaching the estate is invoked against the agent of that estate, the office of judge against the judge, the office of preaching against the preacher, and the office of the state against its bearer. The Christian conservatism of the nineteenth century no longer had this critical power of maintaining orders by unrelenting criticism of its exercise, and for that reason it became reactionary, which is to say impotent as a history-shaping entity. But Luther did not only criticize the persons; rather, he also criticized the state *authority* as such and called upon subjects not to submit to willfulness if it is preparing to infringe upon the obedience of faith under the illusion of God-given authority. Luther saw that the "estate" can turn into a "larva" under which not God's call and command but rather the devil's temptations go out to men. At that point, disobedience becomes a commandment. As an example, a characteristic citation from "Responsibility for the Riot" may form the conclusion which is taken from the writing against Duke Georg when he ordered that the Lutheran usage of the Lord's Supper in Leipzig be punished with disgraceful penalties and expulsions. Luther counsels the "devout people" that they "should rather risk body and good before they deny both species[81] against Christ or take one species at Duke George's command."[82]

> We concede to Duke George that he sits before the world in princely honor and is a laudable, honorable prince of the empire, but before God and in spiritual matters we concede him no honor except the honor of Pilate, Herod, Judas, and the like, who condemn and murder Christ and his Apostles for the sake of God's Word. . . . This is why when I call him the devil's apostle, I do him no injustice, I do not malign his princely honor or his temporal majesty.[83]

---

81. I.e. in the Lord's Supper.
82. [Martin Luther, *Responsibility for the Riot* (1533), WA 38, 86-127, 98,23.24-25.]
83. [WA 38, 99,23-29f.]

> For at first glance, it moves a devout Christian heart (and not without reason) when a commandment comes from the authorities because God has so sternly commanded that obedience, honor, and service should be rendered to the authorities with the whole heart. Thus, so that the good people should not be frightened nor rebel against Duke Georg as their proper prince and authority set in place by God, I wanted to display the masks that Duke Georg put on and how the devil's commandment is held to be a princely commandment, so that they would recognize this mummery, know that such a commandment did not originate from their authorities according to divine ordinance but from the devil and from his disorder, and neither be troubled nor worry that they are resisting their authorities or being disobedient but rather be confident that they are thereby resisting the devil and nevertheless remain devout, faithful, and obedient subjects to their authorities and pay no mind if Duke Georg would interpret such behavior as disobedience and punish it.[84]

Here, Luther distinguishes between the "orderly power and princely authority"[85] and his "larvae and mummery against God and his Word."[86] The holder of state power can issue a commandment under the mask of the authorities that "originated from the devil and his disorder"[87] as if it were issued by true "authorities according to divine ordinance."[88] In this case, Luther sees the sermon as being obligated to destroy this false appearance and to remove the "bad conscience" from the subjects lest they should feel as if they were "disobedient" in resistance against the state. The bad conscience belongs in this case to the duke and not to the Christians living in his land. By them resisting "the devil," they advocate *for* the properly understood authority, for when the office established by God presumes to require that which is contrary to God, then the obligation falls to them to distinguish between the true "estate" of the authorities and the larvae that they put on.

With that said, we are at the end. With the sacrament, such a falsification as an "estate person" can carry out would not be possible. Yet since sacrament and estate are treated in the same way as things established by God, this misuse must slip in as if the *estate* were holy as such and as if resistance against the authorities, at the very most in the form of suffering but not actively in the unmasking of commands that are contrary to God and in a corresponding opposition, were permissible. The estate, even that of the authorities, is not a sacrament, even if it stands under the Word of God. Our position drives toward a new evangelical doctrine of the state.

---

84. WA 38, 100,7-21.
85. [WA 38, 100,22.]
86. [WA 38, 100,22f.]
87. [WA 38, 100,16.]
88. [WA 38, 100,15.]

Chapter 10

ON THE ORIGIN OF LUTHER'S CONCEPT OF THE CHURCH

A CRITICAL CONTRIBUTION TO KARL HOLL'S ESSAY OF THE SAME NAME

Originally published in *Festschrift für Günther Dehn*, ed. Wilhelm Schneemelcher (Neukirchen: Verlag der Buchhandlung des Erziehungsvereins, 1957), 145–66. Cf. Karl Holl, "Zur Entstehung von Luthers Kirchenbegriff (1915)," in *Gesammelte Aufsätze zur Kirchengeschichte*, vol. 1, *Luther* (Tübingen: J. C. B. Mohr, 1921), 288–325.

After the profound divergences in the German Protestantism with regard to the theological understanding of "church" and the following consequences in the "church struggle" of the Nazi era had become apparent, Iwand found the Protestant church in Germany in the course of its organizational formation after the end of the Second World War again confronted with the challenge to clarify its self-conception. A key aspect was the question about the status of confession and in this context the dispute about the Lutheran Confessionalism, which was organized as the "United Protestant-Lutheran Church of Germany" in 1948. Iwand criticized this development and emphasized instead Luther's understanding of church.

In the present article Iwand referred back to Karl Holl's (1866–1926) study, who as a professor of Protestant theology and church history contributed significantly to the so-called Lutheran Renaissance in the early twentieth century. Iwand wanted to review critically Holl's discernments and at the same time to continue them productively in order to address this concern that in his opinion had been overlooked to the detriment of the Protestant church and theology in Germany.

In 1957 this article was published in the commemorative publication in honor of Günther Dehn's (1882–1970) seventy-fifth birthday. Dehn was a professor of practical theology and therefore Iwand's colleague in the Protestant Theological Faculty at the University of Bonn. Both theologians were connected by their joint work for the Confessing Church. The basic ideas of Iwand's article can also be found, in a somewhat varied form, in his lecture "Luther's Theology," which he held in Bonn in the summer term of 1956 and the winter term of 1956/7.[1] *[MB]*

---

1. [Cf. Hans Joachim Iwand, *Luthers Theologie*, NW V, 235–49.]

Karl Holl's essays on Luther's theology have maintained their vibrant, unparalleled charm even until the present day. They revealed another Luther to us. If one considers them a bit more deeply, one will notice how, alongside all of the serious scholarship, a sort of Nicodemus conversation [Jn 3:1-21] extends throughout the entirety of his work. It is the *young* Luther who provoked this in the great scholar from the school of Albrecht Ritschl[2] and with whom he has entered into a continuous theological discussion.[3] This is the charm of these discourses, a charm that has become so unusual today, a certain something that distinguishes all true research and yet is particularly present in Holl's book on Luther. The external form, which attracts the attention of every reader in this anthology of diverse essays—that the descriptive texts almost recede from view in comparison with the vast footnotes, often filling half to two-thirds of the page, mostly splendid citations of Luther—may be seen as something more than merely the habit of German scholarly work. The main thing in this book is *underneath* the text. It is here that one arrives at the word that the author of these essays hears, from which he learns unceasingly, with which he converses, and by which he plainly allows himself to be corrected in his customary theology and comforted and strengthened in his faith. Holl did not read himself and his thoughts into Luther, even though he did attempt to interpret him and presents his own particular view of Luther's theology, but he has through his *method* essentially arrived at the point that the difference between him and his hero was preserved while the latter was able to speak as never before. That is the novelty of Holl's way of having Luther speak—somewhat in contrast to Theodosius Harnack's book from Erlangen's golden age, a book no less rich in citations both in its structure and in its theology.[4] This book also reappeared from obscurity after the First World War. But how different is its style and its structure! In this book, the author identifies himself completely with Luther. One gets the feeling that Luther rose and in the same process fell in this Restoration theology of the nineteenth century. This is the reason for Harnack having no understanding of Luther's doctrine of predestination (it seems too Calvinistic); for that distinction, reminiscent of Schleiermacher, between the world apart from Christ and the world in Christ;[5]

---

2. [Albrecht Ritschl (1822–89) was a systematic theologian, who left a lasting mark on evangelical theology of the late nineteenth and early twentieth centuries.]

3. [Cf. Karl Holl, "Die Rechtfertigungslehre in Luthers Vorlesung über den Römerbrief mit besonderer Rücksicht auf die Frage der Heilsgewißheit (1910)," in idem, *Gesammelte Aufsätze zur Kirchengeschichte*, vol. 1, *Luther* (Tübingen: J. C. B. Mohr, 1921), (111–54) 125 Fn. 1; Iwand, *Luthers Theologie*, NW V, 47–51.]

4. [Theodosius Harnack (1817–89) was an evangelical theologian, who above all researched the theology of Luther and with his work influenced the Luther research of the early twentieth century. Cf. Theodosius Harnack, *Luthers Theologie mit besonderer Beziehung auf seine Versöhnungs- und Erlösungslehre*, 2 vols. (Erlangen: Theodor Blaesing, 1862/1886); Iwand, *Luthers Theologie*, 42–4.]

5. [Cf. Friedrich Schleiermacher, *The Christian Faith*, 3rd ed. (London: Bloomsbury T & T Clark, 2016), §148, 676–8.]

for the analogous understanding of law and gospel, ultimately for the overhaul of Christology and the doctrine of the atonement in the dogmatic schema of the Formula of Concord and the doctrine of the threefold office first developed in the age of orthodoxy. Accordingly, it must look, as they understood it, as if an unbroken line led from Luther to the Lutherans of that day, as if the essentially Melanchthonian formulas provided the legitimate doctrinal framework for reconstructing the unprecedented phenomenon of Luther's theology and domesticating the most irregular dogmatics since Paul into a regular system of doctrine. Holl shakes himself free of all of this. He interprets Luther without any confessional preconditions. In this way, he inaugurated a process of liberation of Luther's theology, a process that no Luther scholar should wish to undo. Unfortunately, this did not play itself out in his school the way one might have hoped. The record is still not finalized on why that is. Indeed, apart from a few brave exceptions, a serious conversation has not even been taken up after the horrible aberrancies that the last decade revealed in the matter of the use and abuse of Luther's name and theology. That Lutheran Confessionalism has remained as the winner following the collapse of the national German fantasies is certainly what we would have expected least of all from the perspective of the 1920s.

Holl's essays have been left behind; the rudiments of an approach begun within them have not yet been brought to fulfillment. In the fight over the theological foundation and witness of the evangelical church that began in 1933, we were lacking the man who had given Luther scholarship such a powerful push. Maybe he would have taken his place—in contrast to Emanuel Hirsch,[6] whom he esteemed so highly—where another great "liberal" and "Protestant" stood, Professor Freiherr von Soden.[7] But wherever Luther scholarship will begin anew, it must attempt to incorporate Holl's scholarship and the meticulousness of his method, even where it will follow new and distinct paths. This is not easy considering a scholarly life that has been driven out in so many areas. Yet if much of what earlier seemed self-evident has been broken and shattered by years of damage to academic freedom and particularly to the *ethos* that was once proper to German scholarship, and if we must laboriously—even as we are far too old!—rebuild it, it is worth it for Luther scholarship to "put out into the deep" [cf. Lk. 5:4] and to reconnect with the men and the research that once brought us to life. Thus, the following should be

---

6. [Emanuel Hirsch (1888–1972) was an evangelical theologian, who had a great impact on the Luther Renaissance of the early twentieth century. During the time of National Socialism, Hirsch supported the ideology as well as the politics of the Nazis. Further, after the end of the Second World War he did not revise his views.]

7. [Hans Freiherr von Soden (1881–1945) was an evangelical theologian who belonged to the leading representatives of the Confessing Church and whose theological thinking after the end of the Second World War was foundational for the establishment of the Evangelical State Church of Kurhessen-Waldeck. Cf. Hans Freiherr von Soden, *Urchristentum und Geschichte: Gesammelte Aufsätze und Vorträge*, vol. 1, ed. Hans von Campenhausen (Tübingen: C. J. B. Mohr, 1951), 25–89.]

understood as an attempt to carry Holl's essay concerning the "Origin of Luther's Concept of Church" a little further. What has been published so far[8] cannot

8. We should recall here Ferdinand Kattenbusch, *Die Doppelschichtigkeit in Luthers Kirchenbegriff* (Gotha: Klotz, 1928), and Ernst Kohlmeyer, "Die Bedeutung der Kirche bei Luther," *Zeitschrift für Kirchengeschichte Neue Folge* 10 (1928): 466–511. On the concept of "communio sanctorum," Paul Althaus has published an important study *[Commumo sanctorum: Die Gemeinde im lutherischen Kirchengedanken.* Vol. I. Luther (Munich: Chr. Kaiser Verlag, 1929)].

Just as the question of Luther's concept of church began to stir in research as a result of Holl's suggestions, the discussion collapsed because the question of the church was transformed from a "historical" question to the defining question of the present. Johannes von Walter, *Die Theologie Luthers* [(Gütersloh: Bertelsmann, 1940)], 281, judges very correctly: "It was Karl Holl who gave Luther research in modern times the impetus that had become urgently necessary precisely at this point by publishing an essay entitled: '"Die Entstehung von Luthers Kirchenbegriff' in the Festschrift dedicated to Dietrich Schäfer in 1915 for his 70th birthday." Most closely related to the concept of the church is the question of church law in Luther. From the shock that Rudolph Sohm's "Kirchenrecht" gave to the Protestant doctrine of ecclesiastical law—his book was published in 1892!), —it has not yet recovered. But cf. the important, if not in all pieces satisfying, monograph by the Munich scholar of ecclesiastical law Johannes Heckel, *Lex Caritatis: A Juristic Disquisition on Law in the Theology of Martin Luther* (1933), trans. and ed. Gottfried G. Krodel (Grand Rapids: Eerdmans Publishing, 2010). What does not satisfy me in this work, which is plausible in its basic conception of *ius divinum* and natural law, convincing in its overall view of "justification and law," and at all stimulating in every direction, is what Sohm has elevated to the central idea, the Protestant truth of that famous sentence: "Ecclesiastical law is at contradiction with the nature of the church." [Rudolph Sohm, *Kirchenrecht*, vol. 1, Die geschichtlichen Grundlagen (Leipzig: Duncker & Humblot, 1892), 1.] This truth comes up short for me in Heckel.

What Sohm says is indeed bold, but so true that it should not be relativized: "The church depends on the material truth, i.e. on the fact that in truth God's word and God's will are proclaimed, offered to the world, put into effect. Law, on the other hand, is fundamentally attached to form (*summum jus summa injuria*), and it must first be attached to form, for only in this way can it arrive at decisions that are above the parties, that impose themselves on both sides as just in spite of opposing interests, and that do not arise from the influences of the moment, but from fixed, transmitted, generally valid principles" (Ibid., 1f.). For this, cf. Joseph Lortz: "One-sidedness was his [i.e. Luther's] undoing, or, conversely, he foundered on the Catholic sythesis" (*The Reformation in Germany* [1939], trans. Ronald Walls, vol. 1 [New York: Herder and Herder, 1968], 488). Related to this "synthesis" is the possibility for the Catholic Church to arrive at juridical principles from theological ones.

On the other hand, it makes sense to me what Heckel says in principle against Sohm: "Whoever had developed a new concept 'faith' and with it a new concept 'church' (Heckel means 'new' in relation to the medieval concept of faith and law), could not continue to be burdened with the traditional concept 'law'. Therefore Luther could not 'naively' adopt the medieval natural-law formulas" (Heckel, *Lex Caritatis*, 12). But the question of law can only be solved together with the other question of the genesis of Luther's concept of church.

make the claim that it has clarified the questions posed by Holl in a productive manner.⁹

In that essay, Holl attempted first to answer the question of the origin of Luther's concept of church from the source materials before the indulgence controversy. "The concept of church with which Luther confronts the Roman hierarchy is already present before the indulgence controversy. It arose in him not as the result of some sort of objection but simply as a result of his fundamental religious ideas," and furthermore, "his *doctrine of justification* was what propelled his new

---

9. Holl's shortcoming, which hinders him at every turn in his investigations of the concept of church, is his recourse to Luther's experience of faith or God. Perhaps Holl is partly to blame for the fact that Lortz was able to write: "Luther was the German Reformation" [Lortz, *The Reformation in Germany*, 428]. This is similarly wrong as if one wanted to say: "Paul is the early Christianity." But also the sentence of Werner Elert: "The morphology, however, does not write Luther's theology. On the contrary, it seeks to discover in Luther's theology only that which is able to carry the whole structure of the historical Lutheranism that followed. This, then would be the impact of the Gospel (evangelischer Ansatz)" (Werner Elert, *The Structure of Lutheranism* [1931], vol. 1, *The Theology and Philosophy of Life of Lutheranism: Especially in the Sixteenth and Seventeenth Centuries*, trans. Walter A. Hansen [St. Louis: Concordia Publishing House, 1962], 11) is hardly able to go beyond this subjectivism of the religio-psychological type in the question of Luther's concept of church. But the "impact of the gospel" depends upon the gospel itself and not upon a human "primal experience (*Urerlebnis*)" (cf. the first chapter of the *Structure*) through which, according to Elert, Luther became *typical* for the distinctive style in his denomination. For the experience of the Reformation is not, after all, the "structure" of a Christian type, called "Lutheran Church," which separated from the "Catholic" and its other "structure" to form two analogous denominations. Apparently, Elert means it this way. "The impression that the early polemics present only fragments of the confessional morphology is rather to be ascribed to the fact that they themselves wrote when things were beginning to take shape. The shaping itself is a process that goes on for centuries; it never ceases while there is still a spark of life. Even today it continues for Roman Catholicism as well as for Lutheranism" [Ibid., 4.]

With this shift from doctrine to experience, from the Word of God to self-understanding, from the truth and the witness to the form and shape, the access to the question of Luther's concept of church is essentially blocked. This must then spring from "Luther" like Pallas Athena from the head of a god and is thus "shaped" as a type from the outset. Most of the self-statements of the reformer, which cannot be listed here in detail, speak against this. As a document for many others, cf. the conclusion of the great self-testimony: Martin Luther, *Preface to the Complete Edition of Luther's Latin Writings* (1545), LW 34, 323-338, 338; WA 54, 186,25-29: "I relate to these things, good reader, so that, if you are a reader of my puny works, you may keep in mind, that, as I said above, I was all alone and one of those who, as Augustine says of himself, have become proficient in writing and teaching. I was not one of those who from nothing suddenly become the topmost, though they are nothing, neither have labored, nor been tempted, nor become experienced, but have with one look at the scriptures exhausted their entire spirit."

conception of the church."[10] To support this, Holl primarily presents statements from the first course Luther taught, the *"Dictata super Psalterium."* The church that "alone deserves to be called *church*, i.e. church of Christ" is a "more intimate group" that is "separate" within the external fellowship. "For them alone is it proper to use the name 'members of Christ.'"[11] And so Holl comes to the conclusion that "this"—and so the actual, true—"church" is "according to its essence *invisible.*" "Nevertheless, one is never to doubt that the church of Christ *truly exists,*"[12] at which point Holl does not evade the question of what sort of *existence* it is, for "the church of Christ is not just always there; it is an actual *fellowship, indeed the only true* fellowship since it is the most inward."[13] Then follows the succinct proposition that we wish to bring up for discussion: *"It is a fully complete, coherent system of thought, rounded off in itself. It is the same concept of church that Luther maintained throughout his life* (emphasis original)."[14]

Holl erects his structure upon the thesis that Emanuel Hirsch, Erich Vogelsang,[15] and recently Johannes Heckel[16] have followed,[17] that Luther's so-called justification

---

10. [Holl, "Zur Entstehung," 289.]
11. [Ibid., 295.]
12. [Ibid., 296.]
13. [Ibid., 297.]
14. [Ibid., 298f.]
15. [Erich Vogelsang (1904–44) was an evangelical theologian who above all researched Luther's development.]
16. [Johannes Heckel (1889–1963) was an evangelical lawyer for the state and the church, who in his work *"Lex charitatis"* (cf. note 9 in this chapter) dealt with Luther's attitude toward canon law.]
17. Special studies on the allegedly primary experience of Luther's justification are Emanuel Hirsch, "Initium theologiae Lutheri," in *Festgabe für Julius Kaftan*, (Tübingen: J. C. B. Mohr, 1920, 150–69); Erich Vogelsang, *Die Anfänge von Luthers Christologie nach der ersten Psalmenvorlesung: Insbesondere in ihren exegetischen und systematischen Zusammenhängen mit Augustin und der Scholastik dargestellt* (Berlin and Leipzig: Walter de Gruyter & Co, 1929). This very interesting work believes to have found the moment where within the interpretation of the Psalms Luther's tower experience can be determined in its literary expression and thus fixed theologically and temporally. Holl himself says: "It seems certain to me that Luther gained the redemptive certainty in the time between his move to Wittenberg and the beginning of the lectures on the Psalms, that is, roughly between the summer 1511 and spring 1513. Likewise, it seems indisputable to me that Luther's breakthrough towards the doctrine of justification must have accrued before the beginning of the lectures on the Psalms" (Holl, "Zur Entstehung" 193). One can see how a certain scheme of experience is applied to Luther from the outset. Does this come from the fact that the experience of justification can now only be imagined in terms of the pietistic breakthrough experience—say, according to August Tholuck, *Guido and Julius: Sin and the Propitiator: The True Consecration of the Sceptic*, trans. Jonathan Edwards Ryland (Boston: Gould and Lincoln, 1854)? I fear that is the case. Karl Bauer, *Die Wittenberger*

experience had already occurred before 1513. This assumption does not hold. What people often call the justification experience—here we are speaking of something like his new understanding of Rom. 1:17 as Luther narrates in his own testimony[18]—cannot have taken place before 1515, for the concept of "*iustitia*" remains internally foreign to him until this point.[19] The fact that we, in spite

Universitätstheologie [und die Anfänge] der [Deutschen] Reformation (Tübingen: J. C. B. Mohr, 1928), approaches our question quite differently. The quote from Luther that he prefaces his work with is significant enough: "I simply believe that it is impossible to reform the church, if one does not eradicate from the foundations the canons, decretals, scholastic theology, and logic as we have these things today, and instead institute different directions of study" [Martin Luther, *Letter to Jodokus Trutvetter in Erfurt from May 05.1518*, Letter No. 74, WA.BR 1, 170,33-36].

This side of the matter is completely missing in Holl, Hirsch, and Vogelsang. It is a turn in the legal conception of the church, also from a philosophical point of view, which initiates the Reformation. The theological turn was then further developed and presented in the confrontation with Thomism, Augustinianism, nominalism, and mysticism in a first but brilliant effort. Wilhelm Link, *Das Ringen Luthers um die Freiheit der Theologie von der Philosophie* [ed. Ernst Wolf and Manfred Mezger, Forschungen zur Geschichte und Lehre des Protestantismus 9.3, Munich], 1940. Unfortunately, Link was taken from us too early by an unfortunate accident.

18. [Cf. LW 34, 336-338; WA 54, 185,12-186,24.]

19. Let us refer to just one single passage in the lectures on the Epistle to the Romans, which reads as follows: "This is the reason (if I may speak of myself) why even hearing the word 'justice' nauseates me to the point that if someone robbed me, he would not bring me such grief. And yet the word is always sounding in the mouths of the lawyers. There is no race of men upon the earth who are more ignorant about this matter than the lawyers and the good-intentioners and the intellectuals. For I in myself and with many others have had the experience that when we were righteous, God laughed at us in our righteousness. . . . Therefore the only complete righteousness is humility." Martin Luther, *Lectures on Romans* (1515-16) [LW 25, 441; WA 56, 449,1-6.8f., on Rom. 12:2]. Cf. Axel Gyllenkrok, *Rechtfertigung und Heiligung* in der frühen evangelischen Theologie Luthers (Uppsala: Lundequistska bokhandeln, 1952).

One might think that Luther had only juridical justice in mind, but this is out of question because of the context. Within *iustitia*, for the Luther of the Letter to the Romans—that is, 1515/16—there is still no bridge to God. Later he can say: "So that, through this same Righteousness God and we are made right, just as through the Word God creates and we are what He Himself is, so that we are in Himself and His being is our being" [Martin Luther, Lectures on the Psalms (1519-21), WA 5, 144,20-22, on Ps. 5:9].

Also this exposition follows *ad vocem* "*iustitia*." When the theological difference between these two statements is recognized, one is urged to the conclusion that a new realization must have taken place in the meantime regarding the biblical term "*iustitia Dei*." When Luther describes this turnaround later, he regularly says to characterize his pre-Reformation stance: "For I hated that term 'righteousness of God'" [LW 34, 336; WA 54, 185,17f.].

of Holl, Scheel,[20] Hirsch, and others, are not in a position to calculate or find a definite, allegedly decisive "justification experience"[21] before or in the *Dictata super Psalterium*, that we are able to find "fully complete" concepts neither in the young Luther's doctrine of justification nor in other areas of his theology, will shift our research methodically to another field, namely from that of experience and a specific self-understanding to that of theology, which is to say to the development of his *doctrine*. We grant that this does not take place apart from experience, that existence and the understanding of existence play a substantial role in this— though how much of a role must still be agreed upon!—but to trace Luther's development according to the analogy of a modern individual, autonomous in his religious experience, is hardly sufficient to the issue. Luther's theological work remains and stands within the context of the *church*. The church is the great entirety of the "*mundus intelligibilis*" [the "intellectually perceptible world"], in which the believer lives, in contrast to the "*mundus sensibilis*" [the "world that can be experienced through the senses"], the world of the unbelievers.[22] The

---

20. [Otto Scheel (1876–1954) was an evangelical theologian, who wrote a significant work on the biography of Luther and attempted therein to discern the date of Luther's "reformation discovery." Cf. Otto Scheel, *Martin Luther: Vom Katholizismus zur Reformation*, vol. 2, *Im Kloster*, 4. ed. (Tübingen: C. J. B. Mohr, 1930), 567–79.]

21. [Holl, "Die Rechtfertigungslehre im Licht der Geschichte des Protestantismus (1922)," in idem, *Gesammelte Aufsätze zur Kirchengeschichte'*, vol. 3, *Der Westen*, ed. Hans Lietzmann, (Tübingen: C. J. B. Mohr, 1928), 525–57, 530f.; cf. Hirsch, "*Initium*" 32–4; Hans Joachim Iwand, "Brief an Rudolf Hermann vom 20.9.1926," in NW VI, 120–4, 120–2. The question of whether and when the "reformation breakthrough" could be dated was already a controversy being discussed in Iwand's day. Cf. Walter von Loewenich, *Luther's Theology of the Cross* (1929) (Minneapolis: Augsburg Publishing House, 1976); Heinrich Bornkamm, "Luthers Bericht über seine Entdeckung der iustitia Dei," *Archiv für Reformationsgeschichte* 37 (1940): 117–28; idem, "Iustitia Dei in der Scholastik und bei Luther," *Archiv für Reformationsgeschichte* 39 (1942): 1–46; Karl August Meissinger, *Der Katholische Luther* (Munich: Leo Lehnen Verlag, 1952); Gyllenkrok, *Rechtfertigung und Heiligung*; Ernst Bizer, *Fides ex auditu*. Eine Untersuchung über die Entdeckung der Gerechtigkeit Gottes durch Martin Luther (Neukirchen: Verlag des Erziehungsvereins Neukirchen, 1958).]

22. Luther speaks of the "*opera Dei*" on Ps. 77:15, Martin Luther, *First Lectures on the Psalms* (1513-15), LW 11, 13; WA 3, 532,38-533, 3: "The first division consists of all the visible works of creation, whether once done within the realm of nature or by a miracle. The second division comprises the works of Christ done for us and the works of the whole new creation, that is, the church [or, the whole new creation, the church], which is the world of the spirit and of the mind" (The phrase between the brackets is in Luther's writing written above as a substitute). This is then followed under "third" the "moral works" and under "fourth" the "works of the coming resurrection." The church coincides with the intelligible reality.

church for Luther is not only a "fellowship of persons"[23] or else his later emphasis on the "*signa ecclesiae*"[24] would be hard to understand. Further, Luther does not become intolerable for the church—as Catholic researchers are in the habit of assuming[25]—because of his exaggerated individualism or because of his inability to synthesize. Rather, he becomes intolerable because he asks about the "proper, old church"[26] and its decay and infiltration by foreign influences, assailing the sacrilegious rubbish and the deliberate lack of discernment of the church of his time and the theology and canon lawyers who support and defend them. He perceives doctrine and the order of this church not as somehow inconsistent

23. [Cf. Holl, "Zur Entstehung," 300, 310, 322; Julius Köstlin, *Martin Luther. Sein Leben und seine Schriften*, ed. Gustav Kawerau, vol. I, 3rd ed. (Berlin: Verlag Duncker, 1903), 300; Paul Althaus, *Communio sanctorum: Die Gemeinde im lutherischen Kirchengedanken*, vol. 1. (Munich: Chr. Kaiser, 1929), 42–80; Dietrich Bonhoeffer, *Sanctorum Communio: A Theological Study of the Sociology of the Church*, ed. Clifford J. Green, Dietrich Bonhoeffer Works, vol. 1 (Minneapolis: Fortress Press, 1998), 285f.]

24. [In 1521, Luther names as "signs of the church" Baptism, Lord's Supper, and Gospel in, Martin Luther, *Ad librum eximii Magistri Nostri Magistri Ambrosii Catharini, defensoris Silvestri Prieritatis acerrimi, responsio* (1521), WA 7, 720,32-721,1; in 1539, he names Baptism, Lord's Supper, Keys, Office of Preaching (*Predigtamt*), Prayer and Confession (*Bekenntnis*), Cross and Suffering in idem, *On the Councils and the Church* (1539), LW 41, 148-167, WA 50, 628,29-644,11; in 1541, he names Sacraments, Keys, Office of Preaching, Confession and Prayer, Marriage, Stance toward Authority, Suffering of the Church in the World and Renunciation of Retaliation in idem, *Against Hans Wurst* (1541), LW 41, 194-198; WA 51, 479,4-485,7.]

25. [Iwand has in view here the Roman Catholic research on Reformation history of the late nineteenth and early twentieth century, especially as portrayed by the Dominican Heinrich Denifle (1844–1905) and the Jesuit Hartmann Grisar (1845–1932); cf. Heinrich Denifle, *Luther und Luthertum in der ersten Entwickelung quellenmäßig dargestellt*, 2 vols. (Mainz: Verlag Kirchheim, 1903–9); Hartmann Grisar, *Luther*, 3 vols., trans. E. M. Lamond, ed. Luigi Cappadelta (London: Kegan Paul, Trench, Trubner & co., 1913–17). In his lecture on Luther's theology, Iwand brought to light the newer Catholic Luther research, above all from Joseph Lortz (1887–1975), and highlighted that this goes "far beyond the normal bounds in recognizing Luther's work" (Iwand, *Luthers Theologie*, NW V, 54).]

26. Later in his writing *Against Hanswurst* (1541), LW 41, 194; WA 51, 478,34.479,17-19: "But what if I prove that we have remained faithful to the true ancient church, indeed, that we are the true ancient church and that you have fallen away from us, that is, the true ancient church, and have set up a new church against the ancient one?"

Martin Luther, *Defense and Explanation of All Articles* (1521), LW 32, 10; WA 7, 313,30f.37-315,2: "They say also that I propose new ideas and it is not to be expected that everybody else should have been so long in error ... I preach nothing new, but I say that all Christian things have perished among the very people who ought to have preserved them, namely, the bishops and scholars. But I have no doubt that the truth has been retained in some hearts to this day, if only in the hearts of infants and their cradles."

with a "justification experience" based upon his own particular experience. Rather, the conflict over the true church breaks out within the church itself, as Luther refers to that category of the *"Verbum Dei"* ["Word of God"] over against ecclesiastical authority, the Word that sustains and defines the church in strict contrast to the word of man and to every *"potestas ecclesiae"* exercised by man.[27]

27. Very instructive is the speech, which cannot be dated with certainty but is probably to be dated early, that Luther prepared for Bishop Georg Mascov (others think for the Lateran Council in Rome in 1516). Note the role that Jas 1:18, "Of his own will he brought us forth by the word of truth," plays for Luther (cf. also Johann Haar, *Initium creaturae Dei: [Eine Untersuchung über Luthers Begriff der 'neuen Creatur' im Zusammenhang mit seinem Versändnis von Jakobus 1,18 du mit seinem 'Zeit'-Denken* (Gütersloh: Rufer Verlag, 1939)].

Martin Luther, *Sermo praescriptus praeposito in Litzka* (1512), WA 1, 14,3-5.8: "For as this sentence is true: 'everything that is born of God and from the Word of God does not sin' (cf. 1 Jn 5:18), so is this also true: 'whatever is born of man and of the word of man sins and is sin and therefore will necessarily collapse in eternity'. . . . The root of this evil is, however, that the word of truth is lacking."

This "defect" of the Divine Word takes the place of the scholastic "lack of original justice (*defectus iustitiae orginalis*)."

WA 1, 13,40-41, 3: "There is therefore no need to look for, compose, or accept any other word, if one does not also want to abolish this birth from God, extinguish the Church and drown the people of Christ in the rivers of Egypt, according to the custom of a Pharaoh, that is, to perish through the words of man."

Martin Luther, *That a Christian Assembly or Congregation Has the Right and Power to Judge All Teaching and to Call, Appoint, and Dismiss Teachers, Established and Proven by Scripture* (1523), LW 39, 301-314, 306; WA 11, 409,2-4: "For the soul of man is something eternal, and more important than every temporal thing. That is why it must be ruled and seized only by the eternal word."

LW 39, 306; WA 11, 409,7f.: "[F]or God's word and human teaching inevitably oppose each other when the latter tries to rule the soul."

Luther's Resolution on the 13th Thesis on the Power of the Pope (1519), WA 2, 217,38-40: "So you see that the gospel is blotted out by the decretals, that the word of God is blotted out by the word of man: and this monstrosity we Christians in the church of Christ worship instead of the word of God."

Martin Luther, *Answer to the Hyperchristian, Hyperspiritual, and Hyperlearned Book by Goat Emser in Leipzig–Including Some Thoughts Regarding His Companion, the Fool Murner (1521)*, LW 39, 137-224, WA 7, 646,19-24: "For not only do you [i.e. Emser] write in the manner of a heretic and of the Antichrist, but you also say what all the devils are not allowed to say, namely, that the gospel is confirmed by the pope, its power is dependent on the pope's

The church is a creature, "*Creatura Verbi Domini*,"²⁸ which is to say: there is the same relationship between the church and the gospel, the Word of God, as there is between a creature and its creator. Wherever the creature rebels against its creator, it is a matter of sacrilege. It circumvents the order of being at the highest level. When this takes place within "Christendom," man transgresses against the

power, and the church has done what the pope does? What heretic has ever so completely condemned and destroyed God's word in one stroke?"

Cf. also *Ad librum eximii Magistri Nostri Ambrosii Catharini* (1521), WA 7, 741,14ff, and the important propositions: "*De potestate leges ferendi in ecclesia*" 1530, WA 30/II, 681-690.

For example, 682,1-3: "So the word is the word of God unadulterated and of its own power, not that of the church, except passively and belonging to the office. So the church is under the word and commission of God and not above it."

682,10.11-14: "Although the gospel can be without the church . . . however conversely, the church cannot be without the gospel. Therefore the gospel is higher than the church, because while the Gospel can be without the church itself, the church cannot (be) without the gospel, because the gospel can be hidden even with the angels or in the depths of God, just as it was before the church."

The gospel always precedes the church in an eternal preexistence.

28. Martin Luther, *Resolutions on the Leipzig Debate* (1519), WA 2, 430,6-8: "For the church is a creation of the gospel, herself incomparably smaller, as it is said by James: 'Of his own will he brought us forth by the word of truth' (James 1:18); and Paul: 'Through the gospel I brought you forth' (1 Cor. 4:15)."

Ad librum eximii Magistri Nostri Ambrosii Catharini (1521), WA 7, 721,9-14: "Truly the gospel is the singular, surest, and chief sign of the church, far more sure than baptism or host, because by the gospel alone they are conceived, made, nourished, born, brought up, fed, clothed, adorned, strengthened, armed, and sustained. In short, the whole life and nature of the church is in the Word of God, as Christ says [Matt. 4, 4.]: 'Man lives on every word that proceeds from the mouth of God.'"

Ad dialogum Silvestri Prieratis de potestate papae responsio (1518), WA 1, 656,13-18: "That you posit the case of a sinner being held to the punishment imposed by a priest, as being similar to that imposed by canon law, and finally to that imposed by God, then it follows from my thesis that a person, having obtained a plenary indulgence, does not go straight to heaven or is not delivered from purgatory; and thus you posit that I would think ill of an act of the church, and smack of heresy. To this I answer: be careful that you, too, do not have such a good opinion about an act of the church that you destroy the work of God."

The opponents are concerned with the facticity of the church, which they find in the visible church endowed with specific orders and rights. The doctrine of the invisible church keeps the question of the true church open in relation to the facticity of the church. One can see from these passages, which could be multiplied at will, that those are wrong who think that the distinction between the Word of God and the word of man is a little modern finding of Dialectical theology and Luther himself rather came from the opposition God-Devil according to the motto: Man between God and demon.

Word of God, which is gospel *and* law at once.²⁹ Thus, the behavior of a church that subordinates the *Word of God* to itself and its judgment—that is, that seeks to make it dependent on human judgment—must be an analogy to that heathen confusion that places the creature in the place of the creator and makes it into a visible location of worship [cf. Rom. 1:25].³⁰ This would come back again in a far greater way in the *Third* Article, which leads in paganism to the divinization of the creature as a transgression against the *First* Article for the purposes of self-made religion.³¹

Holl is correct when he points out that for the young Luther of the first lectures on the Psalms, the church is essentially *invisible*. Yet if one looks a bit closer, he will discover that the concept of "*invisibilitas*" [invisibility] expressed in this period of Luther is closely connected to the Augustinian-Areopagite scheme. Accordingly, the true essence of a thing is hidden to the senses and only comprehensible *to the intellect*. All who "*in fide et spiritu vivunt*" live "*in cognitione et amore invisibilium.*"³² By contrast, the fleshly minded man lives in the visible

---

29. [Since Karl Barth's programmatic Lecture "Gospel and Law" in the year 1935 (K. Barth, "Evangelium und Gesetz," *Theologische Existenz Heute* 32 (Munich: Chr. Kaiser Verlag, 1935), the determination of the relationship and the terminological sequence of "law and gospel" in evangelical theology have been disputed. However, the fact that Iwand speaks here of "gospel and law" does not mean that he distanced himself from Luther's formula, because he demonstrated its importance in his lecture on Luther's theology (cf. Iwand, *Luthers Theologie*, NW V, 75–84), as well as in the lectures he gave in 1937 in the practical seminary of the East Prussian Church and then in 1950/51 in Göttingen (cf. Iwand, Gesetz und Evangelium, NW IV).]

30. On Rom. 1:25: LW 25, 167; WA 56, 185,30f: "Instead they so raise their own opinion to the skies."

31. Martin Luther, *The Babylonian Captivity of the Church* (1520), LW 36, 3-126, 107; WA 6, 560,33-561,1.6f: "For the church was born by the word of promise through faith, and by this same word is nourished and preserved. That is to say, it is the promises of God that make the church, and not the church that makes the promise of God. For the Word of God is incomparably superior to the church, and in this Word the church, being a creature, has nothing to decree, ordain, or make, but only to be decreed, ordained, and made . . . [Otherwise] the church would also be above God, in whom we believe because the church proclaims that he is God."

32. Martin Luther, *First Lectures on Psalms* (1513–15), LW 10, 125; WA 3, 150,28, on Ps. 27:5: "live by faith and in spirit, that is, by the recognition and love of what is invisible."

The definition in Luther's understanding of "fides" in this epoch is consistently and essentially based on the contrast between the visible and the invisible world. There is innumerable evidence for this.

LW 10, 440; WA 3, 498,33f, on Ps. 74:5: "Faith has an exit from visible things and an entrance to the invisible things above, and therefore it is the sign or signs of things that do not appear."

10. On the Origin of Luther's Concept of the Church 183

existence and knows nothing that goes beyond it. This *"vivere in re"* is the mode of existence of *"carnales"*: *"volvuntur in rebus visbilibus."*[33] For this reason, we still find in this stage of Luther's theological consciousness an understanding of the model of the saint that is positive in relation to his later understanding that could be called undialectic. The saint lives *"in spe, non in re."*[34] Only when Luther asserts

---

This definition of *fides* according to Heb. 11:1 is still entirely in the scholastic tradition. The concept of *"signum"* used here has a continuous meaning there, for example for Lombard, especially for the doctrine of the sacraments. Luther did not consciously separate himself from this path of knowledge until the Heidelberg Disputation (LW 31, 35-70; WA 1, 353-374), which is 1518. Cf. Thesis 19, LW 31, WA 1, 354,17f.: "That person does not deserve to be called a theologian who looks upon the invisible things of God as though they were clearly perceptible in those things which have actually happened." This is the rejection of Lombard and the understanding of Rom 1:20 that became authoritative for all scholasticism. It is at the same time the break with Aristotelian epistemology, while that with Aristotle's ethics is already accomplished long before. [Cf. Iwand, *"Theologia crucis,"* NW II, 381-98, 386-9. Cf. *"Theologia Crucis"* in this volume.]

LW 11, 152; WA 4, 3,26.28.32f., on Ps. 85:1: "Righteousness will go before him ... That is, his righteousness will not come from works, but his works will come from his righteousness.... And this is also directed against Aristotle, who says 'by doing righteous things they are made righteous' instead: Through existence, the just do just things."

The concept of justice in the Old Testament abolishes the Greek *paideia*. What a significant moment! The epistemological counterpart to this is the break with the scholastic understanding of Rom. 1:20 in the sense of the *analogia entis* in the Heidelberg Disputation.

Compare this to the "Sentences" of Peter Lombard. Peter Lombard, *The Sentences. Book 1, The Mystery of the Trinity*, trans. Giulio Silano, Mediaeval Sources in Translation 42 (Toronto: Pontifical Institute of Mediaeval Studies, 2007), I. III. 1, 19: "Thus, man was able to perceive, or did even perceive, by the understanding of his mind, the invisible things of God through the things which are made, that is through visible and invisible creatures. For he was assisted by two things, namely nature, which was rational, and by the works which God had done in order that the truth should become manifest to man."

This intelligible knowledge of God is a supernatural, not a rational, philosophical knowledge. In the lectures on the Psalms Luther likes to call this "intellectification," "not ... by human wisdom, but by the spirit and mind of Christ" (LW 10, 145; WA 3, 171,33f., on Ps. 32:1) (This gloss has been left out in the LW, the translation is therefore provided by the editor).

33. LW 10, 125; WA 3, 150,30 on Ps. 27:5. ["So the carnal do not live by faith, but empirically; not in spirit but in the flesh. Hence they are not 'under the cover' but out in the open, and they are involved in visible things."]

34. We still lack an account of the change of Luther's concept of the "holy" (*"sanctus"*). What a change happens here from the still monastic-ascetic understanding of 1513 to the new position, which he presents, for example, in *"De votis monasticis"*! As the break with the medieval form of life of Christian existence is in general very wrongly attributed to the subjective moments and motives in Luther's development. In reality it is about an objective

the "simultaneously" ("*simul*") of Christian existence *in spe and in re*, thanks to his new understanding of the sin that also remains in the Christian, only when he formulates in his exegesis of Rom. 4:7: "*simul peccator et iustus; peccator in vera, sed iustus ex reputatione et promissione Dei certa*,"[35] only when he hazards the paradox[36] that had never been heard before: "*Sancti intrinsece sunt peccatores semper, ideo extrinsece iustificantur semper; hypocrite autem intrinsece sunt iusti semper, ideo extrinsece sunt peccatores semper*,"[37] does that turning point come

breaking of "godless" ("*impiae*") forms and institutions, the whole way of life that was handed down is felt as sacrilegious. That is why the old orders are broken.

Martin Luther, *The Judgement of Martin Luther on Monastic Vows* (1521), LW 44, 243-400, 320; WA 8, 619,21-23: "They all say that their orders are holy, as if orders made those who observed them holy, or as if it were something holy to live under their order, when only the name of the Lord sanctifies and when holiness consists in walking in him alone." How differently Luther still speaks about the "*Sanctus*" or the "*Sancti*" in his *First Lectures on the Psalms* (1513-15), LW 10, 333f; WA 3, 397,37ff., on Ps. 68:14. Significant is the "double sleep, one of the church, the other of the world. . . . Therefore the *world's* sleep is to sleep in the spirit, not to be awake to God. This means to amuse oneself and be totally wrapped up with the love of things. For as a sleeper does not rejoice in real things or is sad about them but is deceived by phantoms and apparitions of things, so, before God and in spirit, all whose joy, hope, fear, or grief has to do with transitory things to the disparagement of eternal things are deceived by apparitions, as Scripture shows in many places" (LW 10, 333.334; WA 3, 397,37.398,5-10).

LW 10, 334; WA 3, 398,27-30: "The church's sleep is to sleep according to the flesh and to the world but to be awake to God, just as others are awake to the world. For as one who sleeps does not see openly the things that are in the world, so as if they do not use them." WA 3, 179,10f., on "*ponens in thesauris*" (Ps. 33:7): "the faith in the invisible is hidden from the carnal men" in invisibilibus fidei absconditis ab hominibus carnalibus" [This gloss is not included in the English translation.]

LW 11, 144; WA 3, 647,38-40, on Ps. 83,4: "The altar is Christ, any saint, or bishop whose example is adopted for imitation, whose words are pondered as a rule."

On the contrary, then, LW 25, 324; WA 56, 335,26f., on Rom. 7:1: "Therefore with marvelous stupidity and with a monkey-sees-monkey-does attitude do these people act who want to imitate the works of the saints and glory in their fathers and ancestors."

35. LW 25, 260; WA 56, 272,17f., on Rom. 4:7: ["(F)or he is at the same time both a sinner and a righteous man; a sinner in fact, but a righteous man by the sure imputation and promise of God."]

36. Martin Luther, *Lectures on Galatians* (1535), LW 26, 168; WA 40/1, 285,10-13, on Gal. 2:20: "If Paul had not used this way of speaking first and prescribed it for us in explicit terms, no one even among the saints would have dared use it. [For] it is unprecedented and insolent." Luther calls this "peculiar phraseology" of Paul "not human, but divine and heavenly" [LW 26, 168; WA 40/1, 285,8f.]. He started using this phraseology in 1515.

37. LW 25, 257; WA 56, 268,27-30, on Rom. 4:7["The saints are always sinners in their own sight, and therefore always justified outwardly. But the hypocrites are always righteous in their own sight, and thus always sinners outwardly."]

about in his theology that a man like Denifle quite correctly perceived to be the definitive break with medieval theology and piety.[38] For the understanding of sanctification and the essence of saintliness that had been just as characteristic as it was vital to the Catholic Church until that point was thereby made impossible at its root. Here and nowhere else is the notion of a universal priesthood, a notion that was often asserted in the Middle Ages and that would later appear in the doctrine of the Office of the Keys at the Leipzig Disputation,[39] reestablished. All of this has its foundation in the fact that the portrayal of the saint had been made impossible: whoever intends or strives to be one, it is precisely that person who is not. The lack of clarity concerning the new life and the new righteousness becomes fundamental, since Luther acknowledges to Paul that the *work* is indifferent;[40] even the one who does a work cannot see from it how his *essence* is before God, his "*iustum esse coram Deo.*"[41] The Luther who is proceeding toward the *Analogia entis* in his exegesis of the Psalms cannot yet see this. He still understands Rom. 1:20 as the core proposition of his epistemological method, and when he speaks of "*fides*," he is thinking first and foremost of Heb. 11:1, where faith is described as "*argumentum rerum invisibilium*,"[42] not of Rom. 1:17.[43]

All of this can be verified in detail. It could also be shown how this transcendence of the metaphysical world of faith turns into something in a certain sense inherent to Luther on the basis of its intelligible understanding. This may be the more profound significance of the multiple senses of scriptural interpretation and the

---

38. [Cf. Heinrich Denifle OP, *Luther und Luthertum in der ersten Entwickelung*, vol. 1, part 2, ed. Albert Maria Weiß OP (Mainz: Verlag von Kirchheim & Co, 1906), 608.]

39. [WA 2, 378,24-379,36.]

40. Martin Luther, *Lectures on Galatians* (1519), LW 27, 329; WA 2, 562,29, on Gal. 5:2: "The external work is immaterial." So already verbatim in the lecture on Galatians 1516/17 [cf. WA 57, 38,3f], of which we only have a "postscript made during the lecture itself" (Karl August Meissinger, "Einleitung" Lectures on Galatians by Martin Luther [1516/17], WA 57, IV).

41. [Cf. LW 25, 247; WA 56, 260,18f, on Rom. 3:21: "no living man is justified before God."]

42. ["an argument from invisible things," cf. Martin Luther, *Lectures on Hebrews* (1517), LW 29, 229-231; WA 57, 226,10-229,5.]

43. One can show how gradually in the course of the first lecture on the Psalms, Rom 1:17 overshadows Heb. 11:1. The question of the "*iustitia Dei*" displaces the other of "faith and understanding" [cf. Anselm of Canterbury, *Proslogion*, in idem, *Basic Writings*, ed. and trans. Thomas Williams (Indianapolis and Cambridge: Hackett Publishing Company, 2007), 75-98; Rudolf Bultmann, *Glauben und Verstehen*, 4 vols. (Tübingen, 1933-65). Only the first volume has been translated into English: Rudolf Bultmann, *Faith and Understanding*, vol. 1, ed. Robert W. Funk, trans. Louise Pettibone Smith (New York: Harper & Harper, 1969); Iwand, *Glauben und Wissen*, NW I, 73-92; idem, *Theologiegeschichte*, NWN III, 246-57.]

preeminence of the tropological method in this phase of Luther's exegesis.[44] By contrast, the decisive question now becomes: Is this concept of *"invisibilitas,"* which belongs to a particular system of values and understanding,[45] which is built upon analogical reasoning according to the Lombard's process in relation to Rom. 1:20 and for this reason always makes reference to the schema of *res* [thing] and *signum* [sign][46]—as *signum* every *res* represents, in accordance with their essential designations, something that cannot be seen—is this concept of invisibility that we encounter here the same one in whose name Luther would later protest against the visible church that made its leadership visible in the Roman pontificate? Indeed, it sounds entirely different when Luther writes in his *"Reply to the Celebrated Romanist at Leipzig"*—referring to the discalced Augustin Alveld—of 1520: "Would it not be a horrible error for these preachers of dreams to count the unity of the Christian community—separated by Christ himself from all physical and external places and locations and given a spiritual place—as a physical community, which is of necessity bound to a place and a location? How is it possible, and what mind may grasp it, that spiritual unity and physical unity are one and the same thing?"[47]

---

44. The problem of the tropological interpretation cannot be solved simply by referring to the scheme of "pro me" [cf. Iwand, "The Misuse of the *pro me*" in this volume]. Cf. the large passage LW 10,367; WA 3, 428,25ff. on our problem. A sentence like the following might be characteristic: LW 10, 373; WA 3, 432,26-31, on Ps. 69:17: "Since, therefore, we do not have actual sufferings and afflictions in our time, it is extremely necessary that we at least inflict them on ourselves in our thinking, so that we might be the kind of people on whom God would have mercy and whom He would safe. So let us be own tyrants, tormentors, heretics, stirring up such attitudes as keep after us and urge us on to better things, lest we be destroyed through peace and security."

This may have been the real motive of the young Luther's "theology of existence." This problem leads Luther to adopt the *"resignatio ad infernum,"* cf. LW 25, 378; WA 56, 388,3-28, on Rom. 8:28. From here I would like to enter into an argument with Lennart Pinomaa about the "existential character of Luther's theology" ([Lennart Pinomaa, *Der existentielle Charakter der Theologie Luthers: das Hervorbrechen der Theologie der Anfechtung und ihre Bedeutung für das Lutherverständnis, Annales Academiae Scientiarum Fennicae,* vol. 47.3] (Helsinki [Suomalaisen Kirjallisuuden Seura,] 1940). This supposed existentialism is likely to be the very theology of immanence that Luther overcomes.

45. The connection between the system of value and the system of knowledge results for scholasticism from the fact that Lombard in his commentary on the *Sentences* starts from the Augustinian difference between *"uti"* ["use"] and *"frui"* ["enjoy"] with respect to the material world. [Cf. St. Augustine, *On Christian Teaching,* trans. R. P. H. Green, Oxford World's Classics (Oxford: Oxford University Press, 1999), 9; Peter Lombard, *The Sentences. Book 1, The Mystery of the Trinity,* trans. Giulio Silano, Mediaeval Sources in Translation 42 (Toronto: Pontifical Institute of Mediaeval Studies, 2007), I. I. 3, 7.]

46. [Cf. Fn. 32.]

47. Martin Luther, *On the Papacy in Rome Against the Most Celebrated Romanist in Leipzig* (1520), LW 39, 49-104, 66; WA 6, 293,35-294,1.

The passage that is decisive at this point says that Christ has "removed" the unity of the church from all places and locations. So when the analogical schema of *res* and *signum* finds its application in the church and the visible church is perceived as the paradigm of this invisible church, this constitutes a betrayal of this Lord who reigns from the invisibility of his kingdom and in the invisibility of faith.[48] The "*Et-Et*" ["both-and"] of invisible and visible church, which could endure through the entire Middle Ages, thanks to the metaphysical understanding of *invisibilitas*—at least for the year of the decision—becomes an "*Aut-Aut*" ["either-or"]. Founded on the concept of the "*Ecclesia invisibilis et spiritualis*,"[49] Luther undertakes his assault on the visible church and proves the incompatibility of these two churches.

Time and again there have been those who have sought to interpret Luther's understanding of "invisible church" as if it were referring to spiritual or even personal ideas.[50] I believe that both of these are insufficient to understand what Luther meant and, above all, *why* the visible church that he encountered and exactly this same invisible church, which is an article of faith and confession, were

---

Ad librum eximii Magistri Nostri Ambrosii Catharini (1521), WA 7, 710,1-4: "Just as the stone [*petra*] is without sin, only discernible by faith, invisible and spiritual, so also must the church be without sin, only discernible by faith, invisible and spiritual. It is particularly important that the foundation is of the same composition as the building."

A proper study of Luther's understanding of Mt. 16:18 would have to follow here; we lack the necessary space for that here. For Luther the stone (*petra*) is not "Simon Barjona," but the "hearer of the Father's (divine) revelation": *Luther's Resolution on the 13th Thesis on the Power of the Pope* (1519), WA 2, 190,8.

Therefore, according to Luther, Christ founds his church in the faith, in which he himself is present. LW 39, 68.69; WA 6, 295,22f.34-36: "Thus it is plain that Christendom is a spiritual community which is [not] to be numbered with the worldly community . . . St. Paul says in Colossians 3[:3] that our life is not on earth but is hidden with Christ in God." Martin Luther, *The Leipzig Debate* (1519), WA 2, 257,18-21.22f: "Therefore one must not listen at all to those who cast Christ out of the militant church into the triumphant one, since it is the kingdom of faith, that is, that we do not see and yet we have our head . . . , that we see the chairs, not the one, who sits upon it, or the king."

48. Luther differentiates three "ways" of the churches being in the writing "On the Papacy in Rome" (LW 39, 65-71; WA 6, 292,35-297,40): the first is "natural, basic, essential and true," the "spiritual internal Christendom"; the second is "man-made and external," meaning the assembly at certain places and under certain forms; the third way to talk about the church is "the houses that are built for worship. The little word 'spiritual' is then further applied to temporal goods. . . . From all this follows that the first Christendom, which alone is the true church, may not and cannot have an earthly head. It may be ruled by no one on earth, neither bishop nor pope. Here only Christ in heaven is the head and he rules alone" [LW 39, 70.71; WA 6, 297,23f.37-40.]

49. *Ad librum eximii Magistri Nostri Ambrosii Catharini* (1521), WA 7, 710,1.

50. [Cf. Ernst Troeltsch, *The Social Teaching of the Christian Churches*, trans. Olive Wyon, vol. 2 (Louisville and London: Westminster John Knox Press, 1992), 516f.]

for him *incompatible*.[51] This can only be the case because these "two churches" stand alongside each other as rivals,[52] and the so-called visible church—the church that considers itself to be bound to places like Rome and persons like the pope or

---

51. LW 39, 66; WA 6, 293,35-294, 1.
Luther's Resolution on the 13th Thesis on the Power of the Pope (1519), WA 2, 239,28f.31-35: "For this is the reason that the church is called a kingdom of faith, because our King is not seen but believed, as it says in 1 Cor. 15, 25 . . . But these people make a kingdom of earthly things out of it, raising up a visible head. For even when a pope has died, the church is not without a head; why, then, in the lifetime of a pope, is Christ alone not held to be the head? Or does he resign when the pope is alive and follow him when he is dead, as a sort of alternating pope? But if he is also the head, when the pope lives, why do we lift up two heads in the church?"
LW 39, 72; WA 6, 298,21-24: "[W]ho has ever seen a live animal with a dead head? The head must instill life. That is why it is clear that on earth there is no head of the spiritual Christendom other than Christ alone."
Luther's Sermons Collected by J. Poliander (1519-21), WA 9, 458,18-24: "For they have now made one thing out of the Pope and Christ, and so they babble that Christ and the Pope are that one [mixed] man, and that Christ is inseparable from the Pope."
It is necessary to keep in mind that especially at that time Roman canonists like Prieras and Catharinus had really "horrendous" theories about papalism. In connection with the Hussite wars, the "monarchioptants" (Dempf) come in the foreground. [Alois Dempf, *Sacrum Imperium: Geschichts- und Staatsphilosophie des Mittelalters und der politischen Renaissance* (1929), 3rd ed. (Darmstadt: Wissenschaftliche Buchgesellschaft 1962), 555.—The ecclesiastical theorists who had previously advocated conciliarism and then turned to the monarchy are referred to as "monarchioptants."]
52. The reference to the "two churches" is there from the outset in Luther, cf. the early sermons collected by Poliander, Eck's former pupil, who went over to Luther after the *Leipzig Debate*, WA 9, 530,7-14: "If one now preaches according to the gospel, then the quarrel lifts up, then on emust stretch the neck to it. But now the pope with his followers has made a declaration and forbidden that one should not preach against them and their authority (meaning the *ius divinum*), that is, that there would not be a riot in the church. Therefore no one must preach the gospel who wants to have the pope as his friend. And thus the whole holy scripture shows us through an d through a twofold people, that there has been from the beginning of the world and will remain to the end." WA 9, 539,13f.: "And yet, those who appear to be the most pious are the vilest, the clerical are the most carnal, as are now the pope, bishops and priests."
Ad librum eximii Magistri Nostri Ambrosii Catharini (1521), WA 7, 740,13-27: "O man, do not aspire to the office of bishop, the office of canon, monasticism, or any spiritual station; there is sheer sin and corruption in it. . . For the one and proper office of the clergy is to teach the gospel, without which there is no clergy, but only the appearance of a clergyman. Nevertheless, that most holy king became strong thereby, so that he completely erased the gospel. And why don't I curse this curse? May the Lord Jesus destroy forever all these idols

the bishops—has stepped into the place of the *ecclesia invisibilis*.[53] For Luther, there is no vicarious standing in of the visible church, its institutions, or its organization, for the invisible church.[54] For precisely this is the true church, the church of the Word and the exalted Lord. The myth of the visible church is preserved by this

of the world, your papacy and office cardinal with all your structures into the abyss of hell, Amen."

It will never be possible to say that Luther gained this concept of the church solely from his justification experience. His antithesis to the papal church and the Canon law is about much more. The doctrine of the church is a matter sui generis in Luther's theology and must not be attributed to his subjectivity in any, even the most sublime, form of the mere experience of grace. Rather, it is a matter of the true and false church.

53. Martin Luther, *Ad librum eximii Magistri Nostri Magistri Ambrosii Catharini* (1521), WA 7, 720,18-21. This writing, along with the other *Vom Papsttum zu Rom* (1520), LW 39, 49-104; WA 6, 285-324, is the main source for Luther's later doctrine of the *ecclesia invisibilis*): "What folly then is it of the most ungodly papists that they bind the church of God, which is above all free, to her place and to certain and necessary (things) of her person, and say that he is not a Christian who does not want to worship even this ungodly Pope who lives in this place?"

On the other hand, is this on the true church, ibid., 720,8-12: "But everything is equal and free: every place is fitting for a Christian and no place is necessary for a Christian, any person can nurture him and no particular person is necessary to nurture him: for here reigns the freedom of spirit that makes all things equal and makes nothing necessary, of whatever is also physical and earthly."

The church on earth exists as *"ecclesia universalis."* WA 2, 430,28f. *Leipzig Debate* (1519) In response to Augustine's saying: "I would not have believed the gospel had not the authority of the Catholic Church moved me in that direction" [Augustin, *Contra epistolam Manichaei* V.6 (PL 42, 176)], Luther wrote, "With this sentence he understands the church neither as the pope nor as Rom. Rather he understands the church here as the universal church spread across the entire world."

LW 39, 66; WA 6, 294,4-7: "Therefore, he who says that an external assembly or unity creates Christendom speaks his mind arbitrarily. And whoever uses Scripture to support this brings divine truth down to the level of his lies and makes God a false witness."

54. *Ad librum eximii Magistri Nostri Ambrosii Catharini* (1521), WA 7, 742,12-15: "If he were teaching the commandments of God, he would not be the placeholder of God. For he is the placeholder of the absent prince, for this reason, that where the placeholder of God rules, there is no god at all. But where God is present, no governor is needed, only servants [are needed]."

Luther's Sermons Collected by J. Poliander (1519-21), WA 9, 458,27-29: "We have shown that the Pope is not the head of the church. Now we will prove that he is not Christ's vicar either. A proxy has the same job, does the same work, as the one he represents. The Pope does not do the same works as Christ."

LW 39, 73f; WA 6, 299,35-39: "But, you laymen, beware of having the hyperlearned Romanists burn you as heretcis, since you want to make the pope a messenger and letter-

visible church pushing aside the invisible church as a metaphysical quantity in the "world beyond" and by stepping in and presenting itself as the *mediator* of those invisible powers for man's terrestrial existence. The present time of salvation, the today of the gospel [cf. 2 Cor. 6:2] and the *certitudo fidei* [certainty of faith] are thus abolished. Everything must now be "mediated" by a specific "institution of salvation," through a priesthood provided with a specific "character" and through means of grace that operate as *res sacrae* because they supply the *gratia invisibilis*.[55] This self-contained work of the mediation of grace is held together by the "spiritual right"[56] that results from this distinction of sacred and profane, otherworldly and this-worldly reference to existence [*Daseinsbezug*], a distinction that is necessary for such an understanding of the church. If I see it correctly, this whole "world beyond," with its powers flowing from there unto us and its

---

carrier. Nevertheless, you certainly have good reason to do so, for 'apostle' in Greek means 'messenger' in German, and this is what the entire gospel calls them."

55. In the Catholic view, all sacraments confer a special "character" on the recipient, with the exception of the Eucharist itself, "and by this same sacrament a character is not imprinted on man (as in the ordination to the distribution of the sacraments); "because it [i.e. this sacrament] does not ordain man to any further sacramental action or benefit received . . . But it contains within itself Christ, in whom there is not the character, but the very plentitude of the Priesthood" (Thomas Aquinas, *The Summa Theologiae of St. Thomas Aquinas*, trans. Fathers of the English Dominican Province, 2nd revised ed. [New York: Benzinger Brothers, 1920] III, q 63 a 6).

The "character *indelebilis*" is based on the assumption that the sacrament conveys the participation ("*participatio*") in the "*sacerdotium Christi*." This, however, is eternal, ibid., a 5: "Consequently, every sanctification wrought by His Priesthood is perpetual."

On the concept of the sacraments as "res sacrae," cf. the fundamental remarks of the Lombard. Peter Lombard, *The Sentences. Book 4, On the Doctrine of Signs*, trans. Giulio Silano, Mediaeval Sources in Translation 48 (Toronto: Pontifical Institute of Mediaeval Studies, 2010), IV. I. 2-4, 3-4: "A sacrament is a visible form of an invisible grace. . . . For a sacrament is properly so called because it is a sign of God's grace and a form of invisible grace in such manner that it bears its image and is its cause."

From this, one can infer the meditorial, representational-figurative ("significans") and at the same time effective-sanctifying character ("sanctificans") of the sacraments. Martin Luther, *The Blessed Sacrament of the Holy and True Body of Christ, and the Brotherhoods* (1519), LW 35, 45-73, 63; WA 2, 751,33f.: "If it is merely an o*pus operatum*, it works only harm everywhere; it must become an *opus operantis*" (emphasis by the translator).

56. LW 39, 70; WA 6, 297,10-13: "This Christendom is ruled by canon law and by prelates within Christendom. Included in it are all popes, cardinals, bishops, prelates, priests, monks, nuns, and all those who are regarded as Christians according to externals, no matter whether they are true and real Christians or not."

hierarchical organization, drops away for Luther and the concept of the church that he recognized as being in accordance with the Scriptures.[57] With the abolition

---

57. Compare for the most important writings: Martin Luther, *Concerning the Ministry* (1523), LW 40, 3-44; WA 12, 169-196; idem, *That a Christian Assembly or Congregation Has the Right and Power to Judge All Teaching* . . . (1523), LW 39, 301-314; WA 11, 408-416.

The core sentence reads, LW 40, 18; WA 12, 178,9f.: "A Priest is not identical with Presbyter or Minister—for one is born to be priest, one becomes a minister."

That means, LW 40, 19; WA 12, 178,21-23: "the New Testament knows of no priest who is or can be anointed externally. If there are such, they are imitators and idols."

LW 40, 19; WA 12, 178,26-30: "For a priest, especially in the New Testament, was not made but was born. He was created, not ordained. He was born not indeed of flesh, but through a birth of the Spirit, by water and Spirit, in the washing of regeneration [John 3:6f.; Titus 3:5f.]. Indeed, all Christians are priests, and all priests are Christians. Worthy of anathema is any assertion that a priest is anything else than a Christian."

LW 40, 20; WA 12, 179,25-27: "Christ has been made the first priest of the New Testament without shaving, without anointing, and so without any of their 'character' or all the masquerade of episcopal ordination."

Here, Luther invokes the *"ius communionis,"* the law of the community. This *ius* is a true *ius divinum*. Whoever elevates himself above others within Christianity and ascribes to his office special functions, as "the Servant of the Word," "baptizing," "consecrating and distributing the sacred bread and sacred wine," "binding and loosing sins," "sacrificing," "praying for others," or "judging and deciding concerning matters of doctrine," breaks the divine law of the community.

LW 40, 33; WA 12, 189,9-12: "We have then altogether the same rights. For if we have in common the name of brethren, then one cannot be especially superior to the other or enjoy more of heritage or authority than the other in spiritual matters, of which we now are speaking" LW 40, 34; WA 12, 189,17-20: "For since we have proved all of these things to be the common property of all Christians, no one individual can arise by his own authority and arrogate to himself alone what belongs to all."

It is therefore more than a *lex charitatis*. The *"ius commune Christianorum"* is a genuine law within the Christian community. As founded in Scripture, it is *ius divinum*, that is, we are not free to act this way or that way, but if we order and build the ecclesiastical institutions differently, if we do not build the "common priesthood of the believers" into the foundation as a legal basis, we act sacrilegiously: "[E]ither they have no other priesthood than which the laity possesses"—thus no difference of the "priests" from the priesthood of the laity!—"or they have the priesthood of Satan" (LW 40, 34; WA 12,189,31f.).

LW 40, 33f; WA 12, 189,14f.: "For we are dealing not with a matter that is optional or permissible, but with a command and a necessity."

The decisive point is that the common priesthood is constituted by the presence of Christ, who is always in the midst of His own.

LW 40, 42; WA 12, 195,4-8: "There is then no reason for you to doubt that the church of God is among you, even if there are only ten or six who have the word. What such would do, along with others who do not yet have the Word but who would give their consent, certainly may be considered the work of Christ if they act, [. . .] in humility and in the spirit of prayer" (The omission is due to the sentence structure of the English translation).

The theme of the other writing takes one point out of the whole, the judging of doctrine. This judgment, according to the Lord's word "my own know me" (Jn 10:14) should belong to the congregation, not to the bishops and theologians, that is, not to those who teach but to those who hear.

WA 11, 409,10-12.14-17: "Human words and laws have established and ordered that the authority to judge doctrine should be left only to the bishops, the educated and the councils. What they have decided should be held by all the world as law and an article of faith. . . . For almost nothing is heard from them other than the praise that they have the authority and right to judge what is Christian or heretical. And the common Christian should wait for their judgement and abide by it."

409,20-22.26-32: "For Christ sets the opposition, takes from the bishops, the educated and councils both the right and the power to judge the doctrine and gives it to everyone and the whole Christian congregation . . . Bishop, pope, the learned and everyone have the power to teach, but the sheep shall judge, if they teach Christ's voice or a strangers voice. Friend, what will those say again who blow water, that scream: Concilia, Concilia, one has to listen to the learned, bishops, the masses, one must look at old traditions and practices? Do you think that for me God's word should yield before your old traditions, practices and bishops? Never."

410,6f.: "that they take the judgement of the doctrine shamefully from the sheep and take it to themselves by their own word and iniquity."

This conception of Luther, which was dominant throughout the great years of the Reformation, of the congregation as a subject—for it is begotten by the word and can therefore bear witness to it! [In the original German, this phrase includes a play of words between "begotten" *(gezeugt)* and "witness" *(bezeugen)*]—could have led to a genuine formation of the congregation. However, it was soon abandoned, and the judgment of the doctrine was once again completely assigned to the *ministerium verbi divini*. Cf. CA XXVIII.21 [KW 95; BSELK 195,4-15]: "Consequently, according to the gospel, or as they say, by divine right, this jurisdiction belongs to the bishops as bishops (that is, to those to whom the ministry of Word and sacraments has been committed): to forgive sins, to reject teaching that opposes the gospel, and to exclude from the communion of the church the ungodly whose ungodliness is known—doing all this with human power but by the Word." This doctrine is much more developed among the Orthodox. Here the definition comes close to the special "character" of the ordained again, even though one holds with the Council of Chalcedon that there can be no "ordination" without a "*vocatio ad certum aliquem locum*" ["call to a particular place"].

Johann Gerhard, *Loci theologici XXIII. 158*, ed. Preuß, VI (Berlin, 1868, S. 109): "Where no call has been extended, ordination may not be carried out."

But cf. Ibid., 178 (S. 121): "On the material cause of office: . . . here it is to be noted that the ecclesiastical bearers of office [clergy] can be called 'matter out of which' (something is made) and 'matter in which' (something is made); the former is the case because this order or estate of the church consists of the ecclesiastical officials as material parts, so to speak;

of the "seeming holiness," that is the declaration that all *opera* are indifferent,[58] that *ecclesia invisibilis* that is thought to be beyond the visible church as its equivalent collapses that it might rise again *positively* in a totally different and new way.

This *"Ecclesia spiritualis et invisibilis"*[59] apprehended in the present day subsists off of a totally different antithesis than that of visible and invisible. That is the antithesis of God's Word and man's word. Luther does not only discover that the concept of holiness can be traced back to God's *gracious verdict* that is pronounced "paradoxically" on the sinner. Rather, he discovers thereby the specific category of the *"Verbum Dei."* He does not only tear down but builds up at the same time. The Word of God does not change to fit man's word, experience, feelings, and so on. Rather, man changes to fit the Word of God. This is the decisive antithesis. "And He thus changes us into His Word, but not His Word into us."[60] What seems to Luther to be an "either-or" is conversely considered by his opponents to be a nearly self-evident "both-and." This becomes clear and tangible as a flashpoint in both Luther's and Eck's interpretations of Mt. 16:18. For Luther, it is an incomprehensible idea that Jesus could transfer his divine *potestas* [power] to fallible, diminishing, mortal men. Not the "Simon bar Jonah" [Mt. 16:17] but rather the *"auditor paternae revelationis* [hearer of the Father's revelation]"[61] transformed in the Word is the *Petrus* that merits the promise that *"ecclesia in perpetuum mansura* [the church endures forever],"[62] even as Eck along with many patristic citations instinctively holds on to

the latter is the case, because the dignity of ecclesiastical service is inherent in them as subordinates, so to speak."

Luther holds on to his position also later. Cf. *Articles Against the Whole School of Satan and All Ports of Hell* (1530), WA 30/II, 420,18-26, theses 5-7: "The Church of God has no power to confirm Articles [of Faith] or Commandments or the Holy Scriptures as if it were doing so by superior power or judicial authority, nor has it ever done so, nor will it ever do so. The Church of God, on the other hand, is confirmed and proven by the Holy Scriptures or the Articles of Faith rather than by a higher power and judicial authority. The Church of God affirms the Articles of Faith and the Scriptures as a subject, that is, she recognizes and confesses them, as a servant recognizes the seal of his master."

Basis for these boundaries of ecclesiastical power: "He who has no power to promise and to give future and present life has no power to establish articles of faith" [424, 32f.]. Luther wrote these theses and had them printed on his own initiative when the negotiations in Augsburg gave rise to fears that Melanchthon would be somewhat permissive. They arrived in Augsburg on July 22.

58. *Ad librum eximii Magistri Nostri Ambrosii Catharini* (1521), WA 7, 720,8: "But everything is indifferent and free."

59. WA 7, 722,6. Ibid.: "Therefore no one sees the church. Rather one believes in it only through the sign of the word."

60. LW 25, 211; WA 56, 227.4f., on Rom. 3:4.

61. [Cf. Fn. 47.]

62. [CA VII.1. KW 43; BSELK 61,1f.]

It would be carrying things too far to even begin to outline the great battle over Mt. 16:18 and the power of the keys here with citations. A few may suffice. *Leipzig Debate* (1519), WA 2, 286,17-24: "He says the same thing in the homily 'That All Priests Pray on the Day

the primacy of Peter, the prince of the Apostles, in the sense of a historical-earthly quantity.[63] Where this point has been conceded, the lot has already been cast as far

of Peter and Paul' where he says: 'on the rock (not 'on you,' but 'on the rock'), which you confessed.' I find the same thing in Ambrosius, although he sometimes speaks differently. At the same time there is that golden gloss, as they boast, about the chapter 'So the Lord' which reads: 'And upon this rock' etc. I do not believe that the Lord has indicated anything other than these words by this saying, which Peter answered the Lord when he said, 'You are Christ, the Son of the living God' because on that article of faith the church is founded. So Christ founded the church on himself."

WA 2, 191,23-25: "For, as I have said, who can deny that the keys are given to him who, by the revelation of the Father, confesses Christ? If this is accepted, then where there is the revelation of the Father and the confession of Christ are necessarily the keys."

191,32-35: "But now, when he is rebuked after the invitation as one who does not know God, it becomes clear that that earlier Peter who received the keys was not Peter the son of Barjonah, but the Church, the daughter of God, who, begotten by the word of God, hears the Word of God, and continually confesses to the end."

193,13f.: "And yet the keys were not taken from him again, because he received them not in his own person but in the person of the Church."

193,36-39: "That the keys were given only to the one who does not obey flesh and blood, but the Father in heaven, that is, [they are given] to one who is holy and righteous in spirit. Otherwise every pope is a satan who does not understand what is God's."

Contra malignum Iohannis Eccii iudicium M. Lutheri defensio (1519), WA 2, 633,36-40: "I will not allow my Eck to apply this word (You are Peter) to anyone other than one who is like Peter, who has Christ's revelation and the Holy Spirit. For these words require such a successor, and make none a successor without the faith of Peter, which must be determined by other words than these."

Defense and Explanation of All the Articles (1521), LW 32, 3-99, 76; WA 7, 423,2-9: "Christ did not give these words [i.e. Matthew 16:19] so that St. Peter might have power to do anything, but they are given to our faith, which is to hold fast to them in order that our sins may be forgiven. St. Peter is only a servant in this matter. He can hold these words up to us, but what he can do with them depends on our faith. He may remit penalty and guilt a thousand times over, and yet accomplish nothing, unless I believe in it. Faith makes the keys effective and powerful, unbelief makes them ineffective and powerless. Without faith there is in these words none of the power which the pope arrogates to himself, deceiving both himself and us."

Assertio omnium articulorum M. Lutheri per Bullam Leonis X (1520), WA 7, 129,14-18: "Therefore I say that it is an ungodly, intolerable blasphemy to understand the rock, which alone is Christ, that is, the Word and the invincible faith in him, as that monarchical power, which is the servant and workshop of Satan. For it is faith in Christ alone that cannot be perverted into any sin by the gates of hell."

Luther's Sermons Collected by J. Poliander (1519–21), WA 9, 522,22.: "He has given his rule to noone on earth."

63. *Leipzig Debate* (1519), WA 2, 292,4-7.11-14: "Eck: 'I answer, it is true that Christ did not expressly name the Roman Church in the gospel, but rather Peter, who was appointed

as the visible church is concerned. All of our Protestant scholars have had to be clear about this—I'm thinking here somewhat of the certainty with which A. Schlatter writes, regarding whether we can overlook the Reformation's interpretation,[64] that whoever says "A" at this point will have to say "B," even at many other points that he could not even dream of. The whole manner of speaking of historical revelation, of the particular apostolic authority, of being eyewitnesses, and so on, will still need to be reviewed in view of that question that was at the center of the Leipzig Disputation and that became decisive for the continued course of the Reformation: the question of visible and invisible church. The church under the Word must always be believed and confessed to be *"ecclesia invisibilis."* "In Psalm 9 the church is called 'Almuth' (hidden) and an article of faith which the holy universal church believes and professes, that it is never and nowhere visible, and keeps from it every [thought of] place and person."[65]

From this point—even when the objection arises that these are the opinions of the "Young Luther," which is, after all, the reformer in his decisive years and writings!—it is necessary to examine this image of the Lutheran Church that was sketched in the nineteenth century by Stahl, Löhe, Vilmar, and Kliefoth[66] and that

prince of the apostles. This is because Peter, who had supremacy, moved the chair from Antioch to Rome by the command of the Lord . . . but this is the opinion of the holy fathers: because Peter was appointed vicar of Christ by divine right, so are all his Followers, just as the Roman popes, wherever they may be, are vicars of Christ.'"

64. Adolf Schlatter, [*Der Evangelist Matthäus: Seine Sprache, sein Ziel, seine Selbständigkeit* (Stuttgart: Calwer Vereinsbuchhandlung, 1929), 507f.] on Mt. 16:18: "The anti-Catholic polemic has taken offense at this phrase, because it described not Peter but his faith and his confession as the rock on which Jesus builds his church. The hypostatization of faith which endows it with effects without the need a believer, belongs to a completely different logic than the one that formed the spiritual life of Jesus and the evangelists. . . . Therefore, when thinking of the beginning of the church, it is not spoken of as a 'belief' or as a term (is belief really a term for Schlatter? Or in general?), but of that person to whom Jesus hands over his work, so that the new church comes into being through him."

In relation to this, Eck is still the better interpreter. He understands our word as *promissio*, which is fulfilled with the resurrection. *Leipzig Debate* (1519), WA 2, 293,11f: "Therefore the decretals rightly conclude from that passage where Christ promised, but only after the resurrection did he fulfill it."

65. *Ad librum eximii Magistri Nostri Ambrosii Catharini* (1521), WA 7, 722,8-10.

66. [Friedrich Julius Stahl (1802-61), Wilhelm Löhe (1808-72), August Friedrich Christian Vilmar (1800-68), and Theodor Friedrich Dethlof Kliefoth (1810-95) were representatives of a restoration of Lutheran Confessionalism. Cf. Friedrich Julius Stahl, *Die lutherische Kirche und die Union: Eine wissenschaftliche Erörterung der Zeitfrage* (Berlin: Wilhelm Hertz, 1859); idem, *Die Kirchenverfassung nach Lehre und Recht der Protestanten*, 2nd ed. (Erlangen: Theodor Bläsing, 1862); Wilhelm Löhe, *The Books About the Church* (1845), trans. James L. Schaaf (Philadelphia: Fortress Press, 1969); August Friedrich Christian Vilmar, *Dogmatik*, ed. Karl Wilhelm Piderit, vol. 2 (Gütersloh, 1874), 181ff;

has contributed so much to the destruction of Luther's doctrine of the church at its root.[67] However, it will also be necessary to move away from the thesis that Luther had subjectively shaped his concept of the church on the basis of the doctrine of justification and had already had it essentially finished in 1513.[68] The tremendous reversal in the understanding of the invisible Church that takes place within the ten years that we are surveying (1513–23) is thus disregarded. I emphasize yet again that Luther is not done justice when this invisible church is understood as

---

Theodor Friedrich Dethlof Kliefoth, *Acht Bücher von der Kirche*, vol. 1 (Schwerin and Rostock: Stiller, 1854).]

67. The criticism of the concept of the church of the Lutheran restoration theology of the nineteenth century is still awaited. Compare a sentence from Friedrich Julius Stahl, *Die lutherische Kirche und die Union*, 57: "On the whole, therefore, the church is a divine institution of grace, an institution, a given material (!) power, a holy foundation which embraces man, seizes him before he does his own deed by the means of grace which are entrusted to her, and prepares him for faith and promotes the faith by those means that lives already in him." It would be a great merit, if Stahl's work, which still widely determines the judgments and prejudices of Lutherans, were thoroughly revised. Pretty much everything developed there is wrong—but it has method! It goes back to the presentations of the nineteenth century, not to the sources, when Max Weber and Ernst Troeltsch refer to the Lutheran church as "*Anstaltskirche*" [institutional church], and emphazise the "*Begriff der Heilsanstalt*" [the concept of the institution of salvation] in contrast to the voluntary community of the "sect."

[Max Weber, "Twelve: The Protestant Sects and the Spirit of Capitalism," in *Essays in Economic Sociology*, ed. Richard Swedberg (Princeton: Princeton University Press, 1999), 168–78; Troeltsch, *The Social Teaching of the Christian Churches*, vol. 1: 331–6; vol. 2: 477–84, 515–18.] Cf. the judicious and valuable work of Holsten Fagerberg, *Bekenntnis, Kirche und Amt in der konfessionellen Theologie des 19. Jahrhunderts* (Uppsala: Almquist & Wiksell, 1952), esp. 195ff and 299ff.

68. Martin Luther, Preface to: "Confession of the Faith and Religion of the Barons and Nobles of the Kingdom of Bohemia" (1538), LW 60, 214-219, 217f; WA 50, 379,25-35: "But after it pleased Him who set me apart from my mother's womb [Gal. 1:15] to reveal to me that son of perdition [2 Thessalonians 2:3], then I did consult with flesh and blood [cf. Galatians1:16] and had quite a few debates with the best men I was able to find, fearing that the light which was in me might be darkness [cf. Matthew 6:23], so unsure was I of my own self on account of the length, width, and depth of papal majesty [cf. Eph. 3:18]. Until then even I myself had not hesitated to believe that it was governed by the Holy Spirit and was unable to err, until I became gradually more confident, while in response to my insignificant skirmishes and some preludes of mine the Papists were whipping up their consternation into a foam, like waves of the wild sea (as Jude [13] says). Then I began to regard the pope with suspicion and little by little came to despise him and finally, even as his defenders were betraying—or, rather, entirely abandoning—him in books more vain than vanity itself [cf. Ecclesiastics 1:2 etc.], I came to recognize him as the very 'abomination in the holy place' [Matthew 24:15]."

a "fellowship of persons." For "*aufertque ab ea omnem locum et personam*" ["and removes from it every place and every person"]. The thing is deeper than that. The church is invisible because in it and through it the *regnum Christi* [kingdom of Christ] is "in the midst of us" [cf. Lk. 17:21] as *regnum fidei* [kingdom of faith]. In this kingdom there is neither sin nor death. What we have now in *faith*—and will have later "with sight and senses"[69]—is intended with the invisible but living present of the *regnum coelorum* [kingdom of heaven].[70]

But now two things come out in Luther. The first is the change of meaning of the "sign" by which the invisible church indicates its presence. The sign no longer has the aim of making the invisible visible—even with the sacrament, this is not the sign's aim[71]—but rather to indicate its presence in such a way that it

---

69. [LW 35, 66; WA 2, 753,15f.]

70. Martin Luther, *A Sermon on Preparing to Die* (1519), LW 42, 94-115, 104; WA 2, 689,11-14: "For Christ is nothing other than sheer life, as his saints are likewise. The more profoundly you impress that image upon your heart and gaze upon it, the more the image of death will pale and vanish of itself without struggle or battle."

LW 42, 105.106; WA 2, 690,17-19.21f.24f: "So then, gaze at the heavenly picture of Christ, who descended into hell [I Peter 3:19] for your sake and was forsaken by God. . . . In that picture your hell is defeated and your uncertain election is made sure. . . . Never, therefore, let this be erased from your vision. Seek yourself only in Christ and not in yourself and you will find yourself in him eternally."

LW 26, 285; WA 40/I, 444,20-23, on Gal. 3:13: "For in fact there is no sin any longer, no curse, no death, and no devil, because Christ has conquered and abolished all these. Accordingly, the victory of Christ is utterly certain; the defects lie not in the fact itself, which is completely true, but in our incredulity."

It would be highly necessary to examine more closely the meaning of "*Glaubstu, dan hastu*" [lit. "You believe, then you have"] in Luther. [Martin Luther, *The Sacrament of Penance* (1519), LW 35, 3-22, 16; WA 2, 719,8; idem, *The Holy and Blessed Sacrament of Baptism* (1519), LW 35, 23-43, 38; WA 2, 733,35; idem, *The Freedom of a Christian* (1520), LW 31, 327-377; WA 7, 24,1-17]. For whoever interprets this phrase in the sense of subjectivity, as Hegel and his school did with the Reformation, has not understood it; that phrase must probably be understood in terms of the resurrection of Christ as being about the *Ecclesia* and her reality.

71. LW 35, 66; WA 2, 753,6-10: "For everything that is bound to time and sense must fall away, and we must learn to do without them, if we are to come to God. For this reason, the mass and this sacrament are a sign by which we train and accustom ourselves to let go all visible love, help, and comfort."

LW 35, 65; WA 2, 752,33-35: "giving us such a gracious sign, by which—if we hold fast to it in faith—he leads and draws us through death and every danger unto himself, unto Christ and all saints."

Promotionsdisputation von Palladius und Tilemann (1537), WA 39/I, 217,12-21: "It has pleased God to take up this corrupt nature of ours, infected with the poison of Satan, and to wrap up in these outward appearances and sacraments so that we may understand Him.

is comprehensible to *faith* as present. Further, the external sign has a "spiritual" dynamic as such. It is of such a nature that it incorporates the believer into this infallible *true church* removed from sin and death. The sign is no longer a *"signum"* of the metaphysical reality that is to be thought of as transcendent by comparison to the world of the senses, a *"signum"* that has been misplaced in visibility. Rather, it is the indication of the *inbreaking* and of the immediate, promising nearness of the kingdom of God *in* the world of space and time. It must be understood as a sign of a dynamic, not as a sign of a higher existence to be grasped ontologically. Yet this is not yet enough. In this new formulation of the *"ecclesia invisibilis,"* the *Word* becomes the decisive *sign*.[72] Now the Word *can be* a sign. In the medieval sacramental understanding, this was only the case insofar as the Word univocally determined the sign as it was given to the senses.[73] This is largely the understanding of our modern treatments of the Lord's Supper with regard to the Word: it is an "interpretive Word."[74] This is nicely Thomistic. But for Luther, the Word is not based on a *res* or an activity, such as the establishment of the Passover meal.[75] Rather, it is based on the divine *promissio*,[76] on the testament. The sign is given to whoever

Thus the Holy Spirit leads us, through those outward things by which He entices and invites us, to the eternal, heavenly, and invisible, which are beyond our comprehension. Just as a fisherman deceives, catches and pulls out the fish by the bait that is cast and brought back in from the sea, so we too are led to the eternal by the action of the Holy Spirit."

These two essentially identical statements are twenty years apart. One cannot simply dismiss those first remarks of Luther about the sacraments of 1519 with the "young Luther."

72. *Ad librum eximii Magistri Nostri Ambrosii Catharini* (1521), WA 7, 721,9f: "The gospel is the only, surest and noblest sign of the church before bread and baptism."

Resolutio disputationis de fide infusa et acquisita (1520), WA 6, 97,5f: "The Scriptures have only one single sacrament which is Jesus Christ."

97,21-23: "Therefore the Word is fellowship in and revelation of this sacrament; but the sacrament itself is Christ, thus he is grasped with faith alone."

73. Thomas Aquinas, *Summa theologica* [cf. Fn. 56] III, q 60 a 7: "Since, therefore, in the sacraments determinate sensible things are required, which are as the sacramental matter, much more is there need in them of a determinate form of words."

74. [Joachim Jeremias, *The Eucharistic Words of Jesus*, trans. Norman Perrin (Philadelphia: Trinity Press, 1990), 218–36].

75. [Cf. Hellmut Gollwitzer, "Bericht über die von der Abendmahlskommission erarbeitete Erklärung," in *Zur Lehre vom Heiligen Abendmahl: Bericht über das Abendmahlsgespräch der Evangelischen Kirche in Deutschland 1947–1957 und Erläuterung seines Ergebnisses*, ed. Gottfried Niemeier (Munich: Chr. Kaiser Verlag, 1959), 19–34, 28f.; Iwand, "Die theologischen Aussagen der Arnoldshainer Thesen," *Kirche in der Zeit* 15 (1960): 327–31.]

76. Martin Luther, *The Babylonian Captivity of the Church* (1529), LW 36, 3-126, 38; WA 6, 513,24f: "A testament, as everyone knows, is a promise made by one about to die, in which he designates his bequest and appoints his heirs."

LW 36, 38; WA 6, 513,34-36.37-514,1: "You see, therefore, that what we call the mass is a promise of the forgiveness of sins made to us by God, and such a promise as has been

believes in this so that he might cling to it. Thus, it is a sign of God's faithfulness for the believer. This is why the sacraments are now called "*seal or token*"[77] and "*marks of notaries*,"[78] because the performance of the testament, that is, the διαθήκη of the new covenant underlies this seal. And it should also be noticed that first of all—precisely from the standpoint of the conclusion of the covenant with the validating death of the testator—the flesh and blood of Christ themselves are understood as true "signs." The sacrificed body of Christ is the seal of God's definitive promise, the seal added by God himself to the *Word* of forgiveness. In this way, the *signa ecclesiae* are understood as *signa* in terms of the *Word* (=*promissio*), no longer in terms of the *res*. And when these signs indicate the presence of the church and its gifts—and they always offer these as present realities—they do this because the Word can never remain empty [cf. Isa. 55:11]. Where the *Word* is, there is *faith*, and where *faith* is, there—and there alone—is the *true church*.[79]

---

confirmed by the death of the Son of God.... A testator is a promiser who is about to die, while a promiser (if I may put it thus) is a testator who is not about to die."

LW 36, 39; WA 6, 514,19: "First of all there is God's Word. After it follows faith."

LW 36, 42; WA 6, 516,30-32: "For God does not deal, nor has he ever dealt, with man otherwise than through a word of promise, as I have said. We in turn cannot deal with God otherwise than through faith in the Word of his promise."

77. Martin Luther, *A Treatise on the New Testament, that is, the Holy Mass* (1520), LW 35, 75-129, 86; WA 6, 359,18f (emphasis added by Iwand).

Cf. also LW 35, 86; WA 6, 359,4-6: "This is what Christ has done in this testament. He has affixed to the words a powerful and most precious seal and sign: his own true flesh and blood under the bread and wine." Here, the "body and blood of Christ" are the signs.

LW 35, 86; WA 6, 359,9-11: "that this sign may be a sacrament, that is, that it may be external and yet contain and signify something spiritual; in order that through the external we may be drawn into the spiritual."

LW 35, 86; WA 6, 359,18-21: "the seal or token is the sacrament, the bread and wine, under which are his true body and blood. For everything that is in this sacrament must be living. Therefore Christ did not put it in dead writing and seals, but in living words and signs."

78. [LW 35, 86; WA 6, 359,2f. (emphasis added by Iwand)].

79. *Leipzig Debate* (1519), WA 2, 208,25-29: "Therefore, wherever the word of God is preached and believed, there is also true faith, this immovable rock; and where faith is, there is the church; where the church is, there is the bride of Christ; where the bride of Christ is, there is everything that belongs to the bridegroom. So faith carries with it all that follows after faith: the keys, the sacraments, the authority of the office, and everything else."

Ad librum eximii Magistri Nostri Ambrosii Catharini (1521), WA 7, 720,34-38: "A sign is necessary, which we also have, namely baptism, the bread and above all the gospel. These three are the symbols, watchwords and emblems of Christians. For where baptism and the

Along with this new formulation of the *"signa ecclesiae,"* Luther carries out a decisive transformation in the distinction of God's Word and man's word.[80] This alternative had previously been the theological problem of the receding scholasticism and had prepared the dissolution of the Thomistic synthesis of creation and grace since Duns and Occam. Indeed, it is truly nothing else than the problem that never dies down in theology, the problem of revelation as such.[81]

---

bread and the gospel appear to be for you, in whatever place, with whatever persons, you shall not doubt that in that place there is a church."

Luther's Sermons Collected by J. Poliander (1519–21), WA 9, 535,6-9.10-13: "That is our sign, whereby we find Christ alone. There is no certain sign of Christ to be found other than the place where the gospel is preached. Pope and bishop do not have this sign. . . . True Christians all walk in the faith of the Gospel. One cannot outwardly know or see them, as Moses had indicated, that under the ark's veil should be placed two poles on which to carry it so that no one could see it."

Ad librum eximii Magistri Nostri Ambrosii Catharini (1521), WA 7, 722,1-7: "These signs, especially of the gospel, seem to have once been formed in the temple of Solomon, where two handles of the poles by which the ark was carried protruded outside the mercy seat, the Spirit signifying that one knows only by the clear and public voice of the Gospel, where the Church and the mystery of the Kingdom of Heaven are. For just as one believed by the handles of the poles as if by signs that the ark, though hidden, was present in the Holy of Holies, so no one sees the church, but believes it solely through the sign of the Word, which only resounds in the church through the Holy Spirit."

721,15: "I am not talking about the written gospel but about the spoken one."

Widder das Wüetende Vrteyl der Pariser Theologisten. Schützred Philippi Melanchthon. für Mart. Luther (1521), WA 9, 755,15-18: "We call a church that which is built by the word of God, and is consecrated, nurtured, educated, and governed by the word of God, in short, that creates all her things by the Gospel, and judges all things, according to the Gospel."

LW 39, 305; WA 11, 408,8-12.16-18: "The sure mark by which the Christian congregation can be recognized is that the pure gospel is preached there. For just as the banner of an army is the sure sign by which one can know what kind of lord and army have taken the field, so, too, the gospel is the sure sign by which one knows where Christ and his army are encamped. . . . Thus we are certain that there must be Christians wherever the gospel is, no matter how few and how sinful and weak they may be."

80. [Cf. Iwand, *Luthers Theologie*, NW V, 243–9.]

81. From the point of view of theological development, it should be possible to show—in contrast to the tendency of the otherwise so valuable history of the Reformation by Joseph Lortz—that we have no reason to see the Reformation in light of the event of the schism of the church which occurred only subsequently, or to lament it, as has become fashionable in certain Protestant circles today. This view of things, essentially under the political aspect of the unification of Europe, was probably first presented in the modern sense by Novalis, *Die Christenheit oder Europa* [*Ein Fragment* (1799); cf. Heinrich Bornkamm, *Luther im Spiegel der deutschen Geistesgeschichte* (Heidelberg: Quelle & Meyer, 1955), 155–60]. Leibniz still argues, namely in the sense of the unity of spirits, for the purpose of their unification in

But the exceptional thing about Luther's way of putting the question is that he comprehends the alternative of man's word and God's Word as a determination that is to be made *within* the church itself, not as a determination between church and world or between faith and reason. The substitution of man's word for God's Word and God's Word for man's word can only take place where God's Word is currently in the picture,[82] which is to say among the people of God itself.

In comparison to this, the questions of church and state, church and world are of secondary importance. They depend upon how the determination is made at that highest point, how it is made at the *absolute* itself. It is in the church alone that this frightful transformation takes place that makes out of God's Word the word of man = man's law.[83] So long as this confusion exists at the highest peak in the

---

"God's State" [cf. *Monadologie* (1714), §§ 83–90], which forms the basis of enlightened humanity that has overcome all previous borders and divisions. Novalis reconstructs the unity. Thus the Romantic view of the Reformation won. Protestantism very soon detached the *"ecclesia invisibilis"* from the *"verbum Dei"* and understood her, similar to the Middle Ages, again as an intelligible realm (Kant) [cf. Kant, *Religion Within the Boundaries of Mere Reason* (1793), trans. Allen Wood and George di Giovanni (Cambridge: Cambridge University Press, 1998), part 3. IV, A 134. B 142], while Catholic theology since Bellarmin has expanded the visibility of the church at the expense of predestination, which is still fundamental for Thomas. These developments have resulted in new problems, which I do not think are historically justified to bring to the origin of Luther's concept of the church. [Bellarmin, "De Conciliis" I.3, c.2, in idem, *Disputationes de controversiis christianae fidei adversus huius temporis haereticos* I-III, Ingolstadt 1586–93.]

82. [Cf. Martin Luther, *"Ein feste Burg ist unser Gott"* (1528), 4th verse.]

83. *Sermo praescriptus praeposito in Litzka* (1512), WA 1, 12,40-13,3: "It is the word of truth alone in which they think they cannot sin, while that is almost the only thing in which a priest as a priest sins. In other things he certainly sins, but as a man; but here, if he omits or falsifies the Word, he sins against his office and as a priest, i.e. far more horribly than as a man."

Widder das Wüetende Vrteyl der Pariser Theologisten (1521), WA 9, 744,22-30: "So it seems to me that Paris does not think they are doing anything evil now, but long ago she was fooled when she started pagan art and spoiled Christian teaching with human learning. Thus we who should be Christ's people are indeed not Moses' people, but rather became Aristotle's."

Ad librum eximii Magistri Nostri Ambrosii Catharini (1521), WA 7, 725,25-28: "For they will not deny the gospel, but along with the pronouncements of the gospel they will fabricate amendments, glosses and statutes, and gradually, subtly and secretly, lead the people away from the royal way of faith to sects of works, with which they will annihilate and destroy the gospel."

To the Christian Nobility of the German Nation: Concerning the Reform of the Christian Estate (1520), LW 44, 115-217, 182; WA 6, 445,26-28: "The evil spirit unleashed by canon law has brought such a terrible plague and misery into the heavenly kingdom of holy Christendom."

ordering of the spiritual cosmos, nothing else is certain in its continued existence. This is why Luther speaks of this exchange of God's Word and human *"potestas"* as coming from Satan, which is to say from the Antichrist.[84] The exaltation of man over the Word of God, which is to say over the Scriptures, is more than satanic.[85] Where this exchange occurs, nothing remains of the true church but *"facies"* ["appearance"] and *"larva"* ["mask"], put another way, a church that is pressing more and more toward the visible. The validity of the church that is attached to its visible form (μορφή) must decline, both that which concerns its own life and its public authority. Only with reform at the peak—by emphasizing the authority of those leading the church as *ius humanum* [human authority][86]—can the God-willed ordering in relation to the state and society be reclaimed, for "if the church is above the word and has power to change the word, then it has the power to

---

84. *Epitoma responsionis ad Martinum Luther* (1520), WA 6, 328,16-18.23-25: "He makes each one of us into a Pope, even an ungodly person into God, and decreed that the power of Scripture, that is, the power of the Word of God, which is God Himself, depends on the authority of that man, even an ungodly one; . . . But now this Satan strengthens the Scriptures through a man. Who is the Antichrist if such a Pope is not the Antichrist? O Satan, Satan! How long will you abuse your Maker's patience to your great misery?"

Ad librum eximii Magistri Nostri Ambrosii Catharini (1521), WA 7, 741,16-19: "But does he not show that he is like God when he teaches his own words in place of the words of God and substitutes his papist righteousness for the righteousness of faith?"

759,30-34: "Therefore this king, who ravages the kingdom of heaven and destroys the simplicity that is in Jesus Christ (as Paul says [2 Cor. 11, 3.]), is none other than that rightful Antichrist, who put works in the place of faith, who teaches deceit instead of truth, who teaches appearances instead of mysteries, who teaches his proposals instead of the gospel, his intrigues instead of sincerity, and his decrees instead of the word of God, and so corrupts the conscience and destroys the spirit."

Luther's Sermons Collected by J. Poliander (1519-21), WA 9, 522,25-28: "But now it has again come to this, that they have taken off the servants' garments and have put on the master's garment. All this would still be endurable, how they deal with us, if they did not suppress our Christ and Christian doctrine."

Cf. *De potestate leges ferendi in ecclesiae* (1530), WA 30/II, 682,37.

85. *Resolutions on the Leipzig Debate* (1519), Conclusio 12, WA 2, 429,36-430,4: "Because they therefore attribute authority to the pope to interpret Scripture, even to him alone. Further, they oppose the same [the saying of Augustine] to all whom they hear doubt or oppose the letters or actions of the popes. Neither Lucifer himself nor all the heretics together conceived a more damnable opinion than this, nor even a similar ungodliness. For it follows that the pope and the scribes of the palace are above the gospel and therefore above God, while Lucifer tried to be like God."

86. *Luther's Resolution on the 13th Thesis on the Power of the Pope* (1519), WA 2, 200,36-201,1: "I have allowed everything that is granted to the Roman Pope these days. I do not

change everything."[87] In this way, Luther's newfound understanding of the *regnum fidei* [kingdom of faith] as the *ecclesia invisibilis* necessarily resulted in the monk's step into the restored world,[88] a step that precipitates a new era in the history of Western Christendom.

That which lit up like a flash during those years, only to disappear rapidly in a moment of church history and world history that was never to recur,[89] remains

---

deny the matter; I do not contradict the fact, but I dispute his right, and I believe that he does not settle such things by divine right, but by decrees of the people."

Leipzig Debate (1519), WA 2, 279,23f: "Even a believing Christian cannot be forced to go beyond the Holy Scriptures, which are actually divine law, unless a new and proven revelation is added."

Here it becomes very clear that all questions about the "ecclesiastical law" in Luther should begin with the question of the authority of Scripture, not with the doctrine of justification. This is a shortcoming in Johannes Heckel's work. Perhaps the question of ecclesiastical law is already decided in the interpretation of Mt. 16:18. Here the concept of "*ministerium verbi divini*" becomes clear in its double fashion. Instead of many quotations, just one: Martin Luther, *Explanations of the Ninety-Five Theses* (1518), LW 31, 77-252, 195; WA 1, 595,40-42: "Pay attention to the word and dismiss the outward appearance of the person. Whether the person errs or does not err, you shall not err if you believe God's word."

If the attempt made here is correct to prove the *ecclesia invisibilis* as Luther's creed, it has far-reaching consequences for ecclesiastical law. The newly emerging demand for private confession in the Protestant church will very soon raise anew the question of the "clerical right" to absolution. Neither the priest nor the pope have such a specific right, according to Luther. For the keys to bind and to loose are given to the whole congregation, that is, to all believers. *De instituendis ministris Ecclesiae* (1523), WA 12, 183,30f: "All we, however, who are Christians, hold the office of the keys together."

87. *De potestate leges ferendi in ecclesia* (1530), WA 30/II, 682,21f.

88. Martin Luther, *Commentary on 1 Corinthians 7* (1523), LW 28, 1-56, 35; WA 12, 122,5-15 on 1 Cor. 7:14: "To a Christian, therefore, the entire world is holiness, purity, utility, and piety. Contrariwise, to a non-Christian the whole world is unholiness, impurity, uselessness, and destruction—even God with all His goodness, as Ps. 18:26-27 says to God: 'With the pure Thou dost show Thyself pure; and with the crooked Thou dost show Thyself perverse.' Why is this? Because the pure, that is, the believers, can use all things in a holy and blessed way to sanctify and purify themselves. But the unholy and the unbelievers sin, profane, and pollute themselves incessantly in all things. For they cannot use anything in a right, godly, and blessed way, so that it might serve their own salvation."

89. It seems impossible to me to treat the Reformation as a heritage in the sense that a continuous line led from Luther through the gnesio-Lutherans to our Lutheran confessionalists. Thus we run the risk of making an event that concerns the whole of Christendom the privilege of a group. The problem of continuity within church history is likely to be different and much more intricate than the history of the world and the culture, with which our "church history" textbooks are concerned. *Luther's Sermons Collected by J. Poliander* (1519–21), WA 9, 620,36-621,3: "Therefore, one should note, that we surrender

valid as a reminder and as a warning, maybe also as hope and consolation, if the evangelical church remains something other than what it proclaims in its name: the church that lives from the gospel, from its certainty, and from the invisible presence of its Lord in Word and sacrament. Whoever has grasped this will not exchange the birthright of the *ecclesia invisibilis* for the pottage of the visible church.

to the fact that right godly life must be called heretical and be highly despised, reviled and scolded. It follows that God's doctrine must be called devilish and be utterly rejected by the great hypocritical saints." In the presentation of the history of the church—if it would be done right—it should be different than in the history of the world! It would have to be the actual and true history of revolution in the history of humanity.

Chapter 11

THEOLOGIA CRUCIS

COMPOSED FOR THE CONVENTION IN BEIENRODE IN THE FALL OF 1959

Originally published as Hans Joachim Iwand, "Theologia crucis," in Iwand, *Vorträge und Aufsätze*, NW II, 381–98.

Iwand gave this lecture at the Beienrode Convention that has been held there regularly since 1951. In Beienrode, which is located in the West German part only a few kilometers away from the border between the two German states, Iwand founded "the house of the helping hands" in 1949. From there, on the one hand the work of the aid organization for the East Prussian Church should be coordinated and on the other hand young widows of deceased pastors of the East Prussian Church and of those who had been killed in the war should find refuge and a new home there. Iwand himself and his wife, Ilse Ehrhardt, who already died in 1950, were buried on the small churchyard in the park of this former estate.

The theology of the cross was a central topic for Iwand. In doing so he refers directly to Martin Luther's theology of the cross and unfolds its importance in the background of the theological and ecclesiopolitical discourses of the twentieth century. The "pastoral character" of the theology of the cross and the new understanding of the "reality," which from his point of view was associated with this, were especially important to him. [MB]

If I am now—at the end of our meeting—following up with a brief outline of Luther's *theologia crucis*, I want to make it clear from the very beginning that it will in no way constitute a conclusive articulation of the subject at hand, nor even something fundamentally new. Of course, this topic has a certain relevance insofar as the old view advocated by Otto Ritschl in his *History of Protestant Dogma*[1]— namely that the *theologia crucis* is the embodiment of Luther's pre-Reformation views and points back to mysticism's piety of *humilitas* [*Humilitas-Frömmigkeit*]—

---

1. [Cf. Otto Ritschl, *Dogmengeschichte des Protestantismus: Grundlagen und Grundzüge der theologischen Gedanken- und Lehrbildung in den protestantischen Kirchen*, 4 vols. (Leipzig: J. C. Hinrichs, 1908–27).]

was recently taken up again by Gyllenkrok[2] and Bizer,[3] and even Barth thinks that the young Luther must be seen in this way.[4] At the same time, the comprehensive and good book by Walter von Loewenich[5] has disproved this understanding of earlier Luther scholarship inasmuch as it deals with the *theologia crucis* in Luther at all. It demonstrated that with the *theologia crucis*, we are dealing with an entirely new treatment of the subject as it has come down from mysticism. Subsequently, I would like to show that with this theological catchword, we are dealing with a theological epistemology with which Luther overcomes the old scholastic method, which was also more or less the Augustinian Neoplatonist method, with resplendent formulas in the Heidelberg Disputation. After the development of the new theological epistemology, he uses it as a basis for the interpretation of the Psalms, which he undertook through the Twenty-Second Psalm. After that he had to go to Worms. But the Twenty-Second Psalm itself becomes for him the pinnacle of an entirely nonmystical understanding of this *theologia crucis*. The suffering of Christ, which he finds prophesied here, represents for him the apostasy of the false church and its attempt to take the kingdom of Christ and make it a kingdom of this world. Thus, this psalm is simultaneously a preeminent document for the original, the radical sense of his distinction of the two kingdoms in the negative and the positive sense. The cross documents the hard and unbending opposition to misusing the name and honor of God for purposes of human wisdom and the most Christian empire. Thus, the fundamental understanding of Paul in the struggle against Gnosticism comes through more clearly than mysticism. Alongside that, I will attend to a third piece from the overall context of the *theologia crucis* that comes a little earlier chronologically but can be understood practically as emerging from that theological root. This third piece pertains to the pastoral character of this theology and will develop the new concept of actuality that arises for faith in the cross. For this early treatment of the *theologia crucis* points in an entirely different direction than Theodosius Harnack indicates in his great depiction of Luther's theology:[6] not in the dogmatic direction of the doctrine of the atonement but rather in the practical direction of a new relationship to reality. Novel insofar as it bears within itself a fundamental reversal of the medieval outlook and contains the

---

2. Axel Gyllenkrok, *Rechtfertigung und Heiligung in der frühen evangelischen Theologie Luthers* (Uppsala: Lundequistska bokhandeln, 1952).

3. Ernst Bizer, *Fides ex auditu: Eine Untersuchung über die Entdeckung der Gerechtigkeit Gottes durch Martin Luther* (Neukirchen: Verlag der Buchhandlung des Erziehungsvereins, 1958).

4. [Cf. Karl Barth, *Church Dogmatics*, vol. 4/1, ed. Thomas Forsyth Torrance et al. (London and New York: T&T Clark, 1956), 526.]

5. Walter von Loewenich, *Luther's Theology of the Cross* (1929) (Minneapolis: Augsburg Publishing House, 1976).

6. Theodosius Harnack, *Luthers Theologie mit besonderer Beziehung auf seine Versöhnungs- und Erlösungslehre*, 2 vols. (Erlangen: Theodor Blaesing, 1862/1885). Cf. especially the forewords of both volumes.

rudiments of the approach where the *theologus crucis* withdraws from the cloister—as opposed to the traditional understanding of monasticism where the piety of the cross is exercised in flight from and overcoming of the world—abolishes its pietistic fundamental principle and encounters God in the actuality of an entirely incalculable historical life suffused with endless and largely unfathomable ups and downs. This third piece with which I would like to exemplify the outlook on life held by the *theologus crucis* is the seven Penitential Psalms, which Luther published in the German translation in 1517 and which, even in linguistic terms, belong to the most beautiful of Luther's works that we possess, which could also be called the handbook of evangelical pastoral care and comfort.

I.

The Heidelberg Disputation, one of the ordinary theological gatherings of the chapter of Augustinian Hermits, took place on April 26, 1518. Luther drew up twenty-eight theses for the occasion that deal with three sets of theological issues: with "works," especially the *opera iustorum*, with the question of the "*liberum arbitrium post peccatum*," and third with the distinction of the "*theologus gloriae*" and the "*theologus crucis*."[7] He does not write first of all about "*theologia gloriae*" and "*theologia crucis*": the theology as such is not in the foreground here but rather the person who engages in it, the theologian, and this is indicative in comparison with the medieval approach to the epistemology. For this medieval approach initially disregards the human situation, which is to say the fact that a fallen, sinful man wants to obtain the knowledge of God; this situation only gets to make an appearance secondarily and incidentally.

These theses are entitled "*theologia paradoxa*," a title by which he appeals to Paul ("if Paul had not preceded him therein") and to Augustine, his "most faithful interpreter." Augustine is the church father who lent the order his name because the order believes him to be the middleman between Paul and itself. He presents his theses "*an bene an male elicita sint*,"[8] and we know a bit of the resplendent way in which the young Luther debated and brought his knowledge to the approval of the younger members of his order. From the letter of Martin Bucer, the later Reformer of Strasbourg, to Beatus Rhenanus: "However hard our principal warriors strained to remove Luther from the saddle, they were not able to gain an inch on him. His charm in responding is wonderful, his patience in listening

---

7. With the works, especially the "works of the righteous" (Theses 1–12), with the question on "free will after the fall" (Theses 13–18), and third with the difference between the "theologians of glory" and the "theologians of the cross" (Theses 19–28). The disputation is found in Martin Luther, *Heidelberg Disputation* (1518), LW 31, 35-70; WA 1, 353-374.

8. LW 31, 39; WA 1, 353,11-14: "so that it may become clear *whether they have been deduced well or poorly* from St. Paul . . . and also from St. Augustine." [The emphasis shows the phrase included into the main text.]

incomparable, etc."[9] The theses have as an appendix twelve theses on philosophy that defend Plato against Aristotle and describe Anaxagoras as the "*optimas philosophorum*" because he takes the infinite as "*forma*."[10] It is apparent that Aristotelianism as a presupposition to theological epistemology is attacked in this assault on the "*theologia gloriae*." If one considers the fact that the introduction of the Aristotelian guiding principle (*analogia entis*) made its imprint on the High Middle Ages since Alexander of Hales and emits until this day the foundation of the Catholic doctrine of revelation,[11] one will see how far-reaching the shock was that Luther administered in the name of the "*theologia crucis*" and its paradoxes.

The formulations are at once elegant and so filled with meaning that they would lose their incisive keenness if translated into German. For that reason, I will present the two most important theses (19 and 20) in Latin and explicate them using the Latin text. They read:

> *Non ille digne theologus dicitur, qui "invisibilia" Dei "per ea, quae facta sunt, intellecta conspicit," Sed qui visibilia et posteriora Dei per passiones et crucem conspecta intelligit.*[12]

Luther illustrates the antithesis in the dialectic of "*intelligere*" and "*conspicere*." He has as an opponent a method—the scholastic method as it can be gleaned in the textbook of scholasticism: the *Sentences* of Peter Lombard—that ascends from that which is visible to the invisible world of God: "*per ea, quae facta sunt*" [through the things which are made]. The formulation likewise originates—and this is what is curious about it—with Paul: "*Invisibilia enim ipsius, a creatura*

---

9. Martin Bucer, *Bericht an Beatus Rhenanus über die Heidelberger Disputation* (1518), WA 9, 162,1. [This same passage has been translated from the Latin in a collection of Bucer's writings: "Although our chief men refuted him with all their might, their wiles were unable to make him move an inch from his propositions. His sweetness in answering is remarkable, his patience in listening is incomparable." Martin Bucer, *Common Places of Martin Bucer*, ed. David F. Wright, Courtenay Library of Reformation Classics 4 (Abingdon et al.: Sutton Courtenay Press, 1972), 19.]

10. Thesis 39.

11. [Alexander of Hales, *Summa theologica*, ed. Patres Collegii S. Bonaventurae (Quaracchi: Editiones Collegii S. Bonaventurae, 1924) no. 21; Thomas Aquinas, *Summa theologiae*, trans. Fathers of the English Dominican Province, 2nd revised ed. (New York: Benzinger Brothers, 1920) I qu. 13 a. 5; Erich Przywara, *Analogia entis: Metaphysics: Original Structure and Universal Rhythm* (1932), trans. John R. Betz and David Bentley Hart (Grand Rapids: Eerdmans Publishing Co., 2014).]

12. LW 31, 40; WA 1, 354,17-20: "19. That person does not deserve to be called a theologian who looks upon the invisible things of God and though they were clearly perceptible in those things which have actually happened [Rom 1:20]. 20. He deserves to be called a theologian, however, who comprehends the visible and manifest things of God seen through suffering and the cross."

mundi, per ea quae facta sunt, intellecta conspiciuntur" (Rom. 1:20). Lombard gives the following articulation: "*Per creaturam mundi intelligitur homo, propter excellentiam qua excellit inter alias creaturas; vel propter convenientiam quam habet cum omni creatura.*"[13] Human cognition is capable of transcending creation—as it is called here, the *creatura mundi*. It has another "*excellentia*" that is denied to the other creatures. It "towers above them," is ecstatic, and is for that reason able to comprehend that which is invisible, which the other creatures are not able to do. At the same time, though, man is himself a creature; he has a particular "*convenientia*" with all creation. He is himself a creation. According to the understanding of scholasticism, man as an intelligible being is the point within the creation where the creation reaches out beyond itself, where it no longer comes into consideration in sensual understanding, that is in a manner that is scattered and diffuse from thing to thing and from impression to impression, but rather does so in a manner that is uniformly grounded on the "*intelligere*," on human "*excellentia.*" This perception of the invisible world, in which the visible world has its unity, is intelligible perception. That is the basis of the scholastic worldview and its doctrine of man amid the created world. Man—the only one capable of intelligible perception—is the center of the creation; here the creation has had its eye set, so to speak, by which it is able to view the invisible essence of God. But this intelligible perception does not skip over that which is created—*ea quae facta sunt*—rather, it ascends from it. Rom. 1:20 is interpreted in this way, and this interpretation remained untouched notwithstanding all the changes in late scholasticism; indeed, one has the single thing from which all knowledge ensues, in the sense of an Aristotelian epistemology that is continually worked out more and more in its irreducible givenness, in order to ascend from it into the invisible world. Here we are running up against a certain idealistic strain within the scholastic knowledge of God, and the concept of the intelligible perception, which we encounter later from *Spinoza*[14] to *Schelling*,[15] has its mooring here. Luther takes up this method of establishing theological knowledge "*per ea, quae facta sunt*" and says, "*Non ille digne theologus dicitur.*" Whoever operates in this way does not deserve the title of theologian. Luther switches the predicate and the participle. The predicate for the scholastics is the participle for Luther and vice versa. Even he speaks of a perception of God and appends to this perception understanding, the *intelligere*. But he does not thereby begin with visible things that are created; in

---

13. Petrus Lombardus, *Sententiae* 1, 3, 1: "By a creature of the world, man is meant because of the excellence by which he stands above all other creatures, or due to the commonality which he shares with each creature." [Peter Lombard, *The Sentences*, vol. 1, *On the Mystery of the Trinity*, ed. Giulio Silano (Rome: Pontifical Institute of Mediaeval Studies, 2007), 18–19.]

14. [Baruch de Spinoza (1632–77) was a Dutch philosopher who represented a rationalistic epistemology.]

15. [Friedrich Wilhelm Joseph Schelling (1775–1854) was a representative of "German Idealism" and founder of a speculative philosophy of nature.]

this knowledge of God, he begins not with the world but with God. God's hidden "*visibilia et posteriora*" are the subject of "perception." They present to us the task of the *intelligere*. Thus it is such a revelation of God that has as its content God who is in our midst as the hidden God, who is nevertheless viewed visibly and "aposteriorly [*aposteriorisch*]," that is to say, viewed first of all in his behavior—not in the things but rather in his *humanitas*.

In the commentary on the theses, which are perhaps a synopsis of the discussion from Luther's perspective, it says:

Quia homines cognitione Dei ex operibus abusi sunt, voluit rursus Deus ex passionibus cognosci et reprobare illam sapientiam invisibilium per sapientiam visibilium?[16]

Did Luther wish to say there that the one who is righteous by works also seeks God in his "*opera*" or that idolatry is the expression of this error that seeks God in his "*opera*"? It almost looks that way. For "*ut sic qui Deum non coluerunt manifestum ex operibus colerent absconditum in passionibus.*"[17] The Incarnation is thus identical with the "*deus absconditus.*" The *theologia crucis* and the principle of the knowledge of God in Christ alone must now coincide. When it is said today that it was always common to differentiate between a natural revelation and a salvific revelation in dogmatics, it becomes clear here that the Reformation stems theologically from the unilateral knowledge of God in Christ. Just as in the first thesis at Barmen, Jn 14:9, "Whoever has seen me has seen the Father," and John 10, "I am the door," are cited as references.[18] The revealed God is the hidden: "*Vere absconditus tu es Deus*" (Isa. 45:15). "*Ergo in Christo crucifixo est vera Theologia et cognitio Dei.*" "*At Deum non inveniri nisi in passionibus et cruce.*"[19]

Thus, if the *theologia gloriae* had a vision as its aim—the vision of God in the intelligible perception—the *theologia crucis* has an "*intelligere*" as its aim, a comprehension and understanding. But what should be comprehended here? This is the further point that will be considered now. I have already said that Luther makes the theologian of the cross, the "man," into the subject of his theses. He really asks what kind of man stands behind the *theologia gloriae* and what kind of man stands behind the *theologia* of the cross. We have also seen that a specific conception of man was essential to the scholastic epistemology: the man between

---

16. LW 31, 52; WA 1, 362,5-8: "Because men misused the knowledge of God through works, God wished again to be recognized in suffering, and to condemn wisdom concerning invisible things by means of wisdom concerning visible things."

17. LW 31, 52; WA 362,8f: "so that those who did not honor God as manifested in his works should honor him as he is hidden in his suffering."

18. [Iwand refers here to the first thesis of the Barmen Theological Declaration of the Confessing Church from 1934.]

19. "Truly, you are a God who hides himself" (Isa. 45:15). "For this reason true theology and recognition of God are in the crucified Christ" (Explanation of Thesis 20. LW 31, 53; WA 1, 362,14.18f.) "God can be found only in suffering and the cross" (Explanation of Thesis 21. LW 31, 53; WA 1, 362,28f.).

God and animal who is distinguished from the realm of creatures by virtue of his intellectual ability—his *"intelligere."* Man related to God as a spiritual being. Luther formulates his theses in such a way that man is first manifest in view of this *"Deus absconditus et crucifixus."* What man is first emerges at this point. *"Qui dum ignorat Christum ignorat Deum absconditum in passionibus."*[20] That is why man has an erroneous sense of self-worth. He is apt to prefer work to suffering. These are the people whom Paul calls *"inimici crucis Christi"* (Phil. 3:18). At this point we encounter the sentence that is so full of substance: *"per crucem destruuntur opera et crucifigitur Adam, qui per opera potius aedificatur."*[21]

Few sentences are so instructive for the theology of the young Luther as this one. Here one can see how the two themes of his theology fit together: the one being law and gospel, the other being the *theologia crucis* and the *theologia gloriae*. The one depends on the other. Of course Luther also says that reason is blind, of course he also fought against the natural knowledge of God because of original sin, rejected the knowledge of God in *"gloria et majestate"*—which Th. Harnack highlighted particularly strongly and Lutherans to this day so passionately emphasize—when it is not bound with knowledge in the *"humilitate et ignominia crucis!"*[22] But it does not stop there. At this point, he defines Adam as one who "is built up by works." Adam has life because he does works by means of which he can stand before himself. The good works are the foxhole in which Adam conceals himself when God calls. We could honestly say: flight before God's Word of grace into achievement, the transformation of the theological situation into an ethical one is an action that is congenial to Adam—thus to our natural man. Luther sees in this "practical" act the roots of the invasion of natural theology. *"Adam per opera potius aedificatur."* Using this sentence like a divining rod, one could walk all the way through theology and its history: it would show us where living water flows. That is why Luther can say later in his commentary on the Psalms: *"CRUX sola est nostra theologia."*[23] For man has lost his judgment of the world; he assesses it incorrectly. He assesses suffering and humiliation as something bad, something evil. He seeks the good where it is not. That is why he lives perversely. He lives

---

20. "He who does not know Christ does not know God hidden in suffering" (Explanation of Thesis 21. LW 31, 53; WA 1, 362,23f.).

21. "enemies of the cross of Christ" (Phil. 3:18). "[T]hrough the cross works are destroyed and the old Adam, who is especially edified by works, is crucified" (Explanation of Thesis 21. LW 31, 53; WA 362,30f.).

22. "Now it is not sufficient for anyone, and it does him no good to recognize God in his glory and majesty, unless he recognizes him in the humility and shame of the cross (Explanation of Thesis 20. LW 31, 52f; WA 1, 362,11-13).

23. "The CROSS alone is our theology." (Martin Luther, *Lectures on the Psalms* (1519-1521), WA 5, 176,32f.

incorrectly. "*Dicit malum bonum et bonum malum, Theologus crucis dicit id quod res est*" (Thesis 21).[24] Here the concept of actuality breaks through.

II.

It certainly would not be saying too much to assert that whoever wants to understand the *theologia crucis* in Luther correctly needs to read the *Operationes in Psalmos*. This commentary on the Psalms is the genuine representation of that which Luther understood to fall under this theological principle. The Psalms and the *theologia crucis* are one and the same. In the Psalms, the *theologia crucis* was lived, confessed, and displayed. In the Psalms it came to expression in the Scriptures. If anyone desires to decode the Psalms, to bring to fresh expression the prayers of those who had spoken therein, to enter into the company of this people of God, he must start from the *theologia crucis*—better yet, he must start from the cross of Jesus Christ. In this suffering—in the face of those who persecuted and scoffed at them—all those were justified who had hoped in God alone. In him alone. Luther contrasts the active and the passive life of the pious, the road goes from action to suffering, and it is in suffering—he asserts—that it first becomes apparent whether I trust in God alone. "*Activa sane vita, in qua multi satis temere confidunt, quam intelligunt quoque per merita, non producit nec operator spem, sed praesumtionem, non secus ac Scientia inflat.*"[25]

So this is once more the "*Adam qui operibus aedificatur.*" This is the "positive Christianity" that one can see and to which one can adhere on one's own just as with others. It is from there that the "*vita passiva*"—suffering—must be accepted. It is at that point where faith is first maintained. "*Addenda est vita passiva, quae mortificet et destruat totam vitam activam, ut nihil remaneat meritorum, in quo superbus glorietur. Quo facto, si homo perseveret, fit in eo spes, idest discit nihil esse, in quo gaudendum, sperandum, gloriandum sit, praeter Deum. Triubulatio enim, dum a nobis omnia tollit, solum utique deum relinquit*"—that is to say, I trust in you alone—"*neque enim deum potest tollere, imo deum adducit.*"[26]

---

24. "A theologian of glory calls evil good and good evil. A theologian of the cross calls the thing what it actually is" (LW 31, 40; WA 1, 354,21f.).

25. "Truly, an active life on which many blindly base their trust and that they view only according to the merits neither brings nor effect hope but rather presumption, no less than knowledge inflates." (WA 5, 165,33-35, on Ps. 5:12a)

26. "To this the passive life needs to be added which kills and destroys the whole active life so that no merit remains in which the arrogant one could glorify himself. Through this, if man endures, hope arises in him, that is, he learns that there is nothing about which he can rejoice, in which he can place his hope, for which he can glorify himself, except God. For the tribulation, because it robes everything from us, leaves only God behind—That is: In you alone I trust—, and it cannot rob God from us; on the contrary: it brings God close." (WA 5, 165,35-166,1, on Ps. 5:12a). [The section between the dashes is added by Iwand].

Here it becomes clear what hope is. In the Middle Ages, hope in God was grounded in the idea that God would reward in heaven that which remains unrewarded here on earth. It is similar to how Kant later conceived of the idea of reward—the certainty that an actuality of the good corresponds to the good action; and this actuality is God. Luther's understanding of *"spes"* is determined entirely by the *theologia crucis*: hoping where there can be no more hope, where nothing else remains for me except the living God and his promise, the pure Word. *"spes purissima in purissimum Deum."*[27] Even God's wrath contributes to the destruction of my trust in myself. In this sort of *Anfechtungen* where the "soul is outstretched with Jesus"—here he means the co-crucifixion of the spirit, the "abandonment by God"—hope is only conceivable as *"patientia,"* as patience. *"Ita ut spem recte quispiam possit patientiam spiritualem seu patientiam in culpis sustinendis appelare."*[28]

Thus Luther understood this passivity not as some state of being dead or empty but rather paradoxically as the highest activity. But an activity of hope that *"fit"*—emerges, is born—in this kind of suffering, that is in the picture as the action of the Spirit. It hopes. It hopes where there can be no more hope. It does not refer to some givenness; rather, it refers only to God. To the fact that God is. Hope consists in the fact that it hopes. The one in despair lives in this hope.

"In his vero conscientiae procellis et meritorum ruinis spes ipsa pugnat contra desperationem et fere contra seipsam, immo contra deum, quem sentit sibi iratum."[29] Luther can depict this hoping in the downfall and breakdown of all *"merita"* as a process of being undressed—for him, death is essentially that sort of process: we are placed naked before ourselves and need to be put to the test to determine whether we trust in the mercy of God alone, whether we live on the basis of that mercy alone. Here we are dealing with the independence of faith from the *"sentire"*—we do not feel anything more of God's grace. But this process is a coming-into-being of man himself: he dies and is made anew. He comes to an end and emerges as one reborn. Schleiermacher later formulated it quite differently from this. Here the new birth is bound together with a death, with a death not only of the bad or old man but of the man as such, of the man who supposes that he cannot live or exist before God without works. Thus this man is baptized by "life." Life is the baptism. That means death. *"Et tamen si perseveret homo et contra spem in spem speret, probatus invenietur et hac tribulatione meritis exutus spe induetur et coronabitur inconfusibili corona in aeternum."*[30]

---

27. "Purest hope in the purest God" (WA 5, 166,18).

28. "So that someone can correctly call hope only spiritual patience or patience to bear offenses" (WA 5, 166,29-31).

29. "Indeed: in these storms of conscience and the ruins of merit, hope itself fights against despair and, in a certain sense, against itself, even against God, with whom it feels him to be angry" (WA 5, 166,25-27).

30. "And yet, if man endures and hopes against hope, he will be found tried and, stripped of merit in this tribulation, clothed with hope and crowned with a crown imperishable in

Passivity—*vita passiva*—is thus something different from the "*vita contemplativa*" as it was known in the Middle Ages. With Luther, the "*vita passiva*" is connected to "*pati*." It is suffering that first makes the man into another. But the fact of the matter lies yet deeper. We become people who hope. By getting a taste of the utter depths of despair, we experience genuine development. Works must be overthrown so that we can find an internal foothold in nothing else—hope comes into being (*fit*) in light of this nothing. It is truly born in us, and the emptiness of life, the nothing in the overthrow of all values, is the flip side that we perceive and that we feel with this birth. In the moment that this faith breaks through, we are able to know ourselves only as those who have fallen away, who doubt and despair. Where our knowledge about ourselves is at home, there is nothing to see. Faith and hope and the ability to love come over us, so to speak, from behind, from the other side. "*Sola vero passive vita purissima est.*"[31] True life is genuine life. Life without pretense. Only the faith that we do not acquire for ourselves is genuine. This coming-into-being of man is a work that God does to us. His Spirit leads into hell and back out again. That is why it also says: "*Quid enim est fides, nisi motus ille cordis, qui credere, Spes motus, qui sperare, Charitas motus, qui diligere vocatur.*"[32] One can see that for Luther, it is a matter of a movement wherein we are those who are moved and God is the mover.

Beginning at this point, he criticizes the scholastic teaching that differentiated between "*habitus*" (= posture, disposition, essence) and act. Luther's theology knows that it proceeds outward from the *theologia crucis*, not from some ethic built on human acts. The action always arises out of a being, a state of being moved that proceeds from faith. The man who moves himself is the man who believes that he has himself in his own hand. Yet the one who is moved by God cannot be moved by God at all without being taken out of himself. And this is precisely what suffering is. This is the hard and barren way.

Yet in this context we encounter an entirely new aspect of the *Verbum Dei*. Perhaps when one begins here, it is possible to understand what "pure doctrine," "*purum verbum*," means for Luther. These powers, namely of faith, of love, and of hope, "*versantur circa purum interne, quo capitur et non capit anima.*"[33] Thus they impart the existence in the Word to the soul, to the human self-consciousness. "*rapitur per verbum in solitudinem.*"[34] Thus one can only have the Word—or rather, it can only have us—if it is everything to us. Everything or nothing. That is the inescapable either-or of the encounter with the Word. That is the "*verbum purum.*"

---

eternity" (WA 5, 166,34-36).

31. "Indeed, a passive life is a truly pure life" (WA 5, 166,11).

32. "For what else is faith but this movement of the heart, which is called to believe, what else is hope but the movement that is called to hope, what is charitable love but what is called to love" (WA 5, 176,9-11).

33. "live around the pure internal word, by which the soul is captured but does not capture itself" (WA 5, 176,16-18).

34. "It is raptured into solitude through the word" (WA 5, 176,19f.).

"*Exuitur tam rebus tam phantasmatibus*,"[35] thus we live neither in actuality nor in fantasy when we live in the Word.

In this way the Word forms the soul. It leads it into nothing. Here, Luther takes up the language of mystical theology. But what comes of it! "*Redacta sum in nihilum et nescivi. In tenebras et caliginem ingressa nihil video, fide, spe et charitate sola vivo et infirmor (idest patior), cum enim infirmor, tunc fortior sum.*"[36]

Luther says that the mystical theologians call this "*ductus*" the ascent above existence and nonexistence. He says that he does not know if they understood themselves correctly when they did so; they would have made "acts" out of them, but it is really a matter of "*mortis inferni passiones*," of suffering death and hell. And then here stands precisely the sentence with which he defines the entire position of the man beset with *Anfechtung*: "*CRUX sola est nostra Theologia.*" Because man is hostile to God from the very beginning, he can only experience God's working on him as suffering, as *Anfechtung* and deprivation, precisely not as an enhancement of life but rather as judgment and death. That is why Luther also rebels against the "*liberum arbitrium*," against the free will. We cannot make a choice for faith—how should we do it then! "*Velle enim illud, quod credere, sperare, diligere iam diximus, est motus, raptus, ductus verbi dei et quaedam continua purgatio et renovatio mentis et sensus de die in diem in agnitionem dei.*"[37]

So Luther can also characterize this process by which a despairing person becomes one who hopes as being recreated: "*Creamur ad imaginem eius, qui fecit nos. Voluntas vero incarnate seu in opus externum effuse recte potest dici cooperari et activitatem habere ... Quare sicut gladius ad sui motum nihil cooperatur, ita nec voluntas ad suum velle, qui est divini verbi motus, mera passio voluntatis, quae tum cooperatur ad opus manuum orando, ambulando, laborando.*"[38]

One could say a lot in relation to this, but one thing should have become clear by now: the *theologia crucis* is neither a merely theoretical expression nor is it simply an antithesis to the *theologia gloriae*; rather, it will be drawn into our life. Starting

---

35. "It [the soul] is stripped of things and also of imaginations" (WA 5, 176,18f.).

36. "I have been called back into nothing and do not know of anything. I trod into darkness and gloom and see nothing. I live in faith, love, and hope alone and am weakened [i.e. I suffer]; for when I am weak, then I am strong" (WA 5, 176,27-29).

37. "For this will, of which we spoke already [i.e. to believe, hope, and love], is a movement, an abduction, guidance by God's Word and, so to speak, a continual cleansing and renovation of the spirit and the senses from day to day towards the knowledge of God" (WA 5, 177,12-14).

38. "We are created according to the image of the one who has made us (Colossians 3:10). The will which has taken shape in life, which expands into external work can rightly be called cooperative and completely active. [. . .] Therefore, as the sword does not contribute in any way to its movement, so the will contributes nothing to what it wants. Rather, that is a movement by God's Word, something the will must simply endure, that consequently contributes to the works of the hands—praying, walking, working" (WA 5, 177,20-22.24-27).

from it we will be able to understand what it means to be one who believes, one who hopes, one who loves—indeed, what it means to be a Christian at all. Because in fact, it is never possible to be a Christian, only to become one. The existence of the Christian is hidden in God. It is not possible to elevate it into consciousness without destroying it. In consciousness we have the flip side, nonexistence. And nevertheless it says: "*Oportet non modo credere, sperare, diligere, sed etiam scire et certum esse, se credere, sperare, diligere. Illud in abscondito tempestatis, hoc post tempestatem agitur.*"[39]

III.

Yet it is possible to appreciate what this theological approach means on a practical level from an analysis of the seven Penitential Psalms. Such a theological analysis does not yet exist in my opinion. Most of the time, the subtleties are read over, and no one notices what a colossal reversal has taken place with respect to Christian existence in this exposition originally produced in the German language.

I begin with Ps. 32:10: "I will instruct you and teach you in the way you should go."

In connection with this verse it says,

> In it I want you. You ask me to redeem you. Do not be sorry, do not teach me. Do not teach yourself either, let me be for you, I will be master enough for you, I will lead you the way, on which you will walk pleasantly. You think it is corrupt, if it does not go as you think, that thinking is harmful to you and hinders me. It must go not according to your mind but over your mind. . . . Not to know where you are going, that is really to know where you are going. My understanding makes you not understand. Thus Abraham went out of his fatherland, and knew not whither. He gave himself into my knowledge and let his knowledge go, and he came the right way to the right end. Behold, this is the way of the cross, which you cannot find, but I must lead you as a blind man.[40]

Thus the way of the cross is a clear, unambiguous reality of our life. It lies ahead of us, so to speak. When we traverse it, that is to say, when we are led upon it, nothing peculiar happens. Real life is the way of the cross. Not the existence that is abstract, self-made, spent in a certain isolation from the world, formed wherever possible by its own ordeals and mortifications. God's call goes out to a particular place—there and only there is it perceptible. And if I evade real life in its heights

---

39. "One ought not believe, hope and love alone, but also know and be certain that one believes, hopes and loves. This happens during the storm in hiddenness, that after the storm" (WA 5, 165,8-19).

40. Martin Luther, *The Seven Penitential Psalms* (1517), WA 1, 171,25-172,2.

and depths, its *Anfechtungen* and consolations, then I do not perceive God's call. For I stand in that place where I have chosen my own place, my own location. If Abraham had remained in Ur, what would God's call have meant to him? We often talk these days about the secularization of the world, and by that we mean that this secularization is the reason why men are turning their backs on the church. It is also possible to see things the other way around. One could ask if a particular preconceived and embedded view of "being pious" and "being Christian" is not the reason why the church is turning its back on men. God's call is absolutely not issued to men where and how the "church" determines of its own accord. Precisely here is where the Reformation's break with the medieval church lies—for the way of the cross that God leads us is not life in the church. Rather, it is the way of God's people in the world.

This way is incomprehensible. It is sealed to our understanding. It is both necessary and permissible to admit that we do not understand God in this way. If we should understand him, it would not be his way but our way. Thus one can only find these two things simultaneously: God, the true God who is the Lord of my entire life, and the actuality of this life in its entire, profound mysteriousness. The most profound and most difficult mystery is in ourselves, in man.

To that I add another passage from Ps. 32:2: "in whose spirit there is no deceit:" "And in his spirit there is no deceit:"

> That is, that his own heart deceives him, or that he is outwardly pious and regards himself as no other than pious, and a lover of God, yet inwardly this view is false.... What evil, false, deceitful trickery most often presents the great-seeming and spiritual people who stand fearlessly for the sake of their pious life and many good works and do not seriously perceive their spirit and inner opinion.[41]

That means that such people do not suffer for themselves. Their works do not have life because of them; they are not the signs and manifestation of their essence. Rather, they have life because of their works. "Nor do they want to take to mind that this deceitful, harmful trickery leaves no man free, but is fully grounded spiritually in all, and is cast out by the grace of God alone."[42]

This evil that is located in ourselves and within ourselves lies on the other side of all our freedom. It is the actual suffering of man—he must do what he does not want. The whole doctrine of his "freedom" is a hollow illusion. That is why the story of his life—but also the history of the peoples—is determined by this unpredictable factor that is located with man, with his passion and folly. "Not a trick that man does and conceives with knowledge against himself or another, but

---

41. WA 1, 167,30-33.34-36.
42. WA 1, 167,36-168,2.

which he suffers and is innate to him, who lets himself be covered and adorned with good life."[43]

However, "Thus lies the evil filth underneath, which the teachers call love of self [amorem sui], desirous love of God [amorem dei concupiscentie], if man is pious for the fear of hell or the hope of heaven, and not for the will of God, but this is difficult to recognize, even more difficult to get rid of."[44]

That is precisely what it is about: how we "get rid of" it. As a consequence, man must not withdraw from the suffering that God has meant for us in the unpredictability of life. As a consequence, marriage; as a consequence, labor; as a consequence, getting out of a prepared form of Christian existence! As a consequence (perhaps it could be said), always being oriented toward the life that is itself the product of our failures and passions.

Once more concerning verse 8:

> Therefore not you, not a man, not a creature, but I myself will instruct you in the way wherein you shall walk. Not the work that you choose, not the suffering that you think of, but what happens to you, but what comes to you against your choosing, thinking, desires; there follow, there I call, there be a disciple, there it is time—your master has come.[45]

Here it becomes evident that we can only walk in this unfathomable way with proper confidence and faith—otherwise, if we go our own way, what do we still need from God! "Have you not read, the eyes of God are open upon the faithful . . . that is in a nutshell nothing else but a right simple faith and firm trust."[46]

But even here the internal struggle of life does not cease. In this transformation before God's eyes, we are simultaneously those who hope and those who give up hope.

> God is so wondrous in his children that he blesses them even in contrary and discordant things. For hope and despair are contrary to each other. They must still hope in despair, for fear is nothing other than an increasing despair and hope an increasing recovery and the two unnatural things must be within us, therefore there must be two unnatural men within us, the old and the new. The old must fear and despair and perish, the new must hope and endure and be raised. And both of these things must happen in one man, yes simultaneously in one work. Just while taking and cutting away what should not be in the wood for the image, the sculptor also forms the shape of the image, so in the fear that cuts away the old Adam, the hope grows which forms the new man.[47]

---

43. WA 1, 168,3-5.
44. WA 1, 168,6-9.
45. WA 1, 172,2-7.
46. WA 1, 172,12.15f.
47. WA 1, 208,9-30, on Ps. 130:5.

This true hope is distinguished from the false one because it does not prescribe for God the "goal, manner, time and measure"[48] in which he should help. Those who do so

> do not wait, they do not await God. God should wait for them and be ready immediately, and not help them in any other way than what they have imagined. But those who wait for God ask for mercy, but they leave it up to God's good will if, how, where and by whatever means he will help them. They do not doubt the help. But they do not give it a name, they let God baptize and name it . . . but whoever gives a name to the help, it will not be given to him.[49]

---

48. WA 1, 208,34.
49. WA 1, 208,37-209,4.4f.

Chapter 12

THE FREEDOM OF THE CHRISTIAN AND THE BONDAGE OF THE WILL

Originally published as Hans Joachim Iwand, "Die Freiheit des Christen und die Unfreiheit des Willens," in *Solange es heute heißt. Festschrift für Rudolf Hermann* (Berlin: Evangelische Verlagsanstalt, 1957), 132–46.

Iwand wrote this text in 1957 for the commemorative publication of his teacher Rudolf Hermann's (1887–1962) seventieth birthday, under whom he had studied at the beginning of his theological studies in Breslau. It was Iwand's intention to resolve in recourse to Luther from a historical and theological perspective what the relation between the freedom of the Christian and the bondage of the will is.[1] Thereby he emphasized the differences between reformatory theology and medieval scholasticism as well as the humanism of Erasmus of Rotterdam on the one hand and the Neo-Protestantism of the late nineteenth and early twentieth century on the other hand. For Iwand the perception of the bondage of the will is an act of liberation, in which God's reality is encountered by the human and bestows him certainty of faith. The relevance of Luther's work, "The Bondage of the Will," for Iwand can be seen in his commentary on this work, which he wrote during his imprisonment in the jail of the National Socialist "Gestapo" (secret state police) in Dortmund in December 1938.[2]
[MB]

This small and, as it relates to the chosen theme, unfortunately quite incomplete essay is written in unfading and thankful memory of those times when we, as young students in the unforgettable lectures and seminars and even in our personal encounters with the then guest lecturer Rudolf Hermann in Breslau,

---

1. [Cf. Hans Joachim Iwand, "Die grundlegende Bedeutung der Lehre vom unfreien Willen für den Glauben," in Iwand, *Um den rechten Glauben*, GA I, 13–30; idem, *Studien zum Problem des unfreien Willens*, ibid. 31–61.]

2. [Cf. Hans Joachim Iwand, "Erläuterungen," in Martin Luther, *Daß der freie Wille nichts sei. Antwort D. Martin Luthers an Erasmus von Rotterdam*, ed. Hans Heinrich Borcherdt and Georg Merz, Ausgewählte Werke, Ergänzungsreihe vol. 1 (Munich: Chr. Kaiser Verlag 1939), 289–371.]

discovered our inner calling to theology. I may say "we," as it was a circle of friends and like-minded individuals, many of whom are no longer among the living, who at that time gathered around Rudolf Hermann and his systematic work. Here we experienced also our first introduction to Luther's theology, which was certainly not as well-known in that time as it is today. Holl's famous essays had not yet come along—they appeared in that same year[3]—and Harnack's depiction of Luther's theology was known only to experts.[4] These were years of great internal movement. The First World War had deeply shaken the European man's sense of life and security, and we sensed the profound transformations that would follow as a result. The "Fall of the West" loomed on the horizon, and the knowledgeable gave voice to this expression in various domains. Those were the years in which Karl Barth's first edition on Romans appeared.[5] Yet we still came from a sheltered world, a world that was not intellectually prepared for the questions and choices that awaited us. In that time we found in the man, to whom these pages are dedicated, a teacher who meant more to us than someone who only taught us. He formed us and has formed us by teaching us how it is necessary to connect the rigor of thought with the unconditionality and depth of faith. He formed us, on the one hand, by returning to the sources, especially to Luther's theology, and, on the other hand, opened up to us the great good of German Idealism as the heritage out of which we all had come, be it more or less consciously. The following is an attempt at such an argument, which is to say an attempt positively to incorporate the thesis of the bondage of the will not only historically but also systematically without selling away the freedom of the Christian but rather basing the latter upon the former. It is intended to be a sign of the enduring thankfulness that I owe to the man to whom this work is dedicated for everything that I have received from him during my time as a student and ever anew in the years following.

I. The Theological Place of the Controverted Concept of Freedom

Among the problems that Reformation theology and the Reformers' understanding of the faith have given us, the thesis of the bound will stand front and center. It would not be an error to assert that the proposition of human bondage virtually constitutes the style guide of all Reformation theology. It is not only Luther who

---

3. [Cf. Karl Holl, *Gesammelte Aufsätze zur Kirchengeschichte*, vol. 1, *Luther* (Tübingen: J. C. B. Mohr, 1921).]

4. [Cf. Theodosius Harnack, *Luthers Theologie mit besonderer Beziehung auf seine Versöhnungs- und Erlösungslehre*, 2 vol. (Erlangen: Theodor Blaesing, 1862/1886).]

5. [Cf. Karl Barth, *Der Römerbrief* (Erste Fassung) (1919), ed. Hermann Schmidt (Karl Barth-Gesamtausgabe 16) (Zürich: Theologischer Verlag Zürich, 1985). According to Barth the first edition is only a "preliminary investigation" (Vorarbeit) and in the second edition "no stone remains in its own place." Karl Barth, *The Epistle to the Romans* (1922), trans. E. C. Hoskyns (London: Oxford University Press, 1968), 2.]

early on attacks the thesis of the *liberum arbitrium*;[6] the other leading Reformers likewise take this as their point of departure in everything that they say concerning man and his lost estate.[7] This demonstrates to us most clearly that the thesis of the bound will is not some expression of weary resignation. Rather, this proposition is established as a new, liberating insight. By it man is able to grasp the basis of what he truly is. "A theologian of the cross calls the thing what it actually is."[8] It is a certain kind of realism that hauls us out of all illusions, not in order to make us despair but rather in order to have us perceive something of the bedrock that is intended to prompt faith. The proposition of the bondage of the will is just as central within the Christianity of the Reformation as the proposition of freedom later became in German Idealism. As a result, it has often later been understood in a way that is strictly opposed to idealism and its philosophy. I wish to say that this is not correct. That would be to oversimplify the problem of the freedom of the will. In the thesis of the *servum arbitrium*, there lies an *intention* that points in an entirely different direction from the understanding that often underlies the apologetic uses of our proposition. Whoever interprets our proposition in such a way that Goethe's "Whoever strives with all his might, that man can we redeem"[9] is led therewith *ad absurdum*, he would be mistaken. With this apologetic use, one

---

6. We find the first statements on the topic in his *Lectures on Romans* (1515/16), LW 25, 375; WA 56, 385,15f., [on Rom. 8:28]: "The free will without grace has absolutely no power to achieve righteousness, but of necessity it is in sin"; in the "three fragments" *on the powers and will of man apart from grace* [cf. Martin Luther, *On the Powers and Will of Man Apart from Grace* (1516), LW 72, (forthcoming); WA 1, 145-151.]. Cf. Carl Stange, *Die ältesten ethischen Disputationen Luthers* (Leipzig: A. Deichert, 1904), 14ff.; Martin Luther, *Disputation Against Scholastic Theology* (1517), LW 31, 3-16; WA 1, 221-228, especially theses 29 and 30 ["29. The best and infallible preparation for grace and the sole disposition toward grace is the eternal election and predestination of God. 30. On the part of man, however, nothing precedes grace except indisposition and even rebellion against grace."]; and theses 13ff of the *Heidelberg Disputation* (1518), LW 31, 35-70, 40; WA 1, 354,5f: "Free will, after the fall, exists in name only, and as long as it does what it is able to do, it commits a mortal sin."

7. Indicative of this turn "from Aristotle to Paul" is the address of the young Melanchthon "The Feast of the Conversion of St. Paul" (25 January 1520): "For, as many of us as were born of Adam, so also are we born as sons of wrath and death and thereby unfortunately driven to failure for nature's sake, such that we cannot be dissuaded by our decision or by our strength. Desires of all kinds exert their tyranny on us, one on top of the other, each allowing himself to be carried away by his desires." (Die Loci Communis Philipp Melanchthons in ihrer Urgestalt nach G.L. Plitt, 3 ed., ed. Theodor Kolde (Erlangen: A. Deichert, 1900), 266).

8. [LW 31, 40; WA 1, 362,21f. (thesis 21).]

9. [Johann Wolfgang von Goethe, *Faust. Der Tragödie zweiter Teil*, Stuttgart 1832, 336. In: Deutsches Textarchiv <http://www.deutschestextarchiv.de/goethe_faust02_1832/348>, accessed January 21, 2021.]

makes out of an *insight* that is looking for its place a *doctrine* used for unknown proposes in such a way that the insight itself remains misunderstood. The application that was later made with the teaching of the bound will, particularly in Christian ethics, amounts to a transplanting of a realization that initially and decisively had its own place into a foreign frame of reference, much as if I were to take a plant only found in the highest mountains and placed it, withered and without roots, into a jar. Whoever wishes to see such a plant in the lowlands will not see it correctly. He will wonder why it has lost its sheen and vigor. In that place where the teaching of the bound will is by its nature at home, it will appear different and end up being a different terrain than where we encounter it in the display window of Christian apologetics.

From time to time some have also tried to sweep our teaching aside by saying that Luther was regressing back into the Middle Ages with this teaching.[10] How could someone believe something so appalling? For Luther appeared to most people to be the founder and discoverer of human freedom according to the understanding of modernity, and it was impossible to grasp that in the center of his theology one would run into the proposition of the bondage of the will. People sought to explain this away by saying that this was the later, anti-Erasmian, antihumanist Luther. But we know now—and this holds objectively true on the basis of the available documents—that with this thesis, the breaking point from the Middle Ages, and directly from the Occamistic theology of the Late Middle Ages, had been reached.[11] These maintained the freedom of the will; Luther denied it. That we today find this so difficult to imagine only demonstrates how far Protestantism has distanced itself from what was thought and taught at its inception, where it understood itself to be particularly near to the "Scriptures." We will need to brace ourselves for an astonishing revaluation of Protestantism and Catholicism on this point. For modern Protestantism—I am thinking here of the line that follows after Albrecht Ritschl until Wilhelm Herrmann and Ernst Troeltsch[12]—may stand closer to Thomism in its teaching of the self-motion of the human will than it does to the Reformation. Even in the High Middle Ages (i.e., with Thomas Aquinas), the teaching of the natural freedom of man's will forms the necessary precondition of the teaching of faith and justification. This is precisely what Luther's denial of

---

10. [Cf. Ernst Troeltsch, *Luther und die moderne Welt* (1908), ed. Trutz Rendtorff (Kritische Gesamtausgabe 8) (Berlin and Boston: De Gruyter, 2001), 59–97; idem, *Die Bedeutung des Protestantismus für die Entstehung der modernen Welt* (1911), ed. Trutz Rendtorff (Kritische Gesamtausgabe 8) (Berlin and Boston: De Gruyter, 2001), 200–316, 225.]

11. [Cf. Gabriel Biel, *Collectorium in quattuor libros Sententiarum*, II d. 25, ed. Wilfried Werbeck and Udo Hofmann, vol. 2 (Tübingen: J.C.B. Mohr [Paul Siebeck] 1984, 480–95).]

12. [Albrecht Ritschl (1822–89), Wilhelm Herrmann (1846–1922), and Ernst Troeltsch (1865–1923) were German evangelical theologians and were among the most important representatives of "liberal theology."]

the freedom of the will is referring to, and it was also those propositions that were condemned so early on by Rome.[13]

It may be paradigmatic how, in the relevant chapters of his *Summa Theologica*, Thomas Aquinas connects the question of the freedom of the will, which he discusses at the beginning, with the teaching of justification, which follows at the end (I a II ae qu. 113). To the question "Whether the will moves itself," he answers with a reference to a proposition of the Aristotelian ethic:[14] "And, in like manner, the will through its volition of the end, moves itself to will the means" (qu. 9 a. 3). The will that is oriented toward the goal must also be able to orient itself toward that which leads to that goal. And yet Thomas says "*similiter*." He doesn't envisage the movement of the will as such but rather in analogy to another movement: that of the *intelligere* in view of the *principia*. Just as the intellect finds the object of its knowledge in itself—the truth is not something given from the exterior—so also does the will have the object of all its endeavors, the *Good*, in itself. That the will must be given a push in order for this movement to begin, that it "is . . . moved by anything exterior" (a. 4) means nothing more than that even this movement requires an impetus from the outside in order to get started, "[w]herefore we must, of necessity, suppose that the will advanced to its first movement in virtue of the instigation of some exterior mover" (a. 4). But this does not concern the direction but rather the elevation of the movement, the transition from the state of potential into the state of action, as it were. Thus, the precondition is given that Thomas falls back on when, after a long discussion of act and virtue, sin and grace, he comes to speak to the decisive question: "*utrum ad eam*"—this is a matter of the infusion of justifying grace—"movement of the free-will is required" (qu. 113 a. 2/3). Here we have come to that nexus of the freedom of the will and justifying grace that signals to us the *place* toward which Luther's antithesis is aimed, and the "*required*" declares unmistakably that the *freedom* of the will is the creaturely precondition that man must bring with him if grace is to prove itself to be effectual to him. At the very least, this is the question that Thomas poses. The answer is clear: "Now God moves everything in its own manner, just as we see that in natural things, what is heavy and what is light are moved differently, on account of their diverse natures. Hence He moves man to justice according to the condition of

---

13. In the bull *Exsurge Domine* of June 15, 1520, thesis 36, the thirteenth thesis of the Heidelberg Disputation was cited verbatim and rejected [Cf. *Enchiridion Symbolorum: Compendium of Creeds, Definitions, and Declarations on Matters of Faith and Morals*, ed. Heinrich Denzinger (San Francisco: Ignatius Press, 2012), 367, 1486]. The first of the rejected theses also belongs in this connection: "It is a heretical, though widespread, opinion that the sacraments of the New Law give justifying grace to those who do not place an obstacle in the way." The *non ponere obicem* [not to put up an obstacle] that the bull wants to preserve as the human precondition for the reception of grace is precisely the demonstration of the *liberum arbitrium*. Cf. *Enchiridion Symbolorum*, 363, 1451.

14. Thomas Aquinas, *Summa Theologiae*, trans. Fathers of the English Dominican Province, 2nd revised ed. (New York: Benzinger Brothers, 1920), Ia IIae qu. 8 a. 2.

his human nature. But it is man's proper nature to have free-will" (a. 3). It may be noticeable that freedom here is seen under the image of movement. We will need to ask ourselves if this analogy of will and movement is appropriate to the object that it serves to clarify.[15] In this connection it is quite obvious that man would sink to the level of a stone, and his being moved would descend to the point where, when he is moved, he does not move from the inside but must rather be given a push. We wish to deny that particular *conditio* of the *humana natura* that Thomas introduces at the beginning with his concept of the *liberum arbitrium*. To whoever has initially occupied his vantage point within this metaphysical system, the assertion of a "bound will" must now appear to be self-defeating and, in view of the connection between justification and sanctification, destructive. God indeed cannot move man from "outside" in the way that he moves a stone. Or should we imagine the *homo impius* in justification to be compelled so "inhumanly" from the outside or seized by an impersonal power and transferred to another place as the wind blows away a leaf? In order to protect the justifying effect of the ecclesial means of grace against the idea of a magical effect from the outside or a *force* that acts independently of man, scholasticism incorporated that *liberum arbitrium* as its dogma in the justification of the ungodly. The nature of man is not eliminated or broken at all but rather redeemed and included in the gracious act of *justificatio*. This nature, however, is the capacity of turning oneself or the personality, which is the fundamental freedom.

"Hence in him who has the use of reason, God's motion to justice does not take place without a movement of the free-will; but He so infuses the gift of justifying grace that at the same time He moves the free-will to accept the gift if grace, in such as are capable of being moved thus." With that last proposition, Thomas limits the *capacitas* in view of the secret predestination of God, but this confession says nothing with respect to the insertion of the *liberum arbitrium* as the *conditio* for how the reception of grace is realized for man. We understand: since God acts where he acts *secundum conditionem naturae humanae*, so within the natural conditions of our human nature, if we are also lifted out of the limitedness of our human nature through grace, then with the *liberum arbitrium*, the bed is already made, as it were, within which the flow of grace finds its way. Quite different from how we often speak of it, the *personal* decision is thus included in the reception of grace in scholastic theology. We are neither children nor are we paralyzed when we receive the sacrament of grace; we are called by God as responsible men with free choice. This understanding of the *free* will leads to the *potentiality* of choice

---

15. Cf. also Luther's relevant remark: "You know that this is why natural philosophy has and always does add something bad and disadvantageous to theology, because every single art has its limitations and its designations which it uses, and these designations have meaning in its materials. When the physical terms were transferred to theology, a certain scholastic theology arose from then on. The penny counts where honor is defeated" (Martin Luther, *Promotionsdisputation von Palladius und Tilemann* (1537), WA 39/I, 229,6-11.22-24; 232,30f.).

enclosed within man by nature. The teaching of justification is delineated within this potentiality. Man with his potentialities, good as well as evil, beneficial to him as well as corrupting, is seen as the partner of God. The *impius*, however, is not man in his potentialities but rather in an *actuality* that is directed in one way and in none other. Here lies the tremendous reversal that is brought about with the teaching of the *servum arbitrium*, which is to say with the doing away with the *liberum arbitrium* from the teaching of justification as an intermediary determination. In the justification of the ungodly, the *actuality* of man comes to light. This is directed in one way and none other—namely, contrary to God. The *justificatio impii* does away with an actuality of man, an actuality that bears not even the potentiality of its own conquering. The Reformers do not begin with the common potentiality of human existence but rather with the special actuality, given in such a way and none other, of the *homo impius sola gratia justificatus*. That is the lever that, once thrown, must change the entire system.

II. The Transformation

The thesis of the "bound will" remains in a curious isolation. It marks the break with the past from which Western theology originates—it is in the best case a regression to Augustine but then proceeds far beyond him—and it leads in turn to the break with the humanism announced by modernity and with its spokesman, Erasmus of Rotterdam. It is not saying too much to claim that this thesis and the view of *man* implied therein contributed to the young humanists finding their way back within the Roman Church, where they would later become the leading forces of the Counterreformation.[16] Thus, our teaching stands in a unique isolation that is characteristic of itself. Even Melanchthon, who at first enthusiastically appropriated it from Luther in the first edition of his *Loci*,[17] slowly retreated from it and later reinserted the teaching of the *liberum arbitrium*,[18] for he thought that he would not be able to develop the ethical responsibility of man in his political ethic and his teaching on society without reintroducing this teaching. As far as I can see, the teaching of the bound will has—with few exceptions in sight—*not* been able to endure within the Protestant school-dogmatic; it has quickly diminished to the level of an acknowledgment of the mere inability to become righteous before God by one's own powers, but that is not its original meaning. This proposition does not intend to say that man *is not able* to fulfill the command of God; rather, the

---

16. [Cf. Johannes Cochläus, *De libero arbitrio hominis* (1525), ed. Hubertus Jedin (Breslau: Müller und Seiffert, 1927).]

17. [Cf. Philip Melanchthon, *Loci communes* (1521), trans. Christian Preus (St. Louis: Concordia Publishing House, 2014), 26–36.]

18. [Cf. Philip Melanchthon, *Loci praecipui theologici* (1559), trans. J. A. O. Preus (St. Louis: Concordia Publishing House, 2011), 56–68.]

provocative thesis of this theologoumenon is that he *does not want to* and *cannot want to*.

"*Non potest homo naturaliter velle, deum esse deum, imo vellet se esse deum et deum non esse!*"[19]

So reads a certain classical thesis of the young Luther that we find in the Disputation Against Scholastic Theology of 1517! One sometimes gets the impression that we are only now for the first time beginning fully and entirely to understand the meaning of this thesis. It's as though Luther already envisions the shadow of the Nietzsche-man behind the humanists of his time, as though he had discovered and endured this human, all-too-human one in himself.[20] He saw and grasped that the natural man is a born *atheist*. At this point, a new discussion of God bursts forth, a discussion that does not involve the relationship of God with himself, this existence-from-him and existence-in-himself. It no longer involves the question with which Thomas initiates his theology: "*Does God exist?*"[21] It also does not involve us becoming aware of our inescapable dependence on God—which Luther never denied but actually far more often developed most splendidly—but in all of this we have not run into the phenomenon of the bound will. No, it is much more the case that from the other side, from *God's* side, a piece of information is set forth that man simply cannot allow to stand: that God is God! We encounter in revelation—that is, in his Word—God, not as that which is behind all created things, the great X that stands invisibly yet tangibly behind all that is visible. God is not the epitome of the metaphysical world that becomes comprehensible to us in faith as the intellectual, intelligible world in contrast to the world of the senses. Rather, God comes onto the scene with his, "I am who I am." He wants us to let him be who he is and to acknowledge him in his righteousness. With respect to this claim of God, Luther realized with a universality and an indispensability (*necessitas*) founded upon who-knows-what that no man by nature can want for God to be God, that there is at this point manifestly an either-or: either the self-willed man will be done away with in view of the actuality of God (which is faith), or he transforms God, this God in his free and very own Self-Existence, into a man-God, into an entity that is relative to him, the man, and customized according to his own measures of value.

Luther can also speak of the law of God in an entirely similar fashion to how he spoke about God being God: here also he discovers a latent opposition to the fulfillment of what is offered that is in one way or another insurmountable. The man of the *liberum arbitrium* wishes that there were no law, "*nullam esse legem et*

---

19. [LW 31,10; WA 1, 225,1f, thesis 17: "Man is by nature unable to want God to be God. Indeed, he himself wants to be God, and does not want God to be God."]

20. [Friedrich Nietzsche, *Human, All Too Human: A Book for Free Spirits* (1878), trans. Alexander Harvey, 2 vol. (Auckland: The Floating Press, 2013).]

21. [Thomas Aquinas, *Summa Theologiae*, Ia qu. 2.]

se omnino liberam" (sc. *voluntatem*).²² The will of man and the command of God are *adversaries, "adversarii implacabiles."*²³ That means that the seemingly inborn knowledge of the *nomos*, as it is repeatedly claimed,²⁴ means nothing for man's actual relationship to the will of the living God. Within man lies an astonishing capability to undress the law of its *true* meaning, the meaning that was originally meant by God, and then make out of it a *value* for himself, thus a *bonum*, that can be sensibly grasped by us in a particular connection of value. And so the commandment, in which God's *will* confronts us, becomes a value whose meaning and usefulness are for us to judge, for which or against which it is for us to decide. But that is naturally never the commandment in which God reveals himself! The commandment doesn't give us two possibilities between which to choose, though it may sometimes seem that way. It means, rather, that man has no choice before God, that his will exists to obey and not to choose, that in his life and over his life he finds a *law* that clarifies him, that he is not left to himself but is rather a person who stands under God's dominion and protection. But the law comes up against man's desire for freedom that is opposed to it. It ignites him and exposes him. In his *liberum arbitrium*, man draws up *his* law for life, in which he hopes to find his freedom: something in the sense of Goethe's Prometheus poem:

Me honor *you*? Why? Have you mitigated the pain of the one who is heavy-laden? Have you quenched the tears of the one in distress? Have not almighty time and eternal fate, my lords and yours, forged me into a man?²⁵

It belongs to the most curious changes within Protestant theology that it was later thought that man could indeed *accept* the law of God in its spiritual sense; he just could not *do* it! As if we met our first defeat at the inability-to-do! If we were able to *want* it, if that *voluntas* were given to us that affirms the *law of God* as God's law, that is rooted in it, that is rooted in it just as our natural *voluntas* is rooted in the law of our own human nature, then the question of doing would no longer be a question. But who transfers our will into the law of God in such a way that it might also become the law of our life?

So Luther also discovers behind the expression of the *liberum arbitrium* an intention that had not yet been seen, an intention that is commonly human but most profoundly *contrary to God*, an intention that does away with God, that transforms the God-ness of God, that does away with the graceful lordship of God—the acceptance of his Word—a human capability to make oneself "Lord of lords and God of gods." There is a point in his great debate with Erasmus where he

---

22. [LW 31, 15; WA 1, 228,13f, thesis 85: "that there would be no law and to be entirely free."]

23. [LW 31, 14; WA 1, 227,26, thesis 71: "implacable foes."]

24. [Cf. Wilhelm Stapel, *Der christliche Staatsmann. Eine Theologie des Nationalismus* (Hamburg: Hanseatische Verlagsanstalt, 1932), 174; Friedrich Gogarten, *Einheit von Evangelium und Volkstum?* (Hamburg: Hanseatische Verlagsanstalt, 1933), 23.]

25. [Johann Wolfgang von Goethe, "Prometheus," in idem, *Schriften*, vol. 8 (Leipzig: Göschen, 1789), 208f., 37–45.]

tells him this: "So by means of this doctrine concerning the governing part of man, man will come to be exalted above Christ and the devil, or in other words, he will become Lord of lords and God of gods."[26]

Luther, without question, overinterpreted Erasmus. Erasmus never understood the nudge that Luther was giving him. In his subjective understanding and his moral view of Christian perfection, he had meant something entirely different with the *liberum arbitrium*. But Luther *sees* the foundation of the matter! He sees the problem of the *liberum arbitrium* with *his* eyes, honed on the Scriptures and his experience. Out of this germ of the *liberum arbitrium* he sees a man grow who will simply be "*anomos.*" His will will be the free, the "*absolutum velle.*" With his absolute desire, he will stand in nothingness; everything that comes to his hand or that meets his eyes, everything that enters into his spirit or his understanding will transform into his, into man's own potentiality. For him—the man of the free will—all actuality will melt away into his very own potentialities. He will no longer find God; rather, the God that he seizes from his free will or that he casts aside will be the God of his intellectual, religious, moral potentialities. This does not mean that God ceased to be actuality nor that man ceased to be connected to him and to be determined and directed by him in all his doing and permitting, but it does mean that man has lost his *access* to his actuality. Luther seeks to preserve man from his own fall by smashing the dream of the *liberum arbitrium*. He wishes to save man from his infinity [*Unendlichkeit*] of groping in the dark. He wants to remind him of his *finiteness* [*Endlichkeit*], of his definiteness that is given in his being in this way and none other. This means first of all the *servum arbitrium*.

Great theological realizations always stand "between the ages."[27] Just as the young Luther's push goes to work deep within scholastic theology and there along with the "*liberum arbitrium*" meets the teaching on justification, so also does his vision in the contest with Erasmus go on far ahead, and he beholds, as it were, behind Erasmus the forms of Feuerbach[28] and Nietzsche. He sees that way that will dissolve theology into anthropology and recast the hereafter of good and evil into a new political morality in its "will to power."[29] He sees the man who will rise from the dead as the nay-sayer to God, sees him coming centuries away. He sees him because he knows him from himself, the man who simultaneously loses his

---

26. Martin Luther, *The Bondage of the Will* (1525), LW 33, 228; WA 18, 744,18-20.

27. [Friedrich Gogarten, "Zwischen den Zeiten," *Die Christliche Welt* 34 (1920/24): 374–8. The title of the essay was then adopted for the journal of the same name, which appeared from 1923 to 1933 and was the public organ of dialectical theology.]

28. [Ludwig Feuerbach (1804–72), in a critical disagreement with his teacher Hegel, developed a theory of religion according to which "God" represents a projection of human ideas and desires.]

29. [Friedrich Nietzsche, *Beyond Good and Evil* (1886), trans. Judith Norman (Cambridge: Cambridge University Press, 2001); idem, *The Will to Power* (1901), trans. Kevin Hill and Michael A. Scarpitti, Penguin Classics (London: Penguin Classics, 2017).]

own actuality, his being in this way and none other, the ahistorical man, the man of the *absolutum velle*.

III. Verdict

Because of that it cannot be said that Luther and Erasmus were completely talking past one another. The point at which Luther begins his dispute with Erasmus, the concrete argument in the matter, the argument that is also comprehensible to Erasmus, was clearly brought out in this controversy. It remains ever profitable to look at Erasmus's formulation and to clarify the outset of the whole difference that became so consequential historically. In his writing on the free will, Erasmus gives a definition that thoroughly says what he *means* and why he is going around and around with Luther. It reads:

"By 'free will' here we understand a power of the human will by which man may be able to direct himself towards, or turn away from, what leads to eternal salvation."[30]

One can say that the controversy concerning the free will is precisely about this definition. Luther responds: "You might perhaps rightly attribute some measure of choice to man, but to attribute free choice to him in relation to divine things is too much."[31] The frame in which Erasmus sees men is clear. Man stands like Hercules at the crossroads. He has freedom of choice, to say yes to grace or to turn away from it. Such a will, Luther scoffs, is a *vertibile arbitrium*, a shifting will [*Wechselwille*]. But this is probably not the point on which the matter depends. Decisive is the fact that, with such an understanding of man's situation before God, everything remains up in the air. One can distinguish between the will in itself, the *merum velle*, and an *act* that is distinct from it, "*by which the action of willing and unwilling is itself produced.*"[32] The *act* may occur one way or another, but the will then remains "free," thus ultimately indecisive. One can do a variety of things, and the will itself is not affected; no *necessitas* stands over it, no real *velle* and *nolle*, no real *amare* and *odisse*!

Thus it is evident that this place of decision where man is moved through such an either-or is a fictitious place where man never stands as he truly is, a man sought and loved by God. In his putatively free decision, he is, in fact, nothing more than his own shadow. This is the surest way not even to encounter the grace of God but rather to relate to it only after the manner of a human potentiality. The half-dead man that had fallen among robbers and was fed

---

30. Desiderius Erasmus, *A Discussion of Free Will/De libero arbitrio διατριβή sive collatio* (1524), trans. Peter Macardle, in Desiderius Erasmus, *Controversies: Collected Works of Erasmus*, vol. 76 (Toronto, Buffalo and London: University of Toronto Press, 1999), 1–90, 21; I b10.
31. LW 33, 103; WA 18, 662,6f.
32. [LW 33, 105; WA 18, 663,6f.]

and saved by the Good Samaritan did not have the potentiality to "relate" to his savior. There remained for Lazarus—as he lay in the grave and heard the call: "Come out"—no free will. In the true encounter with the grace of God, this freedom disappears, the ostensible freedom plunges to that place where the true liberation of man and freedom as a phenomenon from God take place. What, then, is the meaning of *se applicare ad salutem*? To turn oneself toward salvation? Precisely that is what I am not capable of doing. That is the most profound misery of man, that he is not able to accomplish this about-face by his own power, from his own potentialities. The will that drives him, that reigns within him, is an immutably oriented will that refers only to itself. Just as a river that flows along the stream bed is not able to turn around, so also is man not able to *turn himself around*. The true turning toward God lies not in my potentialities; then I would need to cease to be who I am: earthly, fleshly, lost man. This is not to say that they cannot become a phenomenon, but wherever this happens, the limit of all human potentialities has been reached. That is to say, the actuality of my life begins where God's potentiality comes into play. That which is impossible with us is possible with him. For this reason, Luther can say:

"You do not realize how much you attribute to it by this pronoun 'itself'—its very own self!—when you say it can 'apply itself'; for this means that you completely exclude the Holy Spirit with all his power, as superfluous and unnecessary."[33]

Yet at some point we turn these things upside down and see the great *positivum* of our seemingly desperate position. Yet the thought that fills man with desperation is not that he is unable to turn himself of his own free will, that at his core he remains *aversus* with respect to God, but rather that man by that false summons to decision should be whipped as a beast of burden weighed down by its heavy load. This will necessarily end with man left despairing at the wayside. This summons to decision has, in fact, assumed something that it is fundamentally unable to assume: *se applicare ad salutem*. Just as little as the lame man at the pool of Bethesda was able to move himself to the water, so is man unable to cast himself into the purifying flood of grace. The leap of faith is only first successful when faith exists![34]

There is no such thing as a leap out of unbelief into faith. From this point one can understand Luther's polemic against "works" insofar as these are understood as the *acts* of a "free" will that wishes to remain free. For in these works, nothing actually happens, no *turning* is accomplished, and the man who stands behind them remains precisely who he is. These acts are only the appearance of turning that never actually succeeds in being such since the will is unable to move itself; at any rate, it is incapable of bringing itself into motion against itself.

---

33. LW 33, 109; WA 18, 665,13-16.

34. [Søren Kierkegaard, "Fear and Trembeling," (1843), in idem, *Fear and Trembeling and the Sickness unto Death*, trans. Walter Lowrie (Princeton: Princeton University Press, 2013), 87.]

Thus we see that the bound will is not no will (*noluntas*), not some determination from the outside; the bound will *is* the *will* according to its human, ultimate actuality. Just as the stream has a downward slope, so also does the fleshly will have its inclination, and that which is within its own potentiality, and thus our own human potentiality, cannot point us beyond that. Wherever *we* turn ourselves toward salvation, this turning only seems to be so, much like a *Fata Morgana*. We will always seek our salvation, *salus nostra*, which is to say, ourselves. Only when God's salvation *turns toward us*, when a movement from God comes toward us, when God's own doing remains outside the scope of our own potentialities, only then can man believe and be saved. Never where he is active, which is why any psychology of acts [*Aktpsychologie*] in the things of faith is misguided.[35] At this point, no *justitia activa* will be of use. Rather, wherever God's grace truly encounters us, wherever it seeks us out and finds us, we will be *passive*. Passive in the sense that this encounter takes place for us in *suffering*. *Facere quod in se est* means that we are continually moving in circles. The active will *must* revolve around itself. Only *suffering* tears us out of this spell. One will only correctly understand Luther in his fight against works when one sees this inmost connection. The man of the free will lives by his works. "*Adam per opera aedificatur!*"[36] The summons to action is always edifying for the Old Adam, yet "*per crucem destruuntur opera.*"[37] By the cross, all *opera* will be dismantled. Since man conceals himself behind his works, God must dismantle our ability in suffering. There he must set aside all the walls that we have built and continue to build between him and us in order actually to reach us. Only in naked passivity, in the essence of who I am, will his grace find me. Thus God's actuality encounters man's actuality. In this way, each corresponds to the other: faith and passive righteousness.

---

35. [Franz Brentano, *Psychology from an Empirical Standpoint* (1874), ed. Oskar Kraus (New York: Humanities Press, 1973), 88Q, A; Georg Wobbermin, *Systematische Theologie nach religionspsychologischer Methode*, 3 vols. (Leipzig: Hinrichs 1913-25). In Breslau, Iwand attended lectures by Erich Schaeder (1861–1936), who was influenced by Martin Kähler and Hermann Cremer. In 1922, Iwand wrote his theological exam under Schaeder on the topic "Faith and Fate (In the Doctrine of the Certainty of Faith by Karl Heim)" (cf. Jürgen Seim, *Hans Joachim Iwand. Eine Biografie* 2nd ed. [Gütersloh: Gütersloher Verlagshaus, 1999], 32f.). His dissertation he wrote "On the methodological use of antinomies in the philosophy of religion." In Königsberg Iwand composed but did not publish his typewritten licentiate's paper for the local professor for systematic theology Martin Schulze (1866-1943), who himself had studied theology in Halle with Martin Kähler but was rather a Ritschlian theologically. Cf. Hans Joachim Iwand, "Einführung in die gegenwärtige Lage der systematischen Theologie. Vorlesung," (Göttingen, 1949/50), in idem, *Theologiegeschichte*, NWN III, 364-9.]

36. [Cf. LW 31, 53; WA 1, 362,31: "Adam, who is especially edified by works."]

37. [LW 31, 53; WA 1, 362,30: "through the cross works are destroyed."]

IV. Realization

"How much occurs between the mouth and the bite,"[38] as it was once said in this controversy between Luther and Erasmus. "Between the mouth and the bite" means to say between the imperative and the indicative, between "should" and "is." It is manifest that theologians—and philosophers no less so—resort easily to the fallacy that the imperative necessarily implies the indicative, that the "You ought" implies the "You can." And this is true in its own way. How could the "should" be taken seriously if it were not able to come to fruition, if it did not imply the *deed*? Yet between command and deed lies a particular act, and it is a delusion to derive the "is" out of the "should" in the matter of God's command "as if immediately, as soon as something is commanded, it is also necessarily able to be accomplished." This is exactly where the misunderstanding of the divine law lies, that brilliance that dazzles us and deceives everyone who is preparing to follow this light by his natural powers. This collapsing into one another—one is tempted to call it incessant—of command and deed, this "blind" consequence, as if it only depended on providing us with the command, this oversight of man, who is intended by this summons to be not merely a working but also a willing being, leads Luther to postulate at this point of our blindness a particular act of realization that makes a knowing deed out of a blind one. The one who is met by God's call to good deeds must know who he is: he, the man whom God wishes here to make his partner, the *cooperator* of his will and work. The mere glint of the good, that which resides in our spirit as an idea, is not sufficient; faith that one needs only to stretch his hand out to it in order to have it is a delusion, an inevitable delusion to which we must naturally succumb. Here lies the root of everything tragic, both in individual and collective life. It is the delusion of human existence. Right between mouth and biting, in this act of idea and fulfillment that coincide in almost the same moment, a realization flashes down from God, a wonderful opening up before our eyes that makes us see that we are bound, spellbound beings. First, these shackles must fall off so that we may provide our hands and feet, provide all our members to the freedom of divine righteousness. It is not easy to describe this "moment" in which God grabs hold of man, who stands at the precipice of actualizing the good, and sends him his realization: the question of who I am must not be skipped over; I must not "believe" where I am called to realize. There is a faith of man that must give way to realization if we are to find the way from "should" to deed. Ultimately, we are dealing here with the Pauline assertion: "the law brings the realization of sin." Luther added to this a proposition that would be worth a whole essay of its own: "The words of law are spoken, therefore, not to affirm the power of the will, but to enlighten blind reason and make it see that its own light is no light and that the virtue of the will is no virtue."[39] This means, first of all, that *reason*, that very

---

38. [LW 33, 127; WA 18, 677,29f: "For how often there are slips between the cup and the lip."]

39. LW 33, 127; WA 18, 677,7-9.

agency and capacity by which man creates the consciousness of his freedom and his potentialities, must be *enlightened*. Reason is, in a particular way, blind: not because it does not see anything but rather because it is blinded by the radiance of the idea. It is not only the man who is influenced by his senses who succumbs to the blind urgings of his passion; there is also such a blindness on the higher planes of reason, a blindness that is much harder to break through than that blindness of our baser urges, which reason controls. When the conversation concerns the bondage of the will, it is talking about this blindness of reason. Reason is not *able* to comprehend this on its own. Realizing this requires a higher intervention that cannot originate from reason as such. It is missing the intermediary that shows it how it is for man as a rational being. The problem of the self-consciousness of reason, of the *spirit*, breaks in at this point, for is not the spirit just reason directed toward itself? It is in this spirit that Luther places his realization. The man who comes to the call of God realizes his own bondage; whoever does not want the latter cannot have the former. Whoever shrinks away from the proposition of the *servum arbitrium* will forever remain blind. So it is not when man fails in the face of 'reality,' which he encounters with his supposedly good intentions, that he comes to 'consciousness.' The reality that imposes limits on me from the outside can bring me down, but this failure will never enlighten me! I will get myself back together and vainly try yet again in the same blindness, which is to say in the same faith in the supposedly Good, to make that same imperative into an indicative! I will move heaven and earth as long as I have not realized who I am and whom it is with whom I am able to accomplish this. The mouth does not cease to bite, even if it misses again and again.

Luther wrote in his tract to Erasmus a point that makes clear that the *realization of bondage is a realization that comes to us as a revelation*:

> Diatribe persists in representing man to us as one who can either do what is commanded or at least knows that he cannot. But such a man nowhere exists; and if there were such a man, . . . the Spirit of Christ would be in vain. Scripture, however, represents man as one who is not only bound, wretched, captive, sick, and dead, but in addition to his other miseries is afflicted, through the agency of Satan his prince, with the misery of blindness, so that he believes himself to be *free, happy, unfettered, able, well,* and *alive*.[40]

This means, then, that natural man *believes* in his freedom and must believe in it. The freedom of the will is an *article of faith*. With the thesis of the *servum arbitrium*, a faith is broken so that a *realization* might take its place. It is not an exchange of faith and faith that is accomplished here nor an exchange of theory for theory. Rather, a *realization* is sent to us where we were once entangled in a false faith. This is "enlightenment," which is the Spirit of God. This is the function of the *lex spiritualis*, that understanding of the law that is born of the Spirit of God himself.

---

40. LW 33, 130; WA 18, 679,19-22.22-26 [emphasis added by Iwand].

If it does not fulfill its function in us, we cannot be rescued from the delusion of our supposed liberty. Thus, law and realization are related to one another. "They are therefore not absurd but emphatically serious and necessary things that are done by the law."[41]

V. Omnipotence

If one will submit to this realization of the bondage of the human will, it is necessary to accept that a certain point becomes invisible, a point that is otherwise of particular interest to us both within theology and within the psychology that goes together with it: the *transition* from unbelief into faith and thus the question of how the will comes to the act of faith. Together with this question hangs another: the question of why one becomes a believer while another remains in unbelief. As long as one is working with the *freedom* of the will and the *facere quod in se est*, this question needs not become so sharp. One can simply shift the question to men: he didn't *even* do what was in him. But now the question falls back onto God: isn't God *unjust* if he leads and directs, nudges and impels one one way, another another?

Man indeed *must* destroy himself; he cannot turn himself if God does not have mercy on him. This is a part of the *necessitas immutabilitatis* inherent to human desire.[42] One certainly ought not fail to see that it appears unthinkable for Luther that someone who realizes his condition would not immediately know himself to be secure in God's grace. "[I]f men were aware of their misery, he would not be able to retain a single one of them in his (Satan's) kingdom, because God could not but at once pity and succor them in their acknowledged and crying wretchedness, seeing he is so highly extolled throughout Scripture as being near to the contrite in heart."[43] That is to say, no one knows his situation unless he is already secure in the kingdom of grace. With the realization of our sin, we come to understand where it is truly serious and profound, just like someone who rides over Lake Constance.[44] As long as we find ourselves to be in sin's power, blinded and bound by it, we will not be able to fathom it. Only when it is taken from us do we see what sort of an abyss we have been pulled away from. For this reason, whoever lives far from the grace of God does not know it. He lives at the division of existence [*Sein*] and consciousness [*Bewusstsein*]. This represents the *ignorantia invincibilis* asserted by Luther. This is precisely why there is hope for him that he may be saved. The exponents of the free will cannot look upon the "*damnati*" with such hope, for they believe that such people have thrown their salvation away of their own free will, just as they themselves have decided. They do not know that in view of God's

---

41. LW 33, 131; WA 18, 679,36f.
42. [LW 33, 151; WA 18, 693,31: "Necessity of immutability."]
43. LW 33, 130; WA 18, 679,27-30.
44. [An allusion to the 1826 ballad "Der Reiter und der Bodensee" by Gustav Schwab.]

grace, those who see must become blind, and the blind must gain their sight. It is only when one looks out from the perspective of the *servum arbitrium* that the indestructible hope of God's grace stands over the field of death that results from godlessness.

But that is not everything. Far from it! Now, one should see that the teaching of the *servum arbitrium* casts the relationship of the believing to those who reject God in a new light. For they, the believing, are indeed the hope even of these unbelieving: What has happened to these believing, why should it not happen to those unbelieving? Whoever abandons them abandons his own election and makes of his Christianity an achievement, a "*kauchema*."[45] Such a person must slip into the decision-Christianity of the human freedom of the will.

But how, when the rejected ones accuse God himself, that he in his omnipotence drives them irredeemably down the once-trodden path and does not cause them to turn back? When the "for this reason God gave them over that they should dishonor themselves" becomes *history* for them, an irrevocable occurrence? Even here, the *non posse non furere contra deum* [inability to not rage against God][46] must be affirmed. "The ungodly . . . [is] wholly intent on himself and his own affairs . . . and he is incapable of not desiring as of not existing."[47] He must cease to be who he is if he should cease to rage as he rages, "for he is a creature of God, though a vitiated one."[48] He can do no other, as he is *God's* creation, not his *own*, and as such he is subject to the omnipotence of God. "[U]ngodly man cannot alter his aversion." and "God cannot lay aside his omnipotence on account of man's aversion."[49] Luther adds, "This is the well-known fury of the world against the gospel of God."[50] The *impius* is thus not nothing! But what he is he is through the fact that he ever stands under the omnipotence of God as his creation. So whoever would wish for God to abandon the wicked does not comprehend that he is thereby encroaching upon God's divinity that he still exercises in and over the *impii*. Should the Creator and Sustainer of the world be said to stand idle in order to eliminate the *wicked*? They live from the fact that God sustains the world and them in it. The godless should certainly not, for their part, think that he could do otherwise if he wanted to. He must be who he is! "Hence it comes about that the ungodly man cannot but continually err and sin, because he is caught up in the movement of divine power and not allowed to be idle, but wills, desires, and acts according to the kind of person he himself is."[51] This, which man is not able to escape, that his desire should become his history—whether it suits him or not that only the *Gospel* can step onto the field as *victor*, that only faith in God's grace

---

45. ["Pride"—cf. 1 Cor 5:6.]
46. [LW 33, 177; WA 18, 710,16f.]
47. LW 33, 177; WA 18, 710,11.12.17f.
48. [LW 33, 177; WA 18, 710,18.]
49. LW 33, 177; WA 18, 710,7.6.
50. [LW 33, 177; WA 18, 710,19.]
51. LW 33, 176; WA 18, 709,34-36.

in Jesus Christ can do away with the *circulus vitiosus* of guilt and history, or else nothing can—this keeps this teaching of the bound will also within the realm of the *wicked*.

The image of the rider and the horse,[52] the man "possessed" either by God or by Satan, an image that was not invented by Luther[53] but that has made for some difficulties, can be interpreted from this perspective. "For if God is in us, Satan is absent, and only a good will is present; if God is absent, Satan is present, and only an evil will is in us. Neither God nor Satan permits sheer unqualified willing in us."[54] It is clear that the man in this affair is a *passive* entity, that his *desire*, insofar as it aspires to anything, insofar as it is the urge and inclination of his being, must follow a *determination* that lies outside of him. But may we imagine man as a neutral entity between God and Satan? Is it really the case that each one has the same right to man? That is not the case. It is not the case because the work of Satan is simply not a nothing, thanks to the fact that God keeps the wicked in his hand. Even the one who is possessed by Satan continues to belong clandestinely to God; everything he has as far as life and motion are concerned comes from *him*. On the other hand, the man who is propelled and moved by God does not clandestinely belong to Satan. The *deus absconditus* is not a "wicked" God if we are not able to distinguish the identity of the works between the *deus revelatus* and the *deus absconditus*. Much more, that the *impius* under the dominion of his master must be who he is, is not the satanic law of his existence; rather, he owes that to the *omnipotentia* of the God who bears with him in his patience. Yet it must become history, what he *is*. It must not remain a mere potentiality that I can then deny. The thus-and-none-other-way of the history of the man who wishes to be his own lord is the external, if not the internal, refutation of the illusion of human freedom.

VI. Certitude

It belongs to the most thought-provoking matters within theology and probably also of the Christian life of faith that the exponents of the free will argue that *certitude* tumbles down with the thesis of the bondage of the will, even as Luther asserts, on the contrary, that certitude is established only *by* it. Could not this wrestling concerning the certitude of faith in the nineteenth century[55] be illuminated anew from this perspective? Why, then, do the opponents of the free will believe that, with the *liberum arbitrium*, the salvation of man is abandoned

---

52. LW 33, 65f; WA 18, 635,17-22.

53. [Cf. Pseudo-Augustine, *Hypomnesticon contra Pelagianos et Caelestianos* 3,11,20 (PL 45, 1632).]

54. LW 33, 115; WA 18, 670,6-9.

55. [Cf. Hans Joachim Iwand, *Über die methodische Verwendung von Antinomien in der Religionsphilosophie. Dargestellt an Karl Heims "Glaubensgewissheit,"* Diss. masch (Königsberg, 1924).]

to incertitude? It is because the matter now rests outside the control of human consciousness, because it lies *extra me*, that it now "in Christo" coincides with a consciousness, even if a consciousness that was first obtained in faith. Luther, on the other hand, thought that *faith* removes salvation from this immanence of the consciousness, that it secures my life to that rock of hope that lies outside of myself. Certainty and *extra me* coincide in the Reformation sense. That is the sense of the "*assertio*" with Luther. As soon as one attempted to make the "*extra me*" into an "*in me*," the certitude of faith in the *promissio Dei* that is superior to all of the internal and external vicissitudes of life has shattered.

It is thus essential to remember that Luther did not want to see the "*liberum arbitrium*" reestablished for the one who is liberated by God for the freedom of faith. In this he moves beyond Augustine. It is not the potentiality of assurance lying in the interior of man that is the goal and justification for our certitude of faith. Luther shows the lack of restraint and instability of this "interior" along with the insecurity of the ethical process "even if I lived and worked to eternity."[56] Neither psychology nor ethics offers him the objectivity upon which he can securely fasten the anchor of his hope; this is only found in the faithfulness of God, the confidence that "he is faithful and will not lie to me"![57] In other words, in the Word of the mercy of God, a certitude *is* established that in itself demonstrates its superiority over all experience and all of life, a certitude that is not given and founded as a fact of experience but nonetheless governs all experience. Since God "has taken my salvation out of my hands into his,"[58] a position of superior certitude is established that endures in the face of all demons and all *Anfechtungen* (*adversitates*). The question of the certainty of faith is not a question of *certainty*, which is given with the assertion that "God will not lie to me;" it has become perhaps more a question of *faith*. The reality of this *salvation* established *extra meum arbitrium* is accessible to faith alone: if you believe, then you have it. If *sola gratia* defines the *extra me* of salvation in Christ, *sola fide* also defines the *in me*. I must live as a *believer* in order to be able truly to *live* from that certitude. Nonetheless, faith has to do with a reality, with the reality of God himself, where sin and death are not in me but are done away with *extra me* in Christ. The teaching of the bound will cause us to see the problem of certitude as a confrontation between the omnipotence of God and human reason. "*Erasmiani metiuntur dei majestatem secundum rationem* [The Erasmians measure God's majesty according to reason]."[59]

---

56. [LW 33, 288; WA 18, 783,24f: "For my own part, I frankly confess that even if it were possible, I should not wish to have free choice given to me, or to have anything left in my own hands by which I might strive toward salvation."]

57. [LW 33, 289; WA 18, 783,31.]

58. [LW 33, 289; WA 18, 783,29.]

59. An examination of the formula "if you believe, then you have it" that is found very early in Luther is still pending. This formula contains the shortest formulation of the problem of certitude and was very soon subjectively misunderstood and understandably so. It is intended in the sense of the *extra nos*. But to sort out this problem may be a bit

more laborious than that famous philosophical problem of the reality of the external world. We are dealing here with a *judgment* that faith renders differently than reason. Because articles of faith are also articles of judgment, all ontology helps us no further at this point. Cf. the citation above in its whole context: WA 40/I, 360,5-361,11. *Fides est creatrix divinitatis, non in persona, sed in nobis. Extra fidem amittit deus suam justitiam, gloriam, opes etc. et nihil majestatis, divinitatis, ubi nun fides. Vides, quanta justitia fides. . . . Das ist sapentia sapentiarum, religio religionum. Das macht die maxima majestas, quam fides tribuit deo. Quare fides justificat, quia reddit quod debet: qui hoc facit, est justus. . . Fides dicet sic: Ego credo tibi, deo loquenti. Quid loquitur? impossibilia, mendacia, stulta, infirma, abhominanda, heretica, diabolica—Si rationem consulis. . . Monstra sunt, dicit ratio; dicit ista diabolica. Fides hanc rationem occidit et mortificat istam bestiam quam coelum et terra non possunt occidere nec omnes creaturae.* (Reason cannot experience its disclosure in the concept of the world, which is the concept of creation!) *Illa sic dicit de deo: quae ipsa elegit, placent deo. Si deus loquitur, est diabloli verbum, quia non videtur ei congruere. Et Erasmiani metiuntur Dei majestatem secundum rationem.* [Cf. LW 33, 227f: "it [faith] is the creator of the Deity, not in the substance of God but in us. For without faith God loses His glory, wisdom, righteousness, truthfulness, mercy, etc., in us; in short, God has none of His majesty or divinity where faith is absent. . . . To be able to attribute such glory to God is wisdom beyond wisdom, righteousness beyond righteousness, religion beyond religion, and sacrifice beyond sacrifice. From this can be understood what great righteousness faith is and, by this antithesis, what a great sin unbelief is. Therefore, faith justifies because it renders to God what is due Him; whoever does this is righteous. The laws also define what it means to be righteous in this way: to render to each what is his. Faith speaks as follows: 'I believe Thee, God, when Thou dost speak.' What does God say? Things that are impossible, untrue, foolish, weak, absurd, abominable, heretical, and diabolical—if you consult reason. . . . Thus when God proposes the doctrines of faith, He always proposes things that are simply impossible and absurd—if, that is, you want to follow the judgement of reason. . . . When God speaks, reason, therefore, regards His Word as heresy and as the word of the devil; for it seems so absurd. Such is the theology of all the sophists and of the sectarians [—the editors generalized the word *Erasmiani* by translating it as "sophists and sectarians"], who measure the Word of God by reason."]

CONTRIBUTORS

Editors

Benjamin Haupt is Associate Provost and Associate Professor of Practical Theology at Concordia Seminary in St. Louis, Missouri (United States).

Michael Basse is University Professor in Protestant Theology at TU Dortmund University, Germany.

Gerard den Hertog is Emeritus Professor of Systematic Theology at the Theological University in Apeldoorn, the Netherlands.

Christian Neddens is Professor in Systematic Theology at Lutherische Theologische Hochschule in Oberursel, Germany.

Translator

Christian Einertson is in the PhD program at Concordia Seminary in St. Louis, Missouri (United States), and pastor of Trinity Lutheran Church in Farmington, Minnesota (United States).

INDEX

action
    of God 32, 94, 119, 145–7, 150, 152, 160, 198 n.71, 213
    of humanity 23, 29, 30, 32, 42, 56, 68, 71–5, 96, 102, 119, 129, 161, 165, 211–14, 225, 231, 233
activity 14, 23, 32, 43–4, 73, 118, 129, 145, 150, 198, 213
actuality 22, 31, 152, 163–4, 206–7, 212–17, 227–33
Adam 22–3, 43, 52, 54, 60, 63, 211–12, 218, 223 n.7, 233
Alexander of Hales 208
Althaus, Paul 39 n.7, 42 n.11, 49 n.8, 110 n.11, 174 n.8, 179 n.23
analogia entis 183 n.32, 185, 208
analogy 69, 147, 156, 159, 178, 182, 225–6
Anaxagoras 208
Anfechtung 15, 28, 32, 41–2, 57, 95, 155, 213, 215, 217, 239
anthropology 2, 15 n.2, 47–50, 230
apologetics 224
apostasy 16–17, 82, 206
Aristotle 135, 183 n.32, 201 n.83, 208, 223 n.7
Augustin Alveld 186
Augustine 25, 49, 54–5, 142 n.10, 152 n.20, 160, 175 n.9, 186 n.45, 189 n.53, 202 n.85, 207, 227, 239
    The City of God 131, 135
    Confessions 52, 69, 141

baptism 147–61, 179 n.24, 181 n.28, 197 n.70, 199 n.79, 213, passim
Barmen Declaration 2, 88, 110 n.11, 118 n.37, 134 n.21
Barmen Theological Declaration 210 n.18
Barth, Karl 1, 5–6, 13, 67, 93, 100, 135, 206, 222, passim
Baruch de Spinoza 209 n.14

Beatus Rhenanus 207, 208 n.9
Beienrode Convention 9–10, 205
Bizer, Ernst 152 n.22, 178 n.21, 206
blasphemy 56, 160, 194 n.62
Bonhoeffer, Dietrich 2–3, 7–8, 10, 59 n.52, 115 n.29, 127, 133 n.17, 179 n.23
Brentano, Franz 233 n.35
Brunner, Emil 14 n.2, 48 n.5, 108 n.6, 114 n.24
Bucer, Martin 207, 208 n.9
Buddhism 40, 48, 49 n.7
Bultmann, Rudolf 88 n.25, 123 n.44, 140, 141 n.6, 185 n.43

capitalism 99, 116, 196 n.67
certainty of faith, *certitudo fidei* 22, 145, 190, 204, 221, 233 n.35, 239
Christology 5, 22 n.14, 142, 173, 176 n.17
church, *ecclesia*
    Body of Christ 45, 97
    church and state 1–3, 11, 13, 77–8, 83–7
    church catholic 82, 93, 189 n.53
    church struggle (*Kirchenkampf*) 78, 87, 114, 134, 171
    Eastern Church 131
    openness of the church 2, 11, 32, 72–5, 91–108, 125, 181, 222
    Roman Catholic Church 9–10, 65, 83, 91, 112, 115 n.30, 127, 131, 152–4, 158, 174–5, 178, 185, 189 n.53, 190 n.55, 195 n.64, 201 n.81, 208, 224
    visible and invisible church 94, 97, 125, 176, 181–204
    Western church 78, 203, 227
civitas coelestis/civitas terrena 131
commandment
    commandment to love 32, 71
    first commandment 20, 63, 103, 144, 151

community 18, 20, 25, 66, 70, 87, 92–3, 114, 186–7, 191 n.57, 196
compassion 70–1, 73, 75, 121
concentration camps 8, 65, 107, 127, 129
concupiscence, *concupiscentia* 60, 218
Confessing Church 2, 6–7, 37 n.4, 47, 88, 107 n.1, 114–15, 124 n.46, 133 n.17, 171, 173 n.7, 210 n.18
confession
　of faith 23, 84, 87–8, 92–3, 98–100, 110–16, 187, passim
　of sin 52–3, 60–2, 69, 203 n.86
confessionalism/symbolic legalism 78, 86, 90, 113, 171, 173, 195
conscience 19, 21, 71, 98, 129–30, 137, 169
consciousness 28, 43, 53, 69, 105, 112, 127–8, 132, 168, 183, 214, 216, 235–6, 239
consolation 32, 204, 217
conspiracy 1, 3, 133 n.17
　July 20, 1944 attack 129

Dehn, Günther 171
Denifle, Heinrich 179 n.25, 185
Descartes, René 11, 53
despair 15–21, 24, 56, 213–18, 223, 232
devil 16, 54–9, 138, 155–8, 168–9, 230
dialectical theology 48, 108 n.6, 140 nn.5–6, 181 n.28, 230 n.27
dis-enchantment of the world 78–9, 103
Dostoevsky, Fyodor 67, 119 n.39

East Prussia 6–7, 35, 47, 205
ecumenism (*Ökumene*) 95–6
Elert, Werner 110 n.11, 167 n.80, 175 n.9
enlightenment 58, 103, 107, 112, 116, 235
epistemology 144, 183 n.32, 185, 206–10
Erasmus of Rotterdam 221, 227, 229–31, 234–5
ethics 74, 80, 90, 103–5, 109, 224, 239
　ethics of conviction (*Gesinnungsethik*) 120, 143
existence 19–25, 37–9, 53, 59, 69, 94, 117, 144–9, 214–18, passim
extra nos–extra me 63, 141, 239

faith, *fides* 16–22, 30–3, 40–4, 117–20, 141–6, 165–9, 185–90, 193–203, passim
fate 19, 26, 49, 59–60, 113, 118, 229
fault 49, 56, 114, 129
Feuerbach, Ludwig 230
Formula of Concord 173
freedom, *libertas* 18, 65–76, 78, 91–2, 128–30, 221–40
　bondage of the Will, *servum arbitrium* 55, 207, 215, 221–40
　freedom of the will, *liberum arbitrium* 49, 55–6, 223–5, 235–7
friend and enemy (Carl Schmitt) 65, 67

Goethe, Johann Wolfgang von 24 n.18, 30 n.28, 102, 118 n.38, 223, 229
Gogarten, Friedrich 13–14, 42 n.11, 50 n.10, 94 n.38, 140, 149 n.4
Good Samaritan 3, 70–1, 75, 232
gospel 84–90, 115–24, 140, 146, 181, 198–204
　gospel and law 182
grace, *gratia* 24–7, 94–8, 123–5, 189–90, 200, 211, 225–6, passim
Grisar, Hartmann 179 n.25
guilt 31, 50, 68–70, 124, 128, 238
Gyllenkrok, Axel 177 n.19, 178 n.21, 206

Harnack, Adolf von 87 n.23, 109 n.7, 154 n.29
Harnack, Theodosius 172, 206, 211, 222
Heckel, Johannes 133, 174 n.8, 176, 203 n.86
Heidegger, Martin 15 n.2, 52 n.24, 123 n.44
Heidelberg Disputation 15, 43, 61, 183 n.32, 206–8, 223 n.6
Heim, Karl 49 n.7, 233 n.35, 238 n.55
heredity 49
Hermann, Rudolf 4–5, 17 n.4, 60 n.55, 178 n.21, 221–2
Herrmann, Wilhelm 140, 224
Hirsch, Emanuel 59 n.52, 173, 176–8
history 59–60, 66–9, 81–3, 117, 125, 132–4, 203–4, passim
Hofmann, Johann Christian Konrad von 52 n.25
Holl, Karl 68, 162 n.57, 171–204, 222

hope, *spes* 96, 116, 119–25, 204, 213–19, 236–9
humanism 221, 227
humanity 22–3, 59–63, 95–6, 108, 124–5
humiliation, *humilitas* 19, 56, 121, 205, 211

idea 59, 66–8, 88, 102, 105, 111–14
idealism 49–50, 109, 153, 209 n.15, 222–3
idolatry 78, 210
incarnation 22, 63, 88, 97, 117, 210
iron curtain 91
Iwand, Ilse (Ehrhardt) 6, 9, 205

Jesus Christ
head of the church 96–8, 100, 187 n.48, 188 n.51, 189 n.54
Lord 100
John Duns Scotus 200
judgment 101–6, 141–3, 165, 182, 211, 215
justification, *iustificatio* 54, 90, 122, 140–1, 175–80, 224–7

Kant, Immanuel 30, 99, 110, 140–4, 201 n.81, 213
Karma 48
Kattenbusch, Ferdinand 174 n.8
Kierkegaard, Søren 49 n.8, 232 n.34
kingdom of Christ 136, 197, 206
Kliefoth, Theodor Friedrich Dethlof 195
knowledge 28–9, 39–41, 51–8, 62–3, 140–6, 207–17, passim
knowledge of a subject, *Stoffwissen* 66
specialized knowledge, *Fachwissen* 66
Kohlmeyer, Ernst 174 n.8
Königsberg 5–8, 47, 233 n.35
Künneth, Walter 49 n.8

laity 8, 79, 189 n.54, 191 n.57
law 13–33, 53, 69–72, 75, 113–15, 161–3, passim
function of the law, *usus* 17, 23, 26, 99
law and gospel 7, 91 n.34, 110, 163, 173, 182 n.29, 211
Lazarus 89, 119, 232

Lessing, Gotthold Ephraim 58 n.48
liberalism 70, 87, 89, 110
life 17–26, 65–72, 77–9, 116–20, 123–5, 161–8, 213–18, passim
Link, Wilhelm 15 n.2, 48 n.4, 50 n.10, 177 n.17
Loewenich, Walter von 178 n.21, 206
Löhe, Wilhelm 195
Lortz, Joseph 174 n.8, 175 n.9, 179 n.25, 200 n.81
love, *caritas* 15, 32–3, 45, 65–76, 214–18, passim
love for neighbor 25, 70, 72–4
Luther, Martin 14–16, 48–63, 143–5, 148–69, 171–204, passim
Lutheran Renaissance 2, 68 n.9, 171, 173 n.6

materialism 49
Melanchthon, Philipp 91, 143, 173, 193 n.57, 227
metaphysics 30 n.28, 140 n.3, 154 n.29, 208 n.11
Middle Ages 52, 60, 112, 153, 185–7, 213–14, 224
mission 39–40, 42, 45, 71, 93, 96, 121, 125
monasticism 162 nn.57–8, 188 n.52, 207
mortal illness 72
mystical theology 215
mysticism 163, 177 n.17, 205–6
mythical worldview (*Weltbild*) 75

nationalism, nationalist (*völkisch*) 10, 20, 24, 130, 229 n.24
nature of man 54, 61, 105, 144 n.23, 226
neo-protestantism 87–8, 90, 139, 221
Nicholas of Cusa 54 n.29
Nietzsche, Friedrich 17, 20 n.9, 75 n.18, 84, 104–5, 228, 230
nomos 13, 25, 33, 133, 229–30

paganism 79, 182
parables 55, 70–5, 100–2
Pascal, Blaise 52
passion 31, 62, 99, 141, 208–11, 215–18
Paul 37, 40–1, 54–5, 58, 99, 173, 185, 206–8

Pelagius 54
penalty 55, 194 n.62
Pentecost 93-6, 117
person 13-33, 53-7, 70-4, 103-5, 136, 154-9, passim
Peter Lombard 152, 183 n.32, 186, 190 n.55, 208-9
philosophy 23, 33, 51-3, 66, 81, 110-11, 153, 208, 223
piety, *pietas* 43, 56, 95, 132, 185, 205-7
Plato 69, 114, 122, 135, 152, 208
point of contact, *Anknüpfungspunkt* 14-15
potentiality 31, 226-7, 230-3, 238-9
practical seminary 7, 182 n.29
practical theology 43, 163, 165, 171
practice 35, 73, 89-90, 132, 140, 192
praxis 23, 43-4, 75, 168
preaching 13-34, 41, 61, 70, 88, 123-4, 163, 168
predestination 146, 172, 226
predetermination 56
preunderstanding (*Vorverständnis*) 15 n.2
priest, priesthood
    priesthood 15-17, 26, 29, 33, 44, 70, 73, 83, 95, 155, 161, 185, 190
    priesthood of Christ 29
proclamation 13-15, 19-24, 37-9, 79-80, 92-101
Prometheus 18 n.8, 229
promissio 59, 184, 195 n.64, 198-9, 239
Protestantism 79, 86-90, 98, 110-11, 120, 141, 224
Prussian church/union 24 n.17, 157, 205
Psalms 50, 62, 86, 104, 163, 182, 185, 195, 206-7, 212
psychology 17, 23, 233, 236, 239
punishment 49, 55-6, 61, 103-4, 121

reality 44-5, 75, 90, 131-3, 164, 235, passim
realization 36, 60-1, 164, 224, 230, 234-6
reason 26, 40, 61, 131, 136, 140-3, 165-6, 201, 211, 226, 234-9
rebirth 68-9, 97, 129
recognition 31, 35-6, 60, 62-3, 81, 105, 129-31, 139, 165-6

reformation 24, 58, 79, 93, 112-13, 125, 136, 150, passim
religion 16-17, 49, 84, 87, 103, 132, 135, 182
    as opium (Karl Marx) 131
remembering, *memoria/anamnesis* 69, 122
repentance, *paenitentia* 20, 32, 68-9, 74, 81, 93-4, 130
res and *signum* 152-3, 186-7, 198
resistance against state authority 66, 79, 81, 127-38, 169
    killing of tyrants 133-6
responsibility 55, 70, 78, 132, 138, 168, 227
restoration 69, 82-3, 95, 110-11, 172
revelation 22-9, 51-4, 88, 122, 131, 140-1, passim
revolution/counterrevolution 66-7, 81-4, 89-91, 99-101, 110-14, 119, 128, 137, 157
    French revolution 81
    Russian revolution 111
righteousness, *iustitia* 51, 60, 89, 93, 100, 136, passim
    civil righteousness 25 n.19
    divine righteousness 15-16, 63, 75, 93, 119, 144-6, 234
    human righteousness 24, 73, 93, 104
Ritschl, Albrecht 140, 143, 172, 224
Ritschl, Otto 205
romanticism 25, 91 n.33, 112, 129, 201 n.81

sacrament 63, 95, 147-69, 197-9, 204, 226
salvation 16, 26, 41, 56, 59, 73, 95-7, 190, 231-9
sanctification 90, 185, 190 n.5, 226
Sasse, Hermann 116 n.31, 124 n.46
Satan 44, 55-9, 93, 202, 235-8
Scheel, Otto 178
Schelling, Friedrich Wilhelm Joseph 97, 209
Schlatter, Adolf 98, 195
Schleiermacher, Friedrich 78 n.1, 109-10, 172, 213
Schniewind, Julius 6-8, 47

scholasticism 50, 58, 200, 208–9, 221, 226
science 35, 40, 50–1, 110, 116
secular, secularization 82, 111, 141 n.6, 162, 217
Sermon on the Mount 26, 31, 89, 111, 168
sin 22–4, 48–62, 93–6, 99–103, 197–8, passim
  peccata actualia 48, 55, 57–8
  peccatum originale 48–55, 57–62
socialism/socialists 77–81, 84, 87, 90–2, 98–101, 116
social problem 3, 70, 79, 89–90, 110, 113–16
society 15, 67–75, 77–125, 137–8, 147–9, 167–8, 202, 227, passim
sociology 5, 67 n.8, 105 n.50, 179 n.23, 196 n.67
Soden, Hans Freiherr von 88 n.25, 173
Sohm, Rudolph 174 n.8
soteriology 8, 51
soul, *anima* 33, 37, 41, 53, 57, 61, 92, 102, 130–1, 213–15
Spirit (Holy Spirit), Spirit of God 22–3, 38–40, 61, 92–6, 118, 150–3, 213–14, 235
Stahl, Friedrich Julius 91 n.33, 111–13, 149 n.4, 155 n.31, 157 n.35, 158 n.39, 195–6
state 24–5, 70, 74, 77–87, 111–21, 128–38, passim
  authority (of the state) 15, 78, 82, 85, 131–8
  constitutional state 117
  total state 70, 81, 113–14
suffering, *passio* 57, 87, 163–9, 206, 211–18, 233, passim

table of duties (*Haustafeln*) 78
technology 69, 116, 130
temptation 16–17, 31, 36, 56, 168
theocracy 16–17
theologia gloriae 205–20
theology of the cross, *theologia crucis* 10, 35, 42, 45, 86, 205–20
Tholuck, August 52, 176 n.17
Thomas Aquinas 14 n.1, 60–1, 136, 153, 198–201, 224–8
Thomasius, Gottfried 61 n.60
Tolstoy, Lev Nikolayevich 108
total state/totalitarian systems 77, 81–2, 84, 128
Troeltsch, Ernst 22 n.13, 89, 110, 157 n.38, 162–3, 196 n.67, 224
truth, *veritas* 21–4, 40–5, 61–3

unconscious Christianity 92

Vilmar, August Friedrich Christian 112 n.18, 195
Vogelsang, Erich 176–7

Walter, Johannes von 174 n.8
weakness
  of God, Word 15–17, 122
  of humanity 28, 41, 55, 62
Weber, Max 31 n.29, 79 n.3, 86 n.19, 105 n.50, 196 n.67
Wilhelmine empire 108, 129
William of Occam 200, 224
Word of God, *verbum Dei* 154, 180, 193, 201 n.81, 214
work, *opus/opera* 29–30, 193, 207, 210–11, 215, 233
worldview (*Weltanschauung*) 79, 96, 116, 162 n.57, 209

www.ingramcontent.com/pod-product-compliance
Lightning Source LLC
Chambersburg PA
CBHW062133300426
44115CB00012BA/1906